Floating Islanders

Floating Islanders
Pasifika Theatre in Aotearoa

Lisa Warrington
and David O'Donnell

OTAGO

Published by Otago University Press
Level 1, 398 Cumberland Street
Dunedin, New Zealand
university.press@otago.ac.nz
www.otago.ac.nz/press

First published 2017

ISBN 978-1-98-853107-6

Editor: Imogen Coxhead
Design/layout: Fiona Moffat
Indexer: Diane Lowther

Cover: Fiona Collins in *Vula*, 2005, Sydney Opera House. Photo: John McDermott

Printed in New Zealand by Printlink Ltd, Wellington.

Contents

Acknowledgements

First and foremost, we would like to acknowledge the 34 artists who agreed to be interviewed for this book: Dave Armstrong, Anton Carter, Goretti Chadwick, Katrina Chandra, Fiona Collins, Eteuati Ete, David Fane, Dianna Fuemana, Robert Gilbert, Erolia Ifopo, Michelle Johansson, Paul Kieve, Oscar Kightley, Nathaniel Lees, Shimpal Lelisi, Salesi Le`ota, Tom McCrory, Sean Mallon, David Mamea, Kasaya Manulevu, Vela Manusaute, Posenai Mavaega, Mishelle Muagututi`a, Tanya Muagututi`a, Nina Nawalowalo, Anapela Polataivao, Victor Rodger, Justine Simei-Barton, Paul Simei-Barton, Simon Small, Louise Tu`u, Leilani Unasa, Makerita Urale and Sima Urale. Their unswerving patience and kindness as we returned to them for clarification or additional information never wavered. The words of these artists bring to life their experience of writing, rehearsing, devising and performing, the spark of audience connection, and the exhilaration of creating brand new companies and building careers through collaboration and community. We acknowledge and thank them all. Without them, this book would not exist.

Thanks are due to the artists and members of Pasifika communities who kindly replied to email requests, enabling us to expand our understanding of Pasifika theatre practice. They include Iaheto Ah Hi, Barbara Carpenter, Sarah Hunter, Fuarosa Luafutu-Tamati, Samson Samasoni, Rev Mua Strickson-Pua, Mokolagi Tamapeau, Joy Vaele and Albert Wendt. We would also like to thank those who assisted by providing photographs, as well as those who have provided support and information.

We launched our interviews in the office of Pacific Underground at the Christchurch Arts Centre in September 2010, prior to the second earthquake, which rendered the office uninhabitable. This event reinforced how ephemeral the records of our theatre history can be. Much of the material from Pacific

Underground now resides in the archives of the Museum of New Zealand Te Papa Tongarewa.

We would like to acknowledge the dedicated and helpful staff of Te Papa and the Hocken Library at the University of Otago who provided access to archival materials. Thanks are due to the University of Otago and Victoria University of Wellington, and to our colleagues at these institutions who have supported this project in various ways. In particular, thanks to Martyn Roberts for assistance with photographs. Several sections of the book began life at conferences held by the Australasian Association for Theatre, Drama and Performance Studies, Performance Studies International and the International Federation for Theatre Research.

We would like to thank our publisher Rachel Scott at Otago University Press who has been so encouraging throughout the process. In preparing the book for publication, we have received invaluable input from our editor Imogen Coxhead. She did much to clarify our thinking, applying rigorous editorial principles to the work.

We would also like to thank Alison Finigan for her reading and comments on an earlier draft of the manuscript, Kerrin Reeves for her feedback and support and Salesi Le`ota and Murray Lynch at Playmarket, who provided scripts, contacts and other assistance.

Throughout this book we have made every effort to be as accurate as possible. If we have made any errors, we would be grateful to receive feedback on these.

Lisa Warrington
and David O'Donnell

Introduction

In March 1999 on a rare balmy evening on Wellington's waterfront, hundreds of people gather around the concrete stage in Frank Kitts Park. The excited crowd is a mix of Pasifika, Māori and Palagi. The occasion is a free performance of *Romeo and Tusi*, a riotous adaptation of Shakespeare's *Romeo and Juliet* by Oscar Kightley and Erolia Ifopo for the theatre company Pacific Underground. The atmosphere is buoyant and celebratory. Children run and play among the audience; as a band plays infectiously rhythmic music, the actors appear wearing bright costumes. The first lines of the play, amplified by radio mikes, are greeted by gales of laughter. A fa`afafine character, Ruby, delights the crowd with camp humour. A corrupt minister is pursued through the audience. When Tusi's mother warns her against her romance with a Māori boy – 'You are a coconut. He's a kumara' – the crowd goes wild.

Romeo and Tusi was not only popular theatre at its best, it also capped off a remarkable decade in which plays and performances by Pasifika artists had changed the face of New Zealand theatre. How did a relatively small number of theatre practitioners make such a big impact in such a short time? They had brought large numbers of Pasifika people to theatre for the first time and had delighted and challenged audiences of many other cultures. These artists were part of a larger movement of Pasifika creativity in visual arts, music, film, television and literature. They demonstrated a characteristic creative energy, humour and enterprise, and tapped into a spirit of 'non-exclusivity' in their willingness to embrace cross-cultural input and hybridity.

This book tells the story of the phenomenon that is Pasifika theatre, defined here as live performance work created in Aotearoa/New Zealand by artists of Pacific Island ancestry. Since the 1980s there has been an explosion of theatrical voices from artists whose backgrounds include Western Samoa,

American Samoa, Niue, Fiji, Tonga, Tokelau and the Cook Islands. According to Teresia Teaiwa and Sean Mallon (2005), Pacific people are 'one of the most visible minority groups in New Zealand', largely because they are 'prominent on the landscapes of sports and the arts'.[1] Pasifika theatre, with its themes of migration, family, cultural identity and the questioning of stereotypes, has been a major conduit for stories of the Pacific Island diaspora.[2]

'Floating Islanders': Living between cultures

We float – we're not based in one place: we're floating Islanders. MAKERITA URALE[3]

Pasifika people occupy a fluid and mobile position in New Zealand society. As Teaiwa and Mallon argue, '[they] inhabit a social and cultural space in between the tangata whenua and Pākehā and other immigrant groups in New Zealand ... Sometimes the space in between, some state of liminality, can be an anchoring point or a productive site for addressing the instabilities of social and cultural life.'[4]

The migrant experience is often seen as troubled: by standing in two worlds does one effectively stand in neither? Samoan-born Makerita Urale suggests that Pasifika people are used to negotiating across cultures and oceanic borders, and this leads to a positive entrepreneurial energy and an interdisciplinary approach in the work of many Pasifika artists. According to Urale, this 'in-between-ness' has been turned to advantage in Pasifika theatre: 'We're like the coconut tree, how it propagates through the Pacific, through the ocean ... we spread our ideas.'

Urale's image of Pasifika people as 'floating Islanders' links to the work of Tongan writer Epeli Hau`ofa (1939–2009).[5] Born in Papua New Guinea and educated in Tonga, Fiji and Australia, Hau`ofa's career was defined by his travels and connections throughout the Pacific Islands. In his seminal essay, 'Our sea of islands', he argues against the 'belittling' colonialist view of the islands of Oceania as small, remote and therefore insignificant: 'The world of Oceania is not small; it is huge and growing bigger every day ... There is a world of difference between viewing the Pacific as "islands in a vast sea" and as a "sea of islands".'[6] Hau`ofa's view emphasises navigation, exploration, trade and intercultural relationships, 'a large world in which people and cultures moved and mingled, unhindered by boundaries of the kind erected much later by imperial powers'.[7] As Hau`ofa celebrates the role of the ocean in facilitating connections between islands, Urale emphasises the ability of Pasifika artists to collaborate, to break down disciplinary boundaries and to play in the spaces between artforms.

The term 'floating Islanders' also resonates with Italian director Eugenio Barba's concept of 'floating islands': independent, highly-committed theatre companies throughout the world that often receive little recognition – '[l]ike islands without contact between themselves ... determined to survive'.[8] In New Zealand, Pasifika theatre companies have not only survived, they have flourished and become the career seeding ground for a diverse range of artists. Barba warns against idealising such companies, often created because of tensions within a society: 'These are not the islands of Utopia. They are the fragments of a frontier society, the frayed edges of something which is and is not society.'[9] In this spirit, many Pasifika plays explore the marginal status of new migrants, contrasting their Utopian dreams with the reality of living in industrialised cities.

Throughout this book we use Urale's concept of floating Islanders to emphasise the flexibility, fluidity, openness and interdisciplinarity of Pasifika theatre practitioners and companies.[10]

The framework of this book

Floating Islanders came about because of our personal admiration for the achievements of Pasifika theatre artists living in Aotearoa. We write from our position as Palagi theatre practitioners and teachers living and working in Aotearoa. We have been guided by the Tongan/Fijian/Samoan concept of talanoa, which can be defined as 'a conversation, a talk, an exchange of ideas or thinking, whether formal or informal. It is almost always carried out face-to-face ... Talanoa ... literally means talking about nothing in particular and interacting without a rigid framework.'[11]

In the spirit of talanoa, we have held many conversations with Pasifika theatre practitioners over several years.[12] While it has not been possible to meet with every member of the Pasifika theatre community, the views in this book represent a wide sampling of opinions, philosophies and memories covering the first 30 years of Pasifika theatre. We discuss key individuals (primarily writers, actors, directors and producers), document the history of major theatre companies, and analyse many texts and productions. By and large, this is done in chronological order. Our discussions of plays and performances are based on both live and recorded productions and on published and unpublished scripts.

We draw on reviews, programmes, articles, published interviews and other publicity materials. Reviews in particular are one of the most effective ways of assessing the public reception of a work and capturing the atmosphere of a performance. Because the majority of available reviews of Pasifika work are by Palagi, who may occasionally face challenges in understanding the language and cultural context of a work, wherever possible we have endeavoured to include reviews by Polynesian writers.

We consider what is unique and distinctive about Pasifika theatre in New Zealand, and explore its transition from the fringe to mainstream. We examine how Pasifika theatre in Aotearoa relates to performance traditions in the Islands, and to what extent the Polynesian sense of 'family' is embodied in the collective nature of Pasifika theatre. We also acknowledge the importance of the theatre work created by Māori artists since the 1970s and their influence on Pasifika practitioners, and look at some intersections between Māori and Pasifika theatre traditions.

In 2013 the majority of New Zealand's Pasifika population were Samoan (48.7 per cent), followed by Cook Island (20.9 per cent), Tongan (20.4 per cent) and Niuean (8.1 per cent).[13] The proportion of Samoans in the wider population explains why they have such high visibility in Pasifika theatre. As our story evolves, a number of other cultures are represented, including Fiji, Niue, Tonga and the Cook Islands. We also mention writers living in the wider Pacific whose work has made an impact in New Zealand. Although we occasionally also touch on Pasifika film, television, dance, music and cultural festivals where these intersect with our story of live theatre, they are not the focus of this study.

Definitions

We use the term **Pasifika** to define artists of Pacific Island descent working in New Zealand.[14] The term 'Pacific Islander' was commonly used in the past but has fallen out of favour; however, the abbreviation '**PI**' has been re-appropriated by some Pasifika artists, and can also be found in this book. Art historian Karen Stevenson notes: 'As New Zealand-born Pacific Islanders embraced the notion of Pasifika (a self-label that fused their island heritage and their urban reality), they became more comfortable in their role as urban Polynesians.'[15] The term Pasifika is well established as a marker of the distinctiveness of Pacific arts events, visual arts and music. In our definition of Pasifika theatre, Pasifika artists should have primary creative control over the project, especially as producers, directors, writers and devisors. This may include collaborations with Palagi or Māori writers, actors and directors.

Throughout this book we use **Palagi** (a term of Samoan origin also used in other Pacific Islands) or its plural form, **Papalagi**, to identify non-Pasifika peoples involved in or affected by Pasifika theatre. When referring to Māori theatre, we occasionally use the Māori equivalent term, **Pākehā**. We use New Zealand and its Māori name, Aotearoa, interchangeably depending on the context, and occasionally use **Niu Sila**, the Samoan transliteration of New Zealand.

The Samoan concept of **afakasi** (a transliteration of 'half-caste' or mixed-race genealogy) is a prominent theme in works by playwrights such as Victor Rodger, Leilani Unasa and Grace Taylor. Rodger comments, 'As an afakasi, when I go to Samoa they think I'm white, even though I'm not ... I think that's something a lot of half-Samoans feel.'[16] The ambivalence of being afakasi is captured in Taylor's first poetry collection, *Afakasi Speaks* (2013). In a media interview she stated, 'I always refer to myself as Afakasi. I'm about reclaiming, redefining and then putting it back out there.'[17] Artist Sheyne Tuffery, whose work is a celebration of the afakasi, refers to it as 'that confusion of not fitting into either side so you invent your own culture in art'.[18] In theatre, mixed-race genealogy is a powerful dramatic theme because the 'in-betweeness' of being afakasi opens up potent questions of cultural identity as well as new forms of artistic expression.

The Samoan concept of **vā** – the spaces between people and things – is useful as an aesthetic principle for applying to Pasifika theatre. Albert Refiti explains how the vā relates to artistic activity:

> The vā is a spatial ordering concept that exists between things and administers a code of good (ideal) behaviour, an invisible language that enables space and things to be configured in a positive manner. It governed traditional aesthetic appreciation in Samoa, Tonga, Niue, the Cook Islands and Aotearoa from oratory to boat building, tattooing to the fabrication of buildings and space.[19]

Because theatre is a collaborative art form requiring a communal approach to creativity, the vā is particularly relevant. Albert Wendt highlights the link between the vā and group creation:

> A well-known Samoan expression is 'la teu le vā'. Cherish/nurse/care for the vā, the relationships. This is crucial in communal cultures that value group, unity, more than individualism ...[20]

Samoan choreographer Lemi Ponifasio connects the vā to the performing body: '... the notion of the vā is the lived and cognisant body relationship with the world'.[21] Ponifasio's statement proposes a Pasifika framework for understanding and analysing performance that is appropriate to work discussed in this study, whether text-based, devised or choreographed theatre.

**Fa`asamoa**, the 'Samoan way', is the umbrella term for all Samoan customs, beliefs and values. It can influence both the form and themes of Samoan theatre. Sean Mallon makes the point that fa`asamoa is not a fixed concept: 'as a set of cultural practices and values, fa`asamoa is regularly contested and reformulated to suit the needs and criteria of those who practise it'.[22]

Arguably, Pasifika theatre has made a contribution to such flexible re-definitions of fa`asamoa in post-colonial and diasporic Samoan communities. As Wendt has observed, 'Like a tree a culture is forever growing new branches, foliage, and roots.'[23]

Samoan **fa`afafine** are also very important to the story of Pasifika theatre. Fa`afafine are men who live as women in Samoan society, dress in female clothing and take on the 'female' roles in the household. Sometimes incorrectly confused with drag queens, fa`afafine can be very witty and entertaining in a camp way and often appear as comic relief in Pasifika plays.

Fale aitu

The Samoan comic theatre form fale aitu (literally 'ghost house' or 'house of spirits') has strongly influenced the development of Pasifika theatre.[24] Caroline Sinavaiana[25] explains that in this 'house of spirits' performance, pairs of clowns – fa`aluma – are supposedly visited by ancestral ghosts or spirits (aitu). This gives them 'supernatural sanction' to critique authority figures such as 'elders, parents, teachers, religious ministers, government officials and political leaders'.[26] Sinavaiana writes that the 'protective frame of theatre' provides an important outlet for criticism in the otherwise conservative Samoan society, and argues that 'in Samoa's neo-colonial context, the comedy sketch implies an indigenous critique of various forms of Western culture'.[27] She views it as an important part of 'cultural revitalisation'.[28]

Fale aitu is part of a broader practice of clowning that has flourished in Oceania since pre-Christian times. In his major study of clowning in Rotuma, Fiji, Vilsoni Hereniko notes: 'Although the religious significance of sacred clowning has been severely eroded, the urge to amuse others, to satirise the behavior of the stranger or the pompous, or to tell a story in a humorous way cannot be suppressed by westernization or by Christianity.'[29]

Aitu remain important in Samoan society, as Victoria N. Kneubuhl observes:

> Aitu are descendants of the original gods (atua) and ... are associated with chaos, wilderness, danger and darkness ... Samoan society utilises this chaotic world as a restorative power in civilised village life ... When chaos is acknowledged, order is maintained; this symbiosis serves as the basis for ... performance in Samoan culture.[30]

Fale aitu sketches are generally scripted and rehearsed, though performances may contain much improvisation. They typically involve elements of parody, satire, burlesque and slapstick. As Sinavaiana notes, '[normative] status roles are reversed: the high is made low and the world temporarily turned upside down'.[31] Traditionally men, who would also play the roles of women, performed these sketches. John Kneubuhl comments, '... the lead actor or clown in the Samoan faleaitu ... puts on an effeminate persona that is really neither male nor female'.[32] While it is possible for women to perform fale aitu, it remains a largely male-dominated tradition in New Zealand.

Religion and White Sunday

One of the things that marries all Samoans together is religion. ANAPELA POLATAIVAO[33]

Church performance with its mix of music, the sacred and the comic, is a formative influence on Pasifika theatre. Many Pasifika practitioners had their first performing experiences in church as children. For most it was White Sunday (Lotu Tamaiti, literally 'church service of children') on the second Sunday of October each year, when the children of the congregation dress in white clothing, sing, recite Bible passages and perform dramatised biblical sketches. White Sunday provides opportunities to learn rehearsal discipline and the power of performing to a large audience, and parental expectations of excellence help create strong performances in the young actors. Jamie C. Simpson observes that 'the children show an exceptional commitment and focus ... They speak loudly and articulately, rarely breaking serious expression.'[34] Simpson outlines the strict nature of the hierarchy of Samoan society, where children rank at the very bottom: 'Childhood requires deferential humility and service to the older members of the `aiga [family].'[35] On White Sunday, this hierarchy is temporarily reversed in the manner of fale aitu, as 'children "act out" adult responsibilities and experience adult prestige'.[36]

Because White Sunday sketches are not performed in English, they are also an important public way of retaining the speaking of Pacific languages for adults and children alike.

Historical background: Pacific migration to Aotearoa

The relationship between New Zealand and its closest Pacific neighbours is complex. Many South Pacific islands have a history of continuous human occupation for over 2000 years – much longer than Aotearoa itself, where the first Polynesian settlers arrived about 1000 years ago. The social structures and beliefs of Pacific Island indigenous populations were transformed by the arrival of Christian missionaries in the Pacific from the 1830s. Britain, France and Germany all colonised Pacific Islands; New Zealand became involved as a colonial administrator when it annexed the Cook Islands and Niue in 1900, and Tokelau in 1925. These became independent countries in 1965 and 1974 respectively, though the people remain New Zealand citizens.

New Zealand was the colonial administrator of Western Samoa from 1914 until independence was achieved in 1962. New Zealand's track record in Samoa was so poor, however, that in 2002 the then Prime Minister Helen Clark travelled to Samoa to offer a formal apology for what the *Listener* called New Zealand's 'old colonial crimes'.[37] These included failing to quarantine the islands in 1918 to protect the people from the global influenza epidemic – 22 per cent of the population died when the flu-carrying SS *Talune* was allowed to dock in Apia – and the appalling events of 1929, when a peaceful protest march by the Mau independence movement ended in tragedy. New Zealand police opened fire on the crowd, wounding approximately 50 people and killing 11 others including Tupua Tamasese Lealofi III, the much-loved leader of the movement. This incident is a central element in John Kneubuhl's play *Think of a Garden*.

Pacific migration to New Zealand increased significantly from the 1950s as Island people sought work opportunities and the perceived economic benefits of a Western lifestyle – major themes in plays such as *Le Matau* (1984) and *Fresh off the Boat* (1993). Tensions over migration in the 1970s led to the government instituting the infamous dawn raids, in which police and immigration officials raided Pasifika households in search of 'overstayers'. These events were later dramatised in Oscar Kightley's *Dawn Raids* (1997).

Auckland now has the largest Pasifika population in the world. Ninety-seven per cent of Pasifika people live in urban centres and, of these, 66 per cent are in Auckland.[38] This is reflected in the urban settings of many plays, such as *Frangipani Perfume* (1997) and *Club Paradiso* (2015). In contrast, many Māori and Pākehā plays choose small towns or rural settings to explore their themes.

Māori are acknowledged as the indigenous people of Aotearoa – the tangata whenua (people of the land). The relationship between Māori and Pākehā has been contentious since the signing of the Treaty of Waitangi on 6 February 1840. Despite the apparently enlightened actions of the British Crown in making a treaty with the indigenous leaders, the agreement opened up Māori land for sale and led to a massive increase in immigration from the British Isles. After more than a century of resistance to colonial rule, in 1975 a Māori hikoi (march) protesting the loss of Māori land became the catalyst for legislation that eventually led to some iwi being compensated by the Crown for land that had been taken.

The relationship between Pasifika migrants and Māori is complex. Like Māori, Pasifika peoples have been colonised by European nations in the past. As migrants they are technically tauiwi (visitors), but many Māori consider themselves to have a closer kinship with Pasifika people than with Pākehā. Alice Te Punga Somerville sees a strong connection between the urbanisation of Māori in the post-war period, and the large-scale migration of Pasifika people soon after:

> Māori communities were moving to New Zealand's cities at the same time as the first sizeable migrations from the Pacific arrived there – and often in the same suburbs. Māori and Pasifika people have had to scramble for the few resources available to them in the area of employment ... but also in the areas of education, housing, health care, and so on.[39]

The social pressures resulting from the urbanisation of Māori have been dramatised in numerous Māori plays, notably in Hone Kouka's *Waiora* (1996). As Makerita Urale observes:

> Kouka writes about his family, who left their tribal land in the North Island to find work in the forest industry in the South Island. 'Maori people are immigrants in their own country,' says Kouka. 'We have faced the same sense of dislocation from our homes and from our land which Pacific Island immigrants face.'[40]

This shared experience has created a sense of solidarity between Māori and Pacific Island people, but also brings tensions, as Te Punga Somerville notes:

'Māori–Pasifika connections are marked by discourses of relationship and reconnection, but also of disjuncture.'[41] This connection has been dramatised in plays such as *Romeo and Tusi* (1996) and *Once Were Samoans* (2006).

Who has written about Pasifika theatre?

Before we begin this story we must acknowledge those who have already written about the history and art of Pasifika theatre. The first to do so were often practitioners themselves who have provided valuable insights into their practice and philosophy. Alongside often detailed reviews and interviews in the media (crucial in recording the ephemeral flow of work), there are substantial publications by theatre and literary critics, historians and others. Scholarly interest from New Zealand, Germany, Belgium, Hawai`i, Australia and Samoa demonstrates the growing significance of Pasifika theatre, both historically and artistically. In this section, we provide an overview of writing about the subject, picking out common themes and questions that we will investigate throughout the book. It should be noted that this is not a fully comprehensive survey.

In 1986 Samoan actor, writer and journalist Samson Samasoni contributed a piece to *Act* in which he considered the past and future for Māori and Pacific Island theatre.[42] This significant article shows that, in 1986, Māori and Pacific theatre were seen as part of the same movement, the main drive of which was political:

> Throughout the country small groups of Polynesians have set up troupes and dabbled with theatre techniques. The co-operative nature of theatre, as opposed to the individual existence of writers, is becoming more and more attractive to Māori and Pacific Islanders. Black politicos are fast coming to recognise that theatre, or play acting, has a role in the struggle.[43]

The emphasis on collective creation and politics in this article partly explains the appeal of theatre to young Polynesians in the 1980s, notably for Samasoni's own group, TAOtahi (discussed in chapter one). Samasoni pinpoints two of the major themes of Polynesian work at that time: 'The emergence of "black" theatre with a city flavour is reflective of the urban drift and other social phenomena such as the immigration of Pacific Islanders to New Zealand.'[44]

One of the first histories of Pasifika theatre is found in a chapter by Anton Carter in *Pacific Art Niu Sila* (2002). Carter, a former core member of Pacific Underground, provides an insider's view. He notes that theatre is not a 'natural form of entertainment' for Pacific Island communities, and stresses the importance of touring theatre-in-education to break down barriers for younger Pacific audiences.[45] Carter argues that Pacific theatre is unique because it presents collective stories that have never been acted out in a 'public arena' before. He maintains that it has disrupted the myth of the Pacific as 'pleasant and picturesque': some of the works 'are brutal, starkly honest plays focusing on aspects of Pacific culture or personal experiences that are rarely spoken about, especially in public'.[46]

In the same year, Sean Mallon, senior curator for Pacific Cultures at the Museum of New Zealand Te Papa Tongarewa, discussed the history of Samoan theatre in New Zealand in his book *Samoan Art and Artists*.[47] Mallon begins by explaining the use of fale aitu in Samoa, and examines how it has been used and adapted in New Zealand. Like Carter, he explores the significance of key foundational companies such as TAOtahi, Pacific Theatre and Pacific Underground. His account is supported by interviews with some of the leading practitioners.

The influence of Caroline Sinavaiana's studies of fale aitu can be seen in subsequent scholarly work. In her book *Once Were Pacific* (2012), Alice Te Punga Somerville examines the influence of fale aitu on the plays *Romeo and Tusi* and *Once Were Samoans*. She illustrates how these texts use humour to advance their 'political weight'.[48] As the first major comparative study of Māori and Pasifika literature, *Once Were Pacific* is invaluable for its consideration of wider issues of how relationships between tangata whenua and Pasifika migrants are represented through literature.

Sinavaiana's research also feeds into an article by Jamie C. Simpson, who sees a strong connection between fale aitu and White Sunday, noting that both provide 'a ceremonial safety valve' for the least powerful members of society.[49] As Simpson argues:

> Fale aitu provides a release for the common people who, for a moment in time, may laugh and jest at the powers that dictate the circumstances of their lives. Similarly, on Lotu a Tamaiti [White Sunday], children receive momentary relief from the frustrations they experience in the lower class of society.[50]

Christopher Balme was one of the first to write in detail about Māori theatre and has made a major contribution to the study of Pacific theatre. With Astrid Carstensen, Balme co-authored the article 'Home fires: Creating a Pacific theatre in the diaspora', which examines three plays that illustrate the diasporic themes of Pacific theatre: John Kneubuhl's *Think of a Garden*, Hone Kouka's *Home Fires* and Pacific Underground's devised work (with Zeal Theatre),

Tatau: Rites of passage. Balme and Carstensen refer to Kneubuhl as 'the spiritual father of Pacific Island theatre'.[51] They analyse the postcolonial themes of *Think of a Garden* in terms of memory, divided cultural identity and alienation from indigenous culture, and discuss the importance of the spirits of ancestors in both *Think of a Garden* and *Home Fires*. In *Tatau: Rites of passage* they examine the ground-breaking strategy of incorporating sacred ritual within a dramatic framework.

Balme's initial study of Pacific theatre developed into a comprehensive book, *Pacific Performances* (2007), in which he applies a performance studies lens to the colonial history of the Pacific, examining the introduction of European theatre, cultural performances and colonial encounters as performance. A discussion of key works in Pasifika theatre forms the nucleus of his final chapter on the contemporary Pacific. His focus – on *Tatau: Rites of passage*, *A Frigate Bird Sings*, the Naked Samoans comedy shows, and the dance theatre of Lemi Ponifasio's MAU ensemble – demonstrates the diversity of forms in New Zealand Pasifika theatre. Balme argues that New Zealand is the 'theatrical centre' of the Pacific.[52]

Diana Looser has published extensively on Pacific theatre. In her 2011 article 'A piece "more curious than all the rest"', she analyses four examples of pre-colonial theatre in the Pacific Islands, arguing for the existence of indigenous theatre and drama forms that pre-date colonisation, and questioning the usual idea that Pacific Island theatre has arisen from 'the influences of colonial culture and education'.[53] She considers these early performances to be 'antecedents for more recent Pacific theatre'.[54] In 'Moving islands' (2012) she concentrates on theatrical manifestations of the Samoan diaspora by comparing productions from Australia, New Zealand and Hawai`i. She applies the sociological term 'social remittances' to theatrical performance, arguing that theatre carries 'ideas, practices, and identities, both affirmative and subversive', and illustrating ways in which theatre in the Pacific operates as a 'cultural intervention'.[55]

Looser's most important contribution to date is her book *Remaking Pacific Pasts* (2014), in which she surveys indigenous drama from Oceania over the last 50 years, using a historiographic theatre approach to produce detailed comparative case studies of plays from Hawai`i, Aotearoa, New Caledonia and Fiji. She concentrates on works that critically engage with Pacific histories, and shows how representations of the past relate to postcolonial politics and cultural identity. She argues that these performed revisionist histories undertake 'cultural work' that contributes to 'regional dialogues and reinforce[s] regional identities'.[56]

While Looser comparatively examines theatre throughout the Pacific, Hungarian Kata Fülöp specifically examines Pasifika theatre in Aotearoa New Zealand. Her 2012 thesis examines how Pasifika theatre makers construct and perform their identities through theatre, and incorporates a history of Pasifika theatre in New Zealand to 2010 as well as a broader examination of post-colonial theatre and the social role of the artist.[57]

Michelle Keown has published widely on Pacific literature. *Pacific Islands Writing* (2007) contains a section on Pasifika theatre in Aotearoa summarising the achievements of key companies Pacific Theatre and Pacific Underground, and includes an analysis of *Fresh off the Boat*.[58] Keown examines gender, sexuality and the body in Pacific theatre, making connections between Makerita Urale's *Frangipani Perfume* and the subversive comedy of plays such as Vilsoni Hereniko and Teresia Teaiwa's *Last Virgin in Paradise*.

Work by Pacific Underground is also discussed in Karen Stevenson's book on contemporary Pacific art, *The Frangipani is Dead* (2008). Stevenson sites theatre within wider practices of Pasifika art-making.[59] She draws on Carter's work to highlight the significance of Pacific theatre as a 'platform to tell the stories of family, of the previous generation, of issues cultural and social that shaped their lives'.[60] Like Keown and Carter, Stevenson highlights the significance of *Frangipani Perfume* for its focus on the experience of Pacific women, which she says 'refutes the stereotype of Pacific women as voiceless'.[61] The title of Stevenson's book refers to the contested cliché of the frangipani flower as an exemplar of Pacific art:

> For many artists this cliché has been a stumbling block, a constant that they had to work against ... the frangipani, always bright, always colourful, represented the Pacific ... many artists believed that the image represented not who they were but an idealised/mythologised Pacific embedded in the minds of others.[62]

Oscar Kightley and Erolia Ifopo's *Romeo and Tusi* has attracted much critical attention, no doubt due to the fact that this is a post-colonial adaptation and parody of one of Shakespeare's best-known works. In an article tracing the influence of Shakespeare in New Zealand since the 19th century, Mark Houlahan stresses the accessibility of *Romeo and Tusi* to large, less mainstream and 'less Palagi' audiences,[63] and considers the confrontation between Polynesian culture and Shakespeare to have resulted in 'a production that contrives to be both hilariously "local" and movingly "Shakespearean"'.[64] Seven years later Houlahan devoted an entire article to discussing the play.[65] Philip Armstrong ends his comparative study of contemporary versions of *Romeo and*

Juliet with an enthusiastic reading of *Romeo and Tusi*, in which he foregrounds the significance of the fa`afafine Ruby,[66] while Lisa Warrington discusses *Romeo and Tusi* as an 'overtly irreverent' example of the Pacific 'writing back' to the European Shakespearean tradition, and notes the connection to fale aitu.[67] Julie McDougall compares *Romeo and Tusi* with two Māori Shakespeare adaptations as examples of postcolonial 'cultural translation' that give a strong local relevance to canonical texts,[68] and Nicola Hyland contrasts *Romeo and Tusi* with four other cross-cultural *Romeo and Juliet* adaptations (British colour-blind, British Asian, South African and Australian). Her emphasis is not so much on how the Pasifika playwrights have adapted Shakespeare, but on the play's positive depiction of Polynesian youth:

> [Kightley and Ifopo] have produced a text about the state of being young and Brown in New Zealand which can also be read as a message for all post-colonial communities: that othered cultures are both contingent and changeable.[69]

In his book *Transgressive Itineraries* Marc Maufort compares Pacific drama in New Zealand with examples of multi-ethnic drama from Canada and Australia. He examines plays by Kightley and Victor Rodger, concluding that they illustrate 'the coming of age of a Samoan artistic consciousness within contemporary New Zealand'.[70] In his article 'Voices of otherness' Maufort revisits Rodger's work, exploring his portrait of racial tension in New Zealand in the controversial *Ranterstantrum* (2002) and noting the 'double consciousness' of the Samoan protagonist.[71] In 'Positioning alterity', Maufort contrasts work by Toa Fraser and Dianna Fuemana with Māori and Chinese plays, as examples of 'multi-ethnic diversity [that] forces us to redefine the very concept of a monolithic national literature'.[72] Maufort's comparative analysis shows that Pasifika theatre intersects with wider movements of multicultural and migrant theatre internationally. *Performing Aotearoa* (2007), edited by Maufort and David O'Donnell, includes an interview with Samoan actor/director Nathaniel Lees, and an article by O'Donnell that explores the significance of the 'FOB' (fresh off the boat) across a number of Pasifika plays.[73]

Chapter outline

This book is a loosely chronological study of the development of Pasifika theatre in Aotearoa. In chapter one we look at beginnings, including the early careers of Nathaniel Lees, Lani Tupu Jr, Eteuati Ete and Sima Urale. The first Samoan/New

Zealand play *Le Matau* (1984) is discussed alongside Lees' productions of John Kneubuhl's *Think of a Garden* (1993). Chapter two examines the contribution of Auckland's Pacific Theatre company, especially Justine Simei-Barton's role as director and mentor for Pasifika actors and the introduction of fale aitu to New Zealand theatre. In chapters three and four the geographical focus shifts to the South Island, to examine the development of the theatre group Pacific Underground. This includes significant plays, Theatre in Education, music initiatives and the group's artistic collaborations and national tours. Chapter five discusses the diversification of Pasifika playwriting between 1996 and 2007.

In chapter six the focus moves to Pasifika image-based theatre as exemplified by the international recognition of companies The Conch and MAU. Chapter seven examines different approaches to Pasifika comedy, highlighting The Laughing Samoans, The Brownies and The Naked Samoans. Chapter eight explores the significance of the Auckland company Kila Kokonut Krew (KKK), and chapter nine considers the work of a generation of female Pasifika artists, including Tusiata Avia, Courtney Sina Meredith, Grace Taylor, Louise Tu`u, Michelle Johansson, Leilani Unasa and Miria George. In chapter ten we consider the impact of new venues, theatre companies and educational institutions, and assess the overall achievements of Pasifika theatre as a dynamic case study of a migrant theatre tradition.

The voices that matter

In this book we bring together a detailed history of some major companies, an analysis of selected texts and studies of Pasifika theatre artists and performances within Aotearoa. At its heart are the interviews we conducted around the country with many Pasifika practitioners. It has been our prime objective to allow these practitioners to frame their own histories as writers, directors, actors and producers. They represent the voices of experience, the voices of history, and the new voices that are remaking Pasifika theatre on their own terms.

1.
The beginnings of Pasifika theatre

Le Matau *dealt with some deep issues, which Samoans in New Zealand are still trying to come to terms with. In order to survive within a society, you've got to adapt, but then it's about how far you go from your core values.*

ETEUATI ETE[1]

Think of a Garden *was like Bruce Mason for us. If we could one day write a play as good as that then we'd all be happy.*

MAKERITA URALE[2]

This chapter is framed by discussion of two landmark plays performed a decade apart: *Le Matau* (1984) by Stephen Sinclair and Samson Samasoni, and *Think of a Garden* (1993) by John Kneubuhl. While very different in tone and style, these productions were key events in the development of Pasifika theatre in Aotearoa. We acknowledge the inspiration provided by Samoan author Albert Wendt, and survey earlier stage representations of the Pacific Islands. We also chart the rise of the first professional Pasifika actors in the 1980s, and the impact of Toi Whakaari: New Zealand Drama School and The Depot/Taki Rua.

TAOtahi and *Le Matau*

Theatre group TAOtahi was formed in 1981 by a group of Pasifika and Māori students at Wellington High School, supported by English teacher Felicity Day.[3] Group members were Mokalagi Tamapeau, Samson Samasoni, Maria Haenga-Collins (née Duffy), David Saena, Kellee Rei-Harris, Teiana Mavropoulos (née Everitt), Phillip Patau and Danny Karatea-Goddard. The politics of the group were signalled in their name, a combination of the acronym for Theatre Against Oppression (TAO) and the Māori words for 'spear' (tao) and 'one' (tahi).

> We ... were influenced by our families, historical events in Aotearoa, in the Pacific and Afro-American culture, and other parts of the world. The 80s was a most exciting time for the different political events that were occurring within

> Aotearoa, for example the resurgence of Māori activism in particular around the Treaty of Waitangi. Māori language was also making a resurgence, and within Māori and Pacific communities there was animated discussion around the ideologies of black men, black women/feminism, sexuality, unionism, NZ-born identities, overstayers, dawn raids, and a nuclear-free Pacific – to name a few.[4]

The group was initially employed at the Wellington Arts Centre to perform in the annual Summer City festival programme, although its political agenda sat uneasily within the parameters of that event. They devised a short play with music called *Atia*, about a Samoan street kid who is subjected to racism and bullying at school and later imprisoned for petty crime. Eteuati Ete, who was asked to play the lead role, recalls, '*Atia* became too political for the Summer City.' In its place TAOtahi created a 'safe' children's show, *Santa Claus of Rangiora*, written by Rei-Harris and Tamapeau, for performance in Wellington's Botanic Garden. Work continued on *Atia*, however, with the help of Palagi playwright Stephen Sinclair, and it was later presented in both Wellington and Auckland. Ete discovered how empowering theatre can be: 'People in the audience were crying, and the discussions afterwards brought to the fore a lot of issues that we as young kids couldn't really discuss openly with the public and with our own community.'

With the input of the company, Sinclair collaborated with Samson Samasoni on the script of *Le Matau*, New Zealand's first full-length Pasifika play. Opening at The Depot theatre (Wellington) in February 1984, *Le Matau* was a significant step up for TAOtahi in terms of scale and ambition.[5] The central character is a young Samoan man (Ioane Leota, played by Ete) who loses his connection with fa`asamoa through assimilation into Palagi society. Ioane migrates from Samoa to his auntie's Wellington home, where his cousins mock his unfashionable appearance and 'fresh-off-the-boat' naivety. He is employed as a real estate agent by the unscrupulous and ironically named Warren Goodman. Goaded by Goodman, the now-successful Ioane is torn between his duty to his family in Samoa and the enticements of the Palagi world. A crisis occurs when he informs Goodman that he is quitting to care for his sick father in Samoa, but is blackmailed into staying and cuts himself off from all family ties in Wellington. When his auntie berates him for rejecting fa`asamoa, his emotional response illustrates the conflicting pressures on young Pasifika migrants:

> **IOANE**: Ever since I came here everybody says Ioane do your best, find a good job, be a success in the Palagi world. Well I made it! Here I am, this is what you wanted![6]

TAOtahi was creating a new public space for highlighting social and political issues, and indeed, *Le Matau* had a strong political message at a time when many Palagi were either ignorant of, or anxious about, the growing population of Pasifika immigrants. Radically, it included several scenes entirely in Samoan that allowed Samoan-speaking audiences to experience the joy of hearing their own language spoken and sung onstage. The significance of the play's title, which translates as 'the fish hook', becomes clear in the following analogy between salemanship and fishing:

> **IOANE**: These Palagis, they are like fish that rise to the bait; and if the fisherman is wise he will choose the juiciest flesh for his hook ... You see, all I have done is to fish the Palagi way.[7]

The final scene contains a bleak, expressionist echo of this 'fishing' speech, where Ioane rejects his culture and sells his soul to Palagi capitalism.

Le Matau succeeded in attracting Pasifika audiences to theatre. Anton Carter noted, as late as 2002, that 'Pacific Island communities do not normally go to see live theatre; it is not a natural form of entertainment.'[8] Palagi reviewer Mary Paul's review for *Act* highlighted the special feeling of the opening night of *Le Matau* in 1984:

> It was on a hot Saturday night in February that we had the privilege of seeing the first-ever Samoan full-length play ... Instead of buying tickets we made a koha at the door and joined a large Samoan and Palagi audience.[9]

According to Ete,

> Samoans came out, and a lot of them had never seen theatre before. Probably White Sunday is the closest they'd ever come to something like theatre. When the lights came up on the stage, for many Samoans in the audience it was mind-blowing. A review came out in the paper and there was a photo of me, and it was a really good review, it said I did a great performance. And for the first time, my parents decided to come and see something that I was doing. They were really proud of me.

Le Matau introduced key themes for Pasifika theatre that would be explored in later plays, such as the pressures facing new migrants, the dominance of family and church, and racism and prejudice. It also highlighted the richness of Samoan language and music as important performance elements for future Pasifika plays.

After *Le Matau* TAOtahi disbanded. According to Ete, 'Everybody had grown up, and they were in it more for the politics than for the acting.'

Early representations of the Pacific on the New Zealand stage

Prior to the staging of *Le Matau*, Pasifika people were generally invisible in New Zealand drama, something that would be slow to change. As late as 2005 Teresia Teaiwa and Sean Mallon observed, in reference to the *Oxford History of New Zealand Literature* (1998): 'Given the dynamism and range of New Zealand theatre and drama, and contrasted with the relatively more rigorous reckoning given Maori culture in the work of Pakeha playwrights, the lack of attention afforded the Pacific presence in the country and the wider Pacific setting is noticeable.'[10]

A classic example of this invisibility can be seen in poet, novelist and playwright Alistair Te Ariki Campbell (1925–2009), whose cultural identity was masked in his dramatic works. Born in Rarotonga to a Cook Island mother and a Pākehā father of Scottish descent, Campbell was the first New Zealand playwright of Pasifika genealogy. When he was seven his parents died; with his brother he was sent from the remote island of Penrhyn in the Cook Islands to a New Zealand orphanage. Campbell recalled 'trying to rub off his dark skin in the bath: "To survive I felt that I had to make myself invisible."'[11]

Once established as a poet and editor, Campbell began writing radio dramas. None of these specifically reflect his Cook Island ancestry, although he acknowledged his Polynesian heritage in *Sanctuary of Spirits* (1963), which focuses on the raids of Te Rauparaha and was later published as an epic poem.[12] Later in life he had the chance to explore his afakasi identity in his poetry. As Paul Millar writes, 'Recovering his Pacific Island whakapapa (genealogy) through writing became a powerfully therapeutic means of healing childhood's wounds and coping with the harrowing demands of adapting to an alien culture.'[13]

A number of earlier plays by Palagi writers were set in the Pacific Islands and pre-figured some of the themes developed by Pasifika playwrights in later decades. Gordon Dryland's *Unlikely Places* (1979) was considered by Howard McNaughton in 1998 to be 'virtually the only play to address cultural friction between New Zealand and the Pacific'.[14] *The Man Called Jones* (1933) by Eric Bradwell (1908–1988) is a one-act play set on a generic 'island in the South Pacific', which explores the ambivalent position of being afakasi in the post-colonial Pacific.[15] John Thomson notes that Bradwell's theme was 'the supposed wretchedness of the half-caste, despised by both races'.[16] Bradwell was striving for authenticity – the play includes a number of words in the Cook Island language, and in the script he offers his assistance to 'any amateur producer who has no knowledge of island customs'.[17] The play reflects 1930s views on sexual politics in the Pacific: Bradwell's sexualised portrayal of the 'half-caste ... almost pure native'[18] girl, Parau, is reminiscent of Paul Gauguin's exoticised paintings of Tahitian women, a stereotype that would be effectively parodied in 1997 in Sima Urale's mockumentary film *Velvet Dreams*, and Makerita Urale's play *Frangipani Perfume*.[19]

Poet Allen Curnow (1911–2001) made a serious attempt to represent a historical view of the Cook Islands in his verse drama *The Axe* (1948).[20] His use of a chorus of 'ancestral voices of the island' together with a blind and ageing high priest recalls the conventions of Greek tragedy and suggests a desire to re-invent European mythic drama for Polynesia. *The Axe* is based on an account, by Māori scholar Sir Peter Buck, of Christian missionaries on Mangaia in the Cook Islands. In this work, the Christianisation of Mangaia is presented as a period of radical change and anxiety for the Cook Islanders. A deep feeling of unease spreads among the people as a Palagi ship, the 'god with enormous wings' approaches across the sea.[21] To the alarm of his chiefs and priests, King Numangatini, a pawn of the Tahitian missionary Davida, becomes a devout Christian and destroys the traditional gods of the island. This triggers an inter-tribal battle fought over the conflict between traditional beliefs and the new Christian orthodoxy. But the victory of Christianity is soured by the symbolic path of the European axe, which causes a series of tragic deaths including that of Numangatini himself. The axe represents the damaging force of colonisation that creates divisions between Pacific tribes and destroys cultural values and beliefs.

One marker of Pasifika invisibility in New Zealand drama was the practice of white actors sporting brown make-up to play Polynesian roles, a reflection of the centuries-old theatre practice of 'blacking up'. This was how Māori characters were represented on stage in plays like George Leitch's *The Land of the Moa* (1895). The Cook Islanders in the premiere production of *The Axe* at Canterbury University College in 1948 were all played by Palagi actors. In 2012 James Wenley, in an attempt to discover whether the play had relevance for a modern audience, staged a rehearsed reading of *The Axe* in Auckland with a Pasifika cast. Participants in Wenley's experiment predictably criticised its Eurocentric view of Pasifika people, but also found some merit:

> Junior Misimoa, who played Tupia in the reading, originated from the Cook Islands. He responded to the play as a record of a history of his own culture. He writes: 'There is a lot of history in the play that people [nowadays] need to hear about, especially within the Cook Island community. It will hold a lot of truth as a cultural essence that has been missing for a very long time.'[22]

In his play *Hearts of Gold* (BATS Theatre, Wellington, 1983), Craig Harrison created a partly fictional account, set in Samoa in 1916, of Somerset Maugham writing the short story 'Rain', and featuring the prostitute Sadie Thompson. Harrison's play shows Maugham writing the story, intercut with scenes of Rita Hayworth filming *Miss Sadie Thompson* in 1953. Samoan Iosefo Vaifale, a key character sympathetically portrayed by Harrison, has 'signed his life away to the American army'.[23] According to McNaughton, *Hearts of Gold* 'explores some of the parallels between sexual and colonial exploitation developed in Dryland's *Unlikely Places*'.[24]

Albert Wendt and the evolution of Pasifika drama

Samoan author Albert Wendt must be part of any history of Pasifika theatre. According to Victor Rodger he is 'the godfather, the river, the source for all of us. Albert wrote us all into existence with his work.'[25] Wendt's vision for Pasifika art, written in 1976, could be a manifesto for the Pasifika theatre that evolved in the 1990s:

> Our quest should not be for a revival of our past cultures but for the creation of new cultures which are free of the taint of colonialism and based firmly on our own pasts. The quest should be for a new Oceania.[26]

As the first Samoan novelist to come to prominence, Wendt holds a unique place in the history of Pacific and New Zealand literature. His first novel, *Sons for the Return Home* (1973), focuses on Sione, one of the few Pasifika students at a New Zealand university. This foundational text established themes that would continue to be worked through in Pasifika theatre in the years to come. In it, Wendt explores the contradictory pressures on young Pasifika migrants who are expected both to remain loyal to the family and fa`asamoa, and to succeed in the Palagi world. This is compounded by Sione's relationship with his Palagi girlfriend, which dissolves in the face of racism brought on by prejudice against intercultural marriage.

Adaptations of Wendt's fiction have formed the basis of some of the earliest dramatisations of Pasifika migration. Palagi writer and director Paul Maunder made a well-received feature film of *Sons for the Return Home* in 1979; Wendt's short story *Flying Fox in a Freedom Tree* became a feature film in 1989, adapted and directed by Palagi Martyn Sanderson; and his poem 'The contest' was dramatised by Paul Simei-Barton for Pacific Theatre Inc in 1993.

Maunder's film *Sons for the Return Home* featured Uelese Petaia as Sione, with Moira Walker and Lani Tupu (Snr) as his parents and Fiona Lindsay as his girlfriend Sarah. Walker (née MacDonald) had achieved earlier recognition playing opposite Gary Cooper in the Hollywood film *Return To Paradise* (1953), shot in Samoa. *Sons for the Return Home* was partially shot in Samoa and a significant proportion of the dialogue is in Samoan language with English subtitles. The juxtaposition of Samoan and New Zealand scenes throughout the movie highlights the contrast between village and city, and gives the viewer some sense of the disorientation of the Pasifika migrant experience. It was the first substantial dramatic representation to do so; it was also the first New Zealand film to be shown in the marketplace at the Cannes Film Festival, alongside *Goodbye Pork Pie* (1980).

As a Palagi-produced film, however, *Sons for the Return Home* required considerable cultural input from Samoan communities and individuals (including Walker and Tupu, who served as mentors). While Maunder acknowledged these communities, Sarina Pearson argues for the importance of Pasifika people taking artistic control of their own stories:

> Although community participation in image-making is an important dimension of intercultural filmmaking, it does not afford Pacific communities the freedom to represent themselves, nor does it fulfil their desires to tell stories from their own points of view.[27]

This desire was turned into reality not only by writers like Wendt, but also by the emergence of the first professional Pasifika actors who sought to represent their own cultures on stage.

'Being brown': Aotearoa's first professional Pasifika actors

Nathaniel Lees was the first Samoan to become a professional stage actor in Aotearoa. He would later become a leader as director, dramaturg and mentor, taking Pasifika theatre into the mainstream. In 1996 the *Listener* noted, 'Under Lees's impetus, Pacific Island theatre is slowly emerging as a distinct genre.'[28] Actor/playwright Fiona Collins noted in 2016, 'Nathaniel has been to theatre what Albert [Wendt] has been to literature.'[29]

Born in New Zealand to Samoan parents, Lees' personal pathway parallels some of the migration themes common to Pasifika plays. His professional acting debut was in *The Naval Officer* (1979) by Brian McNeill, a play about Captain

Cook's third and fatal voyage to the Pacific. Lees went along with some friends to audition at the Mercury Theatre[30] and was cast as one of the Hawaiians who killed Cook: 'They needed brown people to run onstage and kill him ... and that actually was my introduction to theatre, being brown.'[31] He was disturbed by a lack of authenticity in the production:

> [W]e had to ... wave our wooden spears around, speak what I thought was a nonsense language ... There were Hawaiian words in it, but some of the guys ... had worked in Hawai`i and they said, 'This doesn't make sense.'[32]

Lees remained at the Mercury for several years playing non-Pacific roles. He was inspired by Māori actor George Henare, a long-time member of the company: 'That man's skill in taking on a character and transforming words into a living thing was something that I admired intensely.'[33]

Lees' first opportunity to create Pacific work was with Statement Theatre in South Auckland, where he wrote, directed and acted in Theatre in Education (TIE) tours.[34] Initially Statement devised work based on New Zealand short stories and biographies of important Māori elders, such as Eruera Stirling. Lees felt their work could be more directly relevant to their audience, however; he held workshops with students from primary, intermediate and secondary schools in Otara in which they articulated their own experiences.

> They would tell me about the gangs, the fathers being at the pub all night and coming home, the fights between families, how they felt going to school – and we started creating little scenes. I got them to direct them[selves], so we weren't doing anything that wasn't true to the way they saw it ... I can't say that I've ever done anything since then that has brought me as much creative enlightenment as that period of time ...[35]

One of these students was South Auckland-born Jay Laga`aia. Lees recalls Laga`aia remarking, 'When you guys came over to our school, it was the first time I realised that we could do theatre, that brown faces on the stage were as acceptable as anything else.'[36] By 1985 Laga`aia was acting alongside Lees at the Mercury Theatre, and in 1993 he played the role of Uncle Lilo in Lees' first production of *Think of a Garden*.

While Lees and Laga`aia learned their trade as actors 'on the job', the New Zealand Drama School in Wellington (re-named Toi Whakaari in 1989) was playing an important role in training Pasifika actors.[37] Lani Tupu Jr was the first Samoan to graduate from the school in 1979, followed by Eteuati Ete and Patupatu Ripley in 1984 and Sima Urale in 1989. Iaheto Ah Hi was the first

Tokelauan graduate in 1994, followed in 1995 by Vela Manusaute (Niuean/ Samoan) and Karl Kite Rangi (Cook Islands).[38]

Lani Tupu Jr was born in New Zealand in 1955 to an English mother and Samoan father.[39] Like many Pasifika actors he gained his first performing experience in church plays. He became a company member at Auckland's Theatre Corporate[40] and later the Mercury, playing many classical and contemporary roles, but no Pasifika characters. In 1984 Tupu became the first Samoan actor to play the lead role in a New Zealand television drama series, in this case *Country GP*. His character, Dr Miller, was Māori, reflecting the common practice at the time of treating all Polynesian cultures as one for casting purposes. Although Lees, Laga`aia and Tupu were highly regarded actors, their cultural identity remained largely invisible behind this practice of colour-blind casting.

Like Tupu, Ete began acting while performing in church plays, discovering comedy at a White Sunday performance when he was about five. Ete was born in Samoa in 1962, the second child in a family of eight. His father, Rev Elder Risatisone Ete, was a minister and a lecturer at the Malua Theological College in Samoa; his mother, Fereni, was heavily involved in the work of the church.[41] 'My parents being ministers made my decision to go into theatre harder, as I was supposed to set a better example for young Samoans to seek higher academic rather than artistic achievements.'[42] The family moved to New Zealand when Ete was 12, where his parents led the Samoan Congregational Church in Newtown, Wellington. Ete attended Wellington College: 'At school drama wasn't something that rugby-playing boys were meant to do, so I hung out with the sports crowd.'

After appearing in *Atia* with TAOtahi, which inspired his interest in theatre, he gained a place at the New Zealand Drama School. Ete enjoyed his study, although the roles he played were Palagi: 'There were no Samoan roles. The only thing I struggled with at drama school was all the English accents we had to learn. I couldn't get my head or tongue around that. I just thought, I'm never going to play one of these characters, so why even try?' His opportunity to play a Samoan role came at the end of his first year, when drama school director George Webby gave him special permission to act in TAOtahi's *Le Matau*.

After graduating, Ete joined Rangimoana Taylor's theatre company Te Ohu Whakaari and remained involved in Māori theatre for several years, appearing in Hone Tuwhare's landmark play *In the Wilderness Without a Hat* (1989) and Apirana Taylor's *Te Whanau a Tuanui Jones* (1990).[43] 'There weren't many Māori practitioners coming out of drama school at the time, so I was close enough to fit the bill. I had no difficulties in doing the Māori roles.' In 1987, driven to create work for himself, he wrote, directed and performed the first solo show by a Pacific Islander in New Zealand, a comedy revue with music called *The Johnny Smith Myth*, which charts the rise to stardom of an ordinary Samoan.

Ete spent most of the 1990s as a Pacific Islands arts advisor with Creative New Zealand, advocating for Pasifika artists.[44] In 1999, inspired by the success of comedy groups The Brownies and The Naked Samoans, Ete created *Coconuts*, another solo comedy. This was a series of skits featuring fa`asamoa experiences and cultural misunderstandings. Ete's interest in comedy later evolved into The Laughing Samoans, discussed further in chapter seven.

Sima Urale was born in 1967 in Savai`i, Western Samoa, which she describes as 'pretty much *National Geographic*: grass huts, traditional fales, beautiful. Even right up to [the age of] 12 you didn't have to wear clothes.'[45] The family moved to Wellington when Sima was six and her sister Makerita was nine. Sima was inspired by her father's natural ability as an artist, and credits her mother with fostering ambition in her and her siblings:

> Mum made me dance in front of family and sing songs. From five years old I was already taking the piss out of people. But Mum also had us dancing in little lavalavas and bikini tops doing the hula ... we were doing Samoan siva, Cook Island dancing and hula out in public – so embarrassing![46]

Urale disliked school and, with her mother's blessing, took a year out to consider her future. She encountered Māori director Rangimoana Taylor, who was running a government-funded scheme for unemployed actors. Urale joined the group, performed children's theatre – and discovered a love of acting. After six months Taylor suggested that she audition for Toi Whakaari. 'I loved every moment of Toi Whakaari because I suddenly had these disciplines I had to follow.' Not wanting to be pigeonholed as Samoan, she chose Dame Ngaio Marsh as the subject of a self-devised monologue, and in her 1989 graduation production of Chekhov's *The Cherry Orchard* was cast as Madame Ranyevskaya. Urale was part of what she calls 'the first big brown intake at Toi Whakaari', which included Māori actors Cliff Curtis and Hori Ahipene.[47] 'One of our biggest fears was, who the heck's going to want us?'

On leaving drama school Urale initially found herself cast in Māori roles in productions such as Renée's *Jeannie Once* (1990) and David Geary's *Pack of Girls* (1991). However, in 1991 she also appeared in *The Taming of the Shrew*: 'I thought it was wicked that they were putting me in a Shakespeare – these people [were] acknowledging my talent or craft rather than looking at my colour.'

After graduating from the Victorian College of the Arts film programme in 1994, Urale became the first Samoan female film director. Her credits include the award-winning short film *O Tamaiti* (1997), *Velvet Dreams* (1997) and the feature-length *Apron Strings* (2008). She maintained her theatre associations with leading roles in *Think of a Garden* and *Frangipani Perfume*.

By the end of the 1980s, a core group of professional Samoan actors was building successful careers in New Zealand and beyond. The next step was to create the infrastructure to develop Pacific stories for the stage, encourage collaboration, and build an alternative model to the existing Palagi theatre. The first company to address this need was The Depot in Wellington.

From The Depot to Taki Rua: Support and collaboration

Taki Rua is a positive story of collaboration. MAKERITA URALE[48]

The role of The Depot – later renamed Taki Rua – cannot be underestimated in the story of Pasifika theatre.[49] Opened as an alternative performance space by Downstage Theatre in 1981, it was taken over in 1983 by a collective of independent theatre artists who resolved to stage only New Zealand work.[50] Although there were no Māori and Pasifika members in the original collective, The Depot was the first theatre to welcome extensive input from Māori and Pasifika practitioners, and became a natural home for their plays, devised theatre, rehearsed readings and dance. Sean Mallon recalls how his exposure to Māori theatre at The Depot piqued his interest in Pacific theatre:

> The first play I went to that I wasn't forced to see was a Māori production called *Daddy's Girl* [1990] by Rena Owen. Once I saw the mix of people involved and the stories they were telling, I started to go regularly.[51]

The Depot became a focus for wide-ranging political debate – feminist, Marxist, post-colonial – including ways of representing Māori and Pasifika issues on stage. Such debates came to a head in 1986 when Palagi Simon Wilson made an ambitious attempt to dramatise the colonisation of the Pacific in a parodic musical *South Pacific – The Rainbow* (scored by Rod Dunbar). Wilson deconstructed the colonialist assumptions of the American musical *South Pacific*, exposing the impact of issues such as the Mau protest movement in Samoa, nuclear testing, tourism, exploitation of Pacific workers and the 1985 sinking of the *Rainbow Warrior*. Reviewer Paul Maunder saw the musical as an exercise in portraying 'pakeha guilt', arguing that 'feelings of guilt about the colonial past, while relevant, can simply continue the colonising mode'.[52] In the cast of eight, Polynesia was represented by Eteuati Ete, Samson Samasoni and Māori actress Pona Te Hika. Reviewer Helen White praised these actors but felt they were 'under-used, to the detriment of the whole':

> The experience of the Mau uprising of 1929 was symbolically represented by a spirited slap-dance to fast drumming and the singing of 'Filemu Samoa', 'Peace (for) Samoa', in the context of a bloody war. Samson Samasoni and Eteuati Ete were here allowed to play the heroes of tragedy rather than the victims of farce; we had a sense of the dimensions of what has been destroyed.[53]

White's review demonstrates the potential to create powerful moments of theatre using Polynesian performance elements. But despite good intentions, Wilson's play remained an outsider's view, with a tendency to portray Pasifika people as victims. As White suggests, the dynamic presence of the Samoan actors subverted this view. The most telling critique came from Samasoni, who wrote a piece for the *New Zealand Times* outlining his misgivings about acting in a play which was a 'Palagi vision':

> I began to question why I had accepted a role in Simon Wilson's play when its stance was clearly not a Polynesian one ... *South Pacific – The Rainbow* was written by a Palagi, performed by Palagis, for Palagis. My role, and that of my fellow Polynesian actors, was to support what the Palagis had to say and to help them challenge other Palagis into recognising their past.[54]

Such debates led to The Depot increasing its commitment to Māori and Pasifika artists telling their own stories. In 1994 a name-change – to Taki Rua – reflected the growing partnership with tangata whenua.[55] Taki rua is a Māori weaving pattern in which two strands move together in the same direction, constantly intertwining. The new name was symbolic of the mission to bring Māori and other cultures together to create innovative theatre for Aotearoa. The first Māori company to perform regularly at The Depot was Rangimoana Taylor's Te Ohu Whakaari, whose members included Eteuati Ete and Whetu (Esther) Fala, the latter of Samoan and Māori descent.

During the 1990s Māori practitioners, including Mere Boynton and Hone Kouka, took on management roles in Taki Rua. Makerita Urale, whose sister Vaimaila was the box office manager, recalls, 'There was little colour barrier in Wellington in the 90s. I was in the whānau of Taki Rua at home and in the theatre with Pasifika, Māori, Pākehā and Asian artists.'[56] Makerita went on to produce a number of shows at Taki Rua, including *Women Off the Planet* (a festival of women's performance), and wrote her first play for the venue, a children's show called *Popo the Fairy* (1996), which was performed in Samoan and English and an invented fairy language.[57]

In the same period Taki Rua hosted visiting Pasifika productions such as Pacific Theatre's *The Contest* and *Tusitala and the House of Spirits* from Auckland, and productions by Christchurch-based company Pacific Underground.[58] In 1997, in order for Taki Rua to become a touring production company, the venue was closed. As Taki Rua Productions, the company concentrated on Māori theatre but continued to support Pasifika work by producing plays such as *Sons* (1998) by Victor Rodger and Toa Fraser's *Paradise* (2001).

Setting the bar: *Think of a Garden*

While *Le Matau* was an important milestone in the development of Pasifika theatre, even more significant were two contrasting productions, in 1993 and 1995, of John Kneubuhl's *Think of a Garden*. Although the play was not written in Aotearoa, it was produced at the time when Pacific Theatre Inc and Pacific Underground were evolving into mature companies, and it served as an inspiration for the writing and production of more complex Pasifika works. As Makerita Urale notes, 'John Kneubuhl set the bar.'[59]

Kneubuhl was born in American Samoa, studied with playwright and novelist Thornton Wilder at Yale University, and worked as a professional scriptwriter for many years in Hollywood before returning home in 1968. Over the next 24 years, during which he took a leadership role in education as a lecturer and as programme director of a bicultural education programme, his 'return to roots' demonstrated his deep commitment to Polynesian languages and culture.[60] His writing during this time included the trilogy *Mele Kanikau: A pageant* (1975), *A Play: A play* (c. 1990) and *Think of a Garden*, his most autobiographical work and the last play he wrote before his death in 1992.

Think of a Garden dramatises the disturbing impact of colonialism on Samoan identity. The action unfolds in Leone, American Samoa, in the late 1920s. Aristocratic New Zealand-educated Lu`isa, the granddaughter of a highborn Samoan woman and an Englishman, is married to Frank Kreber, an American plantation owner and lawyer. Their nine-year-old afakasi son (based on Kneubuhl himself) is represented both as a child (David), and an adult (The Writer) who narrates the action. Kneubuhl's championing of the Samoan language and culture is reflected in the fale aitu-inspired character of the housemaid Pito, who speaks entirely in Samoan. The family is excited at the prospect of hosting the leader of the Mau independence movement, Tupua Tamasese, a relative of Lu`isa's. Their anticipation turns to horror when they learn that he has been killed by New Zealand police while leading a peaceful protest in Apia. Subsequent efforts by Lu`isa's brothers Lilo and Frank, to pursue justice on behalf of the Samoan people, come to nothing. Their advocacy reflects the long Samoan struggle for political autonomy that ended with independence in 1962. The fallout from Tamasese's death eventually leads to the break-up of the family.

The portraits of David and Lu`isa powerfully evoke the spiritual contradictions in a colonised people. Christianity is represented by Patrick, a Catholic Marist brother who teaches David, while Lu`isa is torn between a desire to be seen as a progressive, modern Christian and her innate pre-Christian beliefs. Patrick is increasingly perturbed by David's obsession with his 'imaginary friend', a spirit called Veni. David's relationship with Veni leads to a kind of possession until he is visibly transformed: he is 'naked but for a tapa lavalava around his waist' and has 'tried to change the color of his skin to brown with some kind of paint'.[61] This striking image shows a confused attempt by an afakasi child to connect with his Samoan cultural identity. Spiritual symbolism employed throughout the play shows how the loss of political autonomy is only the surface of a much deeper sense of cultural insecurity.

Think of a Garden launched Nathaniel Lees' professional directing career. He was first exposed to the play as an actor in a rehearsed reading for the May 1992 Australasian Playwrights' Workshop in Canberra, alongside Lani Tupu Jr, Sima Urale and Eteuati Ete.[62] According to Lees,

> It affected us so much that tears were shed nearly every time we read it. It was such a joy to read about ourselves and our language that we knew it would reach whosoever came to see it.[63]

Ete commented:

> It was a really special piece that touched upon some major issues for us as a Samoan culture, with the assassination, the Mau independence movement, inter-racial marriages, the clash of the two cultures in the couple – and the young boy, trying to come to terms with all of that.[64]

Directed by Stuart Devenie, the reading was well received, but Lees felt that a Palagi director could not do justice to the play:

> Stuart was looking for little hooks to make it one amazing play, but it was already a great play, had he known how to interpret it ... Being part of that culture, being

> Samoan, I knew about the relationships that he had set up ... We knew it had to be done, Ete, Lani and I ... but we couldn't think of anyone to direct ... In the end I said, 'Alright, I'll do it!'[65]

Lees directed two productions of *Think of a Garden*. The first, at Auckland's Watershed Theatre, opened on 11 February 1993 with Lani Tupu Jr as The Writer and Jay Laga`aia playing Uncle Lilo.[66] The second opened at Taki Rua on 8 March 1995, where Lees played The Writer with Eteuati Ete as Uncle Lilo and Sima Urale as Lu`isa.[67] Lees took a different artistic approach to each production. At the Watershed, out of respect for the mana of the recently deceased playwright,[68] he staged the play exactly as Kneubuhl had intended, following his detailed naturalistic stage directions for set design, lighting and blocking to the letter.

The response to the production from Samoan audiences at the Watershed was overwhelming. As Lees described it,

> People were moved to tears. All the Samoan people ... got up at the end, sang for us and talked to us. At the end of the play we had to sit there and listen to these people saying how happy they were that they were actually alive to see their young people on stage doing these things.[69]

Reviewer Patrick Smith compared the play with *The End of the Golden Weather*, Bruce Mason's 'nostalgic masterpiece': '*Think of a Garden* is a rich and unique experience, and deserves to become as much a part of our Pacific theatre repertoire as Mason's beloved classic.'[70] Lees recalled,

> The joy of it was hearing our language, or my language, spoken on stage ... [Pito] started speaking and the Samoans started falling over themselves laughing. There were quite a few Palagi people there but they were infected by the laughter of the Polynesians and I could see big smiles on their faces.[71]

Lees wanted to bring out the fa`asamoa and spiritual aspects of the play in his 1995 Taki Rua production, and therefore chose a much more stylised approach.[72] This pared-down version dispensed with the naturalistic set and props specified by Kneubuhl and, in another departure from the author's intentions, Lees as The Writer remained onstage as a constant presence observing the action. Lees felt this was a much more Samoan way of telling the story:

> It was the playing with time that Samoans understand. The narrator was much more in the action. He actually sat at the table while they talked to each other. He sat with the boy, who was himself ... Samoans know that the spirits are all around them, and I wanted to keep playing with that.[73]

These experiments allowed Lees to develop his own distinctive directing style, informed as much by his Samoan cultural heritage as his training in Western theatre. This is further demonstrated in his subsequent productions, such as *A Frigate Bird Sings,* discussed in chapter five.

Ete regards *Think of a Garden* as 'one of the pinnacles' of his theatre career: 'A lot of Samoans came and saw the show, and they were really blown away by it. It was a step up from *Le Matau* and, for a lot of our people, it made [the Mau independence struggle] real, whereas before it was just a history lesson.'

Sima Urale, who had played Lu`isa in the Canberra reading of *Think of a Garden*, recreated the role at Taki Rua. She was ready to take on this demanding role despite some misgivings:

> I always felt too young to play Lu`isa. I said to Nathaniel [Lees], 'I wish I was ten years older.' Because of my experience in the village, I could relate more to Pito. But luckily, because I'd played Ranyevskaya [at Toi Whakaari] that really helped with the maturity of the matriarch. They were quite similar characters, tragic figures who want to be something they're not.

Urale's performance attracted special attention from reviewers. Laurie Atkinson felt that she played Lu`isa 'with statuesque beauty and rigid control',[74] while for Patricia Cooke, 'Together with Lees as narrator, her powerful performance was the central focus of the play.'[75]

Reviewers were in agreement that this play and Lees' production of it were exceptional. As Atkinson observed: 'While *Think of a Garden* is not the first Samoan play to be performed in Wellington, it is by far the most distinguished ... The second half builds slowly and inevitably to an explosion of emotions in one magnificent scene that can be compared to the tragic family dramas of Eugene O'Neill.'[76] Reviewer Susan Budd endorsed this view: 'Nathaniel Lees has brought an outstanding tale of the search for cultural identity, on both a personal and national level, to Taki Rua.'[77] The enthusiastic reception by Palagi reviewers was reflected at the 1995 Chapman Tripp Theatre Awards, where *Think of a Garden* was awarded Production of the Year, Director of the Year and Best Female Actor in a Supporting Role for Sima Urale.[78]

As we have seen, there was significant energy in developing Pasifika work in Wellington in the 1980s, in which TAOtahi, The Depot/Taki Rua and Toi Whakaari played crucial roles. Nathaniel Lees' decision to become a director and Makerita Urale's move into producing at Taki Rua provided key leadership. The two landmark productions of *Think of a Garden* proved not only that there was a broad audience for Pasifika theatre, but also that Pasifika practitioners could produce work of the highest quality. This complemented the energy in the companies emerging in Auckland and Christchurch, to be discussed in the next three chapters.

2.

Pacific Theatre Inc: A sense of Pasifika identity

I started 20 years ago and it's been a hard battle. It's extremely difficult for PI stories to be told, because there are not enough resources.

JUSTINE SIMEI-BARTON[1]

Justine Simei-Barton must take a position centre stage in any history of Pasifika theatre in Aotearoa. When she began her work there were no companies or plays in Auckland that provided a sense of Pasifika identity. As director, mentor, facilitator and political activist, and with the support of her husband Paul Simei-Barton, she has provided career-launching opportunities for a new generation of Pasifika practitioners. In 1987 Justine and Paul Simei-Barton founded Pacific Theatre Inc, 'a theatre that would be capable of bringing the vitality of Pacific Island performance traditions into a modern theatrical context'.[2] In particular, they championed the use of the traditional comic art form of fale aitu in Pasifika theatre.[3]

Justine Simei was born in 1961 in Porirua, Wellington. Her parents had migrated from Samoa: her father was from the village of Sasina in Savai`i, and her mother from Solosolo in Upolo. In Wellington her father took a job at the freezing works. The family settled well into their new environment and participated regularly in church activities. Her mother loved to sing and play the guitar around the house, at church, and at family gatherings. Justine attended Porirua College and describes herself as one of the 'naughty girls' there. Clever but easily bored, she skipped occasional classes – yet despite this she discovered an early love of Shakespeare, nurtured by 'a wonderful English teacher'.[4] From this grew an interest in performance for which she became an unofficial director, 'although I didn't know that's what it was'. She credits her teachers with seeing leadership qualities that came easily to her: 'I could gather people; kids would do stuff for me.'[5] Fellow students brought her ideas and scripts for short pieces they had previously enjoyed performing in Sunday school, such as the biblical story of *Tobias and the Angel*. 'If we wanted them to sing or dance, it wasn't a big deal for us to gather a band together, because PI kids are really talented.' Participation was not limited to Porirua College students – a general audition call, perhaps through the church, could attract a range of skilled performers. Parents enjoyed what they saw and often asked for performances to be repeated at church, and Justine valued this level of support from PI elders. Equally important to her was the fact that 'performing arts are respected in the Islands'.

After high school Justine studied for a year at Victoria University of Wellington and worked briefly at Downstage Theatre as an assistant stage manager, where she gained valuable professional theatre experience. She then moved north to study law at Auckland University. She found nothing to relate to in Auckland's theatre scene, as she later told Linda Herrick:

> From being brought up in Porirua where theatre was alive to come to a city that had one of the world's largest Polynesian populations ... it was monocultural. There wasn't anything I could relate to. I'm not saying I didn't understand the texts or the plays, but there were no brown faces apart from Don Selwyn – and I saw a production where Jim Moriarty played Hamlet.[6] Those two inspired me.[7]

Discovering fale aitu

Justine met Paul Barton at Auckland University. Paul was born in Lagos, Nigeria, to a mother of mixed Jewish/Turkish descent and a New Zealand father (an Anglican minister). The family had returned to New Zealand when Paul was three. Justine and Paul were married in May 1987 and shortly afterwards made a trip to Samoa where they visited family in Sasina, Justine's father's village. Here, for the first time, they encountered fale aitu. Justine recalls,

> It was a fundraising event, and there was all this noise happening in this remote village, which just doesn't happen. And so my grandfather sent us down to the fale and everybody was there, from the little kids to the very old people, just laughing, spontaneously cracking up. These old men were playing the clowns. So we'd seen it in action, and we'd seen the impact it had, everybody hanging off the poles of the longhouse and just being free to crack up. I was impressed, because my dad's village is very conservative, and very traditional. But that particular night, it was just freedom of expression.

Paul adds, 'I think seeing the fale aitu in that island context was probably quite a shock. Justine suddenly realised that there was an authentic tradition.'[8] Justine described the concept:

> The fale aitu practitioners were the news spreaders, so if you had something to say or were aggrieved about anything, or the politicians wanted to send a message to the villagers, they would do it through the fale aitu – who would turn it into a comedy skit or satire so that nobody would get offended. The actors would be absolutely protected because the spirits would come down on them, so they were allowed to say and do anything and everything. It was a way of balancing society.

As Sean Mallon notes, Pacific Theatre Inc was 'founded on the concepts and principles of fale aitu to see if what was a very old theatrical practice could offer a theory and technique for a new type of contemporary theatre'.[9] Over the next few years, through a series of workshops and performances, the Simei-Bartons explored fale aitu clowning practice alongside traditions such as the kula ki`i puppet theatre of Hawai`i. These classic forms 'employ oratory, song, poetry, music, dance, puppetry and clowning to create performances both for ceremonial purposes and for popular entertainment'.[10] The company aspired to develop these physical, non-naturalistic, multi-disciplinary forms of theatre.

Feiva/Favour: Sowing the seeds (1987–88)

Justine stumbled across a play script in the Auckland University library that she found herself drawn to. It was *Feiva/Favour*, a musical from Papua New Guinea by John Kolia.[11] Set in a Port Moresby slum, it focuses on the hard-edged, realistic portrayal of an adolescent street gang as they confront welfare officers, the law, sexuality, teen pregnancy, poverty and mortality. The play, filled with song and dance, has a strong political message conveyed with a degree of irony: 'Down here are the poor, the rich are over there.'[12] In act one Murgatroyd, the assistant gang leader, and Zips, his girlfriend, sing about their memories of the villages they come from. Zips provides a romantic view of false paradise by the ocean – a vision quickly shattered when she sings of the truth: heat, dirt, poverty, drunkenness, theft and violence.[13]

Justine immediately saw resonances between the experiences of these Port Moresby teenagers and those of the wider Pacific region:

> The play examines the breakdown of traditional cultural values as young people are forced to leave the security of their villages and migrate to the cities. In a pattern that has occurred throughout the Pacific, these youths find themselves unable to return to the rigidity of village life and excluded from full participation in Western consumer society.[14]

Feiva is infused with 'an earthy sense of humour and an exuberant optimism',[15] and these features, alongside the fact that it was not 'politically didactic', drew Justine most strongly to the work. Galvanised into action, she began to look for a Pacific theatre group who would take it on:

> I thought, 'I wonder if there's a theatre company I could show this to', thinking that there must be several, because Auckland has one of the world's largest Polynesian populations. But there was a huge void. I thought, 'I don't know if I want to do this on my own.' But Paul really encouraged me. He said, 'It can't be that hard.'

The next step was to make it happen herself. Resources that had been open to her in Wellington were not available in Auckland. 'I wasn't associated with any churches [in Auckland], because I hadn't been going for quite some time.' Instead, she drew on her experience at Porirua College: 'I just put out a notice saying, "Is anybody interested in putting on a Pacific Island play?"'

The first person to respond was Sefa Enari, a nephew of the opera singer Iosefa Enari. At the time he was running dance workshops at Auckland secondary schools and he was keen to create choreography for the show. Enari suggested bringing in Kirsten Zemke, a talented composer, and together the three of them looked at the script.

Justine then wrote to John Kolia to sound him out, and asked him to provide a tape of the music for the show. After listening to this, she decided instead to ask Zemke to compose an original score. The result was a blend of 'soul, reggae and funk with traditional Polynesian rhythms'.[16] Choreographer Lemi Ponifasio, whose future career would bring him an international reputation, also came on board.

Justine now required 22 Polynesian actors. She was aware of George Henare (a mainstay at the Mercury Theatre at that time), Lani Tupu Jr and Nathaniel Lees, but felt unable to approach these seasoned professionals. 'I thought, they're already established, they wouldn't want to mess around with a bunch of kids.' The only option was to start from scratch with untrained beginners:

> Sefa [Enari] and I decided to put out a general call in the university, because we come from churches where you just put the word out and you get hundreds. So people started auditioning ... And Dave Fane was one of them.

At that time Fane was a student at Auckland University, interested primarily in rugby and with no significant acting experience or aspiration. He recalls:

> Me and my mates were going for a pub crawl, and we were tanked. And there was a sign outside the Little Maidment Theatre saying auditions for some Pacific Island thing. And so we just bowled on in for a laugh, 'cause it was on the way to the bar, this group of six of us. It was more to take the mickey out of it, 'cause we'd never done anything like it, and we had a good laugh. That was on a Friday, and then on the Sunday, some person rang me and my mate Peter Brown, and said, 'Would you like to be in this Papua New Guinea musical?' And we went 'What? Aw!'[17]

Another young actor who joined the company was Niuean-born Shimpal Lelisi, at that time in his final year at high school. Lelisi remembers the experience that drew him in:

> A friend of mine was stage-managing the production and they were looking for people. She convinced us one Sunday afternoon to come in and have a look. That was the first time I met David Fane, standing in the middle of the floor, getting chairs thrown at him. I thought it was the funniest thing I had ever seen. And I kept turning up for rehearsals from then on.[18]

He was given a small role in *Feiva* as a member of the Rascals gang, led by David Fane. Lelisi had acted in Sunday school plays at the Pacific Gospel Mission in Ponsonby, and had appeared in some school productions, such as *HMS Pinafore*, but this was the next level: 'It was theatre. You had to think about your character, you had to make decisions. I learned all that with Justine at Pacific Theatre.'

With the company assembled, the next step was to form an incorporated society to enable funding applications – and Pacific Island Theatre Inc was born. The name was shortened to Pacific Theatre in publicity and posters. The 25 original members were those in the *Feiva/Favour* company. The fact that the cast consisted of relatively young untried actors reflected the lack of opportunities in Auckland for Pacific Islanders to demonstrate their talent in, as Justine described it, 'a theatre scene dominated by white culture'.[19] From February 1988 fundraising and planning were priorities. They needed $7000 for the production, and received a small grant from the QEII Arts Council. Justine was so determined to make the show happen that she provided $2000 from her own pocket towards costs.[20] The use of the university's Little Maidment Theatre allowed some savings to be made: 'Most of us were students, so we were able to get really cheap rates and use the facilities.'

Rehearsals were held for eight hours a week over two months. Most of the cast of Pacific Islanders and Māori were still in their late teens and were either at school or university. Fane recalls an initially cautious attitude to the process:

> We turned up, and we did the show, but we were still rugby heads, sort of like 'this is a bit strange and artsy'. But there was something about the camaraderie – something about the cast as a team – that connected with me and my mate Peter Brown. We could see some value in it.

Justine had to learn the director's role on the job. Her initial thinking was 'you just get people together and try and guide them'. Although there was a drama diploma offered at Auckland University, at that time run by Mervyn Thompson, she remained self-taught, reading 'a lot of books about theatre and human relationships', including Konstantin Stanislavski, and Peter Brook's *The Empty Space*.[21] She began to attend performances and saw 'hundreds of plays', though she found little to engage her. She wrote to directors Raymond Hawthorne and Paul Minifie at Theatre Corporate and, after meeting Minifie, was invited to come into the theatre and observe rehearsals, which she did whenever she could.

> It gave me ideas, just observing. I used to watch Raymond rehearse the actors, and think, 'why does he keep yelling at everybody like that?' I used to think the sets and costumes, and the way Raymond used the space, was good. And I spent quite a bit of time talking to Paul. He was lovely.

When it came to directing her own cast, it wasn't always easy. She had to contend not only with the raw energy and unfocused talent of her actors, but also with the undercurrent of the relative position of men and women in Pacific society. This was something she struggled with: 'As a Pacific Island woman you are also fighting Pacific Island men, which is another thing I have found quite dispiriting over the years. I have to fight the Palagis and now I've got to fight you bastards as well.'[22]

Vela Manusaute recalls,

> She was very tough. Strong. We were fresh, wanting to act, we just came out of high school, no idea what theatre is. But we all wanted to be on stage. We had all the energy, but in terms of discipline, man it was shocking. I remember she threw chairs. It was only when I was in charge of my own stories that I understood her. She had courage and stood up for Pacific stories to be told on stage and screen. She was a fighter, and looking back now I respect her and what she stood for.[23]

Anapela Polataivao shared this admiration for Justine: 'I admired her because she was the only PI woman that I knew of at that time gathering talent and bringing them together for work.'[24]

Justine may have exercised tough love, but she was very supportive of her young actors. Lelisi remembers that when he and others went to audition for Toi Whakaari, Justine generously paid their audition fees. She also encouraged Manusaute and Fane to audition. According to Fane,

> Justine actually put me onto drama school, saying there was a significant lack of Pacific Island talent coming through. She was really good about pushing people towards studying to get better. It's not enough to have a raw talent, you've got to hone it somewhere. She was great.

Feiva/Favour opened on 4 August 1988 and played for a week. Justine's aim had been to get the piece accepted as professional work – something that would showcase the skills of her performers and create a place in Auckland for Pacific theatre, and she regarded it as a success. As she told the *NZ Herald*, 'In the past, Pacific Island culture has often been regarded on a superficial, tourist dance-and-entertainment level ... For the first time in Auckland, a production is being staged from the Pacific Island perspective, and married with Western theatre techniques.'[25] This hybrid approach was key to the work of Pacific Theatre. Although their first production was from Papua New Guinea, it was infused with a Polynesian perspective, especially through the dance movement and Zemke's original music with its Pacific rhythms.

The play drew many of its audiences from the Pacific Island community. 'We had such a huge cast, and most of them were connected to some kind of church ... they just brought all their families out.'[26] Bringing Pacific Islanders into a theatre to encounter themes that reflected common experience across the Pacific was a significant achievement in 1988, but this was tempered by Bernadette Rae's review in the *NZ Herald*, which found much to criticise.[27] Rae prefaced her remarks by noting that it was 'most painful' to have to apply professional standards to a group whose 'extreme newness and obvious lack of experience' seemed paramount. Praising the energy and enthusiasm of the cast, Rae expressed problems as she perceived them, ranging from direction to diction, from tuneless singers to lyrics lost under the over-loud recorded soundtrack. Defining *Feiva* as 'in many ways a Polynesian *Grease*', she ameliorated her disappointment by commenting on the strength of Pule Simei (Zips) as a key performer. She also favourably noted the male chorus dancing, and the group singing 'when the stronger voices picked up the others and flew'.

Over 20 years later, the sting of this Palagi reviewer's response to Pacific Theatre still has the power to rouse Justine to irritation. 'I thought, how dare they? They think all we can do is just sing and dance, and wave our hips, and show our tits and bums? She doesn't actually think we have an intellect.' Justine does, however, see both sides: 'I guess on reflection it was fair enough.'

The Nine Night: Familiar resonances (1989)

Although disappointing, this critical response motivated Justine to keep the company alive by actively looking for a second play to produce.

> I went out to look for a black play where we could start developing our actors. There were enough white plays out there, so why do that? Pacific Theatre is multicultural and always has been. Our people weren't being cast in anything because there were no roles out there for them.

She chose *The Nine Night* by Caribbean writer Edgar White. His work had been seen briefly in the North Island in 1979, when the Keskidee Aroha project from London toured marae and community centres presenting pieces that included a scene from White's *Lament for Rastafari*.[28] *The Nine Night* provided the black sensibility Justine had been seeking and, with a cast of seven, was a more manageable undertaking than *Feiva*.

White's play has themes that resonate with Pasifika audiences. Set in London, it explores an immigrant Jamaican family whose younger members have adopted European attitudes while the father seeks to have his children respect traditional ways. Several actors from *Feiva* appeared in the play, including David Fane as the father Hamon Williams, Lauiula Muliaumaseali`i as his wife Irene, and Pule Simei.[29] It speaks highly of Fane's innate talent that, while still a very young man, he was able to portray the necessary stature and failings of the family patriarch.[30] Fane pinpoints this production as the time when he began to take acting more seriously and realised that there was 'something a bit beyond the rugby field'.

New to the company for this production was Brian (later Vela) Manusaute, an 18-year-old school leaver who had performed in plays at Selwyn College. He was cast in the role of Izak, Hamon's younger son, described by White as 'a raver and young man of great expectations'. Manusaute's experience reflects Justine's ability to draw together young people who were passionate about theatre:

> I saw a pamphlet that said 'Pacific Theatre. Come and audition.' But there was a bus strike, and I was living in Orakei and the audition was in Point Chevalier. That's a very long way, and our family didn't have a car. But my friend worked in a dairy shop so I went in and I asked him if he could help me out with my dream

to be on stage. He ended up giving me some money and I taxied all the way from Orakei to Point Chevalier. Oh man, I really, really wanted to be in the group. I saw Pacific Theatre and I thought, I can fit in here. Justine heard about the story, I got the role and they dropped me back home.

The Nine Night opened at the Little Maidment on 20 July 1989 and played for a week. Audiences included many students as well as a Pasifika contingent. Reviewing the production for the *Listener*, Bill Lennox took a positive view and singled out Fane and Muliaumaseali`i for praise. While much of the review focused on White's play, Lennox provided strong encouragement for the development of a genuine Pacific writing voice:

> My first thought was that it was a pity to embark on such a worthy enterprise with a foreign play. But Edgar White's script is lively, the message clear and the parallels apparent ... In the absence of local scripts, White seems exactly the right place to start. From this distance we can reject or accept the detail of the parallel as fits our experience.[31]

Lennox's review in a national publication brought Pacific Theatre Inc into wider focus.

Robeson – Song of Freedom (1990)

The third production by Pacific Theatre was another New Zealand premiere, this time by white English actor and writer Andy Rashleigh. *Robeson – Song of Freedom* opened at the Little Maidment in September 1990, featuring Eddie Muliaumaseali`i as the famous black American singer Paul Robeson. Justine recalls:

> [Robeson] was a freedom fighter, an intellectual and an opera singer. My dad was a Robeson fan and a union member, and I saw the connection and parallels between Robeson and my father. And I thought, we can take our score up to a whole new level because they won't be expecting us to be opera singers!

Shimpal Lelisi, who appeared in *Robeson*, recalls how he became more aware of cultural politics through Justine: 'She was teaching us our role and responsibilities as brown players, because there were hardly any brown actors then. You could count them on your hand.'

The play had premiered in London in March 1988, at which point *Guardian* critic Michael Billington had dismissed it as 'emphatically not' a great play, suggesting that its effect was to merely 'diminish a Titan'.[32] Sally Markham, in her review of the Auckland production for the *Dominion Sunday Times*, saw the play as powerful and ironic but felt it needed 'subtle direction to unlock an understanding of the person'.[33] Muliaumaseali`i was an inexperienced actor – Justine recalls that this was his first substantial role – and this was apparent in his performance. While Markham praised his stature and quiet dignity, she considered he was 'less convincing as the man of anger and passion for social justice'; only when he sang was his 'reticence cast off and the theatrical space filled'. As with *The Nine Night*, the actor who shone was a woman – Kenyan Wanjiku Kiarie as Eslander Robeson.[34] Now resident in New Zealand, Kiarie's first visit to the country had been as an actor with the London-based, politically oriented Keskidee, who had toured in 1979.

Markham labelled Pacific Theatre a 'risk-taker', noting that the company was beginning to make its mark by 'building a strong audience in response to its commitment to theatre which explores black issues which have a particular relevance to 1990 New Zealand. It [has] energy which arises from a strong belief in the power of theatre to affect [sic] social change.'[35]

After three productions in three years, it was time for Pacific Theatre to consolidate its position. As Justine notes, 'It was time for us to start learning how to devise our own plays because we had our own stories to tell.'

Lupe and Sina: Devising a new work (1990–91)

> Before your eyes we now unfold
> The ancient legend that is often told
> In the islands of Samoa.
> This is the story of Lupe, the pigeon, and his sister Sina, who takes her name from the woman in the moon.
>
> *LUPE AND SINA*[36]

At about the time the company was producing *Robeson – Song of Freedom*, Pacific Theatre tackled their first devised work. *Lupe and Sina: A love story with cannibals* was based on legends from Samoa, Fiji, the Cook Islands and elsewhere. The intention was to create a children's show – a pantomime. Under Justine's guidance the actors (including Lelisi, Fane, Manusaute, Enari and Mesepa Edwards) experimented in the rehearsal room. Paul Simei-Barton explains the process:

> We did quite a bit of research into traditional myths, and I drew up a synopsis that pulled together four or five different ones – a bare plot outline. We drew on the unpublished collection of myths that Justine got through her family, and on a book by Antony Alpers on the legends of the Pacific.[37]

Justine describes the play as a 'coming of age' story:

> Lupe and Sina lose their parents, so Lupe is told he's got to look after her, and she rebels against his authority and runs away. She meets the Flying Foxes, who are the spiritual guardians of the forest. It's about her adventures and all the different lands that she ends up in. The fishermen find her because she's swept up, and then she falls in love with the village boy. The villagers think that she's a bad omen; they send her away and she gets caught by the cannibals. She cries out to her brother and he flies in as the pigeon to rescue her. And then she realises that his authority is not to oppress her, but to teach her how to grow up to be the young village maiden that she's born to be.

For Justine and Paul, the process of devising went hand in hand with their own learning and training. They sought assistance from skilled practitioners – Alan Brunton and Sally Rodwell of Red Mole, and choreographer Mary Jane O'Reilly, the co-founder of Limbs.[38] As Justine notes, 'We were familiar with Red Mole, with their use of puppetry and masks, and we really wanted to connect with them.' They asked Brunton and Rodwell to run physical theatre workshops to strengthen the actors' skills. This included an introduction to the basics of commedia dell'arte. The group decided to incorporate masks into the piece, and Rodwell conducted a one-day workshop to teach the basics of mask-making using papier maché and clay moulds of the actors' faces. Many of the characters in *Lupe and Sina* would be masked, although the central pair (played by Enari and Edwards) were not.[39]

Paul Simei-Barton has taught art and photography at Massey High School since 1993, and for many years has been a theatre reviewer for the *NZ Herald*, but in 1990 he had never before considered writing for the stage: 'I think that truly was a devised work. But at a certain point, Justine felt it needed a solid script, and I think I just said I could have a crack at it, and we did it.'

The company raised no objection to having a Palagi writer, although the issue was discussed at the time. As Paul notes,

> I initially tried to keep to the background, and be the guy who wrote down the actors' stuff so that it was collaborative and coming from them. I think back then we were possibly over-sensitive about it. [These days] I've rejected that kind of essentialist idea that your genealogy is essential to engage with another culture. But probably back then it was more of a PC kind of time.

In November 1990 *Lupe and Sina* was accepted for workshopping at the annual Playmarket Playwrights' Conference – the first piece with a Pasifika theme to be chosen. Justine was the director with Murray Edmond as dramaturg.[40] The workshop gave Pacific Theatre exposure to non-naturalistic elements from a diverse range of artists, including dancer/choreographer Jamie Bull, musician Phil Dadson and sculptor Matt Pine. Helene Wong conducted a workshop on scriptwriting, and Red Mole offered another based on a deconstruction of Bruce Mason's *Courting Blackbird*.[41]

It took another year to bring *Lupe and Sina* to the stage. It opened at the Maidment on 6 December 1991 in the slot traditionally allocated to children's theatre or pantomime, and played until Christmas – the longest run of any Pacific Theatre show to date. The notion of 'pantomime' in a Pasifika context is an unusual juxtaposition, but in this case, as Peter Calder noted, the production grafted 'ancient Samoan legends onto the traditional European form'.[42] As the majority of cast members had seen little of European theatre they were not familiar with pantomime traditions, but this was pantomime in its loosest sense; there was no attempt to use the common conventions of the form – principal boy, dame and so on – although there were some elements of pantomime theatrics, such as children being brought up on stage and put into a cage to be 'eaten'. Reviewer Mark Amery felt that calling the piece a pantomime was 'a title [that] belittles the product'; the show was 'something special, something you can be proud to call distinctly Pacific'.[43] According to Calder, however, Justine felt the pantomime tradition was ideal: '*Lupe and Sina* incorporates elements of ... fale aitu or ghost house, in which travelling performers entertain villagers with oratory, stories, dance and mime.'[44]

The show broke new ground for the company and allowed for a much stronger combination of Pacific and Western theatre traditions than had previously been possible. It incorporated striking bird masks, physical comedy, dialogue (some in rhymed couplets: another nod to pantomime), choral singing and a stylised fight with spears and drumming. Traditional dance pieces were choreographed by Enari and included a slap dance and a sasa – a dance performed while seated on the ground. This hybrid approach pointed the way to the future of Pacific Theatre.

The politics of staging Shakespeare (1992)

The next project was another jump into new territory. Justine has always loved Shakespeare, '... the language, the characters, the whole drama of it ... his themes are universal. He speaks to all of us, it doesn't matter what colour you are.' She wanted to stage a Shakespeare play. There was a certain degree of bloody-mindedness about this, of not wanting to be pigeonholed into a particular type of work: 'We thought, okay, we'll just show these bastards that we can.' She applied to the Auckland University Students' Association to direct the 1992 outdoor Summer Shakespeare, and invited Alan Brunton to co-direct *Romeo and Juliet* with her.

Working with Brunton gave Justine new insight into the role of the director: 'Alan had such great rhythm and pace and a really good overview. I could see that he was brilliant and that I had so much to learn from him.' By observing his working methods she learned to apply logical structure to the rehearsal process in order to give the actors a clear point of focus and help them to find their rhythm. Part of that process was, each day, to 'always do a run-through of everything that you've learned' and gradually build up the performance, scene by scene. She had the confidence to trust Brunton to edit and adapt the script.

Justine and Brunton saw the production as an opportunity to explore *Romeo and Juliet*'s multicultural potential. They set it during the 1869 land war – the 'war of the Faitasiga' – in Samoa. There were many parallels to be drawn including the notion of two warring families, headed by Laupepa and Talavou – rival claimants to the title of Malietoa – whose 'bloody fray' included breakouts of fighting in the streets where in 'these hot days, is the mad blood stirring'. Mantua became Manu`a, and the humble Apothecary's status was raised to make the character – played by Wanjiku Kiarie – an omniscient narrator, able to intervene and to highlight significant moments. Assuming the Chorus function, the Apothecary's opening speech takes the audience immediately into 'fair Apia [Verona], where we lay our scene'. Tall wooden columns reminiscent of Shakespeare's Globe and the posts of a fale tele reinforced the environment,[45] as did costume, movement, the sound of drumming and the presence of a Germanic brass band.[46] As Justine explained in a television preview, 'The Montagues are presented as a family desperate to maintain traditional Samoan ways, while the Capulets have been influenced by the materialism of Western society.'[47]

Various scenes were coloured with Samoan cultural elements, such as the giving of fine mats, and Pacific music and movement in the Capulet ball scene. When the Apothecary spoke, her text was accompanied by a slap dance. Whole sequences were transformed into siva (Samoan dance) and slow motion, such as the scene in which Friar Lawrence (Bruce Davidson) and the Apothecary – in one of her additional scenes – give Juliet the 'distilled liquor' that will put her into a death-like sleep. Davidson felt the siva was an appropriate way of presenting this scene: 'I had to give her poison, but my intention was good, so I had to give it to her in a happy way, a polite way.'[48] Above all else, the rhythms of the piece were dictated by the text. As Justine describes it, 'We just moved to the rhythm of Shakespeare, so the play was like a dance the whole way through.'

About 90 per cent of the large cast were Pacific Islanders – a mixture of university students and core group members of Pacific Theatre. These included Kiarie, Enari (who played both Benvolio and Paris), Manusaute as Lord Capulet, Andrew Iosefa as Tybalt and Pule Simei as a chorus member. Mario Gaoa, who would later be a key player with The Naked Samoans, appeared as Mercutio, while Romeo and Juliet were played by Faifua Amiga Jr and Louise Cuthbert, who had a major role in *Lupe and Sina*. Justine had a cameo – as a boy – playing Balthasar. Others who made their first appearance with the company would return in later productions, such as Misa Tupou (chorus member) and Aruna Po-Ching (Lady Capulet).[49]

The production attracted controversy. To begin with Justine had to fight to have her bid to direct accepted. 'There was quite a lot of opposition to us putting on *Romeo and Juliet*. I just put it down to racism at the end of the day. They couldn't see how Pacific Islanders could do Shakespeare justice. They didn't want us at all.' As she later told Linda Herrick:

> The university was 'not ready to see people running around in tapa cloths trying to speak English' ... That made me a lot more determined to get this play up and running and we fought a long time for the right to put on a Shakespeare play with Polynesians. We had to be really clever about it. We planted our own actors in the [student association] committee, so when the applications went through, they had the voting power.[50]

But although Justine's strong political sense won the day, the controversy did not end there. Opposition arose from some members of the Samoan community, headed by Elder Leifi Maua Puti Faleauto, editor of the *Samoan Sun*. As he told *Holmes Tonight*, 'It will infer that the head of state of Western Samoa, the Malietoa family, are incestuous ... It's so horrible, you know that people can die for things like this.'[51] He cited the Bible as evidence that the production was essentially tampering with Samoan culture. Academic Michael Neill has explored this incident, noting that Justine's spirited defence of the production was 'an assertion of immigrant confidence, even of cultural sovereignty over the totems of palagi superiority':

> 'They should be really proud that we are venturing the last bastion of Western society ... we're breaking that barrier' ... For Simei-Barton, Shakespeare's play offered a vantage point for critiquing the values of her own society; for the Elder, the application of this alien fable could only result in the falsification of sacred truths – telling lies about the gods and heroes.[52]

Theatre in Education (1990–2006)

One way of growing and establishing the work of Pacific Theatre and providing employment for some of the young developing actors was to set up a Theatre in Education (TIE) programme. This was the closest the Simei-Bartons would come to having a cohesive company as opposed to bringing people together for a specific project. Vela Manusaute recalls they did it not for the money but 'for the passion of the art'. According to Shimpal Lelisi, 'One year there were five guys in a station wagon doing the whole of the North Island, to every school that would take us. It was really good training for us. It was hard, but it was good.'

A shortened version of *Lupe and Sina,* with Faifua Amiga Jr as Lupe, became the basis of one TIE show. Others were devised pieces created by the company during workshops. According to Lelisi, they took excerpts from a number of plays and combined them into one show. 'We'd do a couple of scenes from Shakespeare plays, and then we'd do some Polynesian legends. We found the old Polynesian language was quite similar to Shakespeare, in the descriptiveness and the colour of it all.'

With two devised works they initially toured the North Island in 1993–94 before extending to a national tour in 1995. Both pieces explored conservation issues. *Voices on the Wind* was based on the legends of Kae and the whale, and *Sina and Tigilau* was drawn from Samoan, Cook Island and Tongan versions of the story. The title of the first was borrowed from Katharine Luomala's book, *Voices on the Wind: Polynesian myths and chants* (1992):

> The chant expresses a notion that is common in myths and legends from throughout the Pacific. Characters often listen to the 'voices on the wind' to hear news from distant lands. The wind, constantly blowing across the vast expanses of the Pacific Ocean, unites the diverse island groups that make up Polynesian culture, spreading news, gossip and tales from the legendary past.[53]

The cast at various times included Fane (who briefly re-joined Pacific Theatre after graduating from Toi Whakaari), Tupou, Manusaute, Lelisi, Rachel House, Aynsley Tapuvae, Joe Folau, and Tausili Mose in her first acting job. Anapela Polataivao recalled how she joined the TIE company as a nineteen-year-old, having learned her theatre craft with Samantha Scott, Christian Penny and Anna Marbrook at the Maidment Youth Theatre:

> Tausili [Mose] auditioned for Justine's *Voices on the Wind* show. I went along to have a nosey and Justine hired me. We toured for nine months and loved the experience.

Pacific Theatre's TIE work included the road-safety themed *One More for the Road* (1996), co-written by Lisa Tauoma and Paul Simei-Barton, which played in Auckland secondary schools. The cast included Manusaute in his first acting job after graduating from Toi Whakaari. The group's final work, in 2006, was *Hit the Curve*, for the Land Transport Safety Authority Road Safety Trust and the Wellington City Council.

The Contest: The poem, the bat and the rap beat (1993)

> Art is the devising and disguising
> of tricks that make the leap
> look effortless magical miraculous

ALBERT WENDT, *THE CONTEST*[54]

Pacific Theatre's next mainstage project was *The Contest*, a significant breakthrough in terms of public recognition and bringing together different theatrical worlds. As Peter Calder noted, '*The Contest* seamlessly melded traditional performance styles with palagi technique – and the result was a revelation.'[55] For Paul Simei-Barton, *The Contest* was 'the first play I consider I actually wrote':

> I'd read the Albert Wendt poem, which I thought was fantastic. I had come across it in a magazine [*Landfall*], and as an English teacher in Mangere I had used it with the kids and got a good response. With his permission, we took a little fragment of that poem.

The fragment was the mythological story of Alopese's oratory challenge to find the man who 'can sing all / the seasons through into the future'.[56] The challenge is first met by Mulialofa, who loses the contest and must submit to having the bones removed from his flesh, which are then strung together to make a Bone-Man. Vela – as a flying fox – in turn learns new songs and rhythms that he hears when 'black youths in exotic hides gyrated / to a black singing box / to a beat I'd never heard ...'[57] Armed with this new rhythm as 'holy rock'n'roller',[58] Vela defeats Alopese: 'To win you must catch a rhythm / a way a beat no one can imitate ...'[59]

In adapting elements of this poem for the stage, Paul began with the notion that the new rhythm Vela discovers is the beat of rap music – which at that time was in the early stages of its worldwide rise to popularity. His version of *The Contest* alternates between the world of a teenager, Vela (known as Junior), in present-day Mangere (South Auckland), and his mythological world in ancient Samoa, linked together by the spirit of the pe`a (flying fox). In re-working the material, Paul included a number of direct quotations from Wendt's poem as well as Tongan and other island myths, poems and laments, mixed with a little sample of the rap artist Ice-T.[60] As Paul and Justine stated: 'We have transposed Albert Wendt's Samoan story to a more generalised Polynesian setting to reflect the make up of our group and to emphasise the common origin of Polynesian cultures.'[61]

Junior aspires to be a rapper, giving himself the name MC Ezy V:

> **JUNIOR**: That V is for Vela which means cooked and ready to eat, yeah that's me sweet enough to eat.[62] Well that's what my parents called me, don't ask me why, I think Samoans just get a kick out of giving their kids really weird names ...[63]

Junior has been having strange dreams in which he is visited by a bat-like creature, which his mother identifies as a pe`a:

> **MOTHER**: That's the flying fox, lives in Samoa ... Just like a bat but they cover in fur ... They don't bite, they eat the fruit and they very friendly, before the missionary come they use to be sacred, but now the people eat them.[64]

The two stories run on parallel lines as Vela, in the guise of the pe`a, learns new rhythms and takes them home to win the contest and defeat Alopese. Meanwhile, Junior travels to Samoa in a bid to learn something of his cultural background. The play ends with him in a remote village in Savai`i watching a brief fale aitu performance, much as Justine and Paul had done.[65]

The Contest brought together a variety of rhythmic tones (including rap), and employed different dance styles and movement sequences to advance the narrative, choreographed by Mary Jane O'Reilly, with Sefa Enari as one of five dancers.[66] It was intensely physical. Raewyn White, in reviewing O'Reilly's contribution, describes it as 'very much of the Pacific in its shapes and patterns and rhythms [... with] fragments of Chinese and Balinese traditional forms mixed into the bursts of fa`atupati, sasa and siva.'[67] White makes it clear that O'Reilly came on board 'without a particular knowledge of Samoan dance and performance traditions, but has built on the knowledge of the performers'.[68] O'Reilly herself noted, 'I've been working on identifying what it means to live in the South Pacific for some time now. It's all a process of developing an identity through art.'[69]

Alongside largely naturalistic contemporary Auckland scenes, *The Contest* embraced oratory, story telling, poetic language and mythology. Atmospheric music composed by Mark Dashper, using traditional Polynesian instruments, was considered 'sensationally good. Mixing rap with bird calls, he frames the action with haunting sounds and driving rhythms.'[70]

There was some doubling of roles to connect the two worlds, with Shimpal Lelisi as Vela/Junior and Mele Ah-Sam as the mother of both boys. Two actors (Aynsley Tapuvae and David Fane) worked with the large puppet pe`a created for the performance. Fane also played Mulialofa, with Misa Tupou as Bone-Man and Andrew Iosefa as Kauanui. In reviews, Lelisi and Brian Manusaute as Alopese were singled out for praise, the latter for creating a performance 'tour de force, funny and horrifying by turns'.[71]

Following this production Brian Manusaute took the name 'Vela' when he went to Toi Whakaari in 1994, saying, 'I wanted to go into drama school as a full Pacific Islander. I heard so many stories about drama school turning them white. I wanted to stay brown ...'

As Calder suggested, Pacific Theatre reached a new maturity with this work. Some reviewers voiced minor reservations about the structure of the script, however. For example, although Laurie Atkinson felt the dance and music were filled with vitality, he commented that Junior coming to terms with Samoan traditions felt hastily tacked on at the end.[72] John Parker's set design received praise; Susan Budd described it as 'simple and striking, with bleached nikau palms against a black backdrop and a beautiful curved structure that provides a focus for the dancers'.[73]

The Contest opened in Wellington at Taki Rua Depot in September 1993 and played there for two weeks, then at the Watershed in Auckland. This dual-city production demonstrated a big step forward for the company's public interface. As Paul notes, 'the company was feeling pretty good ... that was the high point for Pacific Theatre'. *The Contest* received several nominations for Wellington's

Chapman Tripp Theatre Awards: Most Original Production of the Year, Shimpal Lelisi (Most Promising Male Newcomer) and Brian Manusaute (Male Actor in a Supporting Role).

For the first years of Pacific Theatre, Justine and Paul were working largely in a void. By 1993, however, Pasifika and Māori theatre in Auckland had 'moved from adolescent to sleek young adult', as Calder described it.[74] No longer were they a voice in the wilderness. February 1993 had seen the revelatory performance in Auckland of John Kneubuhl's *Think of A Garden* and, in Christchurch Pacific Underground had begun to establish itself and was shortly to present *Fresh off the Boat*.

Ma Rainey's Black Bottom: Consolidation (1995)

Eager to continue the forward trajectory of Pacific Theatre, Justine turned to a Pulitzer prize-winning African-American playwright. In choosing August Wilson's *Ma Rainey's Black Bottom* (1984) she was again introducing a significant black writer to New Zealand. The play is set in 1927 when a group of black musicians gather in a Chicago recording studio one afternoon to record songs with Ma Rainey, 'the Mother of the Blues',[75] watched over from a control booth by two white sound engineers – in itself a physical manifestation of an uneasy cross-cultural relationship.

> TOLEDO [Piano player]: As long as the colored man look to white folks to put the crown on what he say ... as long as he looks to white folks for approval ... then he ain't never gonna find out who he is and what he's about. He's just gonna be about what white folks want him to be about.[76]

The play reveals a mixture of bitterness, dissatisfaction, anger, pain and fortitude, and a strong sense of ownership of the blues. As Ma Rainey says, 'This be an empty world without the blues.'[77] She struggles with the notion that, for the white studio bosses, her music is just a commodity.

The powerful material drew a particularly strong cast, including American actor Anthony Ray Parker – in Auckland at that time to film the TV series *Hercules* – as the doomed Toledo. Jay Laga`aia took a leading role as the ultimately tragic Levee who later kills Toledo in a fit of rage, while blues singer Mahia Blackmore played Ma Rainey. African-American jazz bassist and composer Harold Anderson played Cutler, the band-leader, and was also the show's musical director. Other cast members were Alvin Fitisemanu (Slow Drag) and Anapela Polataivao (Dussie Mae), and John Parker once again designed the set. Gaining permission to perform the play was in itself something of a coup, and was achieved because Anderson had a connection to Wilson, who approved the production after receiving information about the company.

When the play opened at the Aotea Centre's Herald Theatre on 31 August 1995, it failed to impress reviewer Bernadette Rae. She felt it exhibited – between bouts of the dramatic and the lyrical – 'long, even tedious tracts of black anger, fizzing with frustration'.[78] She found fault with the music, which was pre-recorded because some of the actors could not play instruments; and while Mahia Blackmore sang with 'enormous style', she was less successful in remembering her lines. Despite the presence of real Americans in the cast, some of the actors had difficulty producing convincing accents, though as Polataivao ruefully recalls, 'we tried'. Justine became aware that the audience attracted to this play was essentially white and middle class rather than the PI community, perhaps because it 'tells the story of Ma Rainey and the jazz era'.

After the three-week season ended, Pacific Theatre – which had done so much to introduce major international black writers to Auckland – now turned away from imported plays to focus exclusively on work of the Pacific region.

Tusitala and the Witch Woman of the Mountain: Developing fale aitu practice (1995–96)

A conviction that fale aitu was a core performance principle for Pacific Theatre led Justine and Paul to continue their study of the art form. Justine saw fale aitu as satirical comedy and a 'political device, in terms of turning the whole world upside down and allowing grassroots people to have their say'. Following their initial village encounter, the pair had watched fale aitu performances at Apia's annual Teuila Festival, and the company had used some basic fale aitu principles in *Lupe and Sina*. Justine and Paul gained a deeper knowledge when they met American Samoan-born academic, poet and story-teller Caroline Sinavaiana, who has written extensively on fale aitu. They spent some time with Sinavaiana in the islands 'just learning from her wisdom', and had the opportunity to read her doctoral thesis on the subject.[79] The two women also worked together for a while in Samoa, going out into communities with fale aitu.

By 1994 Paul had written a draft of a new play entitled *Tusitala and the Witch Woman of the Mountain*, which was selected for the Oceania Playwrights' Workshop held in Auckland in November that year. Colin McColl directed,

Murray Edmond was dramaturg and Rotuman/Fijian playwright Vilsoni Hereniko was a special advisor. Set in 19th-century Samoa in a village on the island of Upolo, the play was designed as a cross-cultural encounter between the Scottish novelist Robert Louis Stevenson and a fale aitu troop. Tusitala, or 'story-teller', was the Samoan name given to Stevenson, while his American wife, Fanny, was known as O le Fafine Mamana o i le Mauga (the witch woman of the mountain).[80] Justine recalled some issues from the workshop, where both Māori and Pacific Island actors were cast.[81]

> Quite a lot of the Māori actors couldn't understand the concept of Samoan people honouring a white guy. In the script Stevenson actually says quite a lot of patronising things, but Samoans accepted it, not because they didn't understand what he was saying, but because they respected his honesty.[82]

As a result of the workshop, Paul reworked the script to bring added prominence to the fale aitu elements.

Justine and Paul initiated a fale aitu workshop, O le Fale Aitu: Feagaia fou, at Auckland's Unitec Performing Arts School around June 1996.[83] They invited Caroline Sinavaiana to give a keynote lecture, summarising her research and personal engagement with fale aitu and advising on the history and significance of the form. She in turn brought fale aitu master practitioner Afioga (Master) Taimalie Siaki from Samoa to teach some basic principles of the art. This was an intensive three-day introduction to a performance style that normally requires at least seven months of apprenticeship, and as such could only provide a taste of fale aitu in action. Still, as Paul noted, the opportunity was 'fantastic': it was 'an exchange with a genuine living practitioner of a very ancient art form'.

Workshop participants included many regular and former members of Pacific Theatre, such as Fane, Manusaute and Lelisi. Also in attendance were actors Canada Alofa and Dianna Fuemana and several members of the newly established Pacific Underground from Christchurch, including Erolia Ifopo and Mishelle Muagututi`a, both of whom had performed in *The Contest*. Fane recalls watching Siaki at work:

> It was fantastic. He was an old man, but every new character, he'd do it – pick the flower from the air, suddenly he's a woman – I suppose you could say it's a bit of commedia dell'arte: there's just that simplicity.

The Simei-Bartons' intention was for fale aitu to be explored and melded 'with contemporary themes relevant to New Zealand Samoans'. However, 'since not all of the participants were fluent in the Samoan language, the usual improvisation of dialogue was abandoned in favour of scripting',[84] and as a result more emphasis was placed on physical comedy. As Lelisi recalls, 'We took a lot from commedia, like the posturing and the [stock] character stuff.' But whereas commedia characters like Arlecchino are very clearly delineated by costume, movement, mask, behaviour and physicality, Paul recognises that fale aitu is less formal.[85] Physicality was to become a fundamental element of the style of New Zealand fale aitu performance, as Justine later defined it for Sean Mallon:

> In Samoa the humorous subtleties and innuendo and the clever and sophisticated use of language are often hidden within the oratory. In New Zealand the humour and performances are a more physical type of theatre, where body language and actions are more important in conveying the message or idea.[86]

From the early days, Pacific Theatre received support, advice and encouragement from Samoan elder Susuga Papali`i Pita Taouma, who would prove a key figure in terms of the company's connection with the traditional Samoan community. Justine explains,

> Pita had a very strong connection with fale aitu practitioners [in Samoa], and was extremely generous in sharing this knowledge with us. He played a key role in the workshop at Unitec, and also provided a lot of support for us when we were being criticised by the more conservative members of the community over *Romeo and Juliet*. He conducted a traditional blessing for all our productions, and was a constant source of inspiration for the company.[87]

With a grant from the Rockefeller Foundation, in 1996 Sinavaiana invited Justine to attend a workshop in Bellagio, Italy, along with artists from the Pacific, Canada, the United States and the Caribbean. Paul reflected on this significant workshop:

> [Caroline's] organisation of this event was an attempt to build on the interest and enthusiasm for fale aitu that she felt at the Unitec workshop. For Justine it was an important validation of her work to see how it was appreciated in a global context and how it related to other indigenous theatrical traditions. The workshop also built on Caroline's idea that fale aitu offered a template for what she called a 'meta-healing' of societies that were still dealing with the damage caused by colonialism. They developed a template for contemporary fale aitu practice and this was later put into effect with a workshop that Justine and Caroline carried out at a community college in American Samoa.[88]

Tusitala and the House of Spirits: Putting fale aitu into practice (1996)

> **SIAKI**: In our custom we can make anyone look ridiculous without fear of punishment. If someone takes offence, well it was the spirits talking. And we cannot be blamed for the actions of an aitu.
>
> *TUSITALA AND THE HOUSE OF SPIRITS*[89]

Revitalised by the workshop and now re-named *Tusitala and the House of Spirits*, the play was first performed at Taki Rua Depot in Wellington from 29 August to 21 September 1996, directed by Justine.[90] The fale aitu influence is evident in the new title. Both European and Polynesian sensibilities are represented within the script, each as a strong imaginative force. Fale aitu performers (fa`aluma) Siaki and Talolo present their version of Robert Louis Stevenson's *The Strange Case of Dr Jekyll and Mr Hyde*.

Stevenson had written an essay called 'A Chapter on Dreams' in *Across the Plains* (1892), in which he described the influence dreams had on his creative imagination. He cites *Jekyll and Hyde* as a story that came to him in part through 'my Brownies ... who do one half my work for me while I am fast asleep'.[91] Stevenson's use of the term 'Brownies' refers to a legendary creature in Scottish folklore, similar to a hobgoblin. Paul Simei-Barton adapted Stevenson's writing, and also created a number of imaginary sequences drawing on the fact that Stevenson had visited the jail in Apia. This enabled him to place Stevenson at fale aitu performances that functioned as a critique of the German colonial regime. In act two, as they prepare to perform, the two fa`aluma consider the similarity between Stevenson's story and the legend of Leaga ma Lelei (Bad and Good); later they point to the story's biblical connection:

> **SIAKI**: Well once Lucifa was one of the Lord's finest angels, but in his pride he turned to the evil side, and became the devil himself. Dr Jekyll is the same, always trying to be so good, but he cannot control the evil inside of him.
>
> **LAULI`I**: Hmmm, the stories are similar.[92] But Tusitala told me that Jekyll and Hyde came to him in a dream. When he sleeps, he is visited by little spirits that give him stories ... He calls them 'Brownies'. Perhaps they are like the spirits of the fale aitu?[93]

When the fale aitu version is performed, Talolo (as Hyde) is overcome by an aitu and attacks his gaoler, the German Captain Wurmbrand. It is only through debate with his creator, Stevenson, that Talolo-as-Hyde can recover himself. At this moment, Brownies and aitu are closely linked.

LAULI`I: Tusitala, you told me that Jekyll and Hyde came to you in a dream. Well, the spirit that haunted your dream now stands before you.[94]

In 'A Chapter on Dreams' Stevenson wrote, 'my Brownies have not a rudiment of what we call a conscience'.[95] Thus, he regarded himself as 'protected', as a writer who did not need to censure himself, in a manner similar to that of the fale aitu performers. Martyn Sanderson, who played Stevenson, later discussed the analogy between 'Brownies' and the aitu:

> What Justine [and Paul were] asking, in effect, is this: were [the Brownies] spirits or weren't they? Stevenson wrote about them exactly in the way a Samoan would talk about spirit possession or conversation with the spirits.[96]

Although this exploration of the 'spirits' lies at the heart of *Tusitala*, the play strongly (and accurately) reflects Stevenson's documented views as a Palagi outsider commenting on what he thinks is best for the people of Samoa. Set in 1893, the framing story tells of the escalating war between the chiefs Laupepa and Mata`afa, in which Stevenson intercedes. It explores the nature of his friendship with the Samoan people and his love for the country where he intends to be buried. A well-developed subplot explores interactions between Samoans and Papalagi, represented by American Joe Strong's crude attempts to seduce Fa`auma, the wife of Lafaele.

Tusitala and the House of Spirits brought a wide audience, which Paul attributes in part to the presence of Sanderson in the cast. However, it met with mixed critical reception. Susan Budd praised the work of Shimpal Lelisi and Iosefa Enari as Siaki and Talolo, claiming that 'their performances are the heart of the play, expressing to a palagi audience more of the essence of Samoa than could – or do – thousands of words'.[97] Laurie Atkinson was unimpressed, asserting that 'it never quite succeeds in merging the theatricality of fale aitu, the historical events and the well-documented private life of a beloved author'.[98] Still, *Tusitala* is clearly Paul's most sophisticated work for Pacific Theatre. It represents the company's aim to explore and work within the precepts of fale aitu – something that had rarely, if at all, been previously attempted in Pasifika theatre in Aotearoa.

Moving on: 1997–2011

Tusitala and the House of Spirits was a highlight in the work of Pacific Theatre and also represented a turning point. The company had hoped to take the production to Auckland for a season at the Watershed but were unable to secure the funding necessary for such a large-scale show. From that disappointing moment onwards, although Pacific Theatre continued as a TIE touring company, the Simei-Bartons turned their attention primarily to television and film-making. Justine had completed a post-graduate diploma in broadcasting at Auckland University in 1991. She was the first Pacific Island graduate of the course, and in 2000 she established New Zealand's first Pacific Island independent professional film company, Tala Pasifika Productions: 'I was told mainstream [media/television] wasn't ready for brown faces. But that had never been tried, so how would they know?'[99] While television and film are not the subject of this book, Justine has served as director, and at times as writer and producer, on a significant number of acclaimed projects. These include short films and documentaries such as *Brown Sugar* (2000), *The Overstayer* (2001), *Coming Home* (2002), *The Trophy* (2008, written by Paul Simei-Barton) and *Snow In Paradise* (2011). She directed the seven-part TV One series *Good Hands – Lima Lelei* (2003), which was nominated as Best Drama Series at the 2005 New Zealand Screen Awards.

In November 2007 Pacific Theatre emerged as an entity once more to stage *Lena*, by Samoan-born playwright/actor Jason Greenwood, at the Herald Theatre.[100] Set in Samoa in 1947 when the country was struggling for independence, the play is based on stories that Greenwood's mother told of her early life. It explores 'the conflict between traditional values and modernity through the story of an afakasi family torn apart by a row over who should control the family plantation'.[101] The cast, led by Olivia Lauiula Muliaumaseali`i as Lena, featured Aleni Tufuga, Nora Aati, Canada Alofa, Jason Greenwood, Mark Webley and Pule Simei-Afamasaga. Sefa Enari again joined the company as choreographer. Justine directed, revealing her continued passion to present Pasifika stories: 'I know there is no one better to do this than us Samoans. I didn't want *Lena* to be handed over to a white mainstream established theatre company that will try to tell us how to be Polynesian.'[102]

In 2007 Justine was appointed artistic director of *Our Street*, an intercultural community theatre project commissioned by the Auckland City Council and performed at the town hall over four days in August 2008. While this was not a Pacific Theatre production, it represents everything that Justine holds dear as an artist and activist. Devised by its communities with dramaturg Fiona Graham, *Our Street* involved three suburbs of which more than half the inhabitants had been born overseas:

> [They included] first and second generation migrants from India, Tonga, China, Rwanda, Fiji, Australia, Samoa, Niue, Somalia, the Cook Islands and Burma ... This project aimed to create new connections, celebrate cultural diversity and encourage community pride.[103]

The show evolved over a period of 12 months of workshops and improvisations, and incorporated music, dance and film. Graham chose to focus the performance event on two weddings, one Samoan–Māori and the other Punjabi–South Indian; not only did this help to bring the communities together in performance, but there was a deliberate degree of cross-pollination. As Graham notes, 'It was powerful to see a young Indian girl performing a Polynesian dance and then the Polynesian youth group doing a Bollywood dance.'[104] The project evoked a passionate engagement from its many participants; Justine refers to it as 'one of the highlights of my theatre career'.

In 2007 Justine Simei-Barton's work was recognised with a Senior Pacific Artists' Award at the Creative New Zealand annual Arts Pasifika Awards. It was an acknowledgement of her contribution to theatre, film and television, something she typically views as a form of motivation for younger artists: 'For many young PIs, it's proof that, as a Pacific Islander, you can make it in the arts.'[105]

> A house is only as strong as its foundations, and by looking back to the very ancient roots and traditions of Pacific Island culture, we hope we have laid a foundation that will see Pacific theatre continuing to grow and bear fruit in all kinds of wonderful and unpredictable ways. PAUL & JUSTINE SIMEI-BARTON[106]

3.

The journey to Pacific Underground

Here in the South Island, in that English Anglican migrant city,
a Pacific grass roots theatre movement was nurtured and unleashed on a world stage.

REV MUA STRICKSON-PUA[1]

They had a brightness about them, something untapped,
something really raw.

DAVID FANE[2]

While Pacific Theatre was concentrating on creating a Polynesian theatre identity in Auckland, a community of young artists was slowly evolving in Christchurch, supported by their elders. A handful of highly motivated individuals emerged from arts organisations and small companies such as Puawai and Whakarite to form Pacific Underground, a multi-disciplinary performing arts group. In this chapter we examine the background and circumstances that led to the emergence of this significant company.

The Polynesian Performing Arts Trust and Puawai

The South Island city of Christchurch has a significant Pacific Island population, third only to those of the Auckland and Wellington regions.[3] In the 1980s the Polynesian Performing Arts Trust (PPAT) was established in Christchurch 'to foster indigenous theatre throughout Aotearoa'.[4] Founding members whose collective vision propelled the trust included the couples Vic Tamati and Fuarosa Luafutu-Tamati, Brian and Maggie Tairakena, and George and Rachel Kahi. According to Luafutu-Tamati, 'There were very few arts institutions that Pacific young people could access in Christchurch without formal training. PPAT became the vehicle whereby [they] could explore their potential and interest in the arts.'[5]

In 1986 the trust began to administer Puawai ('blossoming' in te reo Māori), a new government-funded scheme for unemployed young people. The goal of Puawai was to establish professional standards and equip students for work in the arts industries. Tutors included John Luafutu (music), Sarah Franks (dance) and Guy Ockenden (drama). Student support and assistance was provided by Pacific co-ordinator Luafutu-Tamati, a youth/community worker with a strong interest in the value of the arts as a means of working with Pacific young people.

Puawai was run on a whānau basis, and its open-door policy embraced Palagi as well as Māori and Pasifika students. Simon Small and Robert Gilbert were two Papalagi who joined Puawai in 1988.[6] Small remembers the early days:

> When I joined it was a pretty laid back vibe. Erolia Ifopo was a student and so was Michael Hodgson. The drama group had a room above the Court Theatre in the Arts Centre. The daily routine was morning stretches and vocal warm-ups and cups of tea for the first couple of hours. We would do some dance classes through the week as well as cultural practice, learning Māori and Samoan songs and haka for any special guests.[7]

Between 1986 and 1989 Puawai drama and dance trainees performed several original pieces written by students, including *Miramaze*, a musical that toured South Island marae in May 1988. That same year Christchurch's professional Court Theatre offered places to several trainees, including Ifopo, Small and Gilbert, who appeared in *The Three Musketeers*.[8]

In March 1989 Puawai presented *Sons of Sky and Earth* at the Rolleston Theatre, a story adapted by Palagi actor/director Lex Matheson from Māori legends about the exploits of Maui Tikitiki a Taranga, with original music by George Kahi and Jerry Toto.[9] It featured Ifopo, Small, Andrew Shepherd and Vicki McDowell, with Joseph Otimi as Maui, and afforded Gilbert his directing debut. In July of the same year Puawai produced James K. Baxter's *The Wide Open Cage* at Christchurch's Great Hall, again directed by Gilbert, with Small (Jack Skully), Otimi (Father Tom), Ifopo (Norah Vane) and McDowell (Mrs Bailey), among others. *Press* reviewer Elody Rathgen referred to Gilbert's 'well-intentioned' direction, and lauded the 'well-disciplined, enthusiastic if inexperienced cast working on a super-indulgent text'.[10] Ifopo was singled out for particular praise: 'She presents a vigorous character with intensity and anger. She provides the most powerful moments in the play.'

Whakarite Theatre Company: Being adaptable

Emerging from their Puawai training ground in 1989, Gilbert, Ifopo, Small, Otimi and others were inspired to develop their own company with the primary objective of providing work for Māori and Pasifika graduates of the course –

a move that mirrored the interest in Māori and bicultural theatre that was emerging in Auckland and Wellington. With support from PPAT, Whakarite Theatre Company began in October 1989 with a mixture of Māori, Pasifika and Palagi members. Founding members included Ifopo, Small, Otimi and Linley-Jane Bullen, along with Puawai graduates Karin Joblin, Liz Sugrue, Donna Muir, Rewa Muriwai and Campbell Taylor; Gilbert was director:

> We must have put a proposal to [PPAT's] George Kahi, and [began] with his blessing. George arranged for a kaumatua and they gifted us the name Whakarite. We were told that, roughly speaking, it meant 'adaptable', because we were doing stuff like James K. Baxter and the Māori myths. We didn't feel like we were pioneers, but looking back on it I think we were pioneering something.[11]

In November 1989, just a month after its formation, Whakarite toured in the North Island presenting *The Waitara Purchase* and a school piece, *The Adventures of Hatupatu* by Lex Matheson. *The Waitara Purchase*, Brian Hannam's 1973 satirical documentary drama, 'examines the Māori land question, imperialism in NZ's colonial days and the events that led to the first land wars'.[12] In February 1990 the group presented the Christchurch premiere of *Outside In*, Hilary Beaton's uncompromising 1982 play about life inside a New Zealand women's prison. Gilbert recalls this as a piece the Court Theatre was unlikely to touch, but which played to the strengths of the actors working with Whakarite at that time.

While an early imperative was to promote Māori plays and performers, several Whakarite company members were Pacific Islanders – yet they remained virtually 'invisible' on stage. Ifopo describes her experience:

> In the early days I was playing Māori roles. I'd never really performed alongside other Polynesian actors. When I played Māori roles it was usually because there were no other female Māori actors in the company... and you've got to do it with integrity. Whatever you're doing, you try to be really honest and passionate ... you're being respectful to everyone.[13]

Ifopo's parents had migrated from Samoa in the 1950s. 'Our parents were part of the first wave of Samoans in Christchurch and helped establish the Pacific community there. As kids we watched our parents in cultural performances. Mum was quite the drama queen.' In her solo show *The Native Chef* (2002), Ifopo talks about her childhood experiences:

> When I was growing up in Christchurch the stories told to my sisters and I as children came from my father. Every night after dinner we would gather around, sing hymns, say prayers and listen as our father read from the Bible ...

I went to the Palagi Sunday school in the morning and the Samoan Sunday school in the afternoon, so there was no way of avoiding White Sunday. I would stand in front of the congregation and recite passages of scripture with all the conviction and emotion I could muster, making my parents very proud.[14]

By 1988 Ifopo had found her way to Puawai.

They had all these modules that you could join – dance, music, theatre, sound engineering and catering. And I wanted to go to dance, because I love dance, but when I got there, they said, 'Oh no we're full here, you go see that [drama] guy.' And I said, 'Oh no, it's okay, theatre and drama is the last thing I want to do, because our experience of White Sunday is this trauma, being out in public and speaking; I'd rather dance.' I met Guy Ockenden and he explained that theatre's more than just acting – there's directing, design, stage management. So that made me feel it was more open and there was a lot more scope. He said, 'Just give it a go and see what happens.' Later on I saw Nathaniel Lees playing Othello in the Trinity Pacific Congregational Church in Christchurch. I couldn't believe that he was a Samoan actor playing the lead role in a Shakespeare. It must have meant a lot to me because I cut out an article about him and stuck it in my diary without knowing that later on I would work with him.

Ifopo's family remained uncertain about her new career direction. 'My dad couldn't understand it. He came up one time when I was working at Puawai when we were warming up, and he goes, "Oh, is that all you do – just dance all day? Why don't you get a proper job!"[15] But of course, Dad, Mum and my family came to watch me when I finally started performing in theatre, no pressure.'[16]

After leaving Puawai she became the assistant manager of Whakarite. In addition to the roles she was playing under Gilbert's direction, Ifopo did on-camera work for Television New Zealand in *What Now?* and *Danny's Café*, a weekend children's magazine-style show. By 1991 her contribution to the arts was recognised nationally when she became the theatre representative on the Contemporary Arts Committee set up by the QEII Arts Council during a national gathering of Polynesian performing artists.

In 1989 Whakarite found a new home – the Performing Arts Theatre, converted from the old Cinerama movie theatre near Cathedral Square at 111 Worcester Street. This community-based 200-seat theatre and concert venue was later to become the original home of Pacific Underground. From 1985 the building had served as the Cinerama Youth Centre. Gilbert approached the city council: 'I made an argument for them to give [the theatre] to us for a peppercorn rent. We stripped all the carpet out, repainted inside and got a bar in the foyer.' The theatre became a focal hub for young people getting involved in the arts. Ifopo describes it as 'a playground':

A lot of us met doing events there like Legal Street Dance, which was a one-off fashion show over three days using local designers and our peers – young people, family and friends, instead of models ...We did a show called *Intermission* where we did social and political satire.

Small became the company's writer-in-residence for a year. There was never any question about his acceptance into this largely Polynesian group.

People like Vic Tamati and George Kahi just welcomed me. 'Here's this young white guy keen on the performing arts.' Vic and George had really big visions. I remember having conversations with George at the time where he might say, 'We're going to do a race-relations seminar, and I'd like you to write three five-minute skits about it.' And I'm like, 'But I'm not even Māori!' 'It doesn't matter! Just do it!' So I did. There were all these little opportunities, building confidence all the time.

Sisters Mishelle and Tanya Muagututi`a and musician Posenai (Pos) Mavaega were also involved with the Cinerama Youth Centre. Mishelle and Tanya were born and raised in Christchurch. Their parents, who had migrated from Samoa in the early 1960s, were encouraging, according to Mishelle. 'Dad didn't mind us being involved in the performing arts. We found out later he'd played in one of the only Samoan bands, and his favourite play was *The Merchant of Venice*. He was quietly supportive of everything we did.'[17]

For Tanya, the journey into theatre was a natural progression:

Our whole family was musical, all of us in White Sunday. I loved singing with my siblings ... In high school I studied music, played in the orchestra and did a couple of productions. I finished high school on a student exchange in the US, tried life in Sydney, but ended up back in Christchurch. I met Lester Vaele, who was an accomplished keyboard player and youth worker at Cinerama Youth Centre, where Mishelle was on student placement. Before long, I ended up being a youth volunteer there, programming little events and making posters. I learnt how to jam there, play the guitar, perform in a Samoan and Kapa Haka group, how to organise people and events. It was filled with schoolkids, ex-street kids and a lot of the students of Puawai – mainly PI and Maori – all young and finding their feet. That's where I met Pos, who walked in with his backpack and guitar.[18]

Posenai Mavaega was 21 when he first connected with Tanya (later to be his wife) and Mishelle around 1990–91. He had been a musician since early childhood. 'Where I came from, in Linwood, it wasn't cool to be into music or theatre, or anything like that. It wasn't cool at all.'

I was job searching when I walked into the Cinerama Youth Centre, self-promoting me and my brother Cliff's band Numbers. I started hanging out more

> at the youth centre. With that creative energy, it was magnetic. I was always around, I was always helping. Tanya was a coordinator for a youth programme at that space, and Simon and Erolia were working there. It was a hub of activity with youth off the street and artists. I ended up playing guitar at the youth centre for Chris Searle's band. I was really impressed by Chris's drumming, and the word got out that he was the Palagi drummer with the black 'feel'.[19]

When interviewed by the *Press* in January 1991, Gilbert emphasised Whakarite's commitment to New Zealand work, noting, 'New Zealand writers deserve more support than they have had in the past.'[20] Between 1990 and 1993 Whakarite staged New Zealand works that Gilbert wanted to see performed in the city, the majority of which he directed. For *Big Bickies*, Stephen Sinclair's musical satire about an ordinary family's experience of winning Lotto, the company hired Court 2 (the studio theatre[21]) in August 1990; once again Ifopo drew critical praise for her 'lively expression and unceasing energy'.[22] *Country Killing*, a farcical murder mystery satirising the country and western scene, written and directed by Matheson, played in the newly established Performing Arts Theatre venue in January 1991, followed by Jeff Addison's comedy *Idol Adultery* in December of the same year.

Theatre in Education became Whakarite's main focus, and a company of four toured nationally with new works for primary and secondary school audiences; by the end of 1990 they had performed to more than 800 schools in the South Island alone.[23] The pieces were written by Small (*The Last Kakapo*, *Kumara On Toast*), Matheson (*The House of the People*, *Playing Safe*, *The Adventures of Hatupatu*), and Gilbert, often under the name Hemi Roberts (*Imagine That!*, *Manawhenua*, *The Treaty Makers*, *Manaia Strikes Back*).[24] At least one play each year was based on Māori legend, because, as Gilbert stated, 'Future audiences need to be educated biculturally ... we are trying to create a new pride in that area.'[25]

Legal Street Productions

Around 1990 a loose arts collective was taking shape in Christchurch. Called Legal Street Productions (after the 1980s NZ television show *Street Legal*, which featured Jay Laga`aia), it was planned as a showcase for its members. It arose from Mishelle Muagututi`a's 'first foray into managing a large event and taking risks':

This collective came out of the Legal Street Dance fashion show I organised and choreographed for the Cinerama Youth Centre. A lot of people involved decided to keep going and became 'Legal Street Productions'. We were influenced by the music and dance trends happening around the world and in our local nightclubs at the time.[26]

Anton Carter was 'DJ-ing and doing hip hop music at the time':

Legal Street Productions was formed as a collective of people doing different music or arts things. We'd put on a show together where we'd all showcase ourselves. You had the same backing band with different performers – hip hop, reggae and dancers mixed in with a fashion show.[27]

The collective included Chris Searle, a Puawai graduate and tutor, and later an integral part of Pacific Underground's music team. Victor Rodger, who at that time worked for the *Christchurch Star*, attended Legal Street Dance; his first play, *Sons*, would later be staged by Pacific Underground. As Tanya Muagututi`a describes it,

Victor was a journalist, and he was mates with Mish [Mishelle Muagututi`a]. But he also knew Oscar Kightley, because they did some journalism course together. Victor came to the fashion show and he brought Oscar, and we didn't know him then, and Oscar just thought, 'Oh, this is so dumb', he didn't like it at all! [We] met Oscar a year after, and he says, 'Were you guys in this show ...?'

Gradually the various Christchurch Pasifika performing circles and individuals were intersecting.

First Steps towards a Pacific Theatre Collective

Oscar Kightley grew up in West Auckland.

I was born in Apia in 1969, then was in my dad's village of Faleatiu. I came here when I was four. My parents spoke Samoan at home; the kids just spoke English back to them. I was a bit of a clown at school. I got through by taking the piss and making people laugh. I never performed at school, I was too shy. I always loved reading, so that naturally set me into a path for writing, just because I loved stories. Writing was my favourite subject at school, making stuff up, because it had no discernible rules, you know? Your imagination was what counted.[28]

Kightley gained a cadetship at the *Auckland Star* and worked for four years as a journalist, then moved to Christchurch in 1991 to take up a job as a presenter for a new Television New Zealand children's magazine-style show called *Life in the Fridge Exists* (*L.I.F.E.*). As he observes, 'They wanted a Polynesian guy from

Auckland as part of the team. I fit the bill.' For six months Kightley wrote and presented all his own stories.

When he first arrived he knew only one person in Christchurch – Mishelle Muagututi`a. 'At the time she was doing a dance course and was also involved in Whakarite, a local theatre company. I started hanging out with her and her mates. I didn't even know there were Samoan people in Christchurch.'

At the same time, Erolia Ifopo, as a member of the QEII Arts Council's Contemporary Arts Committee, with Pacific arts advisor Eteuati Ete and musician Pati Umaga was involved in organising a Pacific arts conference at Whitireia Polytech in Wellington.[29] This was to be an opportunity for young Samoan artists to 'meet with seasoned performers, writers, dancers, musicians and visual artists to share ideas and discuss their approach to their work'.[30] The event was attended by Whakarite members Mishelle Muagututi`a and dancer/choreographer Siaosi Mulipola. Mishelle remembers it with enthusiasm:

> That was one of the best conferences! Two days of workshops – everyone circulated and participated in everyone else's artform so we had a taste of dance, theatre, visual arts, music. Then we performed together in a concert. Suddenly, we were realising that there was a much larger Pacific arts scene.

Kightley found himself in the midst of it all:

> I met all these Pacific Islander artists, all with similar stories to mine: Tongan sculptors, Cook Island filmmakers, Samoan visual artists.[31] I met David Fane and Shimpal Lelisi there. That was such an amazing weekend, just being around all this Pacific creativity. And it started opening possibilities in my head towards performance.

Kightley shone as the MC at the conference's final-night concert. According to Ifopo, 'Oscar really stepped up to the occasion. He had us in fits of laughter. To see him get up in front of so many people was a revelation.' Mishelle describes him as 'a natural': 'His intelligence, his charisma, his knowledge, everything combined. He had a great command of the audience, he acknowledged everybody and helped to make us realise we were part of a larger movement.' Simon Small recalls: 'Afterwards I hooked up with Oscar in Christchurch and said, "I'm working on this script, and I'd really like you to be in it."' The role he offered Kightley was originally a Māori character, to which Kightley responded, 'Make him Samoan and I will. I don't feel comfortable playing a Māori – why pretend to be Māori? Just get a Māori!'

The play was *Horizons*, Small's first full-length work written under the pseudonym Francis Serra – a name he had first used when writing *Kumara on Toast* and *The Last Kakapo*.[32] Mishelle found herself drawn to it as well.

> Erolia and Simon were really good at motivating people. Oscar, Erolia, Michael and Simon were flatting together, and one day I went to their place. I thought I was going for a cup of tea, but they were about to start a play reading of *Horizons*. And they said, 'Oh, could you read this part?' I had never acted before. I was in the dance module at Puawai. I read, and they said, 'Oh, you should carry on with that.' That reading was a turning point in my life.

As Ifopo notes, 'All our talents – the dancing, the singing, the comedy – all came together.'

Horizons presented Pacific Island migrant characters for the first time on a Christchurch stage and would eventually draw an audience rarely seen in any local theatre. But the script evolved slowly. An early draft was workshopped by Playmarket in December 1990; Small re-wrote the piece four times before its premiere; and it would later undergo further revision.[33] Directed by Robert Gilbert, *Horizons* (version one) opened on 19 October 1991 for a two-week season at the Performing Arts Theatre in Worcester Street. For the first time in her career, Ifopo (as Ane) was playing a Samoan character.[34] Also in the cast were Papalagi Glen Harley and Linley-Jane Bullen and, in his first acting performance, Kightley. In addition, there were appearances by the Kolours hip hop/funk dance group playing 'friends and cousins who used to hang out at the flat'.[35] Kolours members were Mishelle, Mulipola and Venessa Kidwell, all of whom had trained in dance at Puawai.

Horizons is a romantic comedy that examines Samoan–Palagi relationship issues from a young urban perspective. As Small notes, the play is about 'people growing up in New Zealand and some of the misunderstandings and conflicts that arise when the two influences meet'.[36] Ane, a gifted Samoan painter (Ifopo) and her Palagi partner Lionel, an out-of-work sound engineer (Harley), are seeking a third person to share their flat. They select Ane's big-personality cousin Parry (Kightley), who introduces his Palagi girlfriend Di (Bullen) into the mix. Personality conflicts between the various characters lead to relationship breakdowns, and Ane and Lionel's career choices pull them apart.

Christina Stachurski's review praised the 'deceptively simple' script for its ability to charm and amuse, and to 'present situations from multiple viewpoints without making judgements'.[37] Stachurski identifies Ane's Aunty Sina (Mishelle) as 'an archetypal wise-woman ... a bridge between Samoan and Pakeha cultures'. Aunty Sina's death halfway through the play forces Ane to make a strong decision about her future as an artist, since she must choose between attending her own exhibition opening and the symbolic 'closing' of Sina's life.

From his first stage performance in *Horizons*, Kightley set the tone that was arguably to define his acting in the early years of his career. Stachurski comments on his 'explosive energy' as the 'self-confessed lout' Parry. This contrasted strongly with his 'quiet dignity and wickedly ironic wit' in a second role as Ane's traditional-minded father Tama. According to Gilbert, the show was funny yet honest:

> I remember Oscar stepping over the back of the couch or something, it was hilarious. He spoke with a thick 'Fresh' accent, and audiences recognised this character, this voice, the mistakes that newly arrived Pasifika immigrants might make, and the self-effacing embarrassment that comes out of that. It was just so honest and enlightening, and this was the first time it had ever happened in Christchurch. It was like realising the sky was a different colour. I remember my astonishment at the audience response, different from anything I'd experienced before.

The fact that *Horizons* was written by a Palagi was openly addressed in several interviews given during the subsequent touring life of the play. Kightley publically observed that the play 'accurately depicts Samoan life in New Zealand ... One of the biggest compliments for this show is from Samoans who have seen the play and are surprised that a Palagi has written it, because of how true it is.'[38]

Ifopo was an inspiration for emerging practitioners such as Mishelle and Tanya Muagututi`a. According to Mishelle, Ifopo 'set the bar':

> There are times when the situation is really stressful in theatre productions. Erolia would keep her calm. She would make sure everything was organised. We learnt the theatre discipline that you need from her. We'd be observing her and try to follow suit. To see someone up there, using their craft – we would look at her and be in awe.

Tanya looked to Ifopo as 'a strong role model in terms of Pacific women in theatre'.

> I've always acknowledged her because of that. I saw her working in other plays as other characters and I remember just watching her and thinking, 'I could never do that.' She was supporting us as young people interested in theatre, and she still does. Not just the women, but everyone.

Ifopo is characteristically modest about her own contribution, however:

Mishelle and Oscar were very natural performers. It seemed effortless for them. The laughter, the emotion, the strength – being able to hold the stage. They could bounce off each other. I felt very awkward in comparison.

After the first season *Horizons* received further workshopping and significant re-writes.[39] A sense of Samoan history, myth and spirituality infuses the revised text; Aunty Sina, in an extended role, provides a clear bridge between the two worlds of Samoa and Christchurch.

AUNTY SINA: You know when they first saw the first Europeans? They thought they were gods. They would call out Palagi! Palagi! Who are the people from the sky? ... You know when you stand on the beach, and you look right across, and you can see – the horizon? That's when you see the boat, that's why they say it's from the sky.[40]

The revised work had a new producer (Small), several new cast members and a change of director. Puawai graduate Campbell Taylor and comedy performer Cristal McGill stepped in as Lionel and Di, while Ifopo and Mishelle swapped roles, the former now playing the character referred to in promotional material as 'the adorable Aunty Sina'. Kightley remained as Parry, Tama and a minister who officiates at Sina's funeral. Gilbert, who according to Kightley gave it a 'very traditional' production, was replaced by recent immigrant Bert van Dijk, who 'completely transformed it into a physical piece'.[41] Small attended a physical theatre workshop with him:

I spent a weekend learning so much from Bert. We were doing crazy things like moving huge upside-down paper rubbish bags 30 metres at the pace of a snail without crushing them. I felt that Bert's style with *Horizons* would produce something really mind-blowing.

Mishelle also found van Dijk inspirational:

I learned so much from Bert. His version of *Horizons* incorporated physical theatre into myths and everyday activities, which was new to me and the rest of the cast. During rehearsals we worked a lot on movement and voice. Stylised movement and singing were now incorporated throughout the production, with all cast members involved in the physicality of the play ... In addition, the cast now sang some old Samoan songs, either individually or together.[42]

In an interview with Wellington's *Capital Times*, van Dijk clarified his reasons for adding a physical theatre dimension to the work:

Physical theatre appeals much more to the audience's imagination. People can interpret it in many different ways. I'm not keen on presenting well-chewed, well-digested material. The audience need to do some of the chewing ... The first time we did the play, the audience were mostly Samoan and Polynesian. They were so responsive. They were shouting advice, clapping and cheering. The air was charged with involvement and appreciation.[43]

Van Dijk's exposure to the reactions of a Pasifika audience mirrors Gilbert's experience when directing the play. As Gilbert comments:

I remember them loving the PI humour. [In rehearsal] I didn't know how to handle it as a director, because it was new to me, I just let it happen. I trusted Oscar – he has such an infectious sense of humour and he and Erolia and Mishelle would be in fits of laughter over certain stuff. I remember being surprised at the audience almost being part of the performance – that they broke down that barrier. There were lots of hoots and calling out.

Ifopo recalls,

When I started doing Pacific Island theatre, the audiences switched. When the PIs started coming into that audience, I tell you – for me it was one of my biggest challenges because of their laughter. I mean I'd been in some plays and people were laughing, but the difference with Pacific Islanders was the volume, the emotion. There was more interaction, more response: it's contagious.

Such interactive responses increase the pleasure for performer and viewer, heighten the sense of theatricality, and allow the audience to take ownership of the material presented to them, in a joyously positive way.

Under the umbrella of the Performing Arts Trust, the group took the revised play on tour. *Horizons* (version two) was marketed as 'a new romantic comedy' and 'the first Pacific Island play to tour New Zealand'.[44] Between 5 August and 26 September 1992, it played in Auckland's Galaxy Theatre, Taki Rua Depot and Castle Theatre at the Univeristy of Otago, followed by a triumphant return to the Christchurch Performing Arts Theatre, where Tanya joined the company as the lighting operator.

Pacific Underground is born

By 1992 the key players who would later form Pacific Underground had met and worked together in various combinations, including on a series of school holiday programmes called Culture Shock Youth Forum that were inspired by the Arts Council hui at Whitireia Polytechnic. Tanya took a prominent role: 'We enrolled about 11 kids on the first day, and by the end of the week 50 kids were performing skits directed by Erolia and Oscar, dance pieces choreographed by

Mishelle and Sumara Fraser, and singing in a band tutored by Pos [Mavaega].' These programmes became an integral part of the community from 1992 to 1995, and were a fertile nurturing ground for young Pasifika talent. Among participants were Malo Luafutu, Karoline Tamati and Dallas Tamaira, who would later achieve recognition as Scribe, Ladi6 and the vocalist of Fat Freddy's Drop respectively.

Encouraged by the *Horizons* tour, Small and Kightley agreed it was time to form their own theatre company to tell Pacific stories. Small, Kightley, Ifopo, Mishelle Muagututi`a and Michael Hodgson (a Palagi actor and Puawai graduate) were passionate about the idea, and there was much laughter and excitement at the realisation that they could make it happen. As Fuarosa Luafutu-Tamati describes it,

> I think we were lucky to be in Christchurch, as we were a minority and we were able to just try things without too much interference from anyone. We understood that no one else existed in Christchurch who could project or portray the experience of ourselves as Samoan [and] Pacific within the context of Aotearoa, and specifically from the South Island. It became an effective and successful project that created interest and notice from the general public of Christchurch, [and was] a viable employment option for Pacific young people, who used their natural abilities to represent the characters they had grown up with.

The company name arose from the idea that Christchurch was 'pretty much the underground of the Pacific, the very bottom of the Pacific', according to Anton Carter, and played on the name of one of Kightley's favourite rap groups, Digital Underground. As Mavaega says,

> It's a good name. My parents didn't like the name Underground. But they came to like it, once they'd seen what we were actually doing. A few years later, my dad spoke at a Pacific Underground opening. He was proud of what we were doing, bringing our unspoken underground stories above the ground.

The logo was a target sight over a frangipani design, which represents the Pacific.[45] Enthusiasm stretched to a desire for a jacket that would identify them as members of Pacific Underground, an item that became highly prized. Small recalled the energy of the time: 'Once we had the name, the logo and the jackets, there was just no turning back. We had such confidence in ourselves and our identity.'

Pacific Underground was formed 'with the idea of continuing to create, perform and tour Polynesian theatre and music to people throughout New

Zealand'.[46] The original intention was to produce public shows for adults and, following the Whakarite model, to create TIE work for national school tours. One immediate catalyst for the formation of the company was the possibility of getting a play accepted for a week-long professional workshop at New Zealand Writers' Week. The deadline for this was January 1993 and, with only two months left to create an original script, Kightley and Small (still writing as Francis Serra) were galvanised into action. Kightley recalls sitting in the garden one day and saying, 'We should write a play – it can't be that hard. You just write someone's name on the left, and what they say on the right.'

> We didn't realise how hard it was – we had no idea. We sent it in and, amazingly, got accepted. So we formed a company, Pacific Underground, to do this play, which was *Fresh off the Boat*.

4.

Pacific Underground: The resounding beat

Pacific Underground was a beat that resounded throughout the Pacific Island community in Christchurch. The spirit of family, whānau and friendship became the rhythm for all those that needed recognition, acknowledgement, respect and a sense of pride in being of Pacific or Polynesian descent. It was like a movement that you aspired to be part of.

FUAROSA LUAFUTU-TAMATI[1]

Within three years Pacific Underground would not only be touring nationwide with plays and Theatre in Education (TIE) projects, they would also create their first international collaboration, *Tatau: Rites of passage*. Collectively and individually they began to carve out careers within the theatre and music industries. According to Anton Carter (later the company's manager), the initial impetus was 'to tell our own stories of our experiences growing up in Aotearoa'. He believes the extraordinary energy and commitment in Christchurch arose because of its relative geographical isolation:

> There were no barriers, other than what we placed on ourselves. There wasn't a lot of encouragement either, or established pathways. We were not influenced by anything else. The whole challenge was actually making your own templates. Having fun was a key part of it, seeing what you could achieve. Being able to go to Auckland and perform, and do relatively well and then disappear – it was the whole mystery of it. People would be like, what? You're from where?[2]

Fresh off the Boat: 'A blessed play'

Filled with enthusiasm, Simon Small and Oscar Kightley set about writing a new full-length play, inspired in part by seeing *Hide'n'Seek* (1994) by Hone Kouka and Hori Ahipene, a Māori physical theatre piece in which a young, gay, small-town Māori male comes to terms with disappointing his family's expectations.[3] Small recalls, 'We loved its format – 90 minutes and just power through, no interval. And so that's what we did with *Fresh off the Boat*.[4] As Tanya Muagututi`a notes, 'It grew out of the people who were there at the time' – the founding members of Pacific Underground: Erolia Ifopo, Tanya, Mishelle, Michael Hodgson, Small and Kightley.[5] For Kightley, having a theatre company was 'amazing': 'It's a big thing for a writer, having actors there every day. You know the actors you're writing for.'[6]

As with *Horizons*, the script workshop for *Fresh off the Boat* was funded and organised by Playmarket; led by Stuart Devenie and Lisa Warrington, it helped to bring a tighter focus to the work. As Kightley notes, 'Being taken seriously made it a lot more real.'

Nathaniel (Nat) Lees, who had recently directed the triumphant Auckland production of John Kneubuhl's *Think of Garden*, became an important mentor. Small recalls:

> We wanted Nat to direct it, so we went up to Auckland and he agreed to see us. We gave him the script, and he read it and said he'd like to do it. There we were, 22 or 23, wanting to start our own company with a script. We were really in awe of what he'd achieved, and we had him on a huge pedestal. And for him to join us on the journey was amazing.

Lees' direction encouraged a physical performance style, harking back to the influence of *Hide'n'Seek*. He also played a significant dramaturgical role in encouraging the young writers beyond their immediate comfort zone, and brought gravitas to the work, helping them realise that they could make a difference by taking their work seriously:

> It's a Pacific Island story, so they want happiness. They want singing and they want dancing. 'Those Islanders, they know how to have a good time.' And that's never been the way that I think about theatre. So when we looked at that story, we talked about what it means to be Samoan. For the Samoans who have come here, and for the Samoans born here – what does that mean? And in sharing that, we realised not all these stories are Cinderella stories. We all knew of uncles, aunties, cousins, someone else down the road who had ended very tragically. The idea of trying to find a balance of what is truth and what is perception was something we worked on. What was interesting for me was watching this group of relatively inexperienced Pacific Island actors come to grips with how we actually tell this story truthfully, without making a joke of it.[7]

Parts were tailored to the actors' personalities and played to their strengths as performers. David Fane, who had graduated from Toi Whakaari in 1992, was invited to play the protagonist, Charles. According to Fane, involving Lees was an inspired idea: 'Working with him was a real treat. Nat would remind us of the honesty of theatre, and the power it can bring you.'[8] Mishelle also found the experience invaluable:

> Working with Nathaniel was a huge shift for us. It felt like another step. That was the first time we had been directed by a Pacific director. The weight and experience and understanding he provided was on another level. Working with Nathaniel justified why we had set up Pacific Underground.[9]

Fresh off the Boat explores themes that have a strong resonance for many Pacific Islanders. Karen Stevenson notes that the most important factor driving contemporary Pacific art between 1985 and 2000 was cultural identity,[10] and those driving it were Pasifika artists born in New Zealand, mostly under the age of 30. 'They are from a generation not unlike previous generations, yet one that has a foot in two cultures.'[11] She references humour and 'a generation gap: a rift between the island and the urban'.[12] This is the central theme of *Fresh off the Boat*.[13] The play sees the arrival from Samoa of Charles, seeking work and a new life in New Zealand. Initially speaking only Samoan, he is increasingly bemused and frustrated by the conditions and expectations he encounters in the new country: 'Niu Sila is a big place. Many strange people living here.'[14] At his sister Elizabeth's home he attempts to impose the rules with which he is familiar, saying, 'This is our custom, the way we do things in the Islands.'[15] This does not sit well with Elizabeth (Ifopo), her two New Zealand-born daughters Evotia and Ula (Mishelle and Tanya Muagututi`a), or her Palagi partner Mervyn (Michael Hodgson). Mervyn is obliged to pretend to be just a friend to avoid offending Charles's strong moral sensibilities and incurring his disapproval of mixed-race relationships. Evotia and Ula speculate that their uncle will be a classic 'FOB'. Their friend, teenage New Zealand-born Samoan Englebert (Kightley), has renamed himself 'Samoa' and likes to practise stirring political speeches that he hopes one day to deliver 'to the masses'. His ambition is comically undermined by the fact that he cannot quite begin his imagined life of independence: 'I don't know if my mum would let me go flatting.'[16]

Comedy is offset by Charles' increasing disillusionment, which comes to a head late in the play when he argues with Elizabeth:

> **CHARLES**: I been working in Samoa for the last twenty years, while you've been living in paradise! You get away and have had your fun all this time. Don't have to do what anybody else say, have money to spend and places to go. This is my freedom! This is just like getting out of prison after twenty years. That's what it feel like. I am a free man at last! Of course I get a little bit silly and do crasy things, but it's all right – I'll calm down one day ...[17]

His speech illustrates the complexity of the situation for this newly arrived migrant. Charles can no longer be happy in Samoa, but is struggling to accept the changes dictated by his new environment and the expectations of his family.

The framing of *Fresh off the Boat* exemplifies this almost unsolvable problem. The opening scene, set in a village in Samoa, shows Charles, cross-legged on the floor of his fale, quietly observing the simple pleasures of daily life. In contrast, the final scene shows him dishevelled and lost, staring at New Zealand city life – rubbish trucks, traffic, shops opening – from a bus stop. As Fane notes, 'That was the beauty of it. You don't know where or what he's going to do. My personal theory is that he ended up in Invercargill.'

Fresh off the Boat opened at the Rolleston Ave Theatre in the Christchurch Arts Centre on 17 November 1993, where it received a standing ovation. Small described the scene: 'We staged a traditional Samoan siva and most of the audience came out of their seats to put loving donations on the actors, the director and the producers as we all danced together.'[18] Fane has fond memories of the season:

> It was fantastic, it was a sell-out season. Every night there'd be so many Samoans. Never knew there were so many Samoans in Christchurch. And of course there were Palagi there. And then when we did the show up in Wellington, once again all these Pacific Islanders coming in, and then towards the end of the season I noticed there were a lot more Palagi arriving. And then the Auckland season, it was this really amazing mix of Pacific Island and Palagi audiences. It was quite a blessed play.

Playwright David Mamea recalled his response to seeing the production when it toured to the Wellington International Fringe Festival in March 1994.

> *Fresh off the Boat* came up, and I guess I had my own little version of cultural cringe. What the hell do these guys from Christchurch have to say to me? I think it starts off with Oscar Kightley in a Malcolm X-like kind of pose. And from that moment on I was hooked into that play, because it just took all these things that as a New Zealand-born Samoan I'd picked up through the 70s – the dawn raids and whatever else. But it used them really well, and it was funny. And I laughed and I cried. I really identified with the story, and they did it so well, and I didn't cringe at all.[19]

Reviews were encouraging, with Laurie Atkinson noting its 'dry humour and a strong dramatic climax' and finding particular delight in Kightley's role as Samoa.[20] Susan Budd endorsed the praise of Kightley, but singled out Fane:

> ... a giant of a man, who gives a gargantuan performance. An actor of enormous charm, he charts the path of a man released from 20 years in the prison of his culture to a freedom that proves even more constricting. He portrays beautifully

> the constantly shifting facets of Charles's personality, from bemused innocence to bull-headed stubbornness.[21]

Of Fane's performance Mark Cubey wrote, 'He expertly mixes amazement, stubborn intractability, resentment, playful delight, confusion and anger in a complex portrayal of a fish trying to swim in a mystifyingly foreign sea.'[22] Mike Houlahan praised the dialogue, which he found 'unmistakenly [sic] authentic', and endorsed the quality of the writing: 'For a young company, [it is] an outstandingly mature, hard-hitting and also funny play.'[23]

The initial Wellington season went sufficiently well for the play to be brought back to Downstage for three weeks in April 1995, after which it played in the mainstream Herald Theatre in Auckland, then Apia in Samoa and Brisbane, Australia. It was later recorded by Radio New Zealand and broadcast in New Zealand and Australia. The play won a Media Peace Award, was published in 2005, and continues to be used both as a teaching text and in performances by schools.

The trip to Samoa was a significant step and engendered a different perspective on the play. Mishelle described the scene in Apia: 'We performed for the schools in a covered stadium in Apia Park. You couldn't hear yourself – the kids went wild.' The reaction was thought provoking, as Fane describes:

> When we did the season in Samoa it was a totally different response because of what happened with Uncle Charles. He comes over [to NZ] – the failure, the drive towards alcoholism ... the punch lines and the gag lines didn't work as well in Samoa. And I was talking to my uncle afterwards about it and he was like, 'Well, it's all about failure.' He says, 'But the thing is, when we sent our Uncle Charleses over to New Zealand, they weren't broken. But they come back as broken. So, who's at fault? Is New Zealand at fault for breaking these young men? And then they try to say that's how we all are – we send a perfectly good product over to you, and they come back as broken, we don't understand it.'

Over the years, the view of Pacific Island migration shown in the play has shifted. In 2010 Kightley attended a performance of *Fresh off the Boat* at St Mary's College, an all-girl high school in Ponsonby.

> Strangely, it had dated. A character was making all these political points about the Pacific Islands, 'blah, blah, blah'. But by now, that's changed a little bit. And partly because of Pacific theatre and how that impacted. So it was cool. And I'm sitting there thinking, I'm really glad his lines aren't as relevant as they were in 1993.

Reaching out to the community

Fuarosa (Losa) Luafutu-Tamati, who co-produced the premiere season of *Fresh off the Boat* with Small, also helped to write the constitution for Pacific Underground, among other roles:

> The constitution included a commitment to community development, and to use Pacific stories as a vehicle for change, and to increase awareness of issues that affected Pacific society in Aotearoa and the Pacific region. I also became a fundraiser for PU and was chairperson for a time. In the main, I was the community link for PU and provided support to the young women in the company.

Small recalls: 'Losa and Vic Tamati were so instrumental in making Pacific Underground take off with the Pacific Island community in Christchurch behind it. Losa as a producer reached out to the community to ignite them and make sure they came to see our work. She also dealt with cultural protocol, so we did things right on the night.'[24]

Theatre in Education: The first steps

Drawing on their experiences of touring with Whakarite, the Pacific Underground team turned their attention to writing and touring plays designed for school audiences. According to Anton Carter,

> Theatre in Education essentially was the backbone of Pacific Underground in the early days. That was the key, that we'd actually make regular money and employ people to write a play, and then deliver it for three months. The TIE model was very influential for developing emerging talent and providing a valuable income stream.

Those early days were hard work and the team was 'sleeping on people's couches and touring in a noisy diesel van' as Mishelle recalls. Ifopo reflected on the experience:

> ... you learned your trade on and off the stage, adjusting yourself to administration, writing pamphlets, ringing up schools, booking motels, three or four shows a day, learning to improvise, powhiris, Q&A with the kids, going to the bank. It's stamina – when you came off touring, you were so fit.[25]

The first piece to tour, from April to November 1993, was written by Small and Kightley. *Gifted and Fresh* is a comedy about Mele, a high school student who secretly wants to go to dance school despite her parents' desire that she become a lawyer. Into this story is mixed a quest by two mysterious strangers, Vili and Pili, who have arrived from Western Samoa to find out why so many Polynesians come to Aotearoa.[26] The thrust of the piece was about making vocational and educational choices. Some of the characters wore half masks, an influence which Small traced to Bertolt Brecht and working with Bert van Dijk. The actors who toured this piece were Kightley, Ifopo, Hodgson, and Mishelle, drawing on her background in dance, as Mele.

In term one of 1994 Pacific Underground toured with *Who's the Flavour* by Kightley, then opened the door to a new writer, Victor Rodger, for term one 1995. A journalist with the *Christchurch Star*, Rodger joined Pacific Underground for a short time as publicist, manager and writer. His first project was an early draft of *Absolutely Fobulous*, which Mishelle describes as about 'two sisters who move from their environment to live with their wealthy cousins, and have to learn to live with each other'.[27] A re-drafted version toured secondary schools nationwide in 1995, again with Kightley and Mishelle together with Sara-Lia Tamati and Joy Vaele.

Vaele, who would become one of the long-term members of the company as an actor and playwright, had joined the group via Culture Shock, the holiday programme that Pacific Underground ran at the youth centre in Christchurch,[28] where another future member, Barbara Carpenter, also got her start. Carpenter recalls:

> My first encounter with Pacific Underground was taking part, along with more than twenty other kids, in a school holiday programme called Culture Shock. A fourteen-year-old Fijian/Kiwi girl lost in picking a path for her future, I had dropped out of school and didn't really know what the hell I was doing with my life. Not a troublemaker, but someone lost for direction. I gave this performing arts thing a go. I found Pacific Underground, and the women in particular, to be strong, encouraging and empowered by their passion for performing and expressing themselves. Raised by my Kiwi father, who taught us to 'talk only when spoken to', I was challenged by the likes of Mishelle Muagututi`a, a contemporary dancer, who would have us prancing around like we'd just stepped onto the set of *Fame*, and without batting an eyelid she made me feel like we could do it, and I believed every word she said. It was at the holiday programme I knew that performing and storytelling was something that I was passionate about.[29]

While the main bill shows brought an adult audience and attention from reviewers, it was school touring that paid the wages. Shows such as *Bully For You* (1997, written and directed by Ifopo) tackled issues that could be presented for debate at high schools around the country. Significantly, they also brought a Pasifika presence into the schools. Kightley described the rationale for *Bully For You*:

> Our plays in the past [had] dealt with culture clash, youth expectations, identity crisis and peer pressure, but bullying was something we had not specifically dealt with. Erolia spent a couple of months interviewing students in schools around the country getting stories from bullies and the bullied ... We tried to incorporate this research into the play to present a piece of theatre that [would] be truthful as well as entertaining.[30]

Ifopo's research indicated that girls as bullies were a big issue in schools: 'We were excited to tackle the issue because it meant more strong roles for women. It was the largest cast we had – four women, two men.'

Gifted and Fresh marked the end of Small's time with Pacific Underground, though he remained a friend and supporter. He was accepted by the New Zealand School of Broadcasting in 1994 and had to make a difficult choice. He was confident of the company's capacity to survive, however: 'I thought, if I step out, this is going to continue, because there is a movement going on here.'

Anton Carter joined Pacific Underground when *Fresh off the Boat* reached Auckland in October 1994. Born and bred in Christchurch, he was acquainted with most of the members. He had met Small at Burnside High School, and had been a member of Legal Street Productions with Mishelle and Tanya Muagututi`a and Pos Mavaega around 1990. After leaving polytech Carter had a job with Television New Zealand's *Tagata Pasifika*. His interests in music and documentary video production took him to London for three years, returning in 1994. He stayed with the company as tour manager for about three and a half years: 'Everything was trial and error. There was no blueprint. There was no one else doing what we were doing.'

Sons: An afakasi story

Buoyed by the success of *Fresh off the Boat*, Pacific Underground produced their second mainstage show, *Sons* by Victor Rodger, who named the play in homage to Albert Wendt's *Sons For the Return Home*.[31] Raised by his Palagi mother and grandparents, Rodger used his afakasi experience in writing *Sons*: 'Growing up in Christchurch, you're always being told you're other. You're conscious you're not like the majority population ... When people think "Samoan" they often think of one thing, but I'm very clear that there's a spectrum. I'm very conscious of not being au fait with everything in the culture, yet I still identify as a Samoan.'[32]

In *Sons* Tama MacFarlane (Kightley) is afakasi, with a Samoan father, Manu`a (Fane), who has abandoned the family, and a Palagi mother, Laura (Melissa Miles) who has raised him.[33] On meeting his father and half-brother, Tama begins to explore his Samoan heritage, despite the conflict this causes. While some incidents were created for dramatic purposes, the underlying structure reflected significant elements of Rodger's life and was based on his own experience of meeting his Samoan father for the first time as an adult.[34]

Sons opened at Court 2 in November 1995. Simon Cunliffe in the *Listener* suggested that the play was a 'worthy descendant' of *Sons For the Return Home*.[35] Tusiata Avia notes in her Foreword to the published text, 'One doesn't need to be afakasi or Samoan or cut off from one's culture or family to be touched by this play – for who among us is not the outsider?'[36] Jim Tully in the *Sunday Times* had reservations about the characters, however, believing they needed further development, and felt that the ending, 'though uplifting', lacked impact.[37]

Such matters would be addressed by Rodger when *Sons* was revised in 1998, with Rodger playing the central character, now renamed Noah.[38] On this occasion, Barry Southam claimed that it had 'much the same spell-binding effect' as Eugene O'Neill's *Long Day's Journey into Night*. Rodger's evolution as a playwright will be discussed in more detail in chapter 5.

Tatau: Rites of passage

While *Sons* was in preparation the company was seeding its next project: an international collaboration with Australia's Zeal Theatre, who had a similar interest in telling migrant stories. *Tatau: Rites of passage* explored new territory for Pacific Underground and was the first Pacific theatre international performance collaboration.

Zeal Theatre was founded in Newcastle in 1989 by Stefo Nantsou, who was born in Newcastle to Macedonian parents. Inspired by seeing Steven Berkoff performing *East* in 1977, Nantsou created work with a strong physical basis that showcased 'the cultures of non-English-speaking people in Australia'.[39] Zeal's early work was presented in schools, site-specific locations and workplaces, and was intended 'to tell stories about people who have no voice in mainstream society'.[40]

The two companies met in 1994 when Pacific Underground attended a Zeal workshop in Wellington. The following year they met again at the International Drama Educators Association TIE conference in Brisbane. According to Tanya Muagututi`a, 'Zeal Theatre were presenting their Theatre in Education piece about road safety. They watched our performance of *Fresh off the Boat* and really liked it ... and the conversation started about collaborating.'[41]

Tatau: Rites of passage evolved from that initial meeting and was jointly devised by Erolia Ifopo, Oscar Kightley, Shimpal Lelisi, Mishelle Muagututi`a, Anton Carter and Joy Vaele from Pacific Underground; and Rob Dilley, Meg Dunn and Karen Lantry from Zeal, with Nantsou as co-devisor and director. Mishelle describes the learning curve of the devising process as the Pacific Underground team adapted their text-based approach to Zeal's more physical devising methodology:

> Their approach to creating dialogue was new to us. They would give you a scenario, then you would improvise it [and] the director gave you feedback. We didn't have to learn any lines, it was memory recall. It was very quick.

While the end result was distinctively Pasifika in its subject matter, *Tatau: Rites of passage* speaks universally to the notion of first- or second-generation migrants trying to find their place in the world. The story spans four generations, from the arrival in New Zealand in 1950 of the Petula family, to a gathering 35 years later for a traditional tatau (tattoo) ceremony. Carter notes, 'Essentially, it's about young people coming to a new place and losing their way, then rediscovering it through wanting to get the pe`a [traditional tattoo].' As Michele Hewitson described it in her *Listener* review, 'the tatau also provides the central motif for an ambitious examination of the deeper scars created by the wide-scale migration of Samoan families to a country promising a shot at the Western dream in return for cheap labour.'[42] The over-arching metaphor of the play was the real-life tatau gradually applied in the first 10 minutes at the start of each performance. This painful process of body adornment signals the rite of passage into adulthood and is an ancient Samoan traditional art. It was carried out on stage by Su`a Paulo Suluape II using traditional implements.[43] In Auckland, the person receiving the tatau was Vic Tamati; for the Sydney season it was Fa`amoana Ioane (John) Luafutu. Carter describes the process:

> The Auckland season was three weeks[44] ... Su`a Suluape would ceremonially start the tattooing on the first night, and essentially you'd tell people to come back for closing night, because it'd be completed in three weeks' time ... So the tattooist had to pace himself through those three weeks. And he'd do stuff during the

day as well, so it wasn't all done on stage. The show began with just the person, the tattooist and his two helpers on stage, in low light, and we'd just hold it for almost five minutes, until everyone was in. It was quite painful for the person getting the tatau. But it was also symbolic, because Vic was our chairperson ... It was like the head of the Pacific Underground family was getting tattooed. So there were all these layers to the story. A lot of people were questioning: how could you present it in public? And it's really only because of Su`a Suluape that we would even think of doing something like that. His idea was to show the world the beauty of the art form, because if you didn't it would die.

For Tamati, *Tatau* was 'history in the making for Samoan tattooing, New Zealand theatre, theatre in general, Samoa as a nation, my entire family and for myself personally'.[45]

While applauding the tatau process, which 'mesmerises and intrigues', Hewitson found the device to be 'problematic' and went on to say:

> *Tatau* is never quite sure what it wants to be. At times, it offers documentary and social realism. At others, it extends highly theatrical set pieces; flower power, prison, silly bugger thuggery and a deliciously droll take on the hypocrisy and power of the church in the South Pacific.[46]

The act of tattooing was the focal point of Christopher Balme's analysis of the play in *Pacific Performances*:

> In a certain sense, the tattooing ceremony can be said to 'authenticate' the fictional story presented on stage as it provides a frame of a different kind for the events depicted. In the original Auckland production, further authenticity was added by the fact that the 'body canvas', Vic Tamati, had provided much of the material for the fictional story being enacted. He in effect listened to his own story each night while being tattooed.[47]

Diana Looser elaborates:

> Also included is the longer history recorded in and through the pe`a – the scripts, stories, and relationships encapsulated in the dense inscriptions that cover the man from waist to knees and become part of his own history as he undergoes the process of embodied transformation.[48]

Romeo and Tusi

Theatre in Education remained the backbone of Pacific Underground. One piece in particular was to have enduring impact and widespread popularity, making the transition easily between the school hall and the public stage. This was *Romeo and Tusi*, seeded in Culture Shock workshops, then scripted by Kightley and

Ifopo (who also directed), and taken on a national secondary and intermediate schools tour in 1996. It was then substantially rewritten, 'acquiring an entire band to turn it into a musical, and two more characters: an irreverent reverend and a fa`afafine [Ruby]'.[49] In this form it was publically staged as part of the SummerTimes free theatre season in Christchurch's Mona Vale Gardens in January 1997, and in other cities around New Zealand, and has been revived frequently since then.

The catalyst to action in the work is the meeting and immediate attraction between Anaru Heke, who is Māori, and Tusi Aiu, who is Samoan. Their struggle to have a normal teenage relationship in the face of family and racial antagonism is highlighted by their casting as Romeo and Juliet in a school production.[50] The play interweaves rehearsals and performance of *Romeo and Juliet* with satirical and slapstick family and social scenes. Part parody, part subversive comedy, the entertaining surface masks a deeper theme of racial tension between Māori and Pacific Islanders.

> **MRS AIU**: Tusi, you are a coconut. He's a kumara. Do you know what I'm talking about?
>
> **TUSI**: It doesn't matter what you are. Look Mum, Shakespeare once said a rose is a rose, and by any other name it would smell just as sweet.
>
> **RUBY**: And I once said, a hiding is a hiding and it would hurt just as much. So you better watch your mouth girl, don't mess with your mother.
>
> **TUSI**: You guys are being racist. You don't even know any Māori people. So how can you judge them?[51]

This blatant juxtaposition of politically correct and incorrect statements is a key comedic element of Pacific Underground's writing style. According to Mishelle Muagututi`a, the humour was energetic: 'Oscar and Erolia are the funniest people we know, so when you put them together, the one-upmanship in their humour just made those lines pop.'

Further sources of (often cruel) humour include slapstick and the undermining of authority, even of the original text. As Ruby says, 'it's Shakespeare, some things you aren't supposed to understand'.[52] The early script version showcases American popular culture, with repeated reference, for example, to the *Ricki Lake Show*. The play's climax is interrupted so the actors can mock-debate with the audience on racial prejudice – a section that reinforces the TIE roots of the script. Two familiar figures from Samoan society appear: the outwardly pious, venal minister, who replaces Shakespeare's Friar Lawrence, and the fa`afafine Ruby, whose role – as Anaru informs his disapproving mother in a comically pedantic reprimand – is 'perfectly normal in Pacific Island cultures and comments like yours only serve to oppress her further by making her try to fit a label which is convenient for society'.[53] Many of these comic elements hark back to the spirit of fale aitu. Ruby is simultaneously the director of the school play, Tusi's best friend (and thus a kind of rudimentary, 'feminised' Mercutio) and Juliet's Nurse.

Shimpal Lelisi re-joined Pacific Underground to play Ruby on Kightley's invitation. Moving from the Simei-Bartons' Pacific Theatre to Pacific Underground presented no problem for Lelisi: 'Our aims were the same: create brown works for brown actors. And when we got together it just seemed the natural progression at that time, because there were just so few of us.'[54] He recalls workshopping the script of *Romeo and Tusi*, where Ifopo and Kightley presented the story and 'everyone just threw stuff in'. Ifopo describes the spontaneity of the exercise:

> You're writing, but really when everyone comes together to read the play, and they're improvising different scenes, then it starts developing ... it belongs to everybody, because everyone adds things to the play, and as time passes, and you get more confident, and new people come in, it changes, grows, gets tighter and faster. And the music just punched it out again.

For the first time, the company used a full band. Pos Mavaega describes the musical side: 'The main love song, 'Pure Love', was written by Tanya. Each character had a walk-on musical motif. My arrangements were what was trending at the time – fusion, jazz and funk hip hop, mixed with Island styles.'[55] In *Romeo and Tusi*, Shakespeare's work is clearly being mined for its 'greatest hits', and the light-hearted irreverence shows a healthy disregard for the sanctity and cultural authority of the original text. As Ifopo notes, 'Shakespeare was lucky that he was in our play, that's how we look at it.'

Following the Mona Vale season the show played at free venues in the North Island, including Upper and Lower Hutt, Porirua, Otaki and Frank Kitts Park on the Wellington waterfront.[56] The emphasis was on accessibility, as Ifopo explains:

> ... our main thing was that it was an outdoor free production, because the two groups that we really wanted there were Māori and Islanders, and we would get such a wide variety of people. At first in Christchurch in Mona Vale you'd get people with their little drinks of wine and picnic baskets, and then you'd see the gangs going there, the skinheads – and yet everyone is all together and laughing.

Lelisi describes the efforts to make ends meet: 'There wasn't enough funding to pay us, so at the end of the show we'd stand there with buckets for people's donations. Some nights it was better than getting a weekly wage!'

Romeo and Tusi is remembered with great affection by its participants. Pacific Underground was proud to collaborate with a variety of artists in this project, including graffiti artist Sara-Lia Tamati, who graff-wrote the *Romeo and Tusi* sign on the front of the stage in Wellington, and Moauli Prince, who made canvas sails with Pacific-patterned motifs for the Christchurch production. Mishelle and Tanya's mother made the colour-coded costumes.[57]

Dawn Raids: Exploring migrant history

Kightley's first solo mainstage play for Pacific Underground was *Dawn Raids* (1997), which took as its subject the notorious mid-70s police raids on Pasifika families in Auckland. 'I'd had that idea for a little while, in my head. I think everyone was affected by it ... everyone's got stories of it.'

Dawn Raids is set in 1976 and moves between the ironically named Paradise Honeypot Club, where Sione sings with the Noble Hawaiian Sabretooth Tigers, and his Ponsonby home where he lives with his parents Mose and To`aga, his sister Teresa and his fiancée Fuarosa. It swiftly becomes apparent that Fuarosa, recently arrived from Samoa, is an illegal overstayer whom Sione's family is hiding from the Labour Department and the police until her wedding can be arranged. Fuarosa exhibits the same naïve sense of wonder as Charles in *Fresh off the Boat*, although her aspirations in this new world are limited for comic effect:

> **FUAROSA**: I only wanted to see the dairy. To`aga, you should see all the lollies here. I've never seen them in Samoa. There's the big round colourful ones with the chewing gum inside, the little milk bottles, the wine gums, the K bars ... I just want to eat like a New Zealander, like a Palagi![58]

Instead, she is presented with Islander food such as 'Pisupo ma kapisi' – corned beef and cabbage.

Fuarosa experiences a sense of misplaced shame at being Samoan in a Palagi world. Sione rejects the notion of writing a song about Fuarosa because 'Samoan names have too many syllables to be in a song. You need a nice short Palagi name like Sarah or Tania.'[59] Mose (who seems initially more interested in his copy of *Best Bets* than in family matters) is concerned that if Fuarosa is discovered it will shame the family, even while he is colluding in the secret. He urges her to speak English and to abandon her lavalava in favour of Palagi clothes. He is equally uncomfortable with his daughter Teresa, a university student with strong political leanings, whose 'Brown Panther' uniform of leather jacket, sunglasses, beret and army pants also attracts his criticism.

> **MOSE**: Why you want to dress up like that for? You want to look like a boy? Or maybe you want to look like a Māori.[60]

Shame over clothing is also seen at the end of the play, when To`aga describes her anguish at not being able to supply 'decent' clothing to Bene, Teresa's friend, when he is arrested.

> **TO`AGA**: You should have seen Bene, Mose. Standing in court with a lavalava and singlet. The Palagi look at him like he was a dog ... He wouldn't even look at me. He was too ashamed at what he was wearing.[61]

Typical of Kightley's writing style, the play is filled with jokes that appear to make light of the darkness that lies just beneath the surface.

> **MOSE**: There's nothing wrong with [dawn] raids. It's the only way some of them get up early.[62]

Like Samoa in *Fresh off the Boat*, Teresa uses slogans as political statements: 'Don't be racist, Dad. We are all oppressed indigenous peoples. Now it's time to fight back.'[63]

Sione presents two opposing faces to the world in his attempt to 'belong' to his adopted country. As Sione by day, he works in a 'stinky car assembly plant', bringing home much-needed money to help support the family.[64] As Fabian by night, declaring himself to be part Hawaiian, French and Italian, he lives the dream of independence and acceptance: claiming to have a rock'n'roll lifestyle, imitating Elvis Presley, and – in self-deprecating mockery – reconstructing himself as a suffering hero.[65] 'Remember, Fabian is French for loving vulnerable spirit who carries the burden of pain for his people.'[66] When Sione/Fabian performs Samoan songs with his band, he pretends that they are Hawaiian – because 'nobody likes Samoans' in New Zealand.[67]

Fuarosa also lives a double life, escaping into the soap opera *Search For Tomorrow*, which provides 'the only friends I have'.[68] Sione laughs at her, yet seems unable to make the connection with his own form of escape from harsh reality. Similarly torn between two worlds is Steve, who works as a policeman and struggles to gain acceptance from his Palagi colleagues. He must uphold the law, even when it requires him to take action against his own people. Teresa challenges him:

> **TERESA**: You're Samoan. You should be changing the way things are done, not support them ... Why do you think they let you into the police force? They're using you to help keep our people down![69]

Dawn Raids positions overstayers in New Zealand as persecuted souls who are treated in a manner which echoes that of notorious police states around the world. Teresa and Bene (whose family hides more overstayers) are advised by a police officer to carry passports at all times, since they 'don't look like Kiwis'.[70] Families are dragged from their homes at first light by police officers with dogs. A genuinely tragic note enters the play as To`aga mourns the arrest of her neighbours:

> **TO`AGA**: Do they think we're animals? You know how skinny the dogs are in Samoa. They're the last ones to get fed cos they're not really important. Poor Siosi, he was so scared. Are we lower than dogs, Teresa? Is that what the Palagi think of us? ... Dear Lord. We ask blessings on this house ... We ask that you tell Mr Muldoon to be a good Christian man and to stop arresting us. I know that he is a good man and that if he could see what he is doing to some of our families that he will stop.[71]

That same note of tragic dignity brings the play to its conclusion when Fuarosa, pregnant with Sione's baby, is deported to Samoa to face scorn: 'They'll think I'm a big joke because I got caught and sent back.'[72] But this unfortunate outcome does raise the political awareness of conservative To`aga: 'Sione is driving me to a meeting about the dawn raids at church. It might be too late for Fuarosa but we can't keep our eyes closed to others. It's time to wake up.'[73] Sione finally gets the courage to admit his identity as the leader of the Noble Samoan Sabretooth Tigers, openly performing a Samoan song, 'La`u Lupe Ua Lele'.

One element of the script that particularly pleased Kightley was that it contained sequences of untranslated Samoan dialogue. In scene eight, Steve, who has schooled himself to speak only English in order to be accepted in his job, imagines a telephone conversation with his father, who responds in Samoan. It is Steve's only opportunity to express what Marc Maufort calls his 'divided inner self'.[74] Kightley chose not to follow the tradition of providing a translation for the audience: 'I thought, well, that's not real. That wouldn't happen at home. I think you get the sense of what's happening.'

Dawn Raids premiered at the Herald Theatre and played a two-week season from 11 November 1997 with Kightley directing.[75] Iaheto Ah Hi took the role of Sione, and Erolia Ifopo played To`aga with Ene Petaia as her husband Mose. Samoan actor Mario Gaoa joined the company as Steve, and the remaining roles were played by Joy Vaele (Fuarosa), Mishelle Muagututi`a (Teresa) and Shimpal Lelisi (Bene). When the production was revived in Christchurch a year later, Kightley played Sione while the Samoan opera singer Iosefa Enari played Mose; David Fane stepped into the role of director.

Elizabeth O'Connor reviewed the Christchurch production and found much that was positive, noting in particular that Kightley 'has moved well beyond youth-impro naturalism or TV comedy to a script which has sinew, economy and sound dramatic structure'.[76] What she hoped to see unfolding on stage – a play of open anguish – was kept submerged by 'comic throwaway', demonstrative of Kightley's particular writing strengths. O'Connor, constructing her own vision of the play she hoped *Dawn Raids* could be, felt the central figure should have been Steve. She praised the role as one in which 'the mature moral drama one longs to see played out emerges briefly'. However, Kightley's purpose was to present a cross-section of the Pasifika community on stage, and to see the humour in even the bleakest situation.

Bernadette Rae, reviewing for the *NZ Herald*, was negative about the writing and caustic about the production, casting opprobrium equally on the script, performances and music. 'Tediously long in the pain, puzzlement, anger and despair departments,' she wrote; 'Kightley, as writer and director, adds nothing at all to our understanding of the awful events, neither of their history nor resolution ... The whole performance is actually repetitive, clumsy and uninspired.'[77] Kightley was devastated, saying 'I couldn't write for a year after.' Despite his brief loss of enthusiasm for the stage, he won the 1998 Bruce Mason Playwriting Award, presented annually in recognition of the work of an outstanding emerging New Zealand playwright. He was the first Pacific Islander to receive this award, soon to be followed by Toa Fraser (1999) and Victor Rodger (2001).

Starving and Broke

Younger members of Pacific Underground began to assume leadership positions – one of the secrets of the company's longevity. In addition to touring, Anton Carter and Mishelle Muagututi`a created a new project called Starving and Broke, loosely based on the annual Young and Hungry play festival at Wellington's BATS Theatre. According to Tanya Muagututi`a it was about 'the collective of young ones that were there at the time ... encouraging them and bringing out their stories'.[78]

Starving and Broke represented a significant aspect of Pacific Underground's artistic vision – to plan for the future by encouraging and developing emerging artists – and grew out of a community employment grant scheme. The grant was used to pay young actors and directors to work on new short plays, to be staged monthly in Christchurch. Carter stressed the need to be professional in outlook: 'One of the first questions school kids will ask us when we tour is, "Do you guys get paid for this?" It's important to provide positive role models.'[79]

Short plays included *Merchant of Aotearoa* by Jamie Haugh, directed by Shimpal Lelisi, and *Some Ghost to Watch Over Me* by Tanya Muagututi`a. Tanya had co-devised her first play – *Filo and the Magic Lamp*, based on *Aladdin* – in 1998 after a workshop with Victor Rodger. *Some Ghost to Watch Over Me* was her first solo writing project. It featured two sisters, one of whom dies after a long illness, and incorporated some fale aitu. Tanya describes the play:

> She's the ghost, but she wants to help her troubled sister who's still alive and has this rocky relationship, but she doesn't know how to help her. She's in the spirit world and she meets these two Samoan aitu ... She ends up helping her sister and guiding her ... [The aitu are] comical. They've been stuck in that spirit world because they're too much trouble, and they're from an older time, and they try and get her into trouble.

From being mentored by Kightley, Ifopo and others, Tanya found her own pathway:

> I've always been really staunch about us as women talking about what we want to talk about. I formed a band called Soul Sisters, because I thought it was about time we had our own group.[80] We were always 'Pos's group' or 'Oscar's play', so that's going to rub off on you somewhere. Mishelle and Erolia, who were our senior women back then, they only got to play the mothers. I wrote a play about bullies, and the girl was the bully, as a reaction to all that. My mum's pretty staunch about that, very independent, and she taught all of us independence.

Angels: Soul and gospel

Working on Angels *was a delight for me. My family is very musical. I grew up with five brothers and one sister and our father used to make us sing everywhere – youth group, weddings, funerals, gigs, church, everywhere.* JOY VAELE[81]

Singing in Samoan churches is a key element of *Angels*, by Tanya Muagututi`a and Joy Vaele, co-produced by Pacific Underground and the Court Theatre in 2009. Robert Gilbert reunited briefly with the company to direct the play, which was first performed at Aranui High School (where Gilbert teaches drama) for four days, before transferring to The Forge at the Court Theatre, where it attracted large and enthusiastic Pasifika audiences.

For Vaele, this was a very personal project:

> I grew up in the Assembly of God Church ... church and family was everything. But I am grateful for being part of that life, it taught me a lot ... Working with Tanya was fabulous. Although we grew up in different religions we had similarities within our churches and Tanya and I sang in bands together for years.

The Angels is an all-girl Samoan band specialising in soul and gospel music. Sing (Bronwyn Turei), Stevie (Sela Leavasa), Eleni (Joy Vaele) and Rosie (Cassie Baker) meet as children on White Sunday in 1984. Together they discover a love of performing and develop a band to play in church. Much of their teenage behaviour, such as sleeping with boys and Eleni's drug-taking, is far from angelic. The girls 'borrow' the church's equipment to play secretly at a nightclub, where a Christian music promoter shows interest in taking them to Australia. The group's clandestine lives as musicians transgress the behaviour expected of them as young Samoan women, and Stevie's father, Pastor Samasoni (Ave Sua), orders them to stop performing and leave the club. Unlike the comic minister in *Romeo and Tusi*, Pastor Samasoni is a formidable authority figure with the power to control the girls' destinies. Performance artist Rosanna Raymond has written about the conflict between young Pasifika artists, their parents and church elders:

> Many a career in acting and modelling was ended by parents exerting their control ... but despite the fact that the church still maintained a strong influence over the body and how it was portrayed, new ground had been established for the Island community.[82]

The pastor's rage sparks an argument between rebellious Stevie and Sing, whose love of God is greater than her desire to perform. Sing abandons the group; Stevie moves to Australia, where she becomes a famous singer. In contrast, her friends lead non-glamorous lives: Rosie becomes a nurse, Eleni a druggie, and Sing a solo mother to her child Maia (Monique Togiaso), who has been diagnosed with leukemia.

The play begins with the women preparing to celebrate Stevie's thirtieth birthday. However, in what one reviewer described as 'a twist worth waiting for',[83] we learn that Stevie has passed away in Australia, although the cause of her death is not clear. In a final twist, we discover that Maia is not Sing's child, but Stevie's. Steph Walker's review questioned the non-linear narrative, describing it as 'a lot of flashbacks and flash forwards that get more confusing as we go on'. However, the fragmentary nature of this structure makes sense in hindsight, as we realise that the narrative logic is that of memory. Sing pieces together her memories of Stevie and her inner conflict between spirituality and performance. In *Angels*, fragments from the past illustrate the competing pressures of church and growing up in New Zealand society.

A key scene in their journey towards becoming musicians is the White Sunday performance in 1984, when the girls are about nine years old. It begins with a teacher threatening them with a hiding if they don't sing well enough.[84] They perform the story of Naomi and Ruth from the Bible, which provides a mythical and spiritual framework for their journey: like the story of Sing and her friends, it portrays a strong image of female solidarity, while the hardship of being in a foreign land is highly relevant to the Samoan migration experience in New Zealand. As Gilbert noted, the White Sunday sequence 'resonated with Pasifika audiences particularly and it was enlightening for non-Pasifika audiences'.

Here Muagututi`a and Vaele bring together Pacific Underground's trademark irreverent humour and childish glee with a more serious underlying purpose. According to Muagututi`a, they wanted to honour the place of religion in the community: 'It was important to have White Sunday in the play because we wanted to show that the Bible is such a big part of the belief of Pacific families.' Reviewers of *Angels*, however, saw it as a feminist critique of the authoritarian nature of the Samoan church. Walker argues that the story dramatises 'the heavy hand religion has on Samoan women',[85] while Lindsay Clark writes that for the girls, the band is 'an escape from the strict regime of Church and patriarchy'.[86] Yet even as the play critiques authoritarian social and religious structures, God remains a central part of the characters' lives. Through comedy and song, Muagututi`a and Vaele's writing celebrates the lasting bond between the four Samoan women, leaving the audience with a more complex awareness of the competing pressures facing young Pasifika women.[87]

Evolution: music and events

Music had become central to Pacific Underground's theatre productions, as exemplified by the company's tenth TIE show, *The Prospects* (1998), written by

Kightley and directed by Ifopo, in which four teenagers put together a musical act for a talent quest. They consider performing something Celtic. 'What they end up performing is infinitely funkier, combining slap dancing with pop songs.'[88]

From the early days, Tanya Muagututi`a and Posenai Mavaega had urged for Pacific Underground Music Production (PUMP) to be an intrinsic part of the operation, with Mavaega as producer. It took time, however, for PUMP to find its own path, as Mavaega describes:

> It was actually quite a struggle. I would ask the others if we could include my band under Pacific Underground, and they would say no, because it would confuse the public. 'What is it? Is it a band, or is it a theatre company?' There's a group of us who are just musicians, we used to play as a covers band but we'd also write original material. When we got the opportunity to merge the band with *Romeo and Tusi*, everything took off. There were so many units that came out of Pacific Underground, but the core music production team was Tanya, Chris [Searle] and myself.

Since 1994 Mavaega had served as Pacific Underground's musical director and tutor, working on *Bully For You*, *Rangi and Mau's Fabulous Adventure*, *Romeo and Tusi* and *Sons*. The Hawaiian Sabretooth Tigers in *Dawn Raids* were Mavaega (guitars, vocals), Chris Searle (drums, percussion), Muagututi`a (guitar, ukulele, vocals) and Michael Banks (bass). This unit had been performing together since *Romeo and Tusi*, with musical influences that included R&B, soul, jazz and hip hop.[89] In addition, Muagututi`a had performed with the Soul Sisters.

Pacific Underground's 1999 limited edition CD *Landmark*, produced by Searle and Mavaega, was described as a 'ground-breaking ... compilation album that has the very first recordings of Scribe, The Naked Samoans and Christchurch hip hop pioneers Beats'n'Pieces'.[90] A featured track was Muagututi`a's 'Pure Love'.[91] In 2010 the company released a second CD, *Island Summer*.[92]

Muagututi`a and Mavaega gradually took a leadership role in Pacific Underground as many of its original members left the city. Between 2000 and 2010, under the PU banner, they initiated and ran 10 annual summer Pacific Arts Festivals in Christchurch, each one numbered from a different language: the first Tasi (Samoan), the second Ua (Tongan), the third Toru (Māori) and finishing with Ten. The festivals celebrated the rich and diverse range of Pasifika artists, showcasing writers and poets, artists and master carvers and film and video makers.[93] Many musicians appeared, including Dallas Tamaira and Ladi6, along with performing groups such as The Naked Samoans, The Laughing

Samoans, and shows from the Pacific Underground repertoire such as *Romeo and Tusi* and *Rangi and Mau's Fantastic Voyage*.[94]

In 2003 the couple initiated a new performance event as part of the Christchurch Arts Festival. Island Summer featured traditional and original Pacific Island music, composed and arranged by Mavaega for a 25-piece guitar orchestra.[95] The idea arose following the death of his mother in 2001: 'Our house was full of people singing old songs and hymns to my mum, and I was out the back playing along on my guitar. I arranged some of the music that I was hearing from the house – old traditional hymns – for guitar.'

The event proved so successful that it was included in the Palau South Pacific Arts Festival the following year, and in the Christchurch Festival in subsequent years. In 2009 they organised I Love the Islands, a benefit concert for tsunami-stricken Samoa. Pacific Underground had evolved from a theatre company to a much broader music and events base.

Twenty years of Pacific Underground

Pacific Underground celebrated its twentieth anniversary in 2013. Part of the secret of its longevity has been fluidity: there is no fixed membership, and those who work with the company have diverse musical and theatrical backgrounds. A new generation, including Barbara Carpenter, Joy Vaele and Ave Sua, had taken leadership roles, including writing and directing.

A significant project in 2013 was *Under the Fale*, a response to the rebuilding plans for earthquake-shattered Christchurch. Tanya Muagututi`a had watched the virtual flyover view of the city online. 'I was disappointed. I saw brand new buildings with no history, and that the churches our communities established themselves in were not replaced. *Under the Fale* [celebrated] our community and our traditions like White Sunday, and our banding together in a time of need.'[96] The work was a four-way collaboration with Pacific Underground, the Festival of Transitional Architecture (FESTA), the Free Theatre and Unitec's School of Architecture, whose second-year students had created a sculpture of an abstract fale onto which lighting and images were projected while musicians performed beneath its shelter. At the time Muagututi`a commented, 'The four-way collaboration has been by far the most powerful one we've been involved in. It's everything PU is about: collaboration, innovation and telling stories of our place in New Zealand.'[97]

Samson Samasoni in TAOtahi's *Le Matau* (1984) by Stephen Sinclair and Samson Samasoni, dirs. Helen Jarroe and Stephen Sinclair. Photo: Gerry Vasbenter

Left: Jamie Brown and Eteuati Ete in TAOtahi's *Le Matau* (1984). Photo: Gerry Vasbenter **Above**: Poster for *Le Matau* (1984).

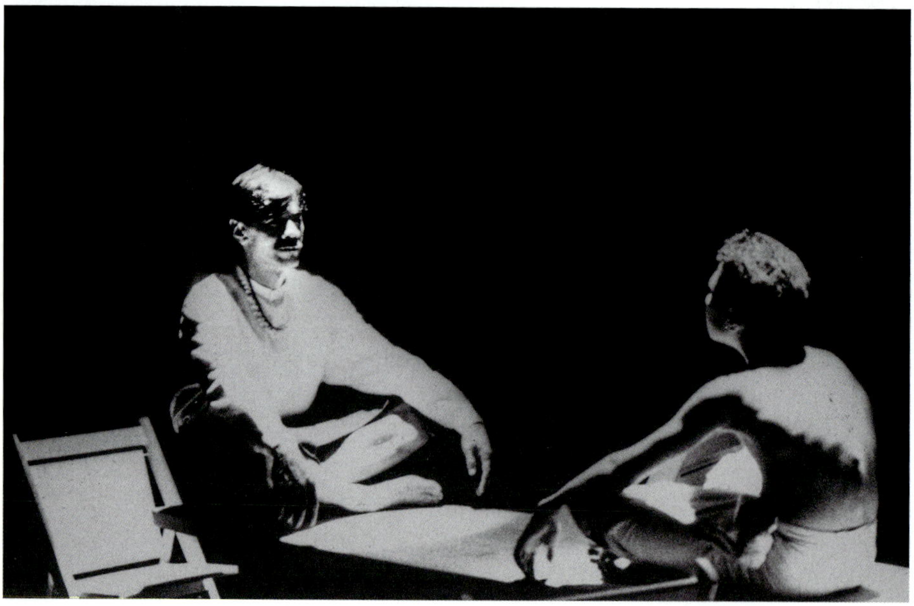

Think of a Garden (1995) by John Kneubuhl, dir. Nathaniel Lees, at The Depot/Taki Rua. **Left**: Nathaniel Lees (Narrator) and Michael Poe Daniel (Young David). **Top**: Michael Poe Daniel (Young David), Eteuati Ete (Lilo) and Le`autuli`ilagi Malaeta Sauvao (Pito). **Above**: Michael Poe Daniel (Young David) and Le`autuli`ilagi Malaeta Sauvao (Pito). Photos: Lisa Maule

Above: Justine and Paul Simei-Barton on a research trip to Sasina in Savai`i, Samoa. Photo supplied by the Simei-Bartons

Above: Faifua Amiga Junior (Romeo) and Louise Cuthbert (Juliet) in *Romeo and Juliet* (1992), dirs. Justine Simei-Barton and Alan Brunton. Photo: Paul Simei-Barton, poster hand-coloured by Mark Adams

Below: *Romeo and Juliet* cast (1992), with Wanjiku Kiarie (centre front). Photo: Paul Simei-Barton

Above: *The Contest* (1993) by Paul Simei-Barton, dir. Justine Simei-Barton. Back row (from left): Aynsley Tapuvae, Shimpal Lelisi, Iosefa Enari; middle: Misa Tupou, Mishelle Muagututi`a, Mele Ah-Sam, Andrew Iosefa; front: Vela Manusaute, Erolia Ifopo, David Fane.
Photo supplied by Pacific Theatre

Left: Justine Simei-Barton (top) with Jay Laga`aia and Mahia Blackmore, in a publicity image for *Ma Rainey's Black Bottom* by August Wilson (Pacific Theatre Inc, 1995). Photo: Paul Simei-Barton

MOKEFRE

Above: Pacific Underground founding members (1993). Clockwise from top: Simon Small, Oscar Kightley, Michael Hodgson, Erolia Ifopo, Mishelle Muagututi`a. Photo: Simon Tobias

Opposite, top: *Tusitala and the House of Spirits* (1996) by Paul Simei-Barton, dir. Justine Simei-Barton. From left, Sylvia Rands (Fanny Stevenson), Olivia Muliaumaseali`i (Lauli`i), Martyn Sanderson (Robert Louis Stevenson). Photo: Haru Sameshima

Pacific Underground logo, designed by Richard Arthur Kingsford.

Opposite, below: *Voices on the Wind* TIE tour. Clockwise from top left): Rachel House, Tausili Mose, Aleni Tufuga, Shimpal Lelisi, Aynsley Tapuvae. Photo supplied by Pacific Theatre

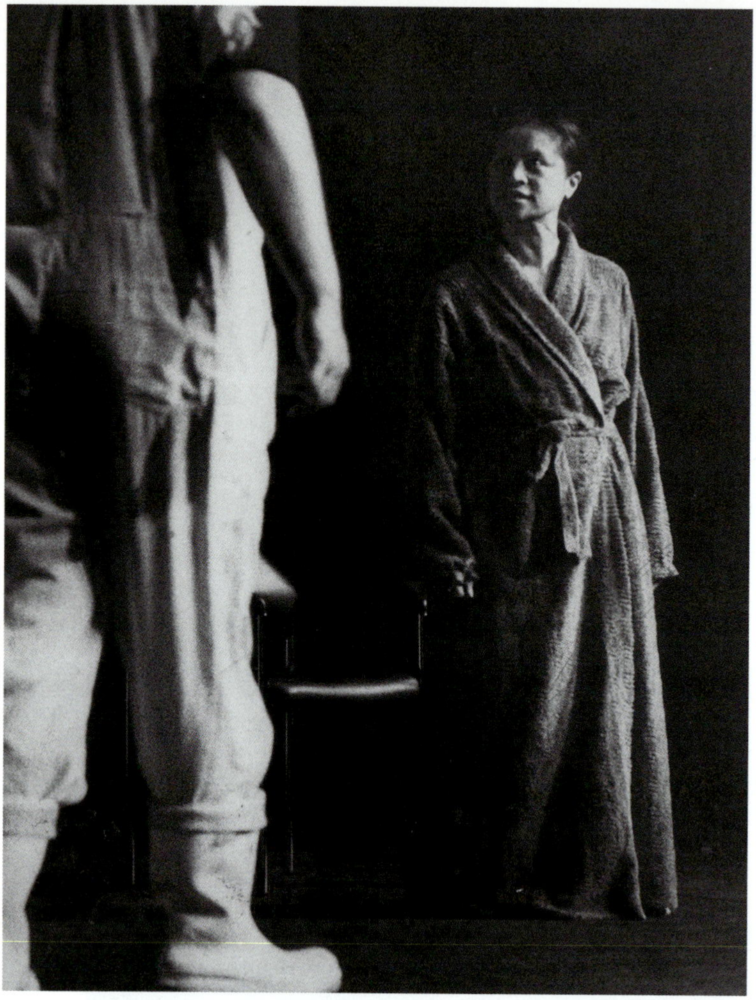

Left: Erolia Ifopo (Elizabeth) in *Fresh Off the Boat* (1993) by Oscar Kightley and Simon Small, dir. Nathaniel Lees.
Photo: Evotia Tamua

Below: Mishelle Muagututi`a and Oscar Kightley in *Sons* (1995) by Victor Rodger, dir. David Fane.
Photo: Sarah Hunter

Poster for *Romeo and Tusi* (1997) at Mona Vale Gardens, Christchurch. Image supplied by Pacific Underground

Poster for *Tatau: Rites of passage* (1996). Image supplied by Pacific Underground

Romeo and Tusi (1997). Back from left: Shimpal Lelisi (Ruby), Erolia Ifopo (Mrs Aiu), Joy Vaele (Tusi), Oscar Kightley (Minister), Dallas Tamaira (Anaru), Mishelle Muagututi`a (Mrs Heke). Front: Michael Banks, Chris Searle, Posenai Mavaega (musicians). Photo: Sarah Hunter

Left: Iaheto Ah Hi (Sione/ Fabian) in *Dawn Raids* (1997) by Oscar Kightley, Herald Theatre production, dir. Oscar Kightley.
Photo: Rakai Karaitiana

Below: Poster for *Dawn Raids* (1998) by Oscar Kightley, Court Theatre production, dir. David Fane.
Design Jacob Luamanuvae; photography Sarah Hunter and Sonya Pegg. Image supplied by Pacific Underground

Left: Ana Tuigamala (Malaga) and Nathaniel Lees (Peseola) in *The Songmaker's Chair* by Albert Wendt (2003), dir. Nathaniel Lees for Auckland Theatre Company. Photo: John McDermott
Right: Ana Tuigamala (Malaga) and Nathaniel Lees (Peseola) in *The Songmaker's Chair* by Albert Wendt (2003), ATC. Set design: John Verryt. Photo courtesy ATC and New Zealand Herald newspix.co.nz

Above: *Rangi and Mau's Amazing Race* (2015) by Tanya Muagututi`a, Joy Vaele, Ave Sua and Raniera Dallas, dirs. Joy Vaele and Troy Tu`ua, Matariki Festival, Te Oro. Centre front: Tanya Muagututi`a, surrounded by (from left): Luse Su`a Tuipulotu, Levi Matautia-Morgan, Jake Arona, David Ray Lelisi, Josephine Mavaega, Joy Vaele, Ella Mavaega. Photo: Pos Mavaega

Above: Joy Vaele (Pomu), Sima Urale (Tivi) and Dianna Fuemana (Naiki) in *Frangipani Perfume* (1997) by Makerita Urale, dir. Erolia Ifopo. Photo: Sarah Hunter

Left: Sima Urale in *Frangipani Perfume* (1997). Photo: Sarah Hunter

Makerita Urale. Photo: Sima Urale

Victor Rodger. Photo: Deborah Marshall

Robbie Magasiva (Gary) in *My Name is Gary Cooper* (2007) by Victor Rodger, dir. Roy Ward for Auckland Theatre Company. Photo: John McDermott

Above: Beulah Koale and Fasitua Amosa in *Black Faggot* (2014 version) by Victor Rodger, dir. Roy Ward. Photo: Karin Williams

Opposite: *Where We Once Belonged* (2008) by Sia Figiel, adapted for the stage by Dave Armstrong, dirs. Colin McColl and David Fane for ATC. From left: Robbie Magasiva, Joy Vaele, Goretti Chadwick, Pua Magasiva, Anapela Polataivao. Set design: Michel Tuffery. Photo: Robert Catto www.catto.co.nz **Left:** *Where We Once Belonged* (2008). From left: Goretti Chadwick, Joy Vaele, Anapela Polataivao, ATC. Photo supplied by ATC. Photo: Tony Rabbit

Tausili Mose in *Vula* (2004) at the South Pacific Arts Festival, dir. Nina Nawalowalo.
Photo: Norman Heke

The Conch's *Vula* (2008) at Brisbane Powerhouse. Photo supplied by The Conch

Erolia Ifopo singles out Tanya Muagututi`a and Posenai Mavaega for praise, saying 'they are instrumental in keeping Pacific Underground alive: inspiring the next generation, bringing together the arts and our community, just like when it started way back, when those who had a vision planted a seed and went for it. Fa`afetai tele lava.'[98]

Into the future – 'a sense of family'

Pacific Underground introduced a lot of families to new cultural experiences, reconnecting people to their 'village performance side', according to supporter Rev Mua Strickson-Pua: 'Pacific Underground gave us a theatre of change, raising social issues to empower our people with a message of aroha and hope. Pacific Underground encapsulates the best of our Pacific humanity.[99]

Barbara Carpenter recalls how the sense of family was embraced in the company:

> Myself and Avefua Sua, Losa and Vic Tamati, Tanya Muagutiti`a and Pos Mavaega, Joy Vaele and Shimpal Lelisi all raised families while being part of Pacific Underground. Taking our children along on tours, to performances and to meetings, was not only a necessity at times, but also something that we embraced. From passing babies around read-throughs to changing nappies at the back of the stage, filling the vans with booster seats and entertaining the children while their parents rehearsed their scenes, we made it work, because we loved what we did. Now those children have found their way to the same stage where we once took the limelight and they are here to tell their stories for their generation.

From their current base in Auckland, Muagututi`a and Mavaega continue their long association with Pacific Underground alongside a younger generation of theatre makers. For the Auckland Matariki Festival in July 2015, Pacific Underground revived *Rangi and Mau's Amazing Race*, written by Muagututi`a, Joy Vaele, Ave Sua and Raniera Dallas and directed by Vaele and Troy Tu`ua. The cast included two of Mavaega and Muagututi`a's teenage daughters, Josephine and Ella Mavaega, as well as David-Ray Lelisi, the son of Joy Vaele and Shimpal Lelisi. Mavaega and Muagututi`a's oldest daughter, Talia-Rae, graduated from the Pacific Institute of Performing Arts (PIPA) in 2015. Family has always been a key to the success of Pacific Underground; with this new generation, the future seems assured.

> Talia-Rae was two years old during the *Dawn Raids* seasons, the recording of *Landmark*, and grew up around the *Romeo and Tusi* and *Rangi and Mau's Fantastic Voyage* tours. We watched her perform two solo pieces [at PIPA], one in dance and

one in theatre. In her dance piece, she performed to a song from our album *Island Summer*. So, here we are, watching Talia-Rae dancing to me singing and her dad playing guitars. For her theatre solo, she performed her earthquake story, and she portrayed me, Pos, her two siblings and my mum and dad. For both shows, we laughed and cried in awe, with such pride. For us, that's Pacific Theatre history and it's full circle, right there. TANYA MUAGUTUTI`A[100]

5.
Pasifika playwriting 1996–2012

Many of the plays discussed so far were created by Samoan writers. But as Pasifika theatre gathered momentum these writers were joined by voices from other cultures. Dianna Fuemana's *Mapaki* (1999) and Karl Kite-Rangi's *Between the Islands* (2002) were, respectively, the first Niuean and Cook Island plays written in New Zealand, while Toa Fraser brought urban Fijian characters to the stage in *Bare* (1998), *No. 2* (1999) and *Paradise* (2001).[1] During this period, Albert Wendt made his playwriting debut with *The Songmaker's Chair* (2003), while Victor Rodger began his ascent as a witty provocateur.

As the Pasifika theatre community expanded it developed a momentum whereby one project led organically to the next. Pasifika playwrights were now inspiring each other to write. Makerita Urale produced Oscar Kightley and David Fane's *A Frigate Bird Sings* (1996), a partial catalyst for her *Frangipani Perfume* the following year. Fuemana acted in *Frangipani Perfume*, an experience that provided the impetus for her own writing career. In his introduction to *The Songmaker's Chair*, Wendt wrote of his debt to Kightley, Urale and Fraser, as well as to Māori playwrights Harry Dansey, Selwyn Muru, Briar Grace-Smith and Hone Kouka. He acknowledged playwrights from other Pacific countries: John Kneubuhl (American Samoa), Vilsoni Hereniko (Rotuma/Fiji) and Victoria Nalani Kneubuhl (Hawai`i).[2] This chain of inspiration demonstrates the rich whakapapa of Polynesian playwriting, which is characterised by a sense of community and connection.

In this chapter we examine the range and diversity of Pasifika playwriting from 1996–2012. The works discussed provide a powerful sense of cultural encounters throughout the Pacific region, from Auckland to Samoa, Niue, Fiji and Los Angeles. Common themes emerge, such as migration, journeys in search of homeland, absent fathers, the re-defining of gender politics and the importance of language in maintaining cultural identity.

A Frigate Bird Sings: Pasifika theatre 'comes of age'

*Contemporary Pacific theatre in New Zealand has come of age. The way every aspect of [*A Frigate Bird Sings*] *has come together to form a beautiful organic whole – and its dramatic lyrical power for a general audience – makes this for me the most important commission of a New Zealand work the Festival [of the Arts] has made ...* Frigate Bird *combines the majesty of Shakespeare's* King Lear *on a contemporary scale with the spirit and humour of Polynesian culture.* MARK AMERY[3]

Mark Amery's review of *A Frigate Bird Sings* by Kightley and Fane is, in effect, a mainstream acknowledgement of what Pasifika theatre had achieved by the mid-1990s. The play was commissioned for the 1996 New Zealand International Festival of the Arts, as Kightley explains:

> After the success of *Fresh off the Boat*, Makerita [Urale] wanted Dave [Fane] and me to write something for the next arts festival. Nat [Lees] became involved as a director. It was his idea to explore fa`afafine, based on times when he'd walk home from work at the Mercury [Theatre] down K Road.[4] Dave and I wrote in his basement at his mum's house, with him riffing and me writing stuff down.[5]

According to Fane, the first draft lacked authenticity:

> When we did the first read-through, Oscar and I were laughing but no one else was. We had invited some of the fa`afafine around, and they weren't laughing either. And then we sat down with them and said, 'Where was it we went wrong?' And they said, 'Well, all those extra characters you added, yeah they're funny and that's great, but there was nothing of the real fa`afafine experience.' And then we talked for the remainder of that day, and it was great. They were just so gracious and giving about their experiences. We had forgotten about the beauty of the fa`afas in our lives. And then we went back to our hotel and wrote all night and we came up with a second draft that was pretty much the show that went on.[6]

A Frigate Bird Sings was produced by Makerita Urale under the guidance of festival director Carla Van Zon, who she acknowledges as 'a significant supporter of Pasifika theatre in New Zealand and a generous mentor for me'.[7] Urale spent a year and a half assembling the production team: 'Nathaniel Lees had to direct it. He added strength to it. Hone Kouka was the dramaturg. In the script workshop we got real fa`afafine to sit in, and I asked Albert Wendt to observe and give feedback.'[8]

The play focuses on the central character Vili's troubled life and family:

VILI: I am Vili Atafa, son of Kapili and Siaea Atafa, brother of Sione. I am the provider and the oppressed. I am the caretaker and the teacher. I am the role model and embarrassment. I am fa`afafine.[9]

While fa`afafine characters often appear in Pasifika plays, *A Frigate Bird Sings* was the first to deal seriously with what it meant to be fa`afafine in the context of New Zealand. Discussing this first production, Niko Besnier outlined some of the contradictions in fa`afafine identity:

> Neither complete men nor full women, fa`afafine waver back and forth between male privilege and the covert authority of women, between status degradation and social visibility. While some position themselves as pillars of the fa`a-Samoa and can ascend the ladders of power and prestige in one or the other sphere of the Samoan social world, others emerge as rebels, whose playful defiance of the received order, particularly in matters of gender and sex, provokes the amusement, consternation, contempt, or a complex blend thereof among mainstream Samoans.[10]

The character of Vili captures all of these contradictions. His mother has passed away leaving him to take on the female role in the household, caring for his sickly father Kapili and his straight rugby-playing brother Sione. Vili attempts a relationship with his brother's Palagi rugby mate, Hugh, but is rejected. He finds his tribe when he befriends two flamboyant fa`afafine, Dejavu and Shaninqua. Tired of being Kapili's nursemaid, Vili leaves home, but his brother blames him for the family's struggles: 'We left paradise to come to this place. Mum and Dad had enough shit to put up with but then you had to fuck around.'[11] The argument ends with Sione viciously beating his brother. In the reconciliatory final scene, Kapili tells his two sons the story of the sacred frigate bird.

> **KAPILI**: This bird is seen as a messenger from the gods. Whenever you saw the bird, it was like a sign that the cyclones were coming ... Some see it as a blessing; some see it as a curse ... when the frigate bird sings, the only song you hear is the pain of its loneliness.
>
> **VILI**: I never want to be lonely.
>
> **KAPILI**: Sometimes, it's not our choice.[12]

The parallel between fa`afafine and the frigate bird gives a mythic and poetic dimension to the story. Yet, as Besnier observes, the play avoids romanticising or over-simplifying the tensions for fa`afafine in New Zealand. For some, however, the public exploration of this role in Samoan culture was challenging. Sean Mallon recalls his parents' reaction:

> *A Frigate Bird Sings* was difficult territory, because it was a play about a fa`afafine. I think it was a bit of a shock for [my mum] to see this story told on a public stage. Sexuality was dealt with in the open. My parents were moved by the play, but they were confronted by the issues.[13]

Performed at Downstage Theatre, the *Frigate Bird* cast included Iaheto Ah Hi (Vili), Stan Wolfgramm (Sione), Iosefa Enari (Kapili), Mario Gaoa (Dejavu), Ole Maiava (Shaninqua) and Geoff Dolan (Hugh). Lees' contribution as director included having a strong influence over the script (for which he was given a writing credit when the play was published) and the set design, by multi-media artist Michel Tuffery in collaboration with Kate Peters.[14]

The production received critical acclaim, with Dennis Welch labelling it 'a landmark in New Zealand theatre'. He recognised the skill of the direction: 'Lees has a terrific sense of timing and atmosphere; he won best director at last year's Wellington theatre critics' awards (for *Think of a Garden*) and, on the strength of this brilliant production, must be a front runner again.'[15] Lees was indeed nominated for the award, once more proving that Pasifika theatre was being recognised at the highest levels.

Another season followed at the Watershed in Auckland in October the same year, and again the critics were reaching for superlatives. Stephanie Johnson recognised the quality of the writing: '*A Frigate Bird Sings* has a wonderful script – by turns comic and tragic, yet always rich with sincerity.' Of the direction she wrote, 'Lees has excelled himself with this production. All elements are cohesive, giving a finished product that shines with honesty and love. Authentic, confident and sensitive.'[16] Anita McNaught wrote, 'This is, at last, a subtle, beautifully observed study of one of the most precious and intriguing gifts of Polynesian culture – the third sex ... Kightley and Fane have written a classic of New Zealand theatre.'[17] In recognition of this 'classic' status, *A Frigate Bird Sings* was published in 2012, and revived in the same year by the Auckland Theatre Company (ATC) at the Mangere Arts Centre, directed by Alison Quigan and featuring Fane as Kapili, with Shimpal Lelisi as Dejavu. It was Lelisi's only experience of playing a fa`afafine: 'I just played my instincts. The hardest thing to get was how you carry yourself, and the attitude you throw out at people. If you get that, everything falls into place.'[18]

Reviewer Johnny Givins acknowledged the previous productions and added, 'This one is special – it has come home to South Auckland.'[19] Givins praised the younger actors, especially Unitec graduate Taofia Pelesasa as Vili: 'He is glittering with a power that ranges from naïve, to vulnerable, to heroic.'[20]

Frigate Bird marked a turning point in the public perception of Pasifika theatre, which Makerita Urale felt had finally 'landed as an industry. People take the work seriously.'[21]

Frangipani Perfume: The first all-female Pasifika play

At the time of writing *Frangipani Perfume* (1997), Urale was part of a close-knit community of Māori, Pasifika and Palagi artists resident in Wellington. She puts her love of the arts down to her upbringing:

> I grew up in my dad's village [Savai'i] by the sea and, around the coast, my mum's village. Our toys were butterflies, our earrings were the pupae of butterflies ... Your whole playground is the ocean, the forest, the sea, the skies, the stars, the fruit bats – and looking back, it was a very magical childhood. Our mum was a teacher [who] had created her own library for us as children in the village. She was very modern, very well-educated, and very liberal.[22]

Urale was inspired not only by her idyllic childhood in Samoa, but by a range of European art forms she had come across in her eclectic career:

> I was quite obsessed with opera. There were two songs I couldn't stop playing – The 'Chants d'Auvergne' and *The Tales of Hoffman* aria ['The Barcarolle']. I kept dreaming and dreaming of those two pieces of music. I was obsessed with them. I don't know why. And so I finally one day sat down and got it out of my system by writing a story that incorporated those damned pieces of music.[23]

Frangipani Perfume opened at BATS in December 1997, directed by Erolia Ifopo, with choreographer Cook Islander Teokotai Paitai and lighting designer Jen Lal, Shigeyuki Kihara (wardrobe), Vaimaila Urale (production manager) and Hori Ahipene (creative advisor). Sisters Tivi, Naiki and Pomu were played by Sima Urale, Dianna Fuemana and Joy Vaele. Critical reception highlighted the innovative nature of the play. Denis Welch's review, for example, described it as 'an all-woman show so fresh and free, so defiant of easy definitions, that it can only be described using words such as pioneering and unique'.[24] Welch felt it blended realism, expressionism and high-energy comedy with Paitai's sensational choreography, which ranged from 'the ditsy to the demonic'.[25]

While *Frigate Bird* examines the complex gender fluidity of the fa`afafine, *Frangipani Perfume* explores female identity in Samoan culture – in more depth than any previous Pasifika play. It brings the experiences, memories and dreams of migrant Samoan women centrestage. As in *Frigate Bird*, the mother of the family has passed away, leaving the younger generation to care for an ailing father. In *Frangipani Perfume* he is an offstage presence, placing the focus on the women's experience. The play opens with the sisters dancing to Offenbach's 'Barcarolle', teasingly evoking the stereotypical image of Pacific women as 'dusky maidens'. Urale's stage direction states, 'We are enraptured by these exotic maidens, their dark lustrous hair draped over their shoulders as they oil their skin, smooth hands over their bodies.'[26] The music stops abruptly and the women drop, scrubbing the filthy floor of a toilet. This juxtaposition signals Urale's intention to challenge the stereotype and present the reality of women engaged in hard physical work as low-paid night cleaners among the smells of 'piss and Janola'.[27] These migrant women are literally cleaning up the filth of white society. Naiki protests, 'I hate cleaning. I hate white.'[28]

The play gains much of its energy from sibling rivalries influenced by the sisters' different responses to living in Aotearoa. Tivi, the eldest, feels a responsibility to keep the family together, upholding conservative Samoan values and dreaming of a white wedding. Rebellious Naiki is attracted to women, preferring the freedom to be herself that she feels in New Zealand; while Pomu, too young to remember Samoa, dreams of a romanticised homeland. Pomu ('bomb' in Samoan) is fascinated by science, especially Einstein's groundbreaking discoveries, which arguably led to nuclear testing in the Pacific, and likens sexuality to quantum physics.[29] In the original production the stage was dominated by a large painting of Einstein by artist Apotala Matapelu.

The sisters' relationships with Samoa are expressed through the symbolism of frangipani perfume. Naiki, rejecting traditional culture, calls it 'stink bush oil': 'Real perfume comes from a real shop and in a real bottle, not a used Coke bottle.'[30] When the tensions between the sisters explode in a cathartic dance with sapelu (machete bush knives), Pomu – like Einstein – acts as peacemaker. Tivi and Naiki share with her their memories of 'home' and women making perfume:

> **POMU**: I see it now ... a million petals free, a shower of white flowers falling and falling like pure rain, a million fragrant kisses on my skin, and I breathe and breathe their secret scent as they brush my cheeks, soft as velvet, soft as a dream. We lie beneath the shelter of the Frangipani Tree and we dream and dream.[31]

This poetic imagery suggests that memories of Samoa and connection with their mother and female ancestors will sustain these women through the challenges of their lives in Aotearoa. As Urale comments, 'The script in some ways is more truthful than the writer, because the play is more about the unconscious – like my eyes were closed when I wrote it.'[32] Actor Fiona Collins was particularly struck by the physical aspects of the piece: '… that machete dance … says more to me than a verbal argument'.[33]

The significance of *Frangipani Perfume* as the first all-female Pasifika play is apparent in its acclaimed local and international life.[34] It was nominated as Most Original Production at the 1998 Chapman Tripp Awards, and in 2000 the *Listener* named it as one of the top 10 plays of the decade.[35]

A restaging in August 1998 at the Auckland Town Hall concert chamber, directed by Hori Ahipene, marked the start of a series of revivals in New Zealand and beyond. In 2006 Māori director Rachel House toured a new production to the Dreaming Festival in Queensland and to five venues in Canada, including the Native Earth Festival in Toronto. The play was part of the Pasifika Styles Performing Arts Festival in Cambridge, UK (May 2007),[36] and in November 2008 there was a staged reading of the play at La Mama in New York as part of a New Indigenous Voices programme.[37] Seasons in Samoa (2013) and Hawai`i (2015) followed. The play was published by The Play Press in 2004 as a 'double-bill' with Dianna Fuemana's *Mapaki* – the first book of plays by Pasifika women.

Coming hot on the heels of critically acclaimed productions of *Think of a Garden*, *Fresh off the Boat* and *A Frigate Bird Sings*, Urale's work confirmed that Samoan playwrights had become a major force in New Zealand theatre. As Welch put it, 'Samoan culture is breaking into New Zealand theatre like an actor kept waiting too long for an audition … You can't ignore it any more … The Samoans have arrived.'[38]

Since the initial production of *Frangipani Perfume* Urale has worked extensively in film production, including directing critically acclaimed documentaries such as *Savage Symbols* (2002), which examined the Samoan art of tatau, and the award-winning *Children of the Revolution* (2007), which focused on the children of leading political activists from the protest movements of the 1970s and 1980s. In 2010 she won a Fulbright–Creative New Zealand writer's residency at the University of Hawai`i at Manoa. She was a member of the first Pacific Arts Committee of Creative New Zealand, and is the Senior Arts Advisor – Pacific Arts for Creative New Zealand, a position she has held since 2011. She places a high value on her experiences in theatre:

> There's pride in people who come from theatre. It's a real craft with love and commitment, and has been the backbone of Pacific artists crossing between theatre, film and television. Theatre is my first home. I love the whānau aspect and the creativity and generosity of the theatre community.[39]

The multi-disciplinary focus of Urale's career exemplifies the inventiveness and entrepreneurship that characterises so many of the Pasifika artists discussed in this book.

Dianna Fuemana: The first Niuean playwright

*[*Frangipani Perfume*] gave me a confidence that I never had before with regard to making theatre.* DIANNA FUEMANA[40]

Dianna Fuemana was born in Auckland in 1973 to an American Samoan mother and Niuean father. She started performing in church plays and at high school, where she was chosen for a short performing arts course run by Jay Laga`aia and Cath Cardiff: 'I got my first feel of what professional theatre would be like at around 17.' While still in secondary school, Fuemana became pregnant: '... children at 16 and 19, married at 18, divorced at 20. It was full-on teenage years for me.' She did a television and production course at Carrington Polytech (now Unitec), and was later admitted into the University of Auckland diploma of drama course with Murray Edmond: 'That's when I really began to delve into the theory of theatre and the training of an actor.'

Acting in *Frangipani Perfume* inspired Fuemana to write and perform a solo piece. Titled *Mapaki* (1999), it was the first Niuean play in Aotearoa. The catalyst for *Mapaki* was the 1991 case of Tania Witika, a Māori woman with a long history of suffering abuse who was convicted of killing her young daughter, Delcilia. The case made an impression on Fuemana, a young mother at that time:

> That was the story that made the case for battered woman syndrome. I guess I identified with that trap as a young, single parent ... it was a really important story ... about what women go through.

Fuemana fictionalised Tania Witika as an abused Niuean woman who kills her partner. *Mapaki* earned Fuemana excellent reviews and a Chapman Tripp nomination for Outstanding New Writer.

Fuemana's second play, *Jingle Bells* (2001), a comedy about three Samoan girls unsuccessfully auditioning for Auckland's Christmas in the Park concert, was followed by *The Packer* (2003), composed as part of her master's degree in creative and performing arts at the University of Auckland. She wrote it as a solo piece for her Palagi friend Jay Bunyan, who was acting in the Australian soap *Neighbours* at the time. *The Packer* premiered at BATS in August and later played around New Zealand, in Australia and at the Edinburgh Fringe Festival. Her third play, *My Mother Dreaming* (2005), was performed at the Herald Theatre in Auckland.

While performing *Mapaki* at the 2000 International Women's Playwrights Festival in Greece, Fuemana met the literary manager of Pangea World Theater who invited her to present it at the company's home base in Minneapolis in 2001. Pangea's artistic director, Dipankar Mukherjee, subsequently commissioned her to write a new play. The result was *Falemalama* (House of Lights), a moving piece based on the life of Fuemana's mother, who had recently passed away. *Falemalama* premiered at Pangea World Theater in 2006 as part of their 10th Indigenous Voices Series, where Fuemana played all roles including that of daughter Tien, a character based on herself. She went on to direct the play in Pago Pago in American Samoa as part of the 10th Festival of Pacific Arts (2008), and in Auckland at Celebrate Pasifika (2009) where she used three actors – her daughter Reid Elisaia, her nephew Ali Foa`i and Fiona Collins.

Falemalama is both a tribute to Fuemana's mother and a story of migration. The title character (Falemalama, or Fale) moves across the Pacific from Pago Pago to Niue and then to New Zealand; the fragmented narrative reflects the disruptions to her life as she seeks a place to call home. The play balances traditional and contemporary Pacific oral storytelling, music and movement, and uses dances and music to evoke settings, such as in scene four, where Niuean movements and gestures illustrate the shift to Niue. Musical director Igelese Ete suggests the songs and the use of traditional instruments evoke 'a sense of Pacific pride, patriotism, identity and nostalgia'.[41]

A Storyteller guides us through Fale's childhood in American Samoa. Beaten by her mother, she leaves home and lives as a street kid in the 'small island city'.[42] Becoming pregnant at an early age, Fale loses the child (Michael) to adoption, then marries Niuean Taniela and gives birth to several more children in quick succession. Taniela moves the family to Niue, a place that Fale despises, so she leaves her children and husband and returns to Samoa with Ikinofo, one of her sons. When Taniela then moves the family to New Zealand for a better life, Fale rejoins them, leaving Ikinofo in Samoa. The reunion is not joyful, however: 'Fale rushed to hug her children, but none of them responded. They stood blank with empty bodies when she embraced them. They didn't want her anymore.'[43] She finds some kind of peace in New Zealand; her youngest daughter Tien is born, but she cannot reconnect with her other children and leaves her family to live in a small flat. Fale's health deteriorates, but reconciliation with Michael and Ikinofo brings happiness in the final years of her life. A celebratory ending features a Samoan dance comprising 42 movements, one for each of Fale's children, grandchildren and great-grandchildren.[44]

Fuemana economically creates a complex portrait of a Pacific woman within a patriarchal society, whose life is characterised by forced migration and a subsequent fragmentation of the family. Yet the play effectively conveys Fale's strength and resilience in a life of struggle. Like *Frangipani Perfume*, *Falemalama* brings sympathetic depictions of real Pacific women to the stage without romanticisation or judgment. The process of creating this play, of theatricalising the specifics of her mother's story to celebrate Pacific women in general, was cathartic for Fuemana:

> It was really emotional because I'd written a draft and I sent it out to my brothers and sisters, and some of them said, 'How could you write that? No, that's not true.' I just had to stand my ground and say, 'Yes, she's our mother, but I'm not writing for you. I'm writing for her.' The stories are pretty much verbatim what she had told me, and I just had to trust that. It was hard for my family at first, but then they got it – that it was, in a way, my process of grieving.

The autobiographical element of Fuemana's work continued in *Birds* (2012), a two-hander portraying the relationship between a Niuean mother and son. It is told 'through the lens of a young boy, growing up into manhood':

> *Birds* was my ode to mothers of young men. I wanted to share that experience of being a single parent, raising a son in Auckland ... It was such a heart project for me ... In essence it is the struggle between a woman and her son and how they get through that.

Birds has travelled the Pacific, including to a festival in Niue and the 11th Festival of Pacific Arts (2012) in the Solomon Islands.[45]

> When we did it in Solomon Islands ... a lot of the audience were older, you had a whole New Zealand delegation watching it made up of Māori and Pacific men and women. And those men, they cried, 'That was just amazing! That's my story with my mum.' I wanted it to be accessible to the community. We were able to do a free performance during Pasifika in Auckland at the Auckland Performing Arts Centre ... Mothers came up to me, and said, 'Oh my God, that's our story.'

Reviewing the Auckland production, Sharu Delilkan praised Fuemana's writing: 'The dialogue is pithy and perceptive, displaying Fuemana's skill as a great observational writer ... it was refreshing to get a Niuean perspective.'[46]

Fuemana has added a significant Niuean voice to Pasifika theatre, and has expanded the female aspects of stories from the diaspora. Fuelled by her own experiences, she has examined challenging dimensions of family relationships that are highly relevant in communities in New Zealand and throughout the Pacific.

Toa Fraser: Fijian voices on the New Zealand stage

In the late nineties a new Pasifika writer brought a distinctive urban, multicultural aesthetic to the stage. This was Toa Fraser, born in England in 1975 to a Fijian father and an English mother. In 1989 the family migrated to Auckland's Mt Roskill, which would later become a setting for two of his plays. Fraser studied English, film and television at Auckland University.

His talent was immediately recognised with the premiere of his work *Bare* at Auckland's Silo Theatre in June 1998. As the title suggests, the play (a two-hander) is deliberately stripped back: it consists of a series of monologues for multiple characters, originally performed by Madeleine Sami and Ian Hughes on a bare stage.

The rapid-fire street language, vivid characterisation and ironic humour in *Bare* won Fraser several major awards in 1999: Outstanding New New Zealand Play and Outstanding New Writer (Chapman Tripp Awards), followed by Playmarket's Bruce Mason Award. In 2001 he held a writer's residency at the University of the South Pacific in Suva.

Bare (director Michael Robinson) played at the 1999 Edinburgh Fringe Festival, as did Fraser's second play, the solo work *No. 2*, which won a Fringe First Award in 2000. Directed by Catherine Boniface, *No. 2* premiered at the Silo in June 1999 and subsequently played in Jamaica, Australia and Britain. In 2006 Fraser adapted *No. 2* to a movie script, which he also directed. Following the success of the film Fraser has worked primarily in the film industry, directing *Dean Spanley* (2008), *Giselle* (2013) and *The Dead Lands* (2014).

His meteoric rise with *Bare* and *No. 2* was mirrored in the elevation of Madeleine Sami to star status. Fraser auditioned 18-year-old Sami for *Bare* when she was acting with the Maidment Youth Theatre, and was 'amazed by her natural talent [and] intelligence ...'[47] Sami also has a Fijian background: her father is Fijian Indian and her mother Irish–New Zealand. One of her roles was Venus, a 'hard-out gym chick' with Fijian heritage.[48] In one of the comic highlights of the play, Venus and her boyfriend Dave re-enact a sexual encounter while standing fully clothed on opposite sides of the stage.

As in *Romeo and Tusi*, the script of *Bare* contains Shakespearian text that is seamlessly integrated with popular culture references. While the play's structure is fragmented, with apparently disconnected people speaking about their daily lives, a narrative emerges as Fijian elder Shakespeare Guy searches for his lost granddaughter (Venus). There are echoes here of the migration themes common to Samoan theatre, as Shakespeare Guy's family settled in New Zealand in the

1950s. Towards the end of the play, after Venus has learned that Shakespeare Guy is her grandfather, he tells her he is dying. A sense of reconciliation, healing and loss is borne out when Venus reveals to the audience, 'I feel like ... my whole world has changed.'[49]

In March 2011 Fraser and Hughes co-produced *Bare* at Auckland's Civic Theatre to raise money for victims of the Canterbury earthquake. The two-person play was transformed into an ensemble piece for 17 actors and included film and TV stars such as Sam Neill, Ian Mune, Keisha Castle-Hughes, Lucy Lawless, Rhys Darby and David Fane (playing Shakespeare Guy). Reviewer Nik Smythe judged it a 'historic evening', reserving his highest accolade for 'the sheer originality and strength of the written work that is *Bare*'.[50]

In *No. 2*, family matriarch Nanna Maria sees the younger generation as the key to securing the family's future. She summons her grandchildren to her Mt Roskill home to a feast of 'all kinds of food from all over the world',[51] at which she will name her successor as head of the family. Eventually she chooses entrepreneurial Soul, whose name and actions suggest he has the necessary spirit and strength.

Nineteen-year-old Sami achieved the considerable feat of playing the Fijian grandmother as well as eight other characters, and the combination of Fraser's evocative and poetic writing with Sami's chameleon-like performance elicited enthusiastic reviews both in New Zealand and internationally. The *Scotsman* (Edinburgh) wrote that the play was 'glorious',[52] while the *Independent* (London) praised Sami's skills: 'With a slight pursing of the lip, a tilt of the head or a change of inflexion, she morphs across age and gender, often poking fun but never resorting to caricature.'[53]

In both works Fraser impressed with his ability to say so much with so little. In contrast, his ambitious third play, *Paradise*, is a large-cast, sprawling epic set mostly in Fiji, which picks up the theme of broken families in the Pacific diaspora. *Paradise* was produced by Taki Rua at Circa Theatre (March 2001), and directed by Tina Cook. As in *No. 2*, there is an ageing Fijian Nanna (Nina Nawalowalo) in an old house in Mt Roskill, complaining about the state of the world. But most of the action is set in a luxury tourist resort in Fiji, where Sunny Smith (John Katipa), a New Zealand-based Fijian professional rugby player, holidays with his pregnant girlfriend Gina (Barbara Carpenter). Sunny intends to confront his father Richard Nelson (Fane), the owner of the resort, who abandoned his family when Sunny was four years old. Richard remains unaware that his guest is actually his son and the anticipated confrontation never occurs, allowing levels of tension and irony to grow. Set in the days leading up to the coup d'état led by George Speight on 19 May 2000, the script boils with a subtext of political and economic tension that undermines the perception of the Pacific region as 'paradise'.

Most critics considered the work to be flawed. Timothy O'Brien observed that the excessive 'chatter' meant 'the play is struggling to wind itself up and get moving'.[54] Nawalowalo, however, speaking from a Fijian perspective, felt that as soon as she read the script, 'I was hearing my relatives. Such a wonderful gift to work on as an actor – the beauty of Toa Fraser's writing.'[55]

Paradise remains one of very few plays to seriously consider the politics of the wider Pacific region and New Zealand's relationship with Pacific islands. In its ambition to capture the mood of a whole era in Pacific politics, and to relate that to personal and family stories, it recalls the plays of Anton Chekhov. The unspoken subtext shapes Fraser's ironic observations of human behaviour and forms the emotional core of the play.

In November 2014 Fraser wrote and directed *Pure and Deep*, a sequel to *Bare* that features Venus and Dave 16 years on. It premiered at Auckland's Herald Theatre with Hughes reprising his role as Dave, and Mia Blake (who was in the cast of the *Bare* earthquake benefit show and the film version of *No. 2*) playing Venus. Once again, the actors play an eclectic range of comic characters 'who capture current trends and obsessions with canny accuracy'.[56] While there are plenty of laughs in *Pure and Deep*, Venus and Dave exhibit their vulnerability as they struggle to make sense of their lives in their thirties. James Wenley sums up the impact of the play: '[Fraser] has serious things to say about the country's masculinity, society and environment ... In film and once again theatre, Fraser really is one of this country's most important storytellers.'[57]

Albert Wendt: *The Songmaker's Chair*

Like the Peseola family, our journeys have been from our ancient atua and pasts to the new fusion and mix and rap that is now Aotearoa and Auckland. We have added to and continue to change that extraordinary fusion, the heart of which is still Māori and Moana-nui-a-kiwa. ALBERT WENDT[58]

The fictional Peseola family in Albert Wendt's first full-length theatre work took the migrant themes of previous Samoan plays to a new level of complexity.[59] In a plot reminiscent of *No. 2*, dying patriarch Peseola summons his large `aiga for a kalakalaga (family meeting) in order to appoint a successor. Peseola is a taulaaitu (shaman), storyteller and 'songmaker' whose songs recount the ancient stories of Polynesia. Nathaniel Lees explains the concept:

> Songmakers and orators are special people. They see who we are, and they make plans for who we could be. So our songs and our storytelling are all about who we are firstly, but then what we could have been.[60]

The chair of the title was gifted to Peseola by his father and represents a connection with gafa (genealogy). While Wendt has not consciously recreated his own family in the play, he has '[long] carried with him an image of his father, sitting in a chair in the family home in Samoa, listening to a large radio'.[61]

Wendt wrote *The Songmaker's Chair* in 1996 as 'a fulfilment of a promise to Nathaniel Lees in the 1970s that I would write a play for Samoan actors'.[62] The play was given rehearsed readings at Downstage in 1997 and at the Auckland Writer's Festival in 2001. The first full production opened at the Maidment Theatre in 2003, produced by ATC for the AK03 Auckland Festival, with Lees directing as well as playing Peseola. The show sold out in Auckland and again at the 2004 New Zealand International Arts Festival in Wellington.

As in *Fresh off the Boat*, *Dawn Raids* and *Frangipani Perfume*, the play highlights the struggles for Pacific migrants in Aotearoa, represented by Peseola and his wife Malaga (Ana Tuigamala) who arrived in the 1950s:

> **PESEOLA**: Didn't know what a flush toilet, or washing machine, or electric stove was.
>
> *They laugh.*
>
> **MALAGA**: Or how to use a public telephone –
>
> **PESEOLA**: Or a public faleuila![63]

More than 40 years later as they prepare for the kalakalaga, they recall the hardships of their early years in New Zealand when Malaga went nursing at night and Peseola worked two jobs so they could save the deposit for their house. They await the arrival of their four children: sons Fa`amau (Ben Baker) and Falani (known as Frank, played by Aleni Tufuga), and daughters Nofo (Grace Hoet) and Lilo (Tausili Mose).

Wendt evokes wider social patterns in Aotearoa through the new `aiga relationships formed as a result of migration. Fa`amau has married Joan (Rachel Nash), a Palagi, while Nofo's marriage to Māori Hone (Tamati Te Nohotu) has produced two children, Mata (Stacey Leilua) and Tapua`iga (Fasitua Amosa). Through these grandchildren Wendt examines the shared Polynesian kinships between Samoan and Māori and the differing worldviews of the younger generation. According to Lees, when writing *The Songmaker's Chair* Wendt was 'very conscious of the influence of the reo from Aotearoa on the way he thinks as a Samoan, and how the culture here is producing a different kind of Pacific Islander'.

> Just within one or two generations a lot has changed. The older brother in the play [Fa`amau] is pivotal in that change. He is having that struggle that my generation did. Am I Samoan, or not?

These questions are reflected strongly in the play through the differing perspectives of the three generations. Peseola and Malaga's children resent the pressures on them to succeed in both the Samoan and Palagi worlds. Lilo (an alcoholic) has been in trouble with the law, and Frank exclaims,

> I got sick and tired of being told off by our elders for not being Samoan enough, Papa! I've never wanted to be Samoan. You've always made me feel unworthy of it ...[64]

When Peseola appoints his oldest son as his successor, Fa`amau initially rejects the offer: 'It's too heavy: the responsibilities, the duty, the history, the honour. And I don't know how to carry it. I'm no good at the Fa`asamoa!'[65]

In the play those of the oldest generation often speak in Samoan, making this one of the most bilingual of the Pasifika plays. They are concerned, however, that the central place of Samoan language in their lives is slipping away.

> **MALAGA**: Why are we talking in English?
>
> **PESEOLA**: Why? (*Pause*). 'Ou ke lē iloa. It's like all the other whys. We've been speaking English because for almost forty years, that's been the language of our lives.[66]

Wendt and Lees both felt it was important to convey how crucial Samoan language is to post-migrant Samoan identity. Lees recalls that before they even began rehearsing, they had to share their understanding of what it meant to be Samoan:

> ... there's a generation, and it was my generation, in the 50s, the first New Zealand-born, who pretty much lost the language. My brothers and sisters and I had to be fluent in Palagi, in English, to help [our parents] relate to this new country. We were encouraged not to speak Samoan at home so that they could learn English. Both Al and I realised that this generation, my generation, lost the language... Tui Atua Tupua Tamasese Ta`isi Efi, our head of state [has] written this beautiful book on what language is to Samoa.[67] And it highlighted again what my generation – or certainly me – understand about what language is to the health and wellbeing of who we are as Samoans.

Central to the play is Peseola's throne-like carved chair, which symbolises his position as head of the `aiga and his role in the community as an orator or 'songmaker', along with myriad other associations. Lees explains:

> The chair itself was meant to be as ornate as possible. It was a colonial chair that the old man's father had acquired. Every time the old man gets troubled he sits in the chair, because that's his kaupapa, that's who he is. The chair itself becomes a character that he has to talk to. His oldest son is uncomfortable sitting in it; the others don't even go near it except for the youngest one [Lilo], who sneaks out and sits in it to find comfort. And we did a lot of work on how comfortable you feel, sitting in this chair, as an individual, rather than as your character.

Reviewer Melani Anae notes, 'Peseola's love and fascination for his "chair" mirrors the centrality of the aiga and faasamoa values that are dominant themes in the play.'[68]

The play explores multiple tensions in the family and concludes with a spirit of reconciliation. Peseola finds peace with himself, rising from the chair to deliver his dying speech. In contrast to the creation story that he chants at the beginning, the play ends with a rap song he has learnt from his grandchildren, which he performs while clicking his fingers to the beat:

> ... Why is it we've stayed this far?
> We think we've found a firm fit to this land.
> To our children and mokopuna it's home.
> That's good enough pe `a o`o mai le Amen
> And Papatuanuku embraces us ...[69]

The incongruity of an old man performing rap illustrates the vastness of the cultural shift that has occurred in the years since Peseola and Malaga migrated to Aotearoa. Peseola has maintained the importance of fa`asamoa in the `aiga, yet the family has shifted towards a wider multi-cultural sense of identity. The words of the rap confirm the 'extraordinary fusion' of contemporary Aotearoa and the link with Māori, also maintained through Peseola's part-Māori grandchildren. It brings a strong sense that Pasifika people 'belong' in Aotearoa alongside tangata whenua.

At the conclusion of the song Peseola collapses on the chair. As he dies, owls (lulu) – the ghosts of departed ancestors, according to Samoan belief – carry him away. Lees describes the effect as played in his production, for which Sima Urale designed the audio-visual effects:

There is the sound effect of the flapping of large wings approaching. His family unrolls two large tapa cloths. Time now becomes overlapping and entwined. They hold the tapa out, as in the ceremonial presentation of tapa and `ie toga [fine mats]. On the screen, a large owl flies toward the audience and perches on the branch overlooking the stage. Peseola stands and completes the rap section of his speech. The family members wrap him in the two tapa cloths, kiss him goodbye and sing the song of farewell. The wife steps forward and kisses the old man goodbye. The family raise the wrapped body over their heads and process off stage singing the Samoan farewell song. The video shows the large owl flapping its wings as it rises and flies into darkness. What I remember clearly and is ingrained in my memory was the wave after wave of emotion from the actors and the audience that washed over the stage.[70]

In reviewing the ATC production, Frances Edmond recognised *The Songmaker's Chair* as 'a significant cultural event', observing that it 'permitted an intimate view into the heart of [Peseola's] family'.[71] Anae praised the 'superb and riveting performances by Nathaniel Lees and Ana Tuigamala' and the spiritual depth of the script: 'What is extraordinary about this play is ... the infusion of the unknown, mysterious, and metaphysical world of death in which Peseola realizes his human frailty and mortality, evidenced by dreams and the presence of aitu.'[72]

The Songmaker's Chair was the first New Zealand-written Pasifika play to be published (Huia, 2004). In 2006 it was produced in Hawai`i at Kumu Kahua Theatre, directed by the theatre's co-founder Dennis Carroll and featuring Wil Kahele as Peseola and Fata Simanu-Klutz as Malaga. The cast also included the leading Hawaiian/Samoan playwright Victoria Nalani Kneubuhl as Nofo. Reviewer Joseph T. Rozmiarek argued that 'the play's message transfers universally to all immigrant groups, while its Samoan focus adds depth and richness'.[73] Māori poet Robert Sullivan also commented on the play's wide relevance, 'crossing as it did from the southern to the northern Pacific'. Like Anae, Sullivan was intrigued by the significance of the chair: 'It has a confessional symbolism that connects it with the spirit world, a silent wisdom handed down from the previous songmakers ... The chair is a representation of the va – a cultural space.'[74]

The play's blend of oratory, song, spirituality and symbolism, and the familiar themes – of Pasifika families re-negotiating their cultural identity in response to the challenges of migration – made a rich addition to the emerging canon of Pasifika playwriting. Wendt recalls the feedback he received:

> When it was on in Auckland people would come up to me in the supermarket and say ... 'We loved your play.' It didn't matter what ethnic group they were from. One Palagi couple came up to me and said, 'We loved the play ... it's about family. It's about us.'[75]

Pasifika collaborations: *Niu Sila* and *Where We Once Belonged*

We all live on an archipelago on the Pacific Ocean called Aotearoa/New Zealand, and while we are of different ethnic backgrounds, this geographical fact creates an opportunity for us to think about how we are connected. Not everyone likes it, but I often tease friends and colleagues, saying we're all Pacific Islanders. There is a way in which, together and through our interactions, we create something that is distinctive about the conditions of living here. Writers like Dave Armstrong, designers like Tony DeGoldi and many other collaborators – I don't see them as being peripheral. Their role and influence is braided into the fabric of what's going on in small and not so small ways, in good and bad ways. So if you think about the whole creative nexus around Pacific theatre, it's not all brown. It's more complex, and Pākehā, Māori and many others help constitute it. SEAN MALLON

Palagi Dave Armstrong has had a long association with Pasifika performance, including major collaborations with both Oscar Kightley and Sia Figiel. He is the author of popular comedies such as *Le Sud* (2009) and *The Motor Camp* (2011). While writing for the TV soap *Shortland Street* he was responsible for Pacific material and conducted research into Pacific health issues at Middlemore Hospital; and as a writer on the comedy series *Skitz*[76] he worked directly with Pasifika issues:

> We went out to Porirua East and said, 'What do you want to see on television?' And the kids said 'Us. We don't want to sit at home talking about Palagis, we don't know any. We sit at home laughing at our minister and our parents.'[77]

Five Pasifika teenagers from Porirua College were hired as story consultants on *Skitz*, feeding raw material to Armstrong who then wrote the sketches. One comic sketch depicting an immigrant family grew into a series of three-minute sketches called *Milburn Place*, which ran for 70 *Skitz* episodes and spawned an entire series, *The Semisis* (1996–97). David Fane, recently graduated from Toi Whakaari, was cast in *Milburn Place*, and Armstrong brought in Oscar Kightley as a scriptwriter: 'I had seen *Fresh off the Boat* and it really impressed me. It was the first play I'd seen about Pacific Island experience in New Zealand.'

Scripts were workshopped with the core cast: Fane (Dad), Hori Ahipene (Mum), Jackie Clarke (Tusi) and Robbie Magasiva (Lagi). Armstrong, who is a trumpeter, likens the process to jazz improvisation – riffing on a theme until the humour emerges.

> I think because Pacific society is communal, you get a group thing happening in a workshop or in a play rehearsal that you don't always get to the same extent in a Palagi situation. Working with PI actors is different. You sit, talk and argue. Sometimes you've got to shut up and listen. Pacific actors often jam on an idea and come up with something better than what you wrote. They have very high, demanding standards of form.

Niu Sila (2004) is part autobiographical, based on Armstrong's experiences growing up in a Wellington inner-city suburb where his best friend was the son of the Niuean family next door. Armstrong nurtured the idea of writing a play about this relationship for several years, and approached Kightley to collaborate on the script.

Originally directed by Conrad Newport, *Niu Sila* is a dark comedy that follows 20 years of friendship between neighbours Ioane Tafioka (Fane) and Peter Burton (Damon Andrews). The immediate effect of this casting was a comic bicultural image – Fane is tall and powerfully built while Andrews is short and blonde. The two also played a large cast of supporting characters: 'parents, siblings, teachers, policemen, a minister and the local Indian cricket team'.[78]

Peter's upward mobility contrasts with Ioane's increasing social isolation as they age. The play is framed by two present-day encounters in the TAB where Peter, recognising his old school mate, initially makes overtures of friendship that are rejected by the sullen Ioane. Ioane becomes a compendium of Pasifika clichés:

> **IOANE**: I've got five kids to three different mothers, I've got four government departments chasing me for money I don't have. I'm up to my eyeballs in debt and I'm a certifiable alcoholic. It's the only certificate I've ever won.[79]

In contrast, Peter has a wife and child, an inner-city townhouse and a 'safe' job as a bicultural advisor. Kightley and Armstrong juxtapose the positive aspects of an intercultural childhood with a deep sense of unease about the growing social and economic disparities between the two men.

The play becomes progressively darker. Peter's politically correct façade finally cracks, and Ioane is disparaging of his job as a bicultural advisor: 'Congratulations Peter, you are richer for having known me. Much richer.'[80] The play rejects an idealised picture of race relations in Niu Sila and implies an unconscious hypocrisy in Peter's liberalism.

PETER: ... I live in a trendy Parnell town house, and there's no Islanders around. The only tapa cloth in the street is at the local café – which does a lovely flat white. In fact, the whole neighbourhood's flat and white ... almost.[81]

Niu Sila won a Chapman Tripp Award for Outstanding New New Zealand play and has had a long performance history, with tours throughout New Zealand and to the UK. It has been published by two separate companies (one version an abridged edition for secondary schools), and has been studied and performed as part of the secondary school curriculum.

Following the success of *Niu Sila*, Armstrong worked with the Samoan novelist Sia Figiel on a stage adaptation of her Commonwealth Prize-winning novel *Where We Once Belonged*, a work celebrated for its frank portrayal of a teenage girl growing up in Western Samoa during the 1970s. The novel is a coming-of-age story about 13-year-old Alofa and, like *Frangipani Perfume*, has a clear feminist orientation. Figiel's stylistic inspiration for the book was the concept of su`ifefiloi, 'the traditional Samoan form of storytelling that strings many different songs and myths together in the form of an `ula, or garland of flowers'.[82] This gives the novel a kaleidoscopic, non-linear structure; it moves freely between different time periods and characters, while maintaining the first-person narrative perspective of the young girl.

In adapting the play for theatre, Armstrong deliberately pursued a more linear time-line, enabling exposition to be revealed at an earlier stage and building towards a series of crises for Alofa. Produced by ATC, the stage adaptation premiered in 2008 at the Wellington International Festival of the Arts, followed by a season at the Auckland Town Hall. Alofa was played by Joy Vaele, with Anapela Polataivao, Goretti Chadwick, Robbie Magasiva and Pua Magasiva in supporting roles, dressed uniformly in white t-shirts and blue lavalava. The production was co-directed by Colin McColl and Fane on a striking perspex set designed by Michel Tuffery, and earned Armstrong and Figiel a Chapman Tripp Award in 2008 for Best New Play.

The play exposes double standards based on gender and keeps intact the novel's critique of the patriarchal system in Samoa. Alofa's grandmother Tausi outlines some of the rules: 'Girls should always volunteer to do housework. Girls should never dry themselves with the same towel a boy or man has used.'[83] Alofa worships her father Filiga, the man she loves most 'besides Jesus Christ and Bruce Lee',[84] despite the fact that he abandoned his first wife for Alofa's mother, Pisa. However, when Alofa discovers her father having sex with her teacher, Mrs Samasoni, she becomes suicidal. Alofa herself succumbs to the advances of Lealofi, the pastor's son, and when Filiga discovers that his daughter has been seen naked on the beach with Lealofi, he punishes her by beating her and cutting off her hair.

Reviewer Lynn Freeman praised the adaptation: 'Armstrong has preserved the freshness of the writing and its unconventional style – Figiel's voice is very much here.'[85] Sian Robertson commented on the wider significance of the story, calling it 'an unabashed and moving tale about the discomfort of change, not just for a growing girl but also for a recently independent Samoa awkwardly deciphering the influence of Western culture, simultaneously rejecting and embracing it'.[86]

In bringing *Where We Once Belonged* to the stage, Armstrong and Figiel offered audiences an insight into the recent history and gender politics of Samoa, adding another dimension to the Pasifika theatre story.

David Mamea: 'A minority within a minority'

The last thing I want to do is to write some kind of screed on how terrible it is to be an Islander in a white man's world. DAVID MAMEA[87]

David Mamea was born in Wellington to parents who had emigrated from Samoa in the early 1950s. His father, a stevedore on the Wellington wharf, would sometimes take his son to work when the child was sick, exposing Mamea to a multi-cultural world of English, Scottish, Eastern European, Samoan and Māori workers, which he would later draw on in his writing. 'I would overhear these conversations, and I would also see the dynamics that they had.' Mamea went to film school in Auckland, following which he scripted films such as the horror-thriller *Five* (2007) and the short film *To`ona`i* (2010). He cites James Cameron and David Mamet as writers who exerted the biggest influence on him:

> I learned structure from James Cameron's scripts. And with David Mamet, it's so smart, it's so sharp, and there's so much more that is not on the page that I have to work really hard for, and that's what I try and do with my finished plays, where I don't offer everything up to the audience. They have to work a little bit.

Mamea's first play, *Skyblue* (2012) – which takes place on a single day in a forensic psychiatric unit – was an award-winning piece for radio. His first play for the stage, which has had several iterations, was *Goodbye My Feleni* (2012–14), set at Papakura Army Camp in 1942. In the 2014 full-length version, two Samoans (Simi and Ioane), a Cook Islander (Tama) and a Niuean (Ete) are soldiers preparing to sail for Egypt as reinforcements for the 28th [Māori] Battalion.[88] As Pacific Islanders, they are likely bound for D ('Ngati Walkabout') Company. Mamea's choice of multiple Pacific Island ethnicities was deliberate: 'One of the things that interested me about the play was looking at a minority within a minority.'

The shadow of survival in wartime hangs over the play, but the immediate focus is on friendship, fun, drinking games, songs and army training. In command is Sergeant Ete Masani, who has already experienced the loss of a friend while fighting in Crete. The three younger men express common sentiments of the uninitiated:

> **IOANE**: Are you excited? ... We've got three sleeps, sole! Three sleeps then we're off to see the world!
>
> **TAMA**: And kill Nazis, uso![89]

While these are familiar tropes for a wartime play, *Goodbye My Feleni* touches new ground in its examination of this group of almost-forgotten Pacific Island soldiers.[90] Mamea lightly sketches the ironies that arise from Pasifika experiences within the Māori Battalion, which in its turn is ruled by 'His Majesty's Royal New Zealand Army'.[91]

> **ETE**: You Pacific Islanders think you're something special, don't you? I can tell you right now you're not ... Your mechanical aptitude might impress the Palagi instructors but you're still a dirty Cook Islander, Private. ... And you, Lance Corporal Bishop – your file could say 'natural leader of men' and 'instinctive strategist' from here to Kingdom Come, but your disciplinary records mark you as just another drunken, useless Samoan.[92]

Originally a one-act play, the inspiration for *Goodbye My Feleni* came from several sources:

> In 2008, I read Patricia Grace's *Tu*, and that really affected me. It was mostly the story about the relationship between the brothers, which I really identified with.[93] In my research on the Māori Battalion, I came across a CD; the last thing I expected to hear was a couple of songs sung in Samoan on a CD that I had just assumed would be a mix of songs in Māori and traditional English. And hearing the songs, it affected me quite deeply and unexpectedly.

One of those songs was 'Goodbye My Feleni', and the play concludes with a performance of this as part of a farewell concert by the troops.[94] As Mamea notes, 'Sure, it's a play with singing, dancing Islanders, but it's also very sad.'

Goodbye My Feleni is a well-crafted play with clean, spare dialogue and a good understanding of subtext. It was awarded 'best play by a Pasifika playwright' at the 2013 Adam New Zealand Play Awards,[95] and the New Zealand Writers Guild award for Best Play. Mamea won the Adam award again in 2015 for *Kingswood*, a play about 'four friends and a Holden station wagon on their way from Auckland to Wellington'. This play was given a rehearsed reading by ATC in March 2016, with a cast including Joy Vaele and Louise Tu`u.

Victor Rodger: Stepping out of the 'blackground'

As discussed in chapter four, Victor Rodger's experiences of growing up as afakasi and without knowledge of his Samoan father provided rich material for his first play, *Sons*, and remain major themes in his work.

> I'm happy to be a spokesperson for my strand of afakasi. Not all afakasis are like that. Growing up, raised by Scottish grandparents and a white mother, I was a Kiwi who happened to have a Samoan father. Around the seventh form, I started to get a bit of a cultural consciousness, had my little Malcolm X militant phase, and then came back into the middle, deliberately celebrating both.[96]

Following his time with Pacific Underground in Christchurch, Rodger trained as an actor at Toi Whakaari, graduating in 1997.[97] From 2000 to 2015 he was a regular writer, occasional storyliner and actor on *Shortland Street*. Rodger's scriptwriting skills have been honed by the discipline of writing for television, and also by his passion for certain playwrights:

> I like my dialogue fast and snappy. Intelligence is something that I like to see on stage. I like smart stuff, but I also like to give a shit, and I don't know that those two things always get combined in New Zealand theatre by and large. I love *Have Car, Will Travel* by Mitch Tawhi Thomas who was in my year at drama school. I always like to have Edward Albee's *Who's Afraid of Virginia Woolf?* by my side because I love that play; *Angels in America* [Tony Kushner] is a terrific play, and so is Marsha Norman's *'night, Mother*. These are all plays I read around the time I was writing *Sons*. David Mamet was also an influence for me – I love *Oleanna*, with its rat-tat-tat-tat dialogue.

Rodger's work has always been a stimulating mixture of provocation and heart. His second play, *Cunning Stunts* (1997), a dark comedy about friendship featuring three afakasi characters, was performed at BATS as part of the Young and Hungry season. As a mark of his growing reputation, he went from writing for youth theatre to having his play *Ranterstantrum* (2002) produced by the New Zealand International Festival of the Arts. This work uses a case of mistaken identity – a white couple assumes a Samoan dinner guest is a burglar – to examine white prejudice towards Polynesian men. 'It's probably the edgiest thing I've done.' But it was *My Name is Gary Cooper* (2007) that revealed the full power of Rodger as a playwright.

> *Gary Cooper* is a landmark for me, and I'm proud of it. I didn't realise, until I read a review, that there were no New Zealanders in it – they're Americans and Samoans. But the reviewer said that it couldn't be written by anyone other than a New Zealand Polynesian.[98]

Like Fraser's *Paradise*, *My Name is Gary Cooper* goes beyond New Zealand shores to embrace the wider Pacific. It responds to the Hollywood movie *Return to Paradise*, shot at Lefaga Beach in Samoa in 1952 and starring Gary Cooper:

> **JENNIFER**: Why is your name Gary Cooper?
>
> **GARY**: It is the name I was given. There are, in fact, several Gary Coopers throughout Samoa.
>
> **NICK**: Actually, now you mention it, I seem to recall when we went there, a few parents named their kids after Coop.[99]

In the movie Cooper plays Morgan, a drifter who arrives in Samoa, liberates the islanders from the authoritarian regime of a Palagi pastor and fathers a child with a Samoan woman, Maeva (played by Palagi Roberta Haynes), who dies in childbirth. Later, he returns to the island to care for his daughter Turia (Moira MacDonald). Rodger reflects:

> Back in the day, Hollywood's portrayal of the South Pacific in films like *Return to Paradise* was resolutely from a white point of view, where white characters entered the brown world and stirred things up. What if ... a brown character entered the white world instead, and stirred things up. What would that look like?[100]

Rodger addresses this in *My Name is Gary Cooper* by inverting the film's premise. A young Samoan, Gary Cooper, arrives in Los Angeles in 1973 seeking his father, Nick White, a fictional American photographer who was part of the *Return to Paradise* film crew. The play is partly a satire on Hollywood's sexualised representation of the Pacific, in which Rodger brings his Pacific characters out of what he calls the 'blackground' and into prominence. He avoids a linear narrative structure, deftly intercutting between 1970s LA, Auckland in 2000 – where the middle-aged Gary attends a screening of *Return to Paradise* – and Samoa in 1952.

Like Urale in *Frangipani Perfume*, Rodger pillories anthropologist Margaret

Mead's controversially discredited research into Samoan sexuality.[101] In the Samoan scenes Nick seduces a young girl, Teuila, then abandons her, not realising she is pregnant with his child (Gary). Teuila seeks refuge with the local prostitute, Salamoana, who teaches her to sell her body to survive: 'Hey mister. You want paradise? Teuila got plenty paradise.'[102] Cut off from her family and crushed by Nick's broken promises, Teuila succumbs to alcoholism and drowns herself, leaving Gary in Salamoana's clutches. In 1970s LA, Gary enacts a symbolic revenge on his father by seducing Nick's daughter Jennifer, his son Joel and his wife Connie. As Natasha Hay notes, 'The LA scenes whiz by like a 70s sitcom ... but beneath the glibness is a tragic, soulful undertow.'[103] Gary photographs these sexual encounters then shows the images to Nick, 'because nothing means more to you than family, right?'[104] Nick reacts with intense anger when he realises that Gary is his son. Despite the family's protestations, he evicts Gary, failing to comprehend that his son's actions are a form of retribution for Nick's own failure as a partner and father.

In a final ironic twist, Gary discovers that he has unknowingly fathered an afakasi child as the result of his affair with Connie. He meets this daughter (T) by chance at the film screening in 2000 and pieces her story together. The play ends with a projected image of Gary in tears. As Diana Looser describes it, 'In the end, Gary turns out to be like his own father, Nick: history repeats, and the cycle of displacement and abandonment is carried on for another generation.'[105]

Gary in 2000 expresses cynicism about T's research on the representation of Polynesia in Hollywood cinema, as she has never been to Samoa; yet they bond over a shared interest in movies as they watch *Return to Paradise*.

> **GARY**: So your thesis – how will you describe the Samoans in *Return to Paradise*?
>
> **T**: Can I be frank? It's yet another example of the white hero helps the oogah-boogahs get it together genre. You've got Gary Cooper, you've got that Palagi priest, and a whole lot of natives with barely a brain between them.
>
> **GARY**: So you don't like it?
>
> **T**: Are you kidding? I love it. It's better than a lot of them. Have you ever seen the one about Queen Emma? They've got a chick from Nicaragua playing her and her mother looks like Helen Mirren with boot polish.[106] Hollywood – I tell you, it's got a lot to answer for ...[107]

Rodger admits to being 'movie-mad', and numerous movie references are seamlessly integrated with the play's subtext. For example, Gary impersonates Trevor Howard in *Mutiny on the Bounty* (1962); he and Connie flirt while watching the musical *South Pacific* (1958) on TV; and, in the most shocking reference, Gary has anal sex with his half-sister, inspired by the infamous scene in *Last Tango in Paris* (1972).

For the 2007 ATC premiere production at the Maidment, directed by Roy Ward, Robbie Magasiva played Gary Cooper.[108] Rodger regards frequent collaborator Magasiva as his muse and wrote this role specifically for him. Designer Mark McEntyre created a set that evoked the LA poolside setting 'with a wall of glass panels, lit up in swimming-pool blues reminiscent of David Hockney paintings'.[109]

Among the audience at the ATC premiere was veteran Samoan actor Moira Walker (formerly MacDonald), who played Turia in *Return to Paradise*. Rodger recalls: 'I was so nervous afterwards, with all the anal sex and everything. I said, "Are you alright?" after she saw it. And she said, "You know, it's 2007, not 1957."'

Reviews of the ATC production reflect the impact of the work. Sian Robertson called it 'erotic, hilarious yet tragic ... challenging the idea of an island "paradise"'.[110] Paul Simei-Barton observed that it 'greatly extends the range of Pacific Island writing'.[111]

Critical interest in *My Name is Gary Cooper* confirms its status as one of the most accomplished Pasifika plays, a multi-layered script with complex themes. Looser praises its ability to dramatise 'the dilemmas and ambiguities of contemporary Pacific Islander identities'.[112] Paloma Fresno-Calleja observes that Rodger 'substitutes the traditional happy ending of the original film for a tragic one, affecting two half-caste children who are both victims of Hollywood's fantasies'.[113]

The play was produced by Kumu Kahua Theatre in Honolulu in January 2015, directed by David O'Donnell and designed by James Davenport, and again received enthusiastic reviews: 'The underlying messages and cultural integrity of this production resonate with experiences far beyond the slopes of Titirangi, the sands of Lefaga beach, Malibu or Waikiki.'[114]

Rodger's collaboration with director Roy Ward has resulted in productions of *At the Wake* (2012) and *Black Faggot* (2013), both of which demonstrate Rodger's confidence and maturity as a playwright.[115] *At the Wake* also draws on aspects of his background, depicting a gay afakasi man (Robert) who returns to New Zealand for his Palagi mother's funeral. The three-hander places Robert in conflict with his grandmother, Joan, and his estranged Samoan father, Tofiala, who is a fundamentalist Christian. A review titled 'In the Wake of Genius' praised Rodger for 'his uncanny ability to write dialogue that's ... refreshing and hard-hitting, [which strikes] the perfect balance' between tragedy and humour.[116]

Rodger's provocative *Black Faggot* was a hit at the Auckland Fringe festival (2013), toured New Zealand, and played at the Edinburgh Fringe as part of the 'NZ at Edinburgh' season, where the *Guardian* called it 'funny and heartfelt as it explores the prejudices and stereotypes faced by young gay Samoans'.[117] On the Australian fringe circuit, the *Sydney Morning Herald* reviewer called it 'a riotously funny two-hander ... [that] touches a deeper nerve, prompting bittersweet reflection as well as irrepressible laughter'.[118]

Like Toa Fraser's *Bare* with its multiple characters, *Black Faggot* is structured as a series of interlinked sketches and monologues performed by two actors on a bare stage. As Rodger describes it, 'The language is quite explicit, the situations are quite explicit, it's filthy, it's fun, but it's also got a point to it.'[119] The play focuses exclusively on what it means to be gay in Samoan society, opening with a punk abusing a gay Samoan as a 'black faggot'. This depiction of homophobia and prejudice escalates into a celebration of the gay lifestyle featuring characters such as a shy teenager, a camp fa`afafine artist, a 'liberal faggot' and an 'anal queen'. At its heart is the coming-out story of James, an 'undercover brother'. Caught by his father looking up a website called 'Big black cocks', James bluffs that he is doing a school assignment about chickens. Beyond the laugh-out-loud and often sexually explicit humour, the scene where James finally comes out to his mother and macho brother is poignant and moving, confirming Rodger's ability to blend emotional truth with commercial success.

Since 2015 Rodger's work has taken a darker turn, as seen in two plays produced in quick succession. The first, *Girl on a Corner*, tells the poignant story of Samoan fa`afafine prostitute Shalimar (Atisone) Seiuli who was arrested in Los Angeles in the car of movie star Eddie Murphy in 1997. The second, *Club Paradiso*, is an intense drama about a P-crazed killer (Robbie Magasiva) who terrorises his hostages during a siege in an Otara bar. Rodger described the piece as 'Quentin Tarantino comes to South Auckland by way of German filmmaker Michael Haneke'.[120] In the claustrophobic, sweaty atmosphere created for this tightly written, raw naturalistic piece, the audience experiences a visceral series of extreme emotions – fear, horror and shock – in response to the violent acts portrayed.

The positive reception for Rodger's plays in the UK, Australia and Hawai`i is proof of the wider relevance of his themes as well as the quality of his writing. Among other honours, he has won the Bruce Mason Playwriting Award (2001), held the Fulbright–Creative New Zealand Pacific Writers residency at the University of Hawai`i (2006) and the Burns Writing Fellowship at the University of Otago (2016). His dialogue is razor-sharp, witty and ironic, blending comedy with deep emotion to riveting effect. He tackles complex issues of sexuality, the often-painful nature of family politics and the paradoxes and ambiguities of afakasi identity, in works that have 'changed the face of Pasifika theatre'.[121]

The rapid development of Pasifika playwriting has been characterised by a powerful sense of community and connection, and a creative chain wherein one writer inspires the next. There are many connections between the themes of their plays: migration, language, cultural identity and family stories remain central, but latterly gender, feminism and sexuality have come to the fore. Audiences are taken beyond the shores of New Zealand to examine the Pacific in a broader context, revealing the fragmentation caused by colonisation and widespread migration.

Makerita Urale's concept of 'floating Islanders' resonates from one play to the next. In reviewing *A Frigate Bird Sings*, Anita McNaught wrote that fa`afafine in the islands 'float free'.[122] The sisters in *Frangipani Perfume* float in their imaginations between their working class New Zealand existence and their memories and dreams of Samoa; Falemalama and her children drift from one island to another; Sunny Smith and Gary Cooper travel across the Pacific Ocean to seek their missing fathers.

Over one decade Pasifika writers made a remarkably rapid ascent to mainstream and international acclaim, their credibility acknowledged with awards and critical accolades. For the first time in the history of New Zealand theatre, the distinctive voices of Pasifika playwrights had moved from the fringes to the centre.

6.

MAU and The Conch: Bodies, images and light

The foundation of my work is the body. I love physical fitness. We train as a company, build stamina, skills, pattern and form. The work has to be bred physically through the way you work as an ensemble.

NINA NAWALOWALO[1]

Alongside a growing sophistication in playwriting, the 1990s and early 2000s saw the development of Pasifika non-text-based theatre foregrounding physicality and visual imagery. Physical image-making had been an important component in several plays like *Tatau: Rites of passage* and *Frangipani perfume*. New Zealand theatre overall had been influenced by alternative theatre companies which emerged in the 1970s, such as Francis Batten's Theatre Action, Paul Maunder's Amamus and Alan Brunton and Sally Rodwell's Red Mole. Like their Palagi counterparts, Pasifika artists were inspired by international theatre innovators such as Jacques Lecoq and Jerzy Grotowski. In writing about that period, Murray Edmond has identified a 'dell'arte line' in the theatre of Aotearoa, derived from the physical, improvised tradition of commedia dell'arte as an alternative to the 'literary theatre' of the mainstream.[2]

For the purposes of this discussion, we define physical image-based theatre as work that originates from the body rather than a written text; it is often non-narrative based, creating its own language of movement, space and imagery, playing between the boundaries of theatre, performance art and dance. Such theatre is exemplified by artists such as the Pacific Sisters, a collective of multi-media artists formed in 1992;[3] Samoan-born interdisciplinary performance artist Shigeyuki Kihara;[4] and the contemporary dance company Black Grace, founded in 1995 by Samoan choreographer Neil Ieremia.[5]

This chapter focuses on the work of two companies: MAU (directed by Lemi Ponifasio) and The Conch (directed by Nina Nawalowalo), whose productions serve as examples of Pasifika theatre where the body and striking visual images take precedence over spoken language.

Lemi Ponifasio and MAU

Internationally renowned Samoan choreographer Lemi Ponifasio has developed a unique pan-Pacific performance style from diverse influences, including Samoan dance, tikanga Māori and Japanese butoh, an avant-garde dance style that emerged in Japan in the 1960s.[6] His approach appears radically different from 'traditional' Pacific dance, yet it is inherently connected to Pacific spirituality and communities.

Ponifasio was born in Western Samoa and moved to New Zealand at the age of 15. He was later based in Tokyo for 12 years where he was choreographing for television, making his own dance work and encountering butoh dance through master Min Tanaka.[7] On his return to New Zealand he became involved with Pacific Theatre when he choreographed Justine Simei-Barton's production *Feiva/Favour* in 1988. He began to gather like-minded people to create dance theatre, preferring to work with young people from the community whom he trained from scratch rather than with trained dancers. According to Makerita Urale, these dancers are 'freer from conventions. They're not predictable. They are more malleable and open. And they can be a lot more authentic.'[8]

In 1993 Ponifasio created one of his first significant works in Aotearoa, *Illumina: The body in crisis*, initially performed with other dancers and later as a solo. Set to music by Henri Gorecki, it has been described as an 'emotionally and strongly conceived allegory of birth, life and death'.[9] Reviewing *Illumina* at BATS, Ann Hunt recalled the butoh company Sankai Juku at the first Wellington International Festival of the Arts (1986), noting that 'appreciation of this difficult dance-theatre form [butoh] has been growing'.[10] While Hunt found parts of the work challenging, she described the stage images as 'arresting in their simplicity and strangeness. The dream-like images hold one's attention, and at times haunt with a strange duality.'[11]

In 1995 Ponifasio formed his own performance group, MAU, variously known as the MAU Dance Theatre and MAU Company. Christopher Balme notes that MAU 'derives from the Western Samoan independence movement Mau, which in Samoan means "vision" or "belief"'.[12] Lisa Taouma argues that MAU does not strictly conform to definitions of dance:

> In many ways Lemi and Mau are aptly described as a theatre group in the sense that they provide imagery and drama to be interpreted by the viewer, rather than any sort of dance narrative.[13]

The influence of butoh was strong in *Lo`omatua: The ancient mother*, which was 'created in Apia in 1995 with local people'[14] and later performed at various festivals. *Lo`omatua: The ancient mother* featured Ponifasio himself alongside near-naked, shaven-headed male dancers covered with white powder. An evocation of Polynesian legends was mixed with the slow-moving butoh aesthetic, highlighting the rippling muscles and slowly shifting torsos of the dancers in dim light. The work established clear links between the origin of butoh – the nuclear holocausts of Hiroshima and Nagasaki – and the history of nuclear testing in the Pacific. The most memorable of many powerful images was that of a dead fish dangling by the tail from the mouth of each dancer, suggesting the aftermath of the nuclear tests in the ocean.[15]

Anton Carter met Ponifasio in 1996 at the first national gathering of Pasifika artists, which was supported by Creative New Zealand's Pacific Arts Committee:

> There are certain people that are influential purely for their genius. He just said, 'I am Samoan, and I dance, therefore it is Samoan dance.' He didn't have to do cultural Samoan siva to be a Samoan dancer. And he has pretty much achieved everything that he wanted to do back then – not compromising, having a clear vision.[16]

Ponifasio has created international partnerships on a scale unprecedented for a Pasifika performing arts organisation. In 2006 artistic director Peter Sellars commissioned him to create *Requiem* for the New Crowned Hope Festival in Vienna, the official celebration that marked 250 years since the birth of Mozart.[17] MAU has subsequently performed at some of the most prestigious opera houses and arts festivals in the world, including Théâtre de la Ville in Paris, the Prague Quadrennial, the Venice Biennale, Holland Festival, Adelaide Festival, Edinburgh International Festival, New York's Lincoln Center and Santiago a Mil International Theater Festival in Chile.[18]

Ponifasio's remarkable hybrid signature performance style owes as much to Polynesian dance traditions and avant-garde art as it does to a Japanese aesthetic. Pacific slap dance, presented in a de-familiarised way, is a continuing image. In *Requiem*, for example, dancers dressed in shirts and trousers perform gentle slap-dance movements with small puffs of white powder rising from their clothing each time it is slapped. The small explosions recall nuclear testing in the Pacific, the Western clothing evokes colonial history, and the slap dancing suggests the endurance of Pacific culture.[19] The work invites contemplation and reflection while also stimulating the imagination. There is a sensual and pleasurable aspect to entering this world of images, as Sam Trubridge observes when reviewing MAU's *The Crimson House* (2014): 'Ponifasio is a consummate editor, composing these seductive images in such a way that their final meaning always eludes the viewer, but keeps them always in pursuit of it.'[20]

The vā as creative collaboration

The va or the body's intentionality is the foundation of all expression, including dance.
LEMI PONIFASIO[21]

Ponifasio explores complex relationships between the body, light and space, recalling the vā – the Samoan concept that governs relationships between people and things, between bodies and the cosmos. He considers the relationship between light and space to be central: 'Light is like skin, it is living. You can touch the light. The light is activating the space.'[22] His long-term collaboration with lighting designer Helen Todd has lead to work in which mysterious images emerge from a monumental black space, reminiscent of te pō, the night that precedes creation in Polynesian mythology.[23] Todd commented on her lighting design for *Requiem*: '[It] requires a sacred space, for ceremony and remembrance. It requires an edge of darkness that inspires prayer, or reflection on inflicted loss of life. I try to define territorial zones that shift us, hovering between reverence and fear, where humans and even angels should tread only tenderly.'[24]

Todd's reputation was already well established when she decided to focus exclusively on lighting MAU's shows. Ponifasio has said, 'Her brain and my brain have merged.'[25] Trubridge comments, 'The stunning work of ... Helen Todd paints the stage in layers of darkness and soft light with all the confidence of Ad Reinhardt, Francisco Goya, or our own Ralph Hotere.'[26]

The vast black stage has become the dominant image in Ponifasio and Todd's work, a visual representation of vā, or of space itself. Albert Wendt reinforces the connections between Ponifasio's work with te pō and the vā:

> Lemi Ponifasio is a modern taulaitu [spirit medium] who fishes out of the depth of our collective being a haunting primaeval imagery and menagerie of creatures who confront us with their basic truth about body, bone and spirit, flesh, the Ao, the Po, silence that chants, fear and hope, and sight, all connected in the Va-Atoa, the Unity-that-is-All.[27]

Ponifasio himself emphasises the vā in his collaborations. He stresses that MAU is 'a community of relationships':[28] 'The people I invited to work with me have profoundly changed the way I think about things.'[29] He has often collaborated with Māori artists and communities. In 2007 Ponifasio cast the Māori political activist and artist Tame Iti as himself in *Tempest: Without a body*, which Iti orated in te reo. *Stones in her Mouth* (2014), inspired by a poem of the same name by Māori artist Roma Potiki was presented as a community leadership project. For this, Ponifasio invited young Māori women to travel and work 'in the community; in marae, schools and rural areas of New Zealand and the world',[30] holding workshops at marae to write oratory, chants and calls in te reo, which they subsequently performed. *Stones in her Mouth* incorporated traditional Māori performance arts associated with women, such as the poi.[31] While the imagery is unmistakably Ponifasio's minimalist aesthetic, the performers' vocal work speaks powerfully to the strength and resilience of Māori women.

Birds with Skymirrors

I watch Lemi's work for its beautiful images. NATHANIEL LEES[32]

Building on the environmental concerns of his earlier works, Ponifasio's *Birds with Skymirrors* (2010) responds to pollution and climate change in the Pacific Ocean, and is inspired by an image he witnessed on the island of Tarawa in Kiribati, of frigate birds with flashing pieces of videotape in their beaks.[33] Here we examine it in some detail as an exemplar of MAU's work.[34] The ensemble for the 2012 staging at the NZ International Festival of the Arts included seven dancers from Kiribati who first worked with MAU in *Requiem* (2006).

Birds with Skymirrors begins with a long period of darkness accompanied by a low, ominous rumble. This darkness is reminiscent of the vā itself – pure space. We hear a haunting, distant karanga. As the stage is gradually illuminated, we see a space intersected by a huge diagonal beam and hung with giant mirrors, recalling the image of the flashing videotape. A softly lit male torso, gently moving, is sharply contrasted with a semi-naked brightly lit woman, who confronts the audience and chants a karanga in a shockingly amplified voice. This exquisitely slow beginning opens up a space for reflection as well as appreciation of the challenging images.

Suddenly, in a violent interruption to the meditative mood, the mirrors are animated by projected static and intersected by a long line of blinding light. Fully robed Kiribati dancers skate rapidly and silently back and forth across the stage in formation, slap dancing with precise hand movements. A video projection now shows the grainy image of a large frigate bird struggling to lift off from an oil slick, its desperate movements reflected in the gestures of the dancers. Loud, distorted sound effects make the image more horrifying. Repeated during the show, this combination of images and sound ultimately becomes excruciating.

The woman returns, chanting 'tihei mauri ora' (the breath of life), voiced with anger, perhaps reacting against the violence of the image we have just seen, the bird's death-throes in the industrialised post-colonial Pacific. This contrasts with the dimly lit backs of male dancers, slowly rippling in the light. The human body is lit to resemble a landscape, suggesting unity of the body and the earth.

The sound changes to transmissions of the first American moon landing, including Neil Armstrong's 'one giant leap for mankind'. There is an overwhelming sense of irony – that as mankind reaches out to the stars, this planet is itself struggling for survival. The electronic static of the space transmissions contains another sense of the vā – of the space beyond the earth. This segues into a poi routine performed by three elegantly dressed Māori women. The poi spin, creating white circles of light that leave a trace on the retina as they whirl in perfect unison. There is a terrifying squeal, and the women chant rapidly in te reo, their hands making intricate wiri movements suggesting the flapping of a bird's wings.

In a radical change of rhythm, a near-naked male dancer appears wearing a huge green bird mask with a long beak, his thighs adorned with Polynesian tattoos. The masked dancer is reminiscent of the imagery we might expect in a surrealist painting.[35] The male dancers perform a disciplined, seated slap dance, while one of the women sings a waiata. These traditional cultural performance elements provide striking contrast with the surreal image of the bird.

In the final sequence several dancers gently pat poi, causing white dust to fall and cover the stage. The dust resembles smoke as it rises, sand as it falls; it transforms the stage from a solid black surface to a soft white one marked by the dancers' feet, like footprints on a beach.

In combining the avant-garde with Polynesian performance skills such as poi, slap dance, karanga and waiata, *Birds with Skymirrors* creates mysterious contrasts between the natural world – expressed through the body – and a disquieting sense of the terror of apocalypse for nations losing their land to the rising ocean.[36] Although *Birds with Skymirrors* powerfully expresses concerns about the ecology of the Pacific region, the work is not polemical. Rather, it opens up the vā as a space for contemplation.

Ponifasio's influence: 'It's very MAU-ish'

I think Lemi Ponifasio influences all Pacific artists, and the whole Pākehā landscape. I have seen [other] people's work – the costumes, the design, the look and style – it's very MAU-ish. MAKERITA URALE

Lisa Taouma considers Ponifasio 'famous' for 'the poignant imagery created by the Butoh/Samoan style',[37] while American dance scholar Sondra Fraleigh comments that Ponifasio's 'Pacific butoh style is the most prominent butoh in New Zealand'.[38] Examples abound of the influence Ponifasio has exerted on other artists. Playwright Louise Tu`u acknowledges the importance of his support and feedback at a reading of one of her plays at MAU's studio in Henderson,[39] while Vela Manusaute considers Ponifasio to be one of his most important mentors, even though MAU's work is radically different from his accessible musical/comic style:

> I'm intrigued by his work. He inspires me to reach for the depth of the work. I learn a lot from just listening to Lemi talk. He's an orator of the space between him as the creator and the audience. He understands that dark world and what makes us human. He teaches me so much.[40]

Nina Nawalowalo and The Conch: 'A bridge between worlds'

We founded The Conch with a very clear mission – to build a bridge between worlds, between what we knew of Western theatre and what we wanted to come into relationship with in the Pacific; to create pathways for the amazing talent and creativity of Pacific people. TOM McCRORY[41]

Like MAU, The Conch has developed a distinctive aesthetic that is the result of a unique intercultural vision. Based in Wellington, The Conch was founded in 2003 by Nina Nawalowalo and her husband Tom McCrory.[42] The company's trademark style is a fusion of Pacific cultural forms with physical theatre, mime, illusion, dance, music and lighting, informed by Nawalowalo's Fijian cultural heritage and the performance skills and knowledge both partners gained in Europe and Aotearoa. The company's mission includes the aim to develop 'new theatrical languages capable of expressing and advancing the core values of Pacific Island people to a broad theatre audience'.[43]

Nina Nawalowalo was born in Wellington in the 1960s. Her mother was a British immigrant and her father came from the Fijian island of Kadavu to study law in New Zealand. The family spent two and a half years in Suva, Fiji, before returning to Wellington. The young Nina excelled at sport: she captained the New Zealand under-20 basketball team, toured with the New Zealand under-23s, and was named in the New Zealand senior women's team in 1985. However, her passion for sport turned towards theatre as a result of the life-changing impression made on her by mime artist Robert Bennett, her drama lecturer at Wellington Teacher's College:[44]

> I had never seen illusionary mime and adored his classes. He invited me to join his company, Mime International, touring New Zealand schools and Tahiti. We were selected as part of a New Zealand contingent for the World Youth Festival and I travelled with them to Russia and Prague.

Nawalowalo, by now a primary school teacher, resigned from her job, withdrew from the New Zealand basketball team and went to Moscow with Mime International. While touring Russia and Poland she attended conferences and discussions on mime and theatre, and mixed with members of the great Russian mime and clown companies. 'I had been very stimulated by the videos that Robert would show us – like Mummenschanz and Étienne Decroux. But seeing the incredible standard of the greats such as Slava Polunin I got excited and wanted to train in mime in England.'[45]

In London she enrolled at the Desmond Jones School of Mime and Physical Theatre, where she met like-minded artists. With a grant from New Zealand, she studied Mask with commedia dell'arte master Antonio Fava in Italy, Le Jeu and Clown with Philippe Gaulier, and Clown with Pierre Byland in London and Italy. Nawalowalo entered into a seven-year collaboration with magician Richard McDougall,[46] and together they created shows that mixed mime, magic and mask. For a year they ran a weekly cabaret magic evening, 'Ever So Sleightly', at London's Battersea Arts Centre, with magicians and performers from London and beyond. 'Through Richard, I had a wonderful opening into the world of magic and access to the Magic Circle. At that time women weren't allowed in.' Nawalowalo also worked with leading illusion designer and magic consultant Paul Kieve, who she would later invite to collaborate on *Masi*.[47]

In 1994 Nawalowalo travelled to Fiji with her father:

> One of my enduring memories is standing in the waves listening to the beautiful sound of women singing in harmony as they waded out to the reef to fish ... Here in the water was a place where so many dimensions of these women were expressed. The female powers of strength, sensuality and spirit were simultaneously those of the water itself ... I knew that one day I would make a piece of work about this.[48]

Her father's declining health was the catalyst for this journey, which would become a key turning point in her career:

> I had a profound sense that I should come back to New Zealand. I knew that time was short with my father. I'd been exploring a very European style of theatre, and I suddenly wanted to explore my identity, the connection through my father to my Pacific heritage.

By this stage Nawalowalo had met and married Englishman Tom McCrory, a graduate of the Jacques Lecoq school. One of their first projects on arrival back in New Zealand was co-devising and performing in *Swish*, a piece about basketball directed by McCrory at Wellington's Phoenix Theatre in 1998. The all-male cast included actor Vela Manusaute and hip hop rapper Fiso Siloata. 'We were seeking to capture the intensity of sport in the theatre.' Nawalowalo sees strong parallels between sports and physical theatre, a factor that made her the ideal director for Hone Kouka's *The Prophet* (2004), which focuses on teenagers playing basketball. She used a highly physical rehearsal process including ball coordination games:

> I base everything on my love of sport. My basketball coaches, particularly Bill Eldred, are huge mentors of all my theatre work. This has parallels when I direct actors. It's all choreography isn't it, patterns? How one directs the audience's eye around the stage; strategy. The balance of a court relates to the theatre floor.

McCrory became head of movement at Toi Whakaari in 1999; later, Nawalowalo came in to direct Samoan students Jerome Leota and Anapela Polataivao at the school. In 2000, together with Māori student Kayte Ferguson, they created a devised piece at BATS called *He Kore Te Wiwia / A Space Without Boundaries / Avanoa Leai Se Mea O Lai*. The other key collaborator in this work was lighting designer Helen Todd, from whom Nawalowalo learnt a great deal about how she 'explores the connection of body and light. This proved a great inspiration to my work *Vula*.' The piece received excellent reviews, critic Timothy O'Brien describing it as 'a beautiful evocation of the Pacific and one of the year's loveliest productions in every respect'.[49]

Vula: A play of light in a Pacific lagoon

Vula means 'the moon' in Fijian. The moon gave me the narrative as a cycle, the cycle of day to night. NINA NAWALOWALO

Nawalowalo's enthusiasm for experimental light-based physical theatre merged with her memories of Fiji and her training as a magician to create an innovative theatre aesthetic in *Vula*, which premiered at BATS in 2002. After the challenges of *Swish*'s all-male cast, she chose to work with a group of strong female actors.

> Fiona Collins was at drama school at the time [2001], and I was waiting for her to come through. Tausili Mose had already graduated from drama school and had been searching for an authentic way to theatrically explore her Christian beliefs and identity. Gareth Farr [composer for *Vula*] suggested that I meet Susanna Lei`ataua who was just back from New York, and so it was a wonderful combination.[50]

For Collins, being cast in *Vula* was an important career milestone. Born in Lower Hutt, she was raised 'strictly fa`asamoa' by her afakasi parents, and had attended acting classes with Sam Scott and Raymond Hawthorne before being accepted for Toi Whakaari at the age of 30.[51]

In *Vula*, Nawalowalo took her first steps towards creating a rich physical language, drawing on her dual Fijian/European heritage.[52] The production was the result of detailed research and workshopping by the director and cast. Set on an island lagoon and incorporating stories from Fiji, Aotearoa, Samoa and Tonga, *Vula* explores Pacific women's relationship to the ocean. Seeking strong images that pre-date Western stereotypes of Pacific women, Nawalowalo studied the earliest historical photographs in the Museum of New Zealand Te Papa Tongarewa. One image, brought to life in the performance, shows a pre-colonial Samoan taupou, a ceremonial dancer representing the powerful essence of fa`asamoa, holding a nifo oti, a large machete-like weapon. Throughout the performance, contrasting images range from the traditionally topless taupou (Lei`ataua) to a deeply Christian Mose dressed in black to the ankles. While they assume 'characters' such as the taupou and a community of women washing in the lagoon, they simultaneously acknowledge their own identities, using their real names. Early in the performance Collins directly addresses the audience, welcoming them in several Pacific languages. Nawalowalo notes that members of the audience often responded to the actor: 'It's very empowering for Pacific audiences to hear Pacific languages on stage. Their enjoyment of the jokes was wonderful.'

Nawalowalo's magic training in the UK and her years spent performing and teaching with Richard McDougall were a major influence on *Vula*. Designer Tolis Papazoglou ingeniously evoked the lagoon in the small BATS space by building a PVC pool and flooding the entire stage in four centimetres of water, with strips of black PVC hanging behind in an arc suggestive of the strands of a vast grass skirt. This scenography resonates in some ways with the darkness of MAU's aesthetic, but was also governed by the requirements of magic and illusion used in the show. Large woven screens, manipulated by unseen hands, drifted across the pool, revealing new scenes that formed in the water as they passed. Fans appeared to traverse the water like stingrays.

The collaboration with lighting designer Stephen Blackburn was crucial to creating these magical effects. His delicate lighting, informed by Nawalowalo's practice of rehearsing with full lights, was often tightly focused on precise images: a hand caressing the water; flowers floating on the lagoon.[53] Collins enjoyed the experience:

> I have massive adoration and respect for how that woman works. The beauty of Nina and Tom's combo is their training in magic, clown, commedia and mask with their love and passion for the Pacific. That really shaped of lot of what happened in *Vula*.

Water, aided by Blackburn's lighting design aesthetic, was key to *Vula*'s visceral theatricality. The women swam, washed, splashed and floated, their active corporeality heightened by almost every move being extended, dilated or reflected in the pool. They were defined by dynamic activity marked by frequent changes in rhythm, such as the alternating of real time with slow motion in a scene in which they wash laundry in the lagoon. Drawing on Nawalowalo's training in commedia dell'arte, the actors also performed comic routines such as protecting a precious television set from a thunderstorm.

Reviewers were delighted by *Vula*'s physical beauty and sensitively poetic images. Jenny Stevenson found it 'both elemental and Gothic in its dense layering of the natural and the mystic',[54] and John Smythe wrote that 'even breathing is a long, slow sigh that elevates the spirit to languid flight'.[55]

In this first production of *Vula*, Samoan was the only language spoken, the text written by actors Collins and Mose. When it was re-mounted in 2003 at Wellington's Te Whaea Theatre, Nawalowalo cast a young Fijian woman, Kasaya Manulevu, and included Fijian dialogue in the script. Manulevu had also been present when Fijian women coached the *Vula* actors in traditional meke (dance) hand movements.[56]

Kasaya Manulevu was born in the village of Muani on the island of Kadavu, where she participated in the Fijian version of White Sunday. After her mother passed away she was sent to New Zealand at the age of five to live with relatives in Porirua. She recalls watching a variety of theatre performances at school, including a touring production by Pacific Underground: 'I always knew that one day I would somehow be on stage.'[57] Initially Manulevu found rehearsals for

Vula daunting: 'It felt like the whole of drama school compacted into six weeks.' She felt supported by the experienced actors, however: 'I was a little shadow for the three women. They were like my backbone. I learnt so much just sitting on the side and watching them every night.' But there were cultural obstacles to overcome in her journey to becoming a professional actor:

> Speaking with a loud voice is something we don't do. We'd sing loud but not speak loud. If you go to Fiji and if you're a loud person they think you're a disrespectful person. Especially for women ... So I had to break a lot of barriers when I was doing my six weeks of *Vula*.

Another recruit for the second season of *Vula* was Salesi Le`ota, a Toi Whakaari graduate born in Nuku`alofa, Tonga. Nawalowalo had taught Le`ota mask work at Toi Whakaari, and his absolute precision with detail caught her eye. She initially employed him as producer for the show, then trained him as an operator/animator, a skill that he developed in subsequent touring seasons of *Vula* and *Masi*. Le`ota found the necessary precision demanding:

> ... because you have to be so precise and specific and calm under pressure. When you're standing there, centre stage, looking at an audience, no-one can see you. There's a beautiful sequence where Kasaya dances the meke and the women appear from mats. They dance and return to the mats which close magically around them. The imagery is complex and stunning. It has very strong classical allusions to Andromeda and the creation myth of Aphrodite. When we were in Palau, people saw it as being like Rapa Nui moai.[58] Maybe it's like the relationship between Islanders and the sea. The sea's such a monster, but it's also the giver of life. People interpret *Vula* in many different ways, and Pacific Islanders will always find more behind it.[59]

At the 2004 9th Festival of Pacific Arts in Palau, Micronesia, *Vula* was performed outdoors in a school compound. Following a day of torrential rain, the skies cleared for the evening performance. Manulevu recalls, 'the moon came out. We had the pool of water; the rain filled it up. It was a perfect night.'

Like MAU, The Conch has achieved success as an international touring company. *Vula* travelled to the 2005 Christchurch and Auckland arts festivals, the Sydney Opera House (2006) and, in 2008, to the World Music Theatre Festival in the Netherlands and the Barbican Theatre in London. Here, Mose and Lei`ataua moved on to other projects and were replaced by Ngapaki Emery (Māori) and Nora Aati (Samoan). Le`ota recalls the show in the Netherlands:

> A whole contingent of Pacific Islanders came ... and all those people were thousands of miles away from home. Before we went on stage we said, 'Let's just take these people home for an hour.' Before the first scene was over, they were

already cheering. They sang along, it was like a rock show, and at the same time it was deeply spiritual and humbling for us as performers.

Tom McCrory feels that performing *Vula* at London's Barbican Theatre symbolised how much The Conch had achieved thus far: '[It] was a huge moment of arrival – we all shed tears because the women were so moved to be the first of their people to bring their stories to such an internationally acclaimed centre.' Nawalowalo's colleague from her magician days, Paul Kieve, attended the show and was deeply impressed, both by the concept of performing in water and by the company: 'Nina had not only raised a family but had got this theatre company together. It was a huge achievement.'[60]

Masi: 'The land is the soul of a people'

Nawalowalo was ready to move on to a larger project, and re-connecting with Kieve in London was the catalyst for a new collaboration. The growing reputation of The Conch led to a commission for the 2012 New Zealand International Arts Festival in Wellington. She recalls:

> When *Vula* went to Palau we attended the festival opening ceremony where each country made a presentation to the king and queen. The Fijian presentation was a gift of masi cloth. Through the rain, a tall, powerfully built chief carried a very long, beautiful masi towards the king and queen, moving in slow motion. It really was like butoh. Here he was, a huge warrior dressed in masi, and in that moment I thought, that's it, there's a doorway of something I connect to.

This powerful image inspired the creation of *Masi*. Masi is the traditional Fijian tapa cloth made from the bark of the paper mulberry tree. Nawalowalo explains its significance:

> It's representative of a culture and a people. It comes from the vanua, the earth, which is the land, the most precious thing ... The land is the soul of a people. The process of masi making, and masi itself, represents the cycle of life. At birth, the baby is wrapped in a masi, and you take a piece of masi as gifting to the mother. It's used in wedding garments, and the body is wrapped in masi at the end of life.

Masi was two years in development and involved a large team, including Kieve, McCrory, composer Gareth Farr, lighting designer Nik Janiurek and set designer Tracey Monastra. Nawalowalo made two research trips to Fiji, the first with Kieve, the second with Farr. She followed traditional cultural protocols, working through the chiefly line of her family to approach villages to gain the necessary permission to work with indigenous artefacts and knowledge. Although Nawalowalo's mana as a bulou (daughter of a high chief) is respected in Fiji, and taking *Vula* there in 2006 had built awareness of her theatre work, it was still a struggle to obtain legal permissions, as McCrory recalls:

> There's rightly very powerful legal protection around traditional knowledge in Fiji, so it's important to go through the proper protocols to approach people to gain their permission to use their patterns on stage. We had to apply for a permit from the government to go to Vatulele. Nina had to sit down with the minister of cultural heritage and be intensely questioned about what she was doing. Nina had to really tune into the qualities that she carries. And she did it: they listened.

On the first trip Nawalowalo auditioned over 100 Fijian cultural dancers, casting members of the Suva-based Kabu ni Vanua Dance Group. She invited masi-maker Ro Miriama Saunayalewa Tubailagi and vakatara (chant soloist) Peni Jeffrey Lala to perform as themselves in the show. On the second trip, Farr recorded the choir of the Suva Conservatorium of Music singing in a carpark at midnight, to avoid the interruption of traffic sounds. As McCrory notes, 'The sung meke is traditionally chanted facing inwards in a circle. Gareth sat with his recorder in the heart of the circular group, surrounded by sound.' Back in New Zealand, Farr interwove the recordings with his original compositions.

Masi's meaning is conveyed through visual imagery, dance, magic, sound and music, with minimal spoken text.[61] It is a memory piece, blending traditional Fijian imagery with the meeting of Nina's parents, Noa and Mary Nawalowalo, in Wellington at a chess club in the 1950s. At the premiere at Te Papa's Soundings Theatre in March 2012 Nina played herself, her intercultural identity expressed through the bringing together of masi with photography and illusion. The theatre's proscenium arch was covered with 13 metres of masi cloth, which endowed the entire performance with its symbolism and mana. Tubailagi sat downstage making masi; opposite her sat Lala, chanting and playing percussion, their presence framing the space with male and female energies. Nawalowalo evoked family memories by opening an album while photographs of her parents taken by renowned photographer Ans Westra were projected behind her.

As the first of many magic illusions, Nawalowalo assembles a box made of masi panels and conjures a spirit/ancestor figure (Kasaya Manulevu) from the box; Manulevu in turn conjures a seedling from behind a piece of masi. Through a series of illusions this grows into a real paper mulberry tree – one of 40 imported from Fiji for the production – from which a piece of bark is taken. Manulevu then simulates the beating of the cloth alongside Ro Miriama because, as Nawalowalo says, 'it wouldn't be right to have one woman alone'.

The meeting of her parents is represented by a series of filmic 'wipes' (sliding screens) manipulated by hidden animators, techniques that were previously used in *Vula*. The sequence reveals 'photographic' images, inspired by Westra's work, of Mary (Victoria Abbott), Noa (Alexander Tarrant) and Nina, standing, sitting, holding a suitcase or a chess piece, walking across the space, sometimes appearing to pass and miss each other. The suitcase establishes Noa and Mary as immigrants and connects to an earlier sequence in which a small suitcase was opened to reveal a miniature version of Nina's home village in Fiji, complete with a tiny masi tree.

Noa and Mary's courtship is portrayed as an elegantly danced game of chess. In striking contrast, the male Fijian dancers fill the stage with movement, energy and colour. Together with the masi maker and the vakatara, the dancers represent the 'spirit' of Fiji as a dynamic embellishment of the courtship story. Nawalowalo notes: 'There's so much about their physical being which is just like my dad, from their calves to their bone structure.'

Dressed in an overcoat and suit, Noa is connected to his Fijian childhood through a movement sequence created by the waving of large pieces of white cloth, representing both masi and a photograph of Noa in 'windy' Wellington, where his coat was whipped by the wind. The adult Noa interacts with his childhood self (Jerry Vakamoce) and the Fijian dancers. Several large masi fans appear to dance and fly of their own accord. For Nawalowalo, this was a key moment in the production, bringing together 'the traditional, the theatrical, the magical and the spiritual'. Finally, Noa appears wrapped in white masi, signifying his passage towards death. The climax is a stylised representation of Noa's funeral in which his coffin is covered by a large piece of masi and, by means of one of Kieve's illusions, levitates and is made to disappear.

The autobiographical nature of *Masi* brought together all the influences on Nawalowalo's career into a powerful image-based theatre piece, which was later re-worked and toured to the Oceania Centre in Suva and the 2013 Sydney Festival of the Arts.

The Conch's activities have continued to expand since this production, both in mainstream theatre and in the community.

The Conch in Pacific communities

Nawalowalo's mentoring of Manulevu was part of her broader desire to support emerging Māori and Pasifika performance artists. In 2009 The Conch launched a youth development initiative named Conchus, with a season at BATS showcasing three solo works of which one, *Yalewa* (Woman), was co-devised and performed by Manulevu. The others were *Te Mahara* (The Memory), created and performed by Kristyl Neho, and *Some Things Can't Be Healed By Bandages*, co-devised and performed by Princess Te Puea Whioke. Conchus has since grown into a regular training programme for young Māori and Pasifika performers.

In 2013 The Conch received major funding from Creative New Zealand to expand its activities. With the aim of encouraging theatrical development in the Pacific, the group created a women's theatre company in the Solomon Islands, a project partially funded by the European Union. The aim was to 'use theatre as a vehicle for reducing violence against women and increasing women's participation in civil society and peace making'.[62] The result was *Stages of Change* (2013–14), devised by Nawalowalo and McCrory in collaboration with local women survivors of domestic violence. The work was entirely movement-based. Nawalowalo recalls, 'As one audience member said, "You have given the women a voice without saying a word."'[63] The work was performed in Papua New Guinea, Samoa and the European parliament in Brussels, as well as in the Solomon Islands.[64]

Back in New Zealand Nawalowalo and McCrory joined forces with Nathaniel Lees to continue Conchus workshops for Pasifika and Māori youth, and took on Manulevu as a trainee director. Working in partnership with Te Papa since 2014, they provide regular workshops that culminate in annual performances at Te Marae. These shows work with illusion and movement sequences using Polynesian artefacts from the museum's collection, and conclude with a fono (community meeting). As Nawalowalo says, the workshop/performances are designed to empower, 'instilling belief into students of their own mana and that they themselves are taonga'.[65]

The Conch's community connections have led to a more political, issue-based strain in their work. This is demonstrated in *The White Guitar* (2015), their first work based on a written text, co-directed by Nawalowalo and Jim Moriarty. In a move away from The Conch's largely female focus, *The White Guitar* deals with masculinity. It tells the true story of Fa`amoana (John) Luafutu (brother of former Pacific Underground producer Fuarosa Luafutu) and his relationship with his sons Matthias and Malo (the rapper Scribe). The three men co-wrote the script, drawing on material from Fa`amoana's autobiographical book *A Boy Called Broke* (1994), with Oscar Kightley as script advisor. Fa`amoana, who had appeared in Pacific Underground's *Tatau: Rights of passage*, played himself opposite his sons, which brought remarkable authenticity to the performance. Tupe Lualua played Fa`amoana's mother Lupepe, who was a taupou in Samoa famed for her playing of a white guitar. In contrast to the characteristic humour of other Pasifika plays, *The White Guitar* uncompromisingly narrates the difficulties and misunderstandings that result from Pasifika migration to New Zealand. The grimness of the men's stories is balanced with a redemptive quality, highlighted by Fa`amoana's therapeutic playing of his guitar. *The White Guitar* blends Nawalowalo's image-based style with Moriarty's confessional theatre, honed through his drama therapy work in prisons.

New performance languages

Image-based devised work has expanded the aesthetic possibilities of Pasifika theatre. Using similar resources as a starting point – Polynesian bodies and movement, precise lighting and striking imagery – The Conch and MAU have nevertheless produced radically different work: the playful commedia-like celebration of women's work in *Vula* is in stark contrast to the dark, butoh-inspired austerity of *Birds With Skymirrors*. Yet both companies thrive on collaborative relationships and interaction with communities. Both have a strong awareness of Polynesian connections with the earth and ocean, and ecological themes. Both companies have developed a pan-Pacific approach, incorporating influences from a range of Polynesian cultures alongside their international training.

Nina Nawalowalo and Lemi Ponifasio have created unique image-based theatre and new performance languages based on an experimental blend of Pacific and international influences. They have built communities of collaborators around their work, allowing it to develop in scale while maintaining their singular visions. Both have been recipients of Creative New Zealand's Contemporary Pacific Art Award, as well as many other awards. Alongside the success of playwrights like Kightley, Fraser and Rodger, MAU and The Conch demonstrate that Pasifika theatre practitioners are operating at the highest levels of arts practice in Aotearoa and beyond.

7.

Comedy for the kitchen or the lounge?

It's all in the way you approach it. In a family setting there's comedy that happens in the kitchen, where the boys will be boys. And then there's comedy that happens in the lounge, where the elders and the parents and the children are. Jokes you tell in the kitchen you will never tell in the lounge.

ETEUATI ETE[1]

Many Pasifika practitioners had a second outlet for their skills in the form of sketch-based or stand-up comedy that attracted large and appreciative cross-cultural audiences. In this chapter we focus on comedy groups The Brownies and The Naked Samoans (both founded in the late 1990s) and The Laughing Samoans (founded in 2003), and explore the balance of Western and Pasifika influences on their humour with particular reference to fale aitu. While there are some common threads, each group has a distinctive comedy philosophy and practice.

By 2015 only The Laughing Samoans were still performing regularly, with a touring circuit that included New Zealand, Australia, England, the US and the Pacific Islands. They had created and sustained a highly successful and stable comedy platform based on a non-confrontational comic style – what Eteuati Ete refers to as 'comedy of the lounge'. The wide acceptance among Pasifika communities of their particular brand of humour speaks to their objective: to tread a path that sits well with the generally conservative nature of Samoan society while still providing gently satirical social commentary. The Brownies were still appearing occasionally under the auspices of Kila Kokonut Krew (KKK), while The Naked Samoans had transformed into the successful animated television sitcom, *bro'Town* (2004–09). In chapter two we examined the first serious attempt, by Justine and Paul Simei-Barton, to incorporate fale aitu into locally written drama. Both The Brownies and The Naked Samoans embraced the political incorrectness of fale aitu in their work with humour that was often transgressive and confrontational – Ete's 'comedy for the kitchen'.

The Brownies and fale aitu: 'In the moment'

The five-day fale aitu workshop run by Pacific Theatre in 1996 was attended by a wide range of Pasifika practitioners, including young actors Vela Manusaute and Canada Alofa, who formed The Brownies comedy duo in 1997 as a result of their revitalised cultural understanding. Manusaute remembers, 'We were sick and tired of white people calling us darkies.'[2] The group's name also recalls Robert Louis Stevenson's Brownies – the disruptive spirits from Scottish legend seen in Pacific Theatre's production of *Tusitala and the House of Spirits* (1996).[3] The duo's first show, *Fools of the Bacific (FOB)*, toured the country in 1997.

The Brownies – the first Pasifika sketch-based company to perform on stage in New Zealand – were following in the footsteps of the Semisi family from TV3's *Skitz* (c. 1995) and *The Semisis* (1996–97). Sarina Pearson defines the humour of *Skitz* as 'broad and parodic, using physical slapstick as well as pun, double entendre, and plenty of sexual innuendo'.[4] Most significantly, what *Skitz* emphasised was '[fale aitu's] social irreverence and ability to offend everyone equally, regardless of gender, race, or religion'.[5] These characteristics were also evident in The Brownies' skit comedy.

In general terms, The Brownies were vocally and physically aggressive. Characterised by slapstick, high energy and political incorrectness, their humour at times was consciously confrontational and divisive. For example, Manusaute riffed on all the 'skinny Palagi' sitting at the back of the theatre while all the 'big people' were sitting down the front. He pointed out that if there were to be a fire in the theatre, the Palagi could escape but all the 'big people' would be burnt to death.[6] This potentially discomforting challenge to the notional privileged position of the Palagi is common to Manusaute's work. In a solo stand-up routine presented as part of KKK's comedy show *Laugh You Long Time* (2011), he provoked a mocking element of separation:

> This is a Pacific Island comedy show where we educate non-Pacific Islanders – that's the Palagi people and Māori people – about our lives ... We are going to have some rules here tonight, and the reason we have rules is for the Palagi people. When you say rules to the Palagi, they get excited ... It makes them say 'we feel safe here tonight'.[7]

A typical Brownies sketch involved physical violence or the broadest of slapstick using a variety of props. For example, their *Comedy At Its Best* DVD features a cooking show sequence in which Alofa, dressed in a short skirt and high heels, plays a woman called Buck-Teeth; Manusaute plays her sister, Poofter. The pair create an extraordinary amount of mess, chopping cabbages with a machete, squeezing bananas in their fists and pouring copious amounts of cooking oil into a pot. Playing with misunderstanding and mispronunciation, they decide the one missing ingredient is 'pepper' and, with a flourish, produce a sheet of newspaper which Manusaute tears up and adds to the pot.

The second Brownies show, *Faleaitu: House of spirits* (1998), was titled to draw attention to this comedic form as a mainspring for their work. Manusaute has likened fale aitu to his own experience of commedia dell'arte at Toi Whakaari:

> With fale aitu you have to be in the moment. It's the only time when commoners can say what they like about society, and most of my work I believe is fale aitu. When The Brownies did *Laugh You Long Time*, we had a strong feeling about fale aitu. We did similar things at drama school [commedia] but we have our own version. They're no different in terms of energy and objective, they just use different language. So for me, when I talk about fale aitu, the house of spirits, it's magic, it's spiritual.

Even though The Brownies may have felt protected by the aitu, evidently the analogy had not occurred to former New Zealand Labour MP Taito Philip Field (Samoan), who reportedly 'disapproved of the way [*Fools of the Bacific*] depicted Pacific Islanders as drunkards who resolved fights with machetes and a culture in which women beat their husbands'.[8] According to Manusaute, The Brownies came from 'a family line of fale aitu or Samoan comics. It's in our blood, but it's also normal for all Polynesians to laugh.'[9]

Manusaute continued to perform stand-up comedy, although the name The Brownies disappeared around 2012. 'Our comedy was a bit rough, but damn, we were fearless, and we took no prisoners.'

The Naked Samoans: 'It's like the Colosseum'

Me and Dave [Fane] went to see the show called The Brownies. We thought, they're so cool, look at what Vela and Canada are doing. And we thought it might be time to do it again. OSCAR KIGHTLEY[10]

The original Naked Samoans, who emerged fully formed at Wellington's BATS in May 1998, were Kightley, Fane, Shimpal Lelisi and Mario Gaoa.[11] According to Kightley the idea came from Eteuati Ete:

> He came to me and said, 'Wanna do a show at the Laugh Festival?' But then when it came to it ... it was hard for him to take the time off. So me and Dave [Fane] asked Shim [Lelisi]. And he said, 'I'll bring my mate Mario [Gaoa]'. So we got together, and we made *Naked Samoans Talk About Their Knives*.

The title was clearly a parody of Harry Sinclair's film *Topless Women Talk About Their Lives* (1997). Though it bears no direct similarity to the film, and in fact contained neither nakedness nor knives, it shared a common actor – Lelisi. If any comparison may be drawn with the film, it lies in the implied confessional nature of the material, the Samoan title clearly satirising both this and the widespread media stereotype of Pacific Islanders as criminals and 'low lifes'.

Like The Brownies, The Naked Samoans exhibited an aggressive and politically incorrect form of humour. They adhered to the model provided by *Skitz* and *The Semisis*, and sought to 'diminish the prevalent Polynesian stereotype by doing the hardest thing of all – laughing at it'.[12] Critic Susan Budd noted: 'Their fierce convictions are ... expressed ... with glorious, manic and generous humour.'[13] Sima Urale reflects:

> Naked Samoans were out there. Wonderfully offensive in your face ... breaking stereotypes and bringing about an Island sense of humour. Because otherwise, people only knew our story from the six o'clock news. Naked Samoans are actually Islanders laughing at anything and everything, including themselves.[14]

The popular original show spawned a series of sequels: *Naked Samoans Go to Hollywood* (1999); *Naked Samoans: Wake me up before you go go* (2000); *Naked Samoans: The trilogy* (2001); *Naked Samoans Go Home* (2003); and *Naked Samoans Go Home (Again)* (2006). The shows were collectively written by company members. Fane describes the writing process:

> The great thing about writing with Oscar and the other Nakeds is you sit there and say, 'Right, point A is where we start, point D is where we end. How's the best way to tell the story, and how funny can it be?' And then we just throw in our ideas, but most of our ideas come from aspects of our life.[15]

This egalitarian and apparently random writing process often created new comic potential, as Fane recounts:

> I ended up playing the woman only for one reason: I was late to a meeting once ... And they said, 'Right Dave, you're playing Vienna, and doing the mum', and I said, 'Why me? Should be someone else.' And they said, 'Nah, you're late to this meeting.' ... I ended up doing the women parts. And there is something nice about seeing a bearded guy being a 17-year-old girl.

The Naked Samoans' style has been described as 'serious comedy, a maniacal romp through some of the more unsavoury undergarments of our social fabric, a splendid blend of parody, slapstick, burlesque and sheer exuberant idiocy, Samoan style'.[16] Their shows – which often break down into a series of comedy sketches with a loose narrative thread, sometimes with surprisingly serious themes – represent the purest expression of an anarchic spirit in Kightley and Fane's writing careers to date. Their background and experience would not allow them to create empty, frivolous work, however, as Kightley explains:

> ... even though we were trying to get away from all that kind of 'issue' theatre, the stuff that we were doing was all about that. It's just that it was straight-out, puerile, overt comedy. We were making jokes, but about those things that we used to do serious plays about. We still told stories, thanks to all that time in theatre.

A case in point is *Naked Samoans: The trilogy*, a compilation of their earlier shows with some added material that focuses on the subject of domestic abuse. It follows the lives and careers of brothers Vale (Kightley), Valea (Lelisi) and their best friend Sione (Gaoa), who pursue a dream of being big-time entertainers. Under the guidance of their inept manager, Mackerel (Fane), they are reduced to performing gigs such as a concert for 'families against family violence'. Fane – who also plays the brothers' father and, later in the performance, their mother – is less than impressed: 'Can't you see everybody is laugh at you? I never thought I'd see the day that it's official that my two sons and their mate Sione are good-for-nothing morons.'[17] During the course of the show the Naked Samoans die in a slow-motion comedy skit-style car crash and arrive at the gates of heaven, where they are confronted by St Peter (Iaheto Ah Hi), who addresses them as 'a bunch of lying, cheating, racist Samoans'. He holds a large book of their transgressions, which he proceeds to enumerate. 'You stole, you didn't pay at the dairy, you blasphemed, you had poor personal hygiene, you were rude at the Chinese takeaway, you robbed the dairy, not to mention being racist to every single culture that exists.' Unphased by this list of shortcomings, Fane responds, 'We're not as racist as that mad Indian dairy owner Rakeesh – the bloody black curry-muncher.' Later in the performance, Rakeesh (Gaoa) makes a retaliatory tirade against the Samoan people:

> I am not your average Indian shopkeeper, oh no my little coconuts ... The white people always pay their accounts on time, even the Māori people, but the Samoan people are always take, take, take ... Always pay your account you stinking, jandal-wearing, taro-eating, afro-haired, big-nosed people ... Pay your money, you dirty Samoans!

Every outrageous, racist insult uttered in the show triggered laughter of recognition from its multi-cultural audience. Indeed, when *Naked Samoans: The trilogy* played at the Edinburgh Fringe Festival (August 2002), the *Scotsman* critic admitted to 'choking with laughter', suggesting the show 'conveys its cultural message as brilliantly and as effortlessly as its gags', mixing comedy and tragedy with 'effortless bravado'.[18] Karen Stevenson points out the purpose of reclaiming language: 'Utilising and owning derogatory terms, such as the term "coconut", enabled the assertion of an identity at the same time as it questioned the stereotype.'[19]

Kightley and his colleagues were very aware of the degree to which they were challenging the proprieties. As he stated, 'We push the racist stuff to the extreme to highlight how ridiculous it is ... By lampooning everybody equally it makes everyone realise how similar we all are ... I don't think brown people can be racist, speaking politically, because we're not in positions of power.'[20]

There is a slightly worrying aspect to this universal laughter, however. Helena Grehan, citing John McCallum, talks about 'doubled irony', defined as 'the use of "ironic or pre-emptive self-deprecation" in performance [where the performers] operate within the discourses of power but also mockingly embrace a self-deprecating style ... Any attempt to read the level of irony that they are employing inevitably implicates the reader.'[21] Grehan goes on to suggest the spectators need 'time to reflect on the material and to allow the laugher "to die on their lips"'.[22]

Fane considers that they achieved this in their final show, *Naked Samoans Go Home*, which was about suicide.

> [It] was actually an ode to my cousin. She'd killed herself and we thought, why is it happening? Why do Pacific Islanders always, you know ... It's such a horrible thing. And we knew where we wanted to end up, but we didn't know where to start. So we started piecing it together, and we worked towards that moment. We created that great story and people didn't see it coming until the slap in the face right at the end.[23]

Fane adds: 'It's what Bernard Shaw said: "When they're laughing, slip a note of truth in there."'

Naked Samoans: The trilogy includes scenes of extreme domestic abuse, such as when the mother (Fane) first beats her defenceless child (Gaoa) with a hot iron, then engages in a boxing match with him, and finally, while the boy lies cowering on the ground, threatens to beat in his head with a golf club. Kightley notes, 'As an entertainer it's gratifying of course to have such a great reaction in terms of laughter, but it just gets really worrying, especially when they clap along to the mum giving the hiding, or cheer whenever a new thing comes out ... It's really weird, it's like the Colosseum, it's like the Gladiators.'[24] The notion of laughter 'dying on their lips' becomes disturbed if the audience is enjoying the violence without any possibility of reflection. However, Kightley trusted their audiences would choose to reflect later on the implications of what they had seen.

From stage to screen: *bro'Town*

The Naked Samoans spawned *bro'Town*, a highly successful adult animated TV series in which the actors voiced 14-year-old versions of their characters. Kightley explains:

> John Barnett [chief executive of South Pacific Pictures] saw The Naked Samoans and asked [writer] James Griffin to explore a movie treatment for a story that could involve those characters – and then my mate Elizabeth Mitchell thought of animating the characters. *bro'Town* was born.[25]

bro'Town prospered for five seasons on TV3 in New Zealand (2004–09) and has been sold around the world. The show became a popular cultural icon, with guest appearances that ranged from Prime Minister Helen Clark (who made a cameo in each series) to the governor-general of New Zealand, and even Prince Charles. Kightley recalls an occasion on which Clark took Prince Charles to see *Niu Sila* at the Auckland Festival:

> Dave Fane was in [*Niu Sila*], so we got to meet Prince Charles in the dressing room after. Dave asked him to record something, and at first he said he couldn't. And then Helen Clark vouched for us. And he went, 'Ah, all right'. So we went, 'Wow, we happen to have this recording device. Can you please say, "Morningside 4 life?"' We kept it simple.[26]

bro'Town clearly brought the 'kitchen' to television with an anarchic flavour similar to such global cultural phenomena as *South Park* and *The Simpsons*.[27]

Griffin and Kightley also wrote the script for the comedy feature film *Sione's Wedding* (2006), which by 2016 was the sixth-highest grossing New Zealand film.[28] It was released in several other countries, including the US, where it was retitled *Samoan Wedding*. Kightley, Lelisi, Ah Hi and Robbie Magasiva play four young men who are banned from their friend Sione's wedding by the minister (Nathaniel Lees) unless they can meet certain conditions, such as demonstrating their ability to conduct serious relationships with girlfriends. Fane and Gaoa play supporting roles. A sequel – *Sione's 2: Unfinished business* – was released in 2012, featuring the same cast. Both films show young Samoan men in an unflattering light, but are less satirical and provocative than either The Naked Samoans or *bro'Town*.

The Laughing Samoans: 'It's a Laurel and Hardy thing'

Eteuati Ete and Tofiga Fepulea`i have worked together since February 2003, when they performed *Laughing with Samoans* at the Wellington Fringe Festival. They present themselves as guileless, non-confrontational, inoffensive and family-oriented – in other words, purveyors of 'comedy for the lounge'. Early audiences referred to them as 'the Laughing-with-Samoans guys', a name that they abridged and adopted.[29]

Ete's parents were key figures in the Samoan Congregational Christian Church in Newtown, Wellington, and it was through this that Ete met New Zealand-born Samoan Fepulea`i:

> I had always watched Tofiga at church, during youth conferences and stuff, and he was a very funny guy who made everybody laugh. At the end of 2002 he approached me and said he wanted to give comedy a really good shot. And I said, 'Well, I'm doing a show next year, in February, you should just come and open, see how you go.' So he came, he was supposed to do five minutes, it became 10 minutes ... 15 minutes ... 20 minutes ... and I thought, this guy's brilliant. And that's how The Laughing Samoans took off.

The pair attract large audiences throughout New Zealand, Australia, North America, Papua New Guinea, Samoa, Hawai`i and Fiji. They regularly sell out concerts in major cities, including Melbourne, Sydney and Brisbane, and have played in London and in places as remote as Kalgoorlie in Western Australia. While the majority of their audiences tend to be Pacific Islanders, their humour is also widely enjoyed by Māori and Palagi and they have a strong following among immigrant populations wherever they perform. As Ete notes, 'Our comedy is very attractive to migrant cultures. We find a lot of Asians really love what we do because they experience the same problems and they can identify with someone speaking English in their own unique way.' Beyond language difficulties, their comedy sketches touch on many familiar circumstances of daily life for migrants. But first and foremost, their comedy comes from a Samoan perspective.

The Laughing Samoans in performance

What is it that strikes such a chord with people of diverse backgrounds? The Laughing Samoans function as any classic comedy pairing, with Fepulea`i generally the comedian and Ete his straight man. Such pairings, which essentially rely on a 'Dumb and Dumber' combination, trace their roots to the slapstick of commedia dell'arte, where Arlecchino cannily outwits his equally foolish cohort. Like Arlecchino, Ete and Fepulea`i may show mild aggression: Fepulea`i may become vocally aggressive or offer to hit his comic foil Ete for some transgression, but this threat of violence is never actually carried out. Ete sees this form of humour as 'literally slapstick – it's a Laurel and Hardy thing'.

Another element contributing to their popularity is the subject matter. It appeals in the first instance to their strong Pacific Island fan base because it delves into familiar territory such as family relationships, the church, immigration, language and communication misunderstandings. To Ete's statement, 'You are so charismatic', Tofiga replies, 'That is what my inhaler is for.'[30] This misuse of language, along with dogged and outrageous puns, is one of the most common attributes of their work.

In structure, content and character, there is consistency and familiarity from one show to the next. Popular characters reappear frequently: blonde-bewigged Aunty Tala with her high-pitched giggle and deceptively simple flirtatious desires; the schoolboys, New Zealand-born Paul and fobbish Victor; and Suavai, the Pacific's number one Elvis impersonator. Naturally, this repetitive use of characters has not been without its critics. As one reviewer observed, 'They know exactly how to get a laugh. And that is part of the problem. It is just a bit too comfortable.'[31]

The Laughing Samoans create wholesome comedy that the whole family can enjoy. They appear non-aggressive and laid back, particularly in comparison to the high-energy, confrontational manner of The Brownies. They often deliver their sketches while seated on a polished wooden rostrum, a relaxed position that is the direct antithesis of 'stand-up'. There is a gentle old-fashioned formality to their shows: there is never any overt vulgarity or bad language, and every sketch concludes with the two performers standing, one at either end of the rostrum, and bowing briefly. In this way they honour the audience and impart a sense of respect for elders and community – both important considerations in Samoan culture.

The work regularly demonstrates a connection with the conventions of fale aitu, in particular the improvisational element. One recurring performance quirk arises from moments where Ete dissolves into giggles at sly comments made by Fepulea`i. These improvisations are evidently designed to unbalance his scene partner, who will eventually make reference to the need to return to the script, but so regularly does this occur that one might suspect it is a manufactured experience designed to elicit audience empathy and laughs – if not for the fact that Fepulea`i is genuinely funny and mischievous.

Sketches in which they play family matriarchs nod towards the fa`aluma's freedom to mock authority figures. For example, in *Off Work* they portray women sitting in church on White Sunday, proudly watching as their grandchildren present Bible stories. The sketch is immediately recognisable to Pacific audiences, while those not familiar with White Sunday respond directly to the classic comedy trope of two bragging grandmothers playing an escalating game of sly one-upmanship. As the scene develops, pride turns to frustration as the children are deemed to be doing a poor job, until Fepulea`i finally announces in mock threat, 'My poor grandson is just a little bit nervous. You see how his tie is not quite straight, I'm going to straighten it for him.' David Fane recalls his own childhood experience of White Sunday:

> White Sundays – where you say your Bible sayings and you always tell the story of Jesus and do the large overacting acting. There'd be the whole youth group doing it. It was awful. All I remember about it really was that the parents would be sitting there saying, 'Speak louder, speak louder.' And then seeing my father undo his belt and coming towards the front of the church with 'Speak louder! Speak louder!' And so you start screaming, 'Oh! Jesus is a saviour! He's trying to save me from this man with a belt!'

Each Laughing Samoans show has a loose thematic thread. For example, *Off Work* (2006) is based around the subject of seeking work. Beneath the easy laughs that are generated, we sense they are touching on the real desperation of an unemployed Islander. The key sketch is a job interview in which Ete, the eternal straight man, playing the boss, questions Fepulea`i on his suitability for a job in his factory. Fepulea`i plays a complex range of responses – part of the secret of his comic success. As a clown he is cunning, naïve, ignorant, full of hyperbole and excessive praise, and see-saws between low and high status as befits the moment. As the sketch begins, Fepulea`i seeks to please by commenting on a photo of the boss's wife: 'She's very beautiful, she's very lucky, she married a good man, a good humble man, a kind heart, to give the community the job.'[32] He talks about being a matai (local chief), by which means he endeavours to raise his status, and when the boss asks whether this title actually means anything, his bravura reply is, 'Not really, but in my village it means I can have anything I ask for, you know, like a food, a money, a job.' The desperation that underpins his claim is instantly clear. We quickly enter typical Laughing Samoans punning territory (with a social subtext) when it transpires that this is a job for a stock-taker and Fepulea`i announces, 'I've been taking stock for a long time. You come by my house I show you.' As the skit proceeds, he becomes more verbally aggressive. 'I don't like the colour of your voice ... I don't like what you accusate [sic] about me.' The aggression is softened by further comedic interplay when Ete says, 'I started this business from scratch', to which Fepulea`i responds, 'Not my fault you have fleas.'

The Laughing Samoans approach race relations in a less aggressive mode than The Brownies or The Naked Samoans. In *Off Work* they discuss how to avoid being caught as an overstayer, an issue that resonates with the older Samoan population. Fepulea`i explains that one has to pretend to be one of the locals, 'so when the immigration officer knocks at the door, I warm up my vocal chords and I greet them like a local. I say kia ora, and after that we do the hangi – that's where you rub the noses.' Ete gently points out that the correct word is 'hongi'.[33] Fepulea`i claims to be fluent in te reo. Ete, expressing mock concern, asks, 'What do you do if they ask what tribe you are from? Are you Ngāti Porou? Ngāti Kahungunu? What Ngāti would you be?' To which Fepulea`i replies, 'I say to them I am Koko-Ngāti.' This line invariably brings the house down, demonstrating The Laughing Samoans' ability to poke fun at Māori/Samoan race relations in a mischievous and non-confrontational manner.

The cheeky charm of such encounters, which flirt with an underlying sense of desperation mixed with a probing of racial stereotypes, lies at the heart of The Laughing Samoans' technique. It is reminiscent of the work of one of New Zealand's most popular comedians, Billy T. James (1948–1991), whose signature characters were irreverent portrayals of Māori stereotypes that invited laughter – and sometimes criticism – as they trod a fine line between truth and exaggeration. The Brownies claim him as a childhood hero, because, as Canada Alofa notes, 'he dared to poke fun at everyone, especially himself and where he came from. He helped open doors and through basic comedy made all people laugh at themselves.'[34] In similar style, The Laughing Samoans provide a social message that unravels some of the prevailing Pacific stereotypes. As Ete expresses it, 'Comedy really works for me. From a Samoan perspective, it's a much easier way of communicating messages. It's softer. Through laughter, you're able to learn a lot without it going in consciously.'

Returning to Samoa

The Laughing Samoans pride themselves on the positive reaction to their shows in Samoa, which, as Ete points out, is highly conservative. It is quite an art to couch their comedy in terms that do not offend those in community leadership roles.

> One thing that makes our comedy accessible to a lot of people is the fact that I was born in Samoa and Tofiga's parents are so Samoan that he might as well have been born in Samoa, so we bring that sensitivity to it, whereas some of the New Zealand-born comedians don't necessarily look at it through that filter. Our comedy is very different to The Naked Samoans, and our audience is not necessarily their audience. When you see a Naked Samoans show, the audience is probably young Europeans or New Zealand-born Samoans and Islanders, whereas you come to our show it's predominantly Polynesian or Māori, and its children up to the grandparents.

This was not the experience of The Brownies, as Manusaute explains:

> We tried to take our fale aitu to Samoa and it didn't really work for us. What we think works here doesn't work there. I think they were quite biased because they knew we were from New Zealand. They were pretty judgemental of our comedy with 'who are you to come and talk to us about these types of issues'. But it doesn't bother me. I'm not there to please them. I'm an artist.[35]

While all three groups appeal to multicultural audiences, The Brownies and the Naked Samoans performed in a darker, more transgressive mode, and drew a younger urban audience, open to the humour 'of the kitchen'. The Laughing Samoans achieve their objectives by travelling the middle of the road with conservative, teasing humour that allows them to reach all generations and to speak to the largely church-going Samoan population. They specifically cater to a family audience in 'the lounge', and gently open the doors on the tradition of fale aitu to audiences who might never otherwise experience it. There are dangers in generalising about the responses of Pasifika audiences, however. In *Fobulous* (2013), The Laughing Samoans question the homogenising of Pacific cultures with sketches such as 'Dance competition', in which Fepulea`i, using intentionally inappropriate images, teaches Ete how to memorise the distinctive choreographies of the Cook Islanders, Tokelauans and Māori. As Dave Armstrong puts it, 'PI society is as diverse as any other.'[36]

8.

Kila Kokonut Krew: 'From the Pacific we rise'

By the end of the 1990s no major Pasifika company had yet emerged from the suburbs of South Auckland, home to the largest Pacific Island population in New Zealand.[1] In 2002 that void was filled by Kila Kokonut Krew (KKK). From South Auckland to venues in the Pacific Islands, Australia and Scotland, KKK brought a volatile cocktail of entertaining and community-oriented political theatre that proved popular with Pasifika and Palagi audiences alike. As well as theatre productions, KKK produced 12 music albums, a TV skit series and a web series.

Kila Kokonut Krew was founded in a garage in Manurewa, South Auckland, by a group of 13 Pasifika artists. The name is political and playful, suggesting the artistic equivalent of a clan or gang. The abbreviation 'KKK' invokes and subverts the racist ideologies of the Ku Klux Klan, signalling the company's mission to translate stereotypes about Pacific Islanders into a dynamic sense of Pacific creative solidarity. The word 'coconut', originally a derogatory term, has been commonly invoked in Pasifika theatre, and Kila Kokonut Krew similarly reclaimed the word in a provocative act of rebranding.

The artistic leaders of KKK were Anapela Polataivao and Vela Manusaute, who live in South Auckland with their three children. In 2014 Polataivao and Manusaute jointly won a prestigious New Zealand Arts Foundation New Generation Award, putting them in the same company as Man Booker prize-winning author Eleanor Catton and filmmaker Taika Waititi. The New Generation awards are designed to recognise 'younger minds [who] are driven by a boundless sense of optimism and approach every day like it is their creation'[2] – an accolade that sums up the achievements to date of this dynamic couple.

Anapela Polataivao: 'I didn't have the typical Samoan upbringing'

Polataivao was born in 1973 in the village of Vailoa in Western Samoa and migrated to South Auckland with her family when she was five. She spoke no

English when she arrived and had to learn quickly to fit in at school. 'I remember my mum saying to me on the plane, "if anyone asks you anything, just say please and thank you", so of course that's all I remembered.'[3] Polataivao began acting in White Sunday performances at the age of eight and credits her family for being supportive and encouraging her interest in theatre.

> My grandfather is from Fagae`e. I acknowledge him in all I do because he was an extraordinary being. Where I am today is because of him and my parents. Both my parents are from Samoa. They're still very much Samoan, and they're free thinkers as well. I didn't have the typical Samoan upbringing. My upbringing was actually quite liberal.

Like the Urale and Muagututi`a sisters, having progressive parents gave Polataivao the freedom to move beyond boundaries imposed on other Samoan children. By the age of 15 she was at Otahuhu College and auditioned for the Maidment Youth Theatre (later Massive Company), run by director Sam Scott. After three shows with this company she was cast by Justine Simei-Barton in Pacific Theatre's *Voices on the Wind*. She was acutely aware that the performing arts world was far removed from her life in the suburbs.

> My family was not well-off. My parents struggled. They were working factory jobs, 12-hour shifts, every single day. It was tough. Sometimes, real tough. And then they had this kid, myself, who wanted to go and do this thing [acting], and wanted bus fare, every single day, for nine weeks of the summer holidays, to bus into town and back to Manurewa. We had no phone, and rehearsals would finish about four or five so my father would have to time it. He would walk from home to the bus-stop, which is out on the main road, to wait for me. They would ask, 'How was your day?' I struggled to articulate 'the day' for them to understand.

Her work with Maidment Youth Theatre and Pacific Theatre inspired Polataivao to apply for Toi Whakaari, although her first audition was unsuccessful:

> That got me back to reality. I worked in cafés and got involved in other stage productions as I waited to re-audition. After being accepted, I remember during a formal introduction being asked where in Auckland was I from, and because I said South Auckland, their response was, 'Wow, is that like *Boyz n the Hood*?' I said, 'Yes I am, that's where I'm from, I'm from the hood.'

From 1998 to 2000 Polataivao lived in Wellington where she embraced the training at Toi Whakaari. In her first year she was inspired by Robert Lepage's production of *The Seven Streams of the River Ota* at the International Arts Festival: 'That was epic. The experience was totally magnificent and satisfying.' She was drawn to devised, political, physical theatre like that of French director Ariane Mnouchkine. This led to a highlight of her time at drama school: devising her own show in her third year with fellow students, Kayte Ferguson and Jerome Leota. Together they raised funds to pay Nina Nawalowalo and Helen Todd to be their mentors. The result was the well-reviewed *He Kore Te Wiwia / A Space Without Boundaries / Avanoa Leai Se Mea O Lai*.

> We had nine weeks to devise this piece. Nina and Helen led us to a space of wonder and fulfilment. Like the title of the show, it really was a space without boundaries, rich and layered, magical and musical, exquisite lighting with defining moments of language and culture.

After drama school Polataivao was cast by Christian Penny in the Duffy Theatre company, created by author Alan Duff as part of his campaign to encourage reading for children. She toured schools throughout the country for six months until she became pregnant with her first child.

In 2003 she and Goretti (Letti) Chadwick travelled to New York to perform in *Island Divas*, an intermedia performance created by Samoan filmmaker Lisa Taouma. This was part of the exhibition *Paradise Now? Contemporary art from the Pacific*, curated by the Asia Society Museum and featuring the work of 15 artists from New Zealand and the Pacific Islands.

> *Island Divas* were Letti, myself and two fa`afafines, Siaosi Mulipola and Edward Cowley. Maybe you know them as Buckwheat and Sha-ne`ne. As a woman on stage with these two, how can you compete? You can't. Once they hit the stage, you're suddenly chopped liver.

Since then Chadwick and Polataivao have collaborated regularly. In 2011 they created the comedy duo Pani and Pani. These characters featured in sketches on the Pasifika television show *Fresh*, and in 2013, in a cross-over relationship, they presented special guest 'Aunty Tala', played by Laughing Samoan Tofiga Fepulea'i, in an 'agony aunt' skit. In addition, they both performed in ATC productions like *My Name is Gary Cooper* and *Where We Once Belonged*, and have leadership roles at PIPA. Polataivao has a busy acting career independent of her work with Kila Kokonut Krew. This includes a major role in the TV series *The Market* (2005), an adaptation of *Romeo and Juliet* set around the Otara markets that also featured Chadwick, Nathaniel Lees and David Fane. She played the lead role in Zia Mandviwalla's short film *Nightshift* (2012), giving a moving performance as a homeless mother working as a night cleaner at Auckland airport while caring for her children in a car parked nearby.

Polataivao's diverse skills have fed directly into her work with KKK as director, writer, producer and actor.

Vela Manusaute: 'The first Niuean to graduate from drama school'

Vela Manusaute is an actor, playwright, director, producer, comedian and musician who moves freely between theatre and other media. As a performer he radiates intense energy, while his writing balances anarchic comedy with a political edge. Manusaute was born in the village of Mutalau on the island of Niue to a Niuean mother and Samoan father. He associates Niuean society with the freedom he feels as an artist: 'Samoa has the Matai, chiefly things, and Tonga's got the royalty. So if you look at their arts, it's also bound by those rules ... in Niue there is culture, but there's no hierarchy.'[4]

The family migrated to New Zealand in 1979 when Manusaute was nine. His politics as a writer have been fuelled by his thoughts about his parents' migratory experience:

> ... why did my parents leave Niue? Most of the stories that I tell are about trying to find the milk and honey dream, because I think New Zealand lied to us about it. They opened the floodgates for our people to come here back in the early 70s. Every Islander finds hardship here.

Polataivao echoes these thoughts: 'My family bought into that too. Did we gain or lose, or are we floating in between?'

Manusaute grew up in Ponsonby and moved to Orakei in his teens. Like Polataivao, he was enthusiastic about acting from an early age:

> I was a small kid ... I couldn't fight the bigger kids, so the only way to survive was to entertain them by telling jokes, re-enacting karate movies in the school playground, or being the funny kid in the class. In intermediate I won an award for playing some silly character at school camp. I dressed up and did some funny dance and everyone was laughing. It was that laughter of accepting, being part of something that I loved, and my teacher saw something and she said, 'You should do drama.' But no one wants to do drama because all the white kids were doing drama, and I was the only brown kid there. But I performed, and I loved the freedom and I loved the laughter and I loved the people saying, 'Hey, that was good!'

At Selwyn College he performed in many plays including Bruce Mason's *The Hand on the Rail*, and was supported by his drama teacher June Renwick: 'She's always been the woman behind pushing for me to get there – she told me it was going to be hard.'

High school drama led to further inspiration to become an actor: 'We took the day off to see a matinee of *The Rover* at the Mercury Theatre and Michael Hurst was playing.[5] He's brilliant. What I remember was his energy. I met him later on and I kept saying, "You're my idol."'

After leaving school Manusaute auditioned for Justine Simei-Barton's production of *The Nine Night* (1989). It was the beginning of a long association with Pacific Theatre. He was hungry to be an actor, and attended workshops and acting classes and took every opportunity to watch plays. Cast as a soldier in Shakespeare's *Richard III* (directed by Paul Gittins and starring his 'idol' Hurst), he realised that he had to make a more radical move to advance his career. 'I was surrounded by these older actors, and I asked them, "How do I get to where you are?" ... and they said, "You must go to a drama school."'

Manusaute's first auditions for Toi Whakaari were not successful, but he was determined to train at the national school.

> The only reason I wanted to go to Toi Whakaari was because it had 'New Zealand' on it. I tried four times to get in. Three times they said, 'No – too angry, can't speak English'. Even the former director of the school told my drama teacher to 'tell that boy to stop auditioning, he's not going to get anywhere in drama'. I don't give in easily. I also changed my name, I was born Brian Bird. Vela is a character from Albert Wendt's poem *The Contest,* the last play that we did before I went to drama school. In the play Vela was a fighter. I wanted his spirit; I wanted to go into drama school as a full Pacific Islander. So I changed my name and I went in there. When I came out of drama school I was so proud of myself, the first Niuean to graduate from drama school.

After graduating in 1995 Vela moved back to Auckland where he formed The Brownies with Canada Alofa. Writing comedy sketches led to the realisation that he wanted to be a playwright: 'Jean Betts [Playmarket's script advisor at the time] told me, "Write from your heart. Say what you've got to say. Don't be afraid." "Don't be afraid," I said, "are you sure? Cause I'm dangerous, I'm going to come out fiery." She goes, "Just write honestly."' Responding to Betts' encouragement, Manusaute wrote his first play, *Taro King*. He acknowledges the contribution of Christian Penny, hired as a dramaturg to help develop the script: 'It was one of the scariest things I did. I was put in the middle of the room and asked questions that I couldn't answer. I had no idea, but in my heart I wanted to be a writer and tell my stories.'[6]

Taro King was produced under the banner of Island Players, formed in 2002 by Manusaute, Polataivao, Oscar Kightley and Teuila Blakely. Polataivao recalls: 'That was precious, that we were able to come together for that very brief moment. We always knew Oscar was gonna go. Oscar became extremely busy. He was taking flight.' *Taro King* premiered with *Island Girls* (co-written by Kightley and Blakely) at the Maidment Studio Theatre.[7] Both plays used comedy to open up the audience to serious themes. *Island Girls*, which marked the acting debut of Pua Magasiva, younger brother of Robbie Magasiva,[8] showed the darker side of a Pasifika love story between Jordan (Magasiva) and 'the ultimate Island girl' Leilani (played by Blakely). Francis Till called it 'an unvarnished window that opens into the real, deeply conflicted world of New Zealand's Samoan women and their suddenly fragile men, all trying to adjust to their new home without losing everything that went before'.[9]

Based on Manusaute's experiences of working in an Otara supermarket, *Taro King* was co-directed by Manusaute and Polataivao with a cast that included Goretti Chadwick and Aleni Tufuga. The fast-paced comedy begins with supermarket manager Sammy welcoming the audience to the 'Garden of Eden',[10] where marketing imperatives – 'sell that taro!' – rule. The narrative arc spans the two months of the Fijian military coup in 2000, inviting us to draw comparisons between that period of unrest and the world of the supermarket. There are many energetic set pieces, such as the hard-sell 'five-minute specials' presented by sales girls Lavinia and Moana wearing 'the best Las Vegas showgirl style outfit that Otara can buy',[11] and sequences where Samoan Filipo and Fijian Indian Raj are cutting taro ready for sale. As in many Pasifika plays, duty to family is an important theme. Filipo is ambitious to become a manager in order to improve life for his wife, son and extended family. He faces an unsolvable dilemma since, despite the fact that he always talks about Samoa and the life there, he recognises how hard that life was and sees New Zealand as a land of opportunity for his son – despite his own inability to rise beyond the rank of supermarket taro cutter. In act two, Filipo's dreams are specifically located in the ambitions of his nephew Vegi, a boxer and a 'son of Samoa ... Just like the great David Tua hailed from Mangere, South Auckland, you too, Vegi, will tread the same boxing path!'[12] But the seeds of a fall from grace are sown when a superhero welcome sequence for Vegi ends with him falling to the ground, drunk.

Despite the celebratory tone of *Taro King*, it contains an inherent pathos. Raj ultimately chooses friendship with Filipo over his allegiance to his own people in Fiji. 'I don't trust them, man, too dangerous. They might have another coup tomorrow. I trust you, uso [brother].'[13]

Taro King was enthusiastically received and, once KKK was established, became a core part of the company's repertoire. After its 2004 season at BATS Manusaute received a Chapman Tripp nomination as best playwright. In August 2012 KKK staged a revised version at the Mangere Arts Centre as their 10th anniversary production; in the same year, *Taro King* became Manusaute's first published play, one of four works chosen for Playmarket's Pasifika anthology *Urbanesia*. Reviewer Johnny Givins praised the 2012 production in which Polataivao perfectly captured 'Samoan mother love, humour, aggression and passionate materialism'.[14] Manusaute played Sammy, as described by Givins: 'Wearing a wild Fijian wig he is a super salesman, a selfish aggressive boss, a sympathetic friend and a con artist. He is pulsing with high-voltage energy, demanding and uncompromising in his manipulation of his staff.'

KKK: 'From the Pacific, we rise'

After *Taro King*, Manusaute and Polataivao decided to form a company to address the lack of work for Pasifika actors. As Polataivao notes, 'we had to create the work ourselves. We deeply understood the importance to do so – for support and networking, and developing us artistically on a much higher level.'

KKK evolved as a collective of artists, but the core was the 'tight five', the artistic and administrative hub of the company: Manusaute and Polataivao (the directors), Stacey Leilua, Aleni Tufuga and Glen Jackson.[15] Leilua and Tufuga had both appeared in *Shortland Street* and in ATC's production of *The Songmaker's Chair* (2003). Leilua is a graduate of Unitec's acting course, and her CV includes the feature film *Love Birds* (2011) and the short film *Tatau* (2012). She held various administrative roles in KKK, including producer. Tufuga's work includes Leilani Unasa's *His Mother's Son* (theatre), *Outrageous Fortune* (television) and feature films *Sione's Wedding* (2006) and *The Tattooist* (2006). Glen Jackson was KKK's musical director and producer of their music albums and videos. The company remained true to the original vision of a support network: they aimed to raise the professional profile of Pacific artists in South Auckland, to develop diverse roles for Pacific women in the arts, and to encourage and mentor new and emerging Pacific artists.[16] Their optimistic ambition is summed up in the motto: 'From the Pacific, we rise.'

KKK's first production, *Playaz Night* (2005), premiered at the New Zealand Comedy Festival in the Auckland Town Hall. Written and directed by Manusaute, it was described in publicity material as 'a paradisical feast of chocolate boys and honey-eyed girls … [a] rare and hilarious hip hop-comedy-strip show'.[17] Polataivao recollects, 'We were on a roll. Our audiences were coming out of their homes and into the theatre, which was so encouraging and heartening.'

Once Were Samoans: 'Afakasi with Māori blood'

Taro King and *Playaz Night* were soon followed by *Once Were Samoans*, also written by Manusaute. This was widely performed between 2006 and 2010, including two appearances at Auckland's International Comedy Festival and a season at the Pasifika Spectacular Festival in Brisbane (2010), and won Best Ensemble Acting at the 2009 Auckland Theatre Awards.[18] *Once Were Samoans* was in part a parody of the hard-hitting movie *Once Were Warriors* (1994), which had done much to cement clichés of South Auckland as a crime-ridden gangland in the public imagination. Manusaute describes the play:

> *Once Were Samoans* was about half-caste Samoans, afakasi, with Māori blood. No one talks about those types of stories, you know? And the mother came here and she finds out at the end that most of her kids are from different fathers, and the father ran off because he was Māori ... it's about growing up in South Auckland, a solo mother trying to control her kids.

In the play, the Tufifi family – a solo mother and her six adult children – prepare for a reunion. Mama Louisa (Polataivao) rules her offspring with 'an iron fist and a rubber jandal',[19] and conflict arises when her daughter Moa (Leilua) begins a romance with Taihape Morgan, the smart Māori golfer next door. *Once Were Samoans* undermines racism and prejudice through heightened comic situations. John Smythe identified a 'Samoan/Niu Sila "Kommedia" style that has evolved from its Pacific Underground roots through the Naked Samoans', and enthused that KKK were 'superb exponents' of this style.[20]

A mark of the growing respect for KKK was an unexpected invitation in 2006 to perform *Once Were Samoans* at Ngaruawahia as part of the entertainment for the coronation of the new Māori king, Tuheitia Paki. Manusaute recalls,

> I'd never been to Ngaruawahia. It's huge! With thousands of people there, and all ready for us. I'm thinking, 'Oh shit, we're the last ones to come on!' But we went up there, did our best, and they loved it. And then people started taking us seriously. Because I think people were afraid of what we had to say. They're not comfortable. Laughing Samoans is comfortable, you can be safe. But when you come see a Kila Kokonut Krew show, you know you're going to be sitting there thinking 'something's going to happen here tonight', and something will happen.

Polataivao recalls: 'I'd always seen our audience as brown because I was creating and serving theatre for them, for us.' But when the play was performed in Rotorua and Hamilton the audience was predominantly white. The recognition that KKK's style could reach out beyond Pasifika communities to attract more diverse audiences fuelled the company's development. *Once Were Samoans* confirmed their signature style: fast-paced politically incorrect comedy with a moral and political heart, distinguished by tightly directed ensemble acting and frequent use of music and song.

Four Women: Supporting a new generation of artists

In 2010 KKK initiated Kila Theatre Creatives, a mentoring programme for emerging Pasifika artists. In that year three young writers presented their work to an audience under the label Young Kila Writers. From this process one play was selected for a full production: *Four Women*, by Leilani Esmae Sieni Salesa. It was the first time the company had produced a non-KKK writer's work.[21] *Four Women* demonstrated KKK's commitment to encourage new writers and bring original Pasifika stories to the stage, while the play's female focus fitted perfectly with the group's mission to foreground Pacific women in the arts. It was produced in partnership with Palmerston North's Centrepoint Theatre in February 2011 and directed by Manusaute, using a simple staging with a multi-purpose clothesline and two boxes. The play featured Leilua and Polataivao as a Samoan teenager (Woman One) and her aunty, with Tavai Faasavalu as a minister.

As in all of KKK's work, serious themes in the play are conveyed through exuberant comedy. Questions are raised about how beauty is perceived across different cultures when Aunty encourages her niece, with her size 11 feet, to enter the Miss Samoa beauty contest. According to Leilua, Woman One is 'confrontational, she goes against stereotypes, she's very much against ... anything that has a whiff of the normal, which is a refreshing new character to be seen on the Pacific stage'.[22] Reviewer John Ross noted: 'There's a marvellous episode in which Woman One, as a school-kid, exploring a butcher's shop's vile-smelling rubbish bin, finds unexpected wonder and beauty in an eye[ball].'[23]

Kingdom of Lote: A full-length Tongan play

KKK's mentoring programme led to the company producing *Kingdom of Lote* in 2011 at the Mangere Arts Centre. This was the first play by Suli Moa, a New Zealand-born Tongan actor/writer who graduated from Toi Whakaari in 2009, and the first full-length Tongan play to be performed in Aotearoa by a full Tongan cast.[24] Directed by Manusaute and Polataivao, the production was a celebration of Tongan culture; a magnificent feast was provided for the opening night audience, which included a pig on a spit and other Tongan delicacies such as raw fish, taro leaves stuffed with corn beef and dumplings.[25]

Kingdom of Lote is written in Tongan and English and focuses on a Tongan family presided over by Lote (Sesilia Pusiaki), who exerts pressure on her son Saia (played by Moa) and daughter Sela (Maile Finau) to succeed in the Palagi world. The play thrives on sibling rivalry and features several lively arguments between Sela and Saia. Lote is overcome with pride and expectation when Saia wins a rugby scholarship to attend a prestigious private school, but Sela struggles to compete: Lote shows no interest in her daughter's invitation to speak at a young leaders' forum at parliament. Lote gives Sela a beating, and Saia has to pull out of rugby after being injured in a selection game, after which Sela defies her mother and leaves home. The final scene shows her delivering her speech at parliament.

The play has similarities to Samoan works like *Fresh off the Boat* – we see a younger generation rebelling against parental pressure, which has been heightened by the experience of migration to New Zealand. Gender themes are also prominent as Lote favours her son's career over her daughter's.

The tensions between Tongans' perception of their homeland and the advantages of living in a democracy in New Zealand give a fresh political dimension to Moa's drama. *Kingdom of Lote* contains many references to Tonga, especially in speeches by Lote's brother Krak, who questions Sela's idealised view of Tonga and reminds her of the pro-democracy riots that destroyed much of Nuku`alofa's business district in 2006. While Sela voices pride in the fact that 'we have never been conquered in the whole of the Pacific ... [Tonga is] the only Pacific monarchy left standing',[26] Krak is highly critical of the Tongan king and argues that it is much better to live in New Zealand.

Producing this full-length Tongan play was another milestone for KKK, as was launching the writing career of a new Pasifika talent; in 2013, Moa won the Emerging Pacific Artist Award.[27]

***The Factory*: The 'milk and honey dream'**

While the company continued the work of promoting young playwrights, they also premiered new plays by Manusaute about his Niuean heritage: *My Father's Hands* (2013), co-written with Stacey Leilua, and *My Name is ... Pilitome* (2014). The latter, a comedy in which a New Zealand-born Niuean visits his parents' homeland, received a warm reception when it was performed in Niue in 2015.[28] Alongside Dianna Fuemana, Manusaute has made a significant contribution to Pasifika theatre by bringing Niuean stories to stages in Aotearoa. His largest-scale work to date is a musical homage to the migration experience of his parents and their generation.

> *The Factory* was inspired by a conversation I had with my mother years after my father passed away: 'When are you going to do something for your father? He worked hard for you kids.' A week later at a KKK meeting I said, 'We are going to do a new work, bigger than all the works we've done before and it's going to be a musical!' The look on my team's face ... VELA MANUSAUTE

According to Polataivao, the motivation behind *The Factory* came from Manusaute's perception of their parents and grandparents as 'the forgotten generation in New Zealand history... it was a tribute and celebration of them, for them. Because we are their sweat and tears, their "milk and honey dream" and we exist because of them.'

The Factory – A Pacific musical is a tribute to all Pasifika people who made the difficult transition to Aotearoa in the 1970s, and translates those experiences into a full-scale musical. It was a big step up in terms of moving into mainstream performance venues, international touring and attracting funding, and marked the first occasion on which KKK received a large grant from Creative New Zealand. It had its world premiere in a four-week sell-out season at the Mangere Arts Centre in 2011. A new production with a revised script was presented at the 2013 Auckland Arts Festival alongside international productions from France, China, England, Scotland and Colombia.

Although many Pasifika plays feature songs and music, *The Factory* was the first work to use the full conventions of musical theatre, whereby much of the narrative and emotion is developed through song. Samoan stage and screen composer Poulima Salima created a fusion of musical styles, including gospel, funk, soul and rap mixed with the rhythms of Pacific drumming. Manusaute feels the music supported a spiritual dimension to the performance: 'The opening of *The Factory* was a Niuean song, but it was calling all the gods, the release of the spirit, to bless this house because we are about to release our souls to the audience.'

In the 2011 version the narrative follows a Samoan family who move to Auckland after the devastating tsunami of September 2009. They are employed in a factory run by a tyrannical Samoan who has no qualms about exploiting workers from his own culture. The show contains a critique of Islanders who sell out to the New Zealand hegemony, and the Samoan boss is portrayed as someone who fails to 'represent' his culture. Reviewing the show in the *Herald*, Paul Simei-Barton saw the journey from the islands to the city as a pilgrimage of Biblical proportions, a parallel to 'the Old Testament journey to the Promised Land', while the factory jobs that greeted the Islanders subjected them to 'a modern form of slavery'. He had unreserved praise for the form and content of the work: '*The Factory* demonstrates that musical theatre is the ideal form for expressing the heightened emotions and indomitable optimism of the immigrant story.'[29] Reviews stressed the energy and polish of the musical routines, and also commented on the political themes, such as the use of several generations of Pacific Islanders as cheap labour.

Selection for the 2013 Auckland Arts Festival signalled mainstream acceptance for the company. Their political voice could now be heard in the centre of the city at Queen Street's Q Theatre, where they played to culturally diverse audiences. For this production KKK completely re-worked *The Factory*, and internationally acclaimed Māori musician Tama Waipara joined Salima as musical director. The new script was set in 1974 at the height of Pacific migration to New Zealand.

Re-framing the story as a period piece allowed the company to revisit perceptions of New Zealand's attitude to Pacific migration in the 1970s, and strengthened the politics of the work.[30] The 70s was the period of greatest conflict over the issue of Pacific migration, and the era of the controversial dawn raids, already dramatised by Oscar Kightley and Pacific Underground in *Dawn Raids*. These are alluded to in the 2013 script in a song about overstayers, during which policemen appear and examine the workers' passports.

An emphasis on the history of racism in New Zealand is an important tenet of Manusaute's writing. In the later version the factory boss (Mr Wilkinson, played by Ross Girven) is no longer Samoan but Palagi, reflecting the realities of the earlier time frame. He is portrayed as a melodramatic villain who views the Islanders as 'monkeys', exploits his low-paid workers and refuses to provide them with basic amenities. According to Manusaute, Wilkinson's stereotypical racist comments were taken verbatim from white interviewees in 1970s documentaries.

The Factory (2013) begins with a medley of Niuean and Samoan song. Father and daughter, Kavana (Aleni Tufuga) and Losa (Milly Grant-Koria), leave Samoa to travel to New Zealand where they take up jobs in Wilkinson's clothing factory, the workforce of which is composed entirely of Pacific immigrants. Because he cannot pronounce their names, Wilkinson re-names Kavana as Kevin and Losa as Lucy and informs them that only English is to be spoken on the factory floor. The two Samoan newcomers swap their colourful lavalava for grey smocks and overalls and express their shock as they sing 'leave your dreams at the door'. The pressure rises when Wilkinson reduces the workers' breaks so as to fulfil a big order, and faulty wiring causes the lights to blow. A union representative, Mose

(Taofia Pelesasa), tries to stir up the workers to take action for better working conditions, but his efforts are futile since the migrants are fearful of losing their jobs and being deported. Although Mose dresses like Che Guevara, suggesting a revolution to come, he becomes instead the factory foreman: this is a theatre of resistance rather than revolution.

Broadway-style song and dance routines are interspersed through the narrative, but some of the most powerful scenes feature traditional Island cultural practices. In one sequence, Losa nostalgically recalls Samoa. As she sings in Samoan about her memories of the islands, the cast appear in lavalava and enact stylised ceremonial actions: one group drinks kava; a man receives a tatau; Kavana becomes an orator. The sequence highlights the elegance and dignity of the rituals. Stacey Leilua says, 'It's the traditional moments that the audience responds to the most. You can hear them going really quiet at those points.'[31] The moments where untranslated Island languages are used are often the most theatrically potent.

Respect for Samoan ritual and culture is the key factor in the musical's climax, when Wilkinson is accidentally electrocuted by faulty wiring. Given the melodramatic representation of his racist invective, there could have been cheers or laughter from the audience as the villain is killed by his own failure to provide a safe working environment, yet the abrupt change in rhythm at this point created the opposite effect: there was a stunned silence as the audience waited for the workers to react. After a significant pause, with slow and beautiful choreography the workers, singing a Samoan hymn with exquisite harmonies, respectfully carried the corpse offstage in a stylised representation of a funeral. This moment reinforces the respect for the dead in Samoan culture, endowing the workers with dignity and integrity as a powerful balance to Wilkinson's oppressive workplace practices.

The final song ends with the line, 'my life started at the factory', suggesting that for these migrants there is no going back to the Islands, that the factory is their new reality; the joyful exuberance of the music signals their determination to survive and succeed in Niu Sila. The factory has become an extension of Samoan family and societal structures.

The musical celebrates and interrogates the power struggles between several generations of low-wage workers and their employers, encouraging a sense of empathy with the migrants. Reviewer Janet McAllister called *The Factory* a 'triumph for the Kila Kokonut Krew'.[32]

The Factory web series

In 2013 KKK worked in partnership with producers Janet McIver and Robin Scholes, scriptwriter Michael Bennett and director Joe Lonie to adapt *The Factory* into a web series.[33] The project broadened their interface with Pacific communities: while half the actors employed were professionals, the others were first-time actors recruited through auditions conducted in South Auckland locations such as supermarkets and schools. Online viewers were able to post on blogs, extending the sense of community involvement, and the series included blogs ostensibly written by the fictional characters, which provided insights into their future ambitions.

The Factory web series returns the action to the present day and focuses on three generations of the Saumalu family – grandfather Tigi, parents Kavana and Lilly, and their teenage children Tavita, Losa, Moana and Billy. Tigi, Kavana, Lilly and Tavita are employed at the same South Auckland factory, illustrating, as in the musical, that the workplace becomes an extension of family life and of the migrant community. The narrative highlights conflicting intergenerational cultural expectations.

The KKK legacy

In 2014 *The Factory* toured Australian venues from Adelaide to the Gold Coast, attracting large audiences that included many Pasifika people. It made one reviewer 'long to hear more of these authentic Islander voices'.[34] From Australia the company went to the Edinburgh Fringe Festival as part of the NZ at Edinburgh season, an initiative that showcased New Zealand arts and featured strong Pasifika representation such as Victor Rodger's *Black Faggot* and Lemi Ponifasio's *I Am*. Houses in Edinburgh were disappointing, however, and many reviewers failed to understand the cultural significance of the work.

Shortly afterwards KKK was wound up. Polataivao and Manusaute moved on to other projects: they created a new umbrella organisation with Stacey Leilua – Halamoana (the way to the ocean) – and worked with Rodger's new company FCC (Flow, Create, Connect).[35] In 2015 the couple co-directed Rodger's *Girl on a Corner*, which had a sell-out season at the Basement Theatre. This was followed at the same venue by FCC's inaugural production, *Club Paradiso*, directed by Manusaute and featuring Polataivao in a leading role. Manusaute's taut, precise direction drew out all the tension inherent in the script, while Polataivao's moving performance was a still centre to the dark and troubling drama.[36]

Simultaneously entertaining and politically challenging, KKK's work drew audiences across cultural divides while at the same time raising uncomfortable questions about mainstream New Zealand's attitudes to Pasifika migration. Anapela Polataivao and Vela Manusaute – creative catalysts and mentors to a new generation of Pasifika artists – exemplify Makerita Urale's concept of 'floating Islanders': adaptable, inventive, multi-skilled and driven by a deep passion for the arts.

Nina Nawalowalo in *Masi* (2012), dirs. Nina Nawalowalo and Tom McCrory at Soundings – Te Papa. Photo: Phillip Merry

Nina Nawalowalo in The Conch's *Masi* (2012). Photo: Phillip Merry

Top: Kasaya Manulevu and Nina Nawalowalo in *Masi* (2012). **Centre**: The Conch's *Masi* (2012). Alexander Tarrant in foreground. **Bottom**: The Conch's *Masi* (2012). Photos: Phillip Merry

Fa`amoana John Luafutu in *The White Guitar* (2015), Hannah Playhouse, dirs. Nina Nawalowalo and Jim Moriarty, The Conch. Photo: Sam Hema

Matthias Luafutu, Fa`amoana John Luafutu, Malo Luafutu/Scribe in *The White Guitar* (2015), The Conch. Photo: Paul Lambert

Naked Samoans Talk About Their Knives (1998). From left: David Fane, Oscar Kightley, Mario Gaoa, Shimpal Lelisi. Photo: Sarah Hunter

The Laughing Samoans (Tofiga Fepulea`i and Eteuati Ete) in *Fink About It* (2015). Photo: Big Mark Photography

Vela Manusaute (The Brownies) performs stand-up comedy. Photo supplied by Vela Manusaute

Goretti Chadwick and Anapela Polataivao as Pani and Pani (2014). Photo: Tikilounge Productions

Vela Manusaute and Anapela Polataivao in Edinburgh (2014). Photo supplied by Vela Manusaute

Above: Kila Kokonut Krew's 'Tight Five': Glen Jackson, Aleni Tufuga, Stacey Leilua, Vela Manusaute, Anapela Polataivao, in *Strictly Brown 2* (2009). Photo: Vinesh Kumaran

KILA KOKONUT KREW
FROM THE PACIFIC WE RISE

Left: Kila Kokonut Krew logo, designed by Siliga David Setoga.

Below: Kila Kokonut Krew's *The Factory: A Pacific musical* (2013) by Vela Manusaute, composer Poulima Salima, dirs. Vela Manusaute and Anapela Polataivao. From left: Paul Fagamalo, Joanna Mika-Toloa, Troy Tu`ua, Sela Faletolu-Fasi, Suivai Autagavaia, Mileta Sally Sakalia, Tavai Fa`asavalu, Taupunakohe Tocker. Photo: Vela Manusaute

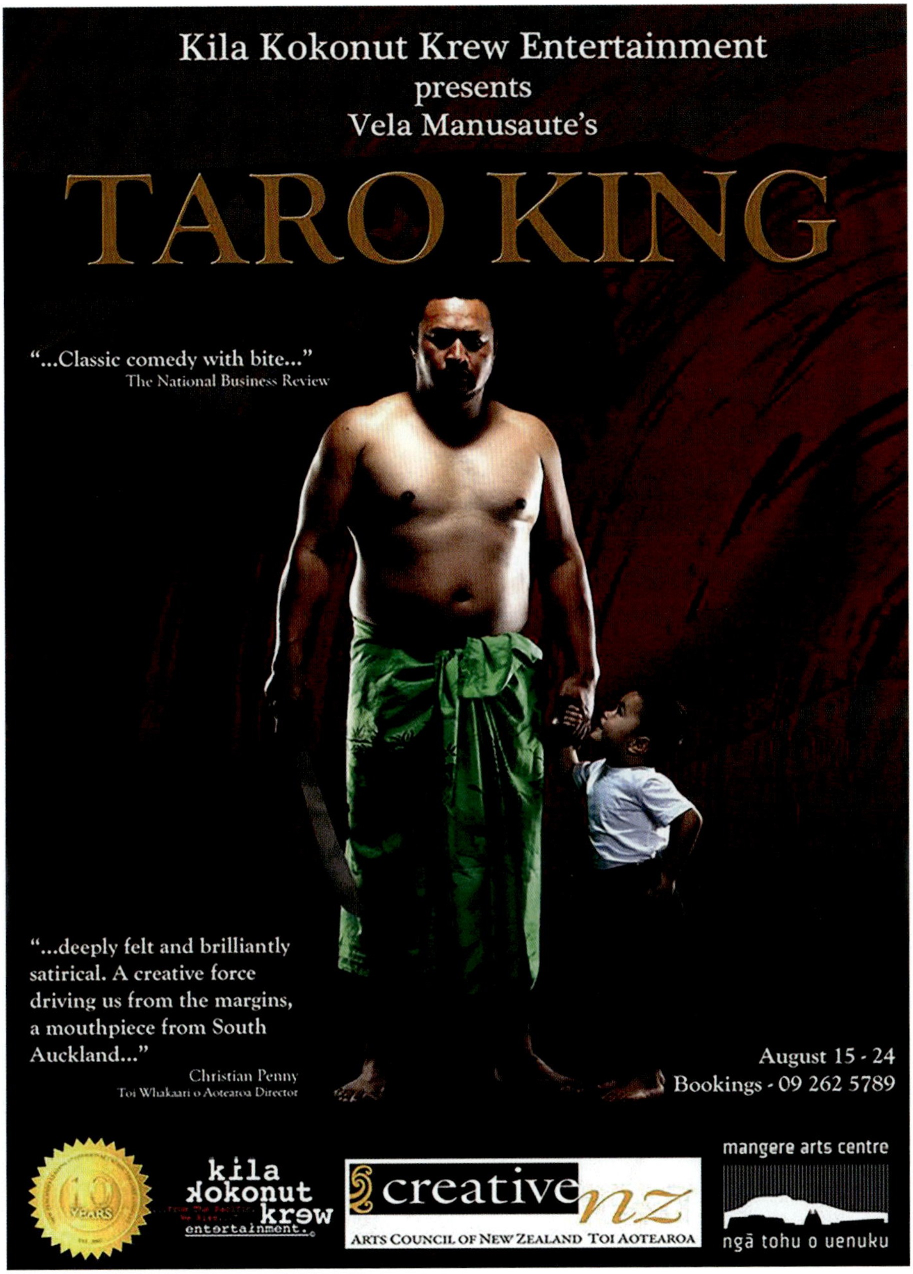

Aleni Tufuga (Filipo) and Solomon A. Tufuga (Solomon) in the tenth anniversary production of *Taro King* (2012), dirs. Vela Manusaute and Anapela Polataivao.

Poster design: Junior Farani. Photo: Vela Manusaute

Left: Louise Tu`u.
Photo: Andi Crown Photography

Opposite: Grace Taylor and Fasitua Amosa in *My Own Darling* (2015) by Grace Taylor, dir. Mia Blake.
Photo: Michael Smith, supplied by ATC

Below: Lafitaga Matua and Nisha Madhan in *Gaga: The Unmentionable* (2012), written and directed by Louise Tu`u/We Should Practice. Photo: Colette Waaka

Mangere Arts Centre. Photo: Lisa Warrington

Above: Iva Hitila in *Mele Kanikau* by John Kneubuhl, performed at Fale Pasifika, University of Auckland (2013), dir. Michelle Johansson. Photo: Joanna Forsberg

Following page: Waikiki Pageant cast perform the final hula 'Hano Hano Hanalei' in *Mele Kanikau*. Photo: Joanna Forsberg

Top: Denyce Su`a and Lauie Tofa as Lady Macbeth and Macbeth in Black Friars' *Macbeth* (2016), dirs. Billy Revell and Michelle Johansson. Photo: Penina Momoisea
Above: Vitinia-Gabrielle Togiatama, Akinehi Munroe and Irene Folau (The Witches) in Black Friars' *Macbeth* (2016), dirs. Billy Revell and Michelle Johansson. Photo: Penina Momoisea

Above: From left: Taofia Pelesasa (Vili), David Fane (Kapili) and Troy Tu`ua (Sione) in *A Frigate Bird Sings* (2012) by David Fane and Oscar Kightley, dir. Alison Quigan, Auckland Theatre Company at Mangere Arts Centre. Photo: Michael Smith, supplied by ATC

Left: Fasitua Amosa (Ioane) and David Van Horn (Peter) in *Niu Sila* (2013) by Dave Armstrong and Oscar Kightley, dir. Ben Crowder, Auckland Theatre Company at Q Loft. Photo: Michael Smith, supplied by ATC

Left: *Digital Winds* (2013) by Iaheto Ah Hi, dirs. Leilani Clarke and Iaheto Ah Hi at Mangere Arts Centre.
Photo: Diana Hu

Below: *Polly Hood in Mumuland* (2011) by Lauren Jackson, dir. Goretti Chadwick. Auckland Theatre Company and PIPA at Mangere Arts Centre.
Photo: Michael Smith, supplied by ATC

9.

Pasifika women writers 2002–15: 'Born restless'

There was nowhere in the world to turn and see my people shine – my burgeoning order of ambitious young Pacific and Māori women, born restless, born to realise the dreams of our ancestors while honouring our own contemporary will.

COURTNEY SINA MEREDITH[1]

Women have always taken strong leadership roles in Pasifika theatre as directors, writers, teachers, actors and producers. We have already discussed the foundational work of Justine Simei-Barton and Pacific Theatre, the influence of Erolia Ifopo with Pacific Underground, Nina Nawalowalo and The Conch, Anapela Polataivao as co-founder of KKK and Makerita Urale's work as writer and producer, among others. In this chapter we celebrate a diverse new generation of Pasifika women practitioners, many of whom cite being afakasi as a key element of their work. Most of them have studied creative writing and/or theatre at university and all bring a high level of polished craft to their work.

The majority of these female theatre artists are based in Auckland. Their personal stories acknowledge their Pasifika communities and evoke a cosmopolitan present and future. Their work embraces the unequivocally urban environment that most Polynesians inhabit – 'urbanesia', a word coined by Courtney Sina Meredith in her play *Rushing Dolls* (2012). The empowerment of Pasifika women through storytelling – often in heightened, poetic language – is evident in the work of performance poets Tusiata Avia, Meredith and Grace Taylor. Like them, playwrights Louise Tu`u, Leilani Unasa, Miria George and Michelle Johansson often emphasise the political, question society's failures, and offer a strong sense of celebration and hope.

The performance poets

Performance poetry has added another dimension to Pasifika theatre in which strong and passionately committed women 'create new shapes on the page and in the mouth'.[2] They break down the boundaries between literature and performance.

Tusiata Avia

Tusiata Avia completed an MA in creative writing at Victoria University's International Institute of Modern Letters (IIML) in 2002 and attended the writing programme at Iowa University in 2003. She was born in Christchurch in 1966 to a Palagi mother and Samoan father and identifies as afakasi. 'Tusiata' means 'artist', which Avia regards as 'a very fortunate name'.[3] Among other awards she has held the Fulbright–Creative New Zealand Pacific Writers' Fellowship at the University of Hawai`i, and won the Janet Frame Literary Trust Award in 2013.

While she has published several acclaimed volumes of poetry, such as *Fale Aitu: Spirit house* (2016), we focus here on her first collection, *Wild Dogs Under My Skirt* (2004). Before publishing the text Avia toured it extensively as a solo theatre performance, both within New Zealand (where it premiered at the Dunedin Fringe Festival in October 2002) and internationally. Over a period of eight years she has performed the work in Honolulu, Hamburg, Vienna, Jerusalem, and at festivals in many other cities.

The genesis of *Wild Dogs Under My Skirt* was Avia's response to travel writer Paul Theroux's 1992 suggestion that Pacific Islanders were 'savages' – which she says 'made me laugh out loud and made me quite angry as well'.[4] In her poetry Avia explores savagery and violence in the domestic context, especially towards children: 'My aunty is as cruel as three years of spiders. / If a child passes she grabs it by the hair and shakes it.'[5] She evokes images of cannibalism, as in 'Fa`afetai mo mea ai':

> Everyone eats up to their elbows
> We are direct descendants of flesh-eaters.
> Try ripping apart a steaming pig and tell me
> That doesn't feel good.[6]

Wild Dogs Under My Skirt considers issues of identity and stereotypes, especially of Pacific women, and makes much use of humour despite its frequently dark subject matter. The title refers to 'the traditional Samoan tattoo for women that runs from the upper thigh to the lower knee and traces the story of the origins of the island'.[7] It serves as a metaphor for an exploration of what is hidden beneath the surface. Like her cousin Victor Rodger, Avia plays with memories of the Gary Cooper film *Return To Paradise* (1953). In a poem of the same name, one of her characters recalls an uncle who played Cooper's body double in long shots when it was considered too hot for the Palagi actor to venture outside.[8] The disruptive nature of the American film company's presence in Samoa is suggested in 'After paradise', in which a house-girl takes to 'wearing her clothes loose / and sleeping late'; her dead abandoned child is 'very small, very white / with strange blue eyes'.[9]

In the performed work Avia plays six distinct characters, including 'a Russian cabaret singer pretending to be a Hawaiian hula girl, a Middle Eastern woman living in New Zealand, a 10-year-old Samoan girl and a frightened Samoan aunty';[10] their monologues range from subversive to confrontational to feminist.

Nicholas Wright connects Avia's writing with the vā, which he views in *Wild Dogs* as 'all those spatial and temporal relations that exist in language within and between cultures, between people, between the present and the past'.[11] Reviewer Sue Gough, who regards Avia as 'Samoa's answer to Germaine Greer', offers a description of the visceral, sly humour of the opening moments of the work in performance:

> When Tusiata Avia ... sashays onto the stage to the sentimental strains of a Pacific melody, all girlish giggles and lovely hula hands, you can almost smell the frangipani. But this is just her way of crossing the stage to where her cane knife is waiting. She plunges the knife into a two-kilo tin of Pacific corned beef and saws it open. Fatty red goo oozes over the sides and onto her hands. Licking her fingers lasciviously, and acknowledging her ancestors' penchant for 'long pig', she eyes the audience with the kind of greedy hunger you'd normally lavish on a rare fillet steak.[12]

In 2016 FCC brought new life to this significant work when the play was produced with a cast of six women (including Stacey Leilua and Nora Aati), directed by Anapela Polataivao.[13]

Avia has engaged in other theatre activities: for example, she acted in *Vula* (2006) and *Polynation* (2008), which she also directed. The latter piece showcases poetry performed by writers such as Selina Tusitala Marsh and Mua Strickson-Pua, with several pieces relating 'to the question of representation and stereotyping'.[14] Avia is highly respected as 'a leading voice in contemporary Pacific Island theatre and literature'.[15] As Bill Manhire, former poet laureate and founder of Victoria University's creative writing courses has noted, her work 'enlarges the way you see the world'.[16]

Courtney Sina Meredith

I could not find myself or my peers online, on TV, in books, in history or in the back yard.
COURTNEY SINA MEREDITH[17]

A similar subversive humour aligned with a highly charged poetic voice can be found in the work of Courtney Sina Meredith, an award-winning and internationally recognised performance poet. Born in 1986 and of Mangaian, Samoan and Irish origin, she is both a musician and a fiction writer, and holds a degree in English and political studies from the University of Auckland. She launched her first book of poetry, *Brown Girls in Bright Red Lipstick*, at the Frankfurt Book Fair in 2012.[18] Her first play, *Rushing Dolls* (2012), received a public presentation in the form of a script reading at Auckland's Herald Theatre in April 2015 under the auspices of Working Titles.[19]

Rushing Dolls is an exhilarating mixture of short, ironic scenes about job hunting and the art world, interspersed with vibrant poems. It creates a framework for the adventures of poet Cleo (Samoan) and her artist cousin Sia (Māori/Tongan). Cleo is 'contemplating the move away from home in pursuit of the perfect job and the perfect life',[20] and is depicted as a young woman with a certain naivety masked by a deep sense of irony. Meredith encapsulates the bonds of family in pure, simple strokes: 'Ma pushed out the sun every morning, she hoisted the moon at night with her bare hands.'[21] The language of the play is passionate, flamboyant, clear-sighted and occasionally both funny and defensive. 'You're forgetting Ma left the factory to look after us. She loves who we are: we're just like her, but in HD.'[22] Meredith has a gift for creating memorable, heady imagery in her performance poetry:

> Shells and bone in the mail, perfumed paper,
> Reading your kisses on the link bus late,
> You inked a pe`a on the moon's white thighs
> Our shadows cry centipedes that taper ...[23]

Rushing Dolls engages strongly with its raw urban environment and contemporary Pasifika politics. It celebrates belonging and yet difference, summed up in its repeated refrain – which plays with the notion of the Russian nesting doll:

> I want to be an activist but my country is sleeping
> I thought I'd be an actress but my ethnicity's hungry
> Me versus the monkeys on how to beat the junkies

I'm not a 'luck' advocate but I'm sick of fate
Or – faith in the new world with its old name.
I'm a girl in a girl in a girl in a girl
I'm a Rushing Doll.[24]

Victor Rodger has described Meredith as 'the embodiment of the new breed of Pasifika writers: unapologetically ambitious, and someone who demands and commands attention'.[25]

Grace Taylor

My father wanted one of my names [Teuila] to be after a flower and my mother wanted a Samoan name to reflect my heritage. My cultural heritage and identity is a massive part of my poetry. GRACE TAYLOR[26]

Poet, writer, director and teacher Grace Taylor was named the Creative New Zealand Arts Pasifika Awards Emerging Pacific Artist in 2014,[27] and was a co-founder of the influential South Auckland Poets Collective. Born and raised in South Auckland to a Samoan mother and English father, she identifies as afakasi. Her first book of poetry, *Afakasi Speaks* (2013), is Taylor's 'navigation of being Afakasi'.[28] It is a term she recognises 'would be offensive to some. It's dependent on the environment you're in and the historical context in which it landed. I don't think Afakasi should have to go out of usage ... I always refer to myself as Afakasi. I'm about reclaiming, redefining ...'[29]

Afakasi is hybrid
they said
as if we are scientifically designed
injected
synthetic
realigned
into an unnatural state of being
I'm Alive!
I'm Afakasi-stein[30]

In July 2014 Taylor, who co-founded the Rising Voices Youth Poetry Movement and is an experienced youth development worker, directed *Skin*, which was presented as part of the ATC's youth show *Selecta: The next big thing* at the Basement Theatre. The ten young poet-performers in the cast delivered 'spoken word meditations on their lives, experiences and attitudes',[31] drawing on 'themes of "skin politics" – gender, cultural identity and multiplicity, self-image, entrapment, body horror'.[32] Taylor and choreographer Jahra Rager Wasasala received praise for the stage movement of the piece, which created 'poetry in motion' through its strong rhythm and visual sense.[33] Taylor's first play was *My Own Darling*, directed by Tongan-born Mia Blake for ATC at the Mangere Arts Centre in October 2015. It was inspired by Alice Walker's poem 'Be nobody's darling', and was intended as a social commentary 'using the dynamics of theatre to bring poetry to life'.[34] According to reviewer Paul Simei-Barton, the work 'takes us on a poetic journey into an unseen city that reveals its secrets through intensely personal stories, seasoned with down-to-earth humour and unexpected beauty'.[35] The central role – Teuila, a young afakasi poet facing single motherhood – was played by Grace Taylor. Teuila is 'journeying from South Auckland into the city's centre on a kind of vision quest, observing what she encounters with her articulate gift for analogy and insight'.[36] Fasitua Amosa and Gabby Solomona played the supporting characters, including South Auckland solo mother Grit Girl, Man from the Maunga, and the Lady Next Door – a Samoan 'aunty' figure who delivers hard truths masked by humour. According to Taylor, 'Auckland is really the sixth character – it's my lover and my muse. I want Aucklanders to see themselves in this show.'[37]

The playwrights

Louise Tu`u

I am a playwright but I see myself as a cross-disciplinary artist. I'm a fervent believer in writing about New Zealand-born experiences here and now. LOUISE TU`U[38]

One of the most innovative, experimental and driven of the younger generation of Pasifika theatre artists is writer, director and producer Louise Tu`u. In 2005 she was the first New Zealand playwright to be selected for the Royal Court Theatre International Residency in London with her first play, *Le Tauvaga*, and in 2007 was invited to present *Le Tauvaga* at the inaugural World Indigenous Theatre Reading Series at the Martin E. Segal Center in New York. She has also taken her work to Berlin and London, and has written and directed a number of short films.

In 2009 Tu`u founded the company We Should Practice, of which she remains the director, with the objective of creating live performance, moving image and public art. The independent organisation aims to be 'proactive in community and public projects … to develop and present … processes and performances'.[39] In 2013 she was invited to be one of five jury members for the international festival Zürcher Theater Spektakel. As a cross-disciplinary artist generally working outside the mainstream, she brings a new spirit and impetus to her work for the theatre.

Tu`u was born in Auckland in 1978 to Samoan immigrant parents who met in Auckland, having both arrived in New Zealand in 1966.[40] At 17 she went on a school exchange to Italy where her interest in drama was awakened: 'We did *A Midsummer Night's Dream* in Italian. They made me a fairy who couldn't speak Italian or English properly … It was a comic role and it was really fun.' Tu`u had no desire to attend drama school, however: 'If I was going to learn anything that was going to help me on stage, surely life would run me over, then that would teach me.' Tu`u completed a degree in German and Italian at Auckland University, and in 1999 spent five months in Samoa learning about her family background and reviving her knowledge of the Samoan language. She gained professional acting experience during 2002 when she toured New Zealand schools with the Duffy Theatre company, and had a brief role in *Shortland Street* playing a Samoan cleaner for which, ironically, she had to be taught how to do a 'FOB' accent.

When she was 25 Tu`u saw a Pasifika play that made her angry: she felt the questions asked by the protagonist were inane and inappropriate. 'I went, right, what's the most productive use of my time? I have to write a play.' Her high school, Auckland Girls' Grammar, provided a starting point for *Le Tauvaga* (The Competition), which is centred around the cultural competition, Polyfest.[41] In the 1980s the school had a high success rate in the Samoan section of Polyfest, though Tu`u herself had only performed with the Samoan non-competitive group.

> I went for Creative Communities funding. I got the funding first and I thought, oh shit, better write a play. So that was my journey into playwriting. We put it on at Metro Theatre in Mangere East. Opposite KFC. In my funding application I said I wanted to target Pacific Island teenagers and this is how I'll do it, staging it in community centres. I wasn't interested in putting it on at the Silo [Theatre]. That was too big a risk in my brain 'cause I didn't know anything, I hadn't made anything before.

Le Tauvaga – directed by Tu`u – premiered on 22 March 2004, playing to good houses. From the beginning she demonstrated confidence and originality in her dramatic structure and writing.

> It was about a young man called Dash, trying to audition for the Samoan [Polyfest] team. He's a head boy, captain of the first fifteen – I tried to jam all the classic over-achiever stereotypes in this character. And this was the one thing that he couldn't get into, and his girlfriend [Taimane] is one of the leaders. So it tests their relationship. I structured the play in the form of a competition, opening with the ulufale.

The ulufale, customised for the play, is an entrance song traditionally used at Polyfest. There is a series of scenes involving Dash, Taimane, his father Sione and cousin Mantis, among others, interspersed with the developing movements of the competition, and ending with the ulufafo (exit song). Dash speaks very poor Samoan, which he blames on his father's failure to teach him, and has little grasp of the cultural tools necessary for the competition.

> **DASH**: Can you just help me with the claps?
>
> **MANTIS**: Ei, fanau i Niu Sila! Open your eyes. You were born here, you idiot. You have freedom beyond your wildest dreams. Those crazy rednecks in the Beehive ...
>
> **DASH**: Is it 'Fa`atalofa fo`i' or the other word?
>
> **MANTIS**: ... who never wanted us here except to keep those unskilled labour quotas filled, slaughter their dairy products in the blood-drenched abattoirs or pack their fridges.
>
> **DASH**: Do I start with the left or right hand?[42]

The play avoids simple solutions, instead posing questions and challenges to the status quo, such as in the speech by Samoan-born Mantis in scene nine in which he speaks bitingly of revolution and reality:

> **MANTIS**: ... I will tell you why this school should not be involved in next year's Polyfest ... How are we meant to be self-sufficient, capable of determining our own destinies? Why are we still disenfranchised from what is rightfully ours? ... I mean, sweethearts, where will you go after the festival, start doing the rounds on cruise ships?[43]

Tu`u's second play, *Providence*, first performed in 2009 then revived in 2010 and 2012, tackles urban homelessness. Two factors led to the writing of this play, the first of which was the tragic death in 2007 of Folole Maliaga, an Auckland woman whose life support failed when a power company turned off her electricity, causing public outcry. The second factor stemmed from Tu`u's trip to New York for the reading of *Le Tauvaga* as part of the World Indigenous Theatre Reading Series. Here she was affected by advertising regarding homelessness: 'There was one poster that I remember, of the Statue of Liberty in a blanket, shivering, and I went, that's really good advertising.'

> I worked as an usher for almost three years at The Edge and you see homeless people hanging around Aotea Square. I think the square is probably a metaphor for something of the city, because of its transformation, the urban jungle becoming more concrete. And homeless people have this point of convergence.

Providence went through several distinct drafts, with dialogue in an early version written in French – the intention being to create a disorienting effect.[44] Tu`u had significant support, such as a workshop of an early draft provided by the Read Raw Playwrights Collective in Auckland,[45] directed by Gary Henderson, and work with the Playwrights' Studio under the guidance of Michelanne Forster. Creative New Zealand also awarded funding for a further full-time workshop of the script. The play's creation process reveals the writer's determination to be authentic in her work.

> I also wanted to challenge myself ... to write about something I didn't know anything about. I've always had quite a strong problem with this work in the ethics involved – how can I write about somebody's experiences that I have no [knowledge of], and don't want to emulate?

Tu`u realised she needed to experience the viewpoint of the homeless: 'We decided that we would go and sleep rough as a company.' She and her actors, Te Paki Cherrington[46] and Moeroa Marsters, slept out in discomfort; Tu`u also stayed overnight at a homeless shelter and spoke with homeless people.

The first performance was given exclusively for the homeless community in central Auckland, where the company had to overcome preconceptions – including the notion of privilege:

> We had a homeless heckler with a filthy mouth. He was like, 'Oh, this shit isn't funny' ... Ten minutes into the play I wrote this joke about the *New Zealand Herald* only being good for toilet paper and he laughed at that and shut up.

For its production at The Basement (October 2010), Tu`u wanted the audience to have a disorienting experience; they were led into the theatre from a car park via a 'staff only' door. The stage space was filled with cardboard boxes, a traditional 'home' for the homeless, which were then transformed into all the set pieces and props required for the performance.

Providence touches on moments of violence, poetry, childhood memories and family dysfunction. The two actors played multiple roles with the primary focus on brother and sister pair, Ken and Tamsen. A recurring motif is the knocking down of cardboard towers, painstakingly erected by Ken. The play ends with the lines:

KEN: ... I've had enough of myself
Maybe I could become a cone and crap myself on somebody
Have some sense
My sense and land on people who need it
I am not going to be remembered and that cuts me up
They will say
What happened to that guy with the green blanket
And no one will reply
Because it's too hard
To think About anyone else.[47]

Janet McAllister and Paul Simei-Barton in their 'Best of 2010' review noted: 'Louise Tu`u's *Providence* masterfully led its audience into "experiencing a replica aspect of homelessness" feeling vague and confused and unsure of what was expected of them – by deliberately breaking the rules.'[48] This was borne out in *Providence*'s February 2012 revival at the Aotea Centre, where reviewers clearly experienced precisely the sense of uncertainty Tu`u was trying to create. Vanessa Byrnes was 'left disappointed, slightly annoyed at unfulfilled promises'.[49] James Wenley observed, 'There are hints of drug use, ambivalence to the world, pain, a brother/sister relationship in breakdown, but I find it very difficult to sense out.'[50] Tu`u has responded to such reviews:

> The areas I play with in my work involve a vague cageyness, engage with a multiplicity of individuals, organisations and random [elements], therefore making it difficult to interpret or understand. It also highlights the conservatism of theatre criticism here, and the compartmentalisation of live performance in NZ.[51]

The exploration of language was a key element of Tu`u's third play, *Gaga: The unmentionable* (2012), which 'looks at the writer's mother tongue, Samoan, through the eyes and experiences of her first language teachers, her parents ... Gaga comes from the hacking of the Samoan word Gagana, which refers to the language.'[52] As with all her writing, *Gaga: The unmentionable* avoids naturalism and is filled with comedy, surprises and apparent non-sequiturs during a series of short but compelling scenes. There are contemporary dance sequences set to music by Michael Jackson, Usher, Kings of Leon and others, and a waltz and a slow siva performed by 'Elderly Woman', who we later discover is Tu`u's real-life mother, Lafitaga Matua. Physical movement is strongly represented, from a man skipping in a lavalava to two actors enthusiastically forming their bodies into letters of the alphabet. Tu`u plays herself, as writer and director of the show, entering the stage space from the audience while attempting (and failing) to do handstands across the stage.[53] She speaks in incomprehensible Finnish for the first four scenes then reverts to English, while her mother addresses her primarily in Samoan, which Tu`u in her on-stage persona struggles to comprehend. Issues of cultural appropriateness are raised and deliberately tested. For example, in scene seven, 'Short Woman' and 'Young Woman' address the purpose of the lavalava the former is wearing:

> **SHORT WOMAN**: The first thing I thought was how culturally appropriate it could be ... Well, let's say one day I need to go to another fa`alavelave. I can use it as a nifo oti for my dance to gather money. *She starts to dance and tosses the lavalava into the air, incorporating it into her taupou dance.*
>
> **YOUNG WOMAN**: They call it crowdfunding now. Oh yes, and when I go to a wedding I can wear it as a sari ... Or I can cross boundaries and wear it as a turban.[54]

Although Tu`u's work lies outside the mainstream, as an innovative, experimental artist with a strong and independent point of view she is clearly a voice to be reckoned with.

Michelle Johansson and Black Friars

Our vision is embedded in our community. I love the space where theatre meets education. MICHELLE JOHANSSON[55]

Writer, teacher, director and producer Michelle Johansson has taken a leadership role in inspiring young people to pursue performing arts careers. In 2006, with Billy Revell and others, she co-founded Black Friars, a company that has developed a repertoire of productions including original Pasifika works as well as appropriations of European classics.

Johansson was born in Auckland to a Tongan mother and Palagi father and was brought up in a vibrant Tongan community in South Auckland. As a child she performed in church as part of Faka-Me (children's day), the equivalent of Samoa's White Sunday. Her entry to theatre was not through performing, however, but through writing and education. She attended Wesley College in Pukekohe (which she describes as 'Little Tonga'), but after a spate of 'badass' behaviour ('wagging and tagging and stealing and dealing') was 'exiled' to Tonga for six months.

In 2003, at the request of the principal, Johansson began teaching drama at Wesley. The core members of that class – Revell, Vau Atonio, Lauie Sila and Misipele Tofilau – in October 2006 became the founding members of Black

Friars. The company was named after Blackfriars Theatre, where Shakespeare's company performed when the Globe burned down.[56] According to Johansson, Black Friars' objective was 'burning down the old infrastructures and proving that Polynesians can do it after all'. Because the company was primarily comprised of young men, it was also about being 'brothers'.

Black Friars made its debut with *Being Brown*, Johansson's first script. A 20-minute segment was performed in the 2007 Pasifika Festival with the encouragement of actor Ole Maiava. *Being Brown* was programmed in the International Comedy Festival back-to-back with a Johansson-scripted pantomime, *Goldilocks and the Three Little Puaka*. In *Being Brown*, four friends meet up and recall their schooldays through a series of flashbacks, while *Goldilocks* was 'a mash-up of fairy tales'. Both were popular and made money for the fledgling company as well as 'a little bit of reputation'. *Being Brown* was performed in many other venues, including at the opening of the Mangere Arts Centre in 2011, while *Goldilocks* remained in the company's repertoire for several years.

By 2008 Black Friars was ready to perform its ambitious *Othello Polynesia*, with the encouragement of Shakespeare scholar Michael Neill. Directed by Johansson, the play was first performed at the Fale Pasifika at Auckland University followed by other venues, including Downstage Theatre (2009). Set against the backdrop of a giant tapa cloth and with an all-Polynesian cast, Island drumming and music, it had a strong Pacific flavour.

Other European classics performed by Black Friars include Aristophanes' *The Frogs* (2009), and Shakespeare's *The Merchant of Venice* (2014) and *Macbeth* (2016).

As Black Friars evolved, Johansson studied for a master's and PhD in theatre at Auckland University under the supervision of Murray Edmond. In 2011 she became a tutor and guest lecturer in drama and Pacific studies at the university, and later became head of performing arts at Manukau Institute of Technology.

As one of the first Tongan playwrights in Aotearoa, Johansson has brought a distinctive Tongan voice to Pasifika theatre. In 2010 she directed her play *Six Lessons and a Wedding* at the Drama Studio, University of Auckland, followed by a season at the Mangere Arts Centre in March 2011. Written as part of her master's in drama, the solo play featured Samoan Lauie Sila but was viewed from a Tongan perspective. Sila played Sefo Salesi, a young deaf man who is marginalised by his family and called a 'retard' by others. Relegated to preparing the food for his sister's wedding, he observes family dramas from the sidelines as he tends the umu and roasts a pig on a spit. Johansson creates a vivid picture of a whole community as Sila switches between the roles of Sefo, members of his family and a corrupt minister. Sefo's narration hinges on six 'rules of island culture', including rule number three: 'know thy enemy'.[57] He is in a perfect position to observe the proceedings: 'Back here. I see everything ... Even if I don't hear it.'[58]

His observations ensure that his sister's cheating boyfriend gets his comeuppance, expose the minister, and help recover the exorbitant tithe paid by his mother to the church. Sefo gives a succinct overview of Island politics where, as his final 'rule' states, 'reputation is everything'.[59] *Six Lessons and a Wedding* recalls fale aitu in its light-hearted critique of parental authority and the church, but telling the story from the point of view of a disabled young man provides poignancy and originality. Albert Wendt commented, 'It is a marvellous script and a stroke of genius to see a Samoan wedding from the viewpoint of an intellectually challenged youth. It was also one of the best performances I had ever seen.'[60]

In 2013, as the creative component for her PhD on John Kneubuhl, Johansson directed his play *Mele Kanikau: A pageant* at the Fale Pasifika at the University of Auckland. She had been introduced to Kneubuhl's work by Nathaniel Lees, who came to the opening night of *Othello Polynesia* in Wellington – a meeting Johansson describes as 'a pivotal moment in my theatre life'. *Mele Kanikau* ('song of mourning') is the second play in Kneubuhl's trilogy written in 1975, nearly 20 years before *Think of a Garden*. Set in Hawai`i, it examines a cultural group preparing to perform hula at a tourist pageant. In her article about the play Johansson notes that it focuses on debates around cultural authenticity. She argues that 'Kneubuhl's afakasi status afforded him licence to make these comments about the declining state of Polynesian culture, and to caution the audience and reader to treasure their heritage and to honour and remember their past.'[61] She quotes Albert Wendt on the historical importance of Kneubuhl's work: 'Before Kneubuhl there were no Samoan playwrights in the Western sense of theatre.'[62]

Johansson's staging of *Mele Kanikau* was only the second production of the play, the first being in Hawai`i in 2001. The cast included Black Friars' core group members alongside experienced Pasifika practitioners such as Ole Maiava and choreographer Aruna Po-Ching, a former member of Justine Simei-Barton's Pacific Theatre. Reviewer Aaron Taouma commented on the effectiveness of the transformation of the Fale Pasifika to accommodate a transverse stage with 'billowing tapa plumes from the ceiling', and the fluidity of Johansson's direction. He praised the acting, especially that of Leroy Lakamu (as Noa) with his 'earthy, erotic and passion-filled hula (choreographed by Po-Ching) bringing out the essence of what it means to be Hawaiian in the space where dark and light meet'.[63]

Black Friars has toured extensively to New Zealand schools and tertiary institutions as well as throughout the Pacific, including performing *Six Lessons and a Wedding* at the National University of Samoa (2013) and *Kiwa* at the Oceanic Performance Biennial in Rarotonga (2015). The company's kaupapa is to share stories in pan-Polynesian ways, and to engage young Polynesians to 'walk that line between theatre and education': for every new show, Black Friars invites young people 'to come play with us'. Several Black Friars members have gone on to study at Toi Whakaari or Unitec, and others, such as Revell, Denyce Su`a and Timote Mapuhola, have become playwrights.[64]

Johansson uses three Polynesian principles in both theatre and education: talanoa (the telling of stories openly and without a fixed agenda); teu le vā (respecting the relational spaces between people); and tuakana/teina (big sister/brother peer mentoring). Her influence extends well beyond the productions she has written and directed, however, and she has links with other Tongan companies such as the Tongan Creatives Collective and Suli Moa's Tales from the Kava Bowl. Her work in South Auckland represents a significant commitment to the future of Pasifika theatre, and her production of *Mele Kanikau* is a milestone in the relationship between Pasifika theatre in Aotearoa and the legacy of theatre in the wider Pacific region.

Leilani Unasa

> **TASI**: I had friends who would talk about Samoa all the time! Their necks were permanently bent from looking backwards. (*HIS MOTHER'S SON*)[65]

Leilani Unasa grew up in South Auckland. While working in Wellington she was inspired by the creative energy she experienced in the theatre scene, and in 2008 completed a master's degree in scriptwriting at Victoria University's IIML. Unasa's first play, *Tautala*, is set in a karaoke bar and is about three friends whose relationships are disintegrating: '... they go out on the town to sing and try and forget about it'.[66] Unasa directed the play herself, using a cast of singers, and staged it at the Blue Note Bar for the 2003 Wellington Fringe Festival. It paved the way for her second piece, *His Mother's Son*, which drew in part on her own experience as afakasi – with a Pākehā mother, and a Samoan father who came to New Zealand as a teenager from a small village in Upolu:

> When I first wrote *His Mother's Son*, I'd probably be too shy to say it was about my family, but it is. The places that I've put them are all places that, for me, were very domesticated – the garage, rugby clubrooms, riding around on the buses all weekend. Doing things that you only experience in Auckland's dense suburbs. That's where my mind is always going.

First performed in Wellington at BATS (January 2007) directed by Katrina Chandra, *His Mother's Son* featured Fiona Truelove, Aleni Tufuga, Helen Jones and Shadon Meredith.[67] It was the second piece staged by Chickenhead Productions (Kylie Brown and Unasa), whose objective was to present 'quality work on stage that gives voice to Māori and Pacific stories'.[68] While the play has undergone several re-writes, the 2012 version consists of 19 short scenes in two acts, which weave backwards and forwards in time to reveal the relationship and subsequent divorce of Samoan Tasi Siaosi and his Palagi wife Rachael, and the effect on their son Stephen.[69] At the same time, we learn Tasi's background and see how he has been affected by issues of abandonment in his childhood village in Samoa.

In this play about cycles of neglect and abuse, afakasi Stephen tries to come to terms with the past. In the final scene, when it is established that Tasi has been dead for some years, the play's fourth character (Sita, herself a ghost presence) reveals to Stephen that she is Tasi's teenage mother, who gave him up for adoption, thus setting the course of their lives.

> **TASI**: I used to tell people that I had no mother, that she was dead. But they all knew. In that tiny place nothing is secret. The shame of her stuck to me my whole life. I thought that coming here to New Zealand would wash it off. But it still followed me.[70]

Sensitively written and with a comedic tone, *His Mother's Son* is one of the first plays since Victor Rodger's *Sons* to deal with the consequences of being afakasi.[71] The play explores some Samoan customs, filtered through both the arcane language of a library book on myths and legends of Samoa, and Tasi's down-to-earth responses to the book's pronouncements. Unasa addresses social welfare issues in passing, pointing out the different rules for rich and poor, brown and white, and exploring gender themes. 'I'm also looking at the politics of ethnicity in New Zealand, as well as social class and poverty. For me that's really important.'

Chandra has a Fijian Indian father and part-Māori, part-Pākehā mother, identifies as afakasi, and felt a particular affinity to the play:

> Seeing an afakasi story on the stage, and the differences in culture, was significant for me. My father was raised not to let women have any role of importance, my mother was a strong, opinionated woman, and they just clashed. My parents got divorced, and I always feel the difference in their cultures was a major issue. You don't really see a lot of that in New Zealand theatre.[72]

Unasa has since co-produced works by Māori playwrights Whiti Hereaka and Chris Molloy and, with Michelanne Forster, written the children's play *Sapai and the Yam Snatchers*, which was published by Playmarket in 2014.[73] Her theatre career has been balanced with community work and social activism within the Pasifika community. She is the co-founder of Oceania Interrupted, 'an Auckland-based collective of Māori and Pacific women committed to undertaking public interventions to raise awareness for issues that affect Pacific people in Aotearoa and throughout the Pacific region'.[74]

Miria George

Protest, for me, is how we can care for ourselves and each other and the ecology around us ... that's what theatre is to me. It's my form of protest. MIRIA GEORGE[75]

Among Leilani Unasa's classmates at the IIML was Miria George, who was already an established playwright when she completed an MA in scriptwriting in 2008. The daughter of a well-known Cook Island visual artist, the late Ian George, Miria also has Māori ancestry; the majority of her plays are highly political and respond to Māori issues. As Alice Te Punga Somerville notes, very few Māori writers deal with the relationship with Pasifika people: 'The obvious, and complex, exceptions to this are the creative people like Miria George and [hip hop/reggae artist] Che Fu who are of mixed Māori–Pasifika descent.'[76] George won the Fulbright–Creative New Zealand Pacific Writer's Residency at the University of Hawai`i in 2016.

George has frequently written Pasifika characters into her plays. *Urban Hymns* (2009) commissioned by Young and Hungry, depicts young Māori, Pasifika and Asian characters coping with the economic consequences of the 2008 global financial crisis. Her best-known play *and what remains* (2005) created controversy and drew a response that was 'fierce, polarised and unprecedented'.[77] Set in the future in the transit space of an airport terminal, Mary is the last Māori woman to leave New Zealand as a result of government policy to rid the country of the so-called 'Māori problem'.[78] The characters reflect New Zealand's increasingly diasporic population, contrasting Mary's plight with other migrant characters who have made New Zealand their home. Among them is Solomon, a middle-class Samoan about to embark on his first 'OE'.

George pays homage to her Pasifika ancestry in *Sunset Road* (Wellington, 2012), one of the first Cook Island plays since Karl Kite-Rangi's *Between the Islands* (2002). *Sunset Road* is a semi-autobiographical migration story depicting a Cook Island family adjusting to life in Rotorua in the 1970s. Teenage twins Luka and Lucia struggle with their identity and ambitions, while their father Ina works in a sawmill and does battle with his inner demons.[79] *Sunset Road* deals with the intergenerational clash of values brought on by the migration experience, with a particularly Cook Island inflection. In reviewing the revised Auckland production (Q Theatre, 2014), Sharu Delilkan noted the universality of this story: 'The journey from Areora, Atiu, Cook Islands to 76 Sunset Road, Rotorua, is beautifully re-told through the somewhat innocent eyes of the twins Lucia and Luka. It's essentially a voyage that many who've settled in Aotearoa from the Pacific Islands will be able to relate to.'[80]

and what remains and *Sunset Road* were produced by Tawata Productions, founded in 2004 by Hone Kouka and George. Tawata also runs the annual Matariki Development Festival in Wellington, which is designed to develop new work by indigenous playwrights. Pasifika writers featured in the festival include Natano Keni, James Nokise, Moana Ete and Taungaroa Emile (who played Ina in *Sunset Road*, 2014). In December 2015 Tawata Productions won the Critics' Wildcard Award at the Wellington Theatre Awards, primarily for this initiative.

As both playwright and producer, George has played a prominent role in bringing the politics of Māori and Pasifika issues to the stage.

'Born restless'

One of the things that is most obvious to me – here in South Auckland and in New Zealand as a whole – is the ... flowering of Pacific and Māori arts. It is quite extraordinary, and I believe it has a huge transformative power. The arts has been one of the most positive ways that things Pasifika have penetrated the fabric of this country.

TUSIATA AVIA[81]

Courtney Sina Meredith's vision of ambitious young Polynesian women creating art that marries tradition with the contemporary is realised in the unique voices of these women. They are aesthetically innovative, create new initiatives, empower other artists and bring a younger generation to the stage; they blend gender issues with questions of cultural identity and provide new insight into being afakasi in New Zealand; they portray domestic scenes of family life, migrant concerns and broader political issues. They are catalysts for change and demonstrate the strength of Pasifika women in the arts of Aotearoa.

10.

Building the future

What I need to see in Pacific theatre now is the next generation of stories. Not the same first wave migration stories. We've seen those. We need second- and third-generation New Zealand Pacific stories.

KATRINA CHANDRA[1]

In recent years a younger generation of Pasifika actors, writers, directors and producers has benefitted from a number of initiatives that did not exist for the first practitioners. New venues, theatre companies and educational institutions, particularly in Auckland, have expanded the community of artists, increasing public engagement with their work and ensuring the future of Pasifika theatre in Aotearoa.

The most significant developments are the Mangere Arts Centre – Ngā Tohu o Uenuku and the Pacific Institute of Performing Arts, both of which provide support for a wide range of Māori and Pasifika performance. There has been a proliferation of new production companies, each with its own initiatives and agenda, and many with members in common. There are writer-focused initiatives for emerging Pasifika playwrights, and work by writers from the whole Pacific diaspora is coming to the stage. Some continue to explore familiar themes such as family and migration; others represent the voices of second- and third-generation Pasifika people, often with very personal stories.

Mangere Arts Centre – Ngā Tohu o Uenuku: A sense of community[2]

I strongly feel theatre should represent and reflect its audience. KATRINA CHANDRA

Since 2010 Mangere Arts Centre has provided its multi-ethnic South Auckland community with a dedicated venue for celebrating the arts. A sense of place and purpose was carefully considered in the creation of this space:

> The building needed to demonstrate a strong cultural connection to New Zealand, iwi and Pacific Island communities ... [with] appropriate spaces to display

large artworks, including textiles such as tapa cloth. The layout was specifically designed to support pōwhiri and other formal greetings and gatherings, with flexible spaces ... to encourage cultural meetings and celebrations as well as the delivery of educational programmes.[3]

The significance of this 'home base' for Māori and Pasifika arts and culture cannot be underestimated. Katrina Chandra, whose diverse theatre career included work as a technican, director, dramaturg and administrator, was appointed the first theatre manager in March 2010.[4] In its initial year of operation the centre held more than 70 theatre events, 11 gallery exhibitions and a range of community exhibitions and public programmes.[5] The centre's inaugural theatre production in September 2010 was a revival of Kila Kokonut Krew's *Once Were Samoans*, recently returned from Australia.[6] This was followed by the Pacific Institute of Performing Arts' graduate show, *Where We Once Belonged* (November 2010), and Kinetic Wayfinding's *Tautai* by Iaheto Ah Hi, directed by Oscar Kightley (December 2010).[7]

Ah Hi went on to develop what he called the 'Stingray Trilogy', following *Tautai* (set partly in Tokelau) with *Plantation* (2012, set in 1950s Samoa and present day South Auckland), and *Digital Winds* (2013). All were staged at Mangere Arts Centre where the sense of the location was tangible, as one reviewer commented:

> *Digital Winds* ... starts with a wonderful fire dance, slap dance and water ceremony in the outside centre court of Mangere Arts Centre being suddenly invaded by two street thugs chasing and attacking a guy for his shoes. We then follow the escaping crew into the theatre to witness the Aotearoa Battle Championships where two B-Boy teams dance up a storm of provocative break-dance gymnastics matching insults with sexual confrontation and bravado ... This is going to be a night of South Auckland in all its myriad dimensions.[8]

The centre has showcased both established artists and emerging talent. Other companies whose work has played there include Tales from the Kava Bowl,[9] Black Friars, and dance/theatre company LIMA Dance Productions, led by choreographer Olivia Taouma-Levy. The Pacific Dance Choreographic Laboratory has presented work by emerging choreographers of Pacific descent under the mentorship of Neil Ieremia, artistic director of Pasifika contemporary dance company Black Grace.[10] Community projects have also been welcomed.

In February 2011 the Auckland Fringe Festival presented Pacific Fringe at the centre: a weekend of Pacific performance, visual art and tradition that included *Mixed Nuts* by LIMA. The event – a variety showcase for 26 Pasifika dancers, actors, singers and comedians – took place in multiple spaces around the venue. There were songs from the Dusky Maidens,[11] contemporary dance offerings and a physical theatre piece entitled *Take That!*[12] In the courtyard, Tongan-born New Zealand visual and performance artist Kalisolaite `Uhila presented his first solo work since leaving art school. *Pigs in the Yard* explored 'the importance of this animal to his native Tongan culture and ongoing colonial concerns in the Pacific Islands'. In this early manifestation of a work that he has subsequently revisited, `Uhila 'reversed the normal relationship of people and animals, so the pigs ran free and the audience and I were behind the fence watching them.'[13] The history of Pasifika theatre itself has been celebrated, with revivals of *A Frigate Bird Sings* by Kightley and Fane (October 2012), *Niu Sila* by Kightley and Armstrong (October 2013) and Rodger's *Sons* (October 2014), all staged as collaborations between Mangere Arts Centre and ATC. *Romeo and Tusi* played there in September 2013 as part of a tour by Jandals Inc, under the direction of Sasha Gibb,[14] and Suli Moa's *A Heart's Path* (Tales from the Kava Bowl, 2012).

In reviewing *A Heart's Path*, Sharu Delilkan commented on the community spirit generated at the centre:

> The theatre was packed with people ... and you could feel the anticipation. What happened next would only happen in South Auckland – which is why I love coming to Mangere Arts Centre. One of the venue's staff members ... stood in front of the crowd on stage and bellowed, 'If there's a seat next to you where you are please squash in because there are more people coming.' Needless to say when the show started the theatre was bursting at the seams ... with plenty of Tongan community support.[15]

Mangere Arts Centre caters to its South Auckland Māori and Pacific Island audiences with pride. As Katrina Chandra has noted, 'You don't get that many brown faces to come into central Auckland to see shows.'

Pasifika theatre in Central Auckland

While Mangere has become an unprecedented hub for Pasifika theatre, work has also been presented at key venues in central Auckland. From 1993 to 1996 the Watershed Theatre hosted Pasifika productions including *Think of a Garden*, *The Contest* and *A Frigate Bird Sings*. The Fale Pasifika at the University of Auckland, which reviewer Aaron Taouma describes as 'Auckland's largest piece of Pasifika architecture ... the spiritual home of the university's Pacific community', has become a theatre venue for works including Michelle Johansson's *Mele*

Kanikau.[16] Silo Theatre presented the premieres of Toa Fraser's *Bare* and *No. 2*. In 2008 this venue was renamed The Basement and hosted works such as *Providence*, *Black Faggot*, *Girl on a Corner*, *Club Paradiso* and *Puzzy*.[17] Like BATS in Wellington, The Basement has become an incubator for new playwrights.

Educational and training opportunities

Companies

There has been steady growth in initiatives for Māori and Pasifika actors. As previously discussed, several Pasifika companies, including The Conch, KKK and Black Friars, have developed mentoring and/or training programmes alongside their main production activities. Massive Company (formerly the Maidment Youth Theatre, founded in 1990), while it is not a Pasifika company, has also provided career development opportunities for a number of Pasifika actors, including Anapela Polataivao and Beulah Koale. Under the direction of its founder Sam Scott, Massive has brought challenging topics affecting young Polynesians to the stage through scripted and devised theatre, including *The Sons of Charlie Paora* (2002, by British playwright Lennie James), and *The Brave* (2015).

Educational institutions

New Zealand's longest-established drama training programmes at Toi Whakaari: New Zealand Drama School (Wellington) and Unitec (Auckland) have welcomed students from the entire Pacific diaspora.[18] The University of Auckland's drama programme (led by Murray Edmond until his retirement in 2015) supported the career development of Toa Fraser, Dianna Fuemana, Michelle Johansson and Denyce Su`a, among others. TAPAC (the Auckland Performing Arts Centre based in Western Springs), in operation since 2003, is both a theatre venue and the home of the Western Springs College Performing Arts School. It hosts a significant collection of arts companies, including The Actors' Program, Touch Compass, Massive, Prayas Indian Theatre Co and DANZ, as well as independent arts practitioners and community performance groups.[19] Whitireia Performance Centre in Wellington offers diplomas in stage and screen arts, dance and singing, and a bachelor of applied arts that teaches a range of Pacific dance genres.[20]

Pacific Institute of Performing Arts: 'Like an `aiga'

Toi Whakaari and Unitec: you are on notice. I have seen the future of drama schools. It is fresh. It is brown. It is glorious. VICTOR RODGER[21]

In 2008 a new theatre-training programme with a distinctive Pasifika philosophy emerged: the Pacific Institute of Performing Arts. PIPA grew out of a theatre certificate programme within the BEST Pacific Institute of Education in Auckland, where Goretti Chadwick began teaching in 2004. Chadwick recalls how she and and Sean Coyle, both experienced theatre practitioners, introduced a diploma in 2008:

> Students would pass our course then go into programmes with other institutions, so we thought, why don't we run our own? We started with about 15 to 20 students and then the next year, over the three intakes, it shot up to 75.[22]

The school offers arts training for the performance and screen industries through its bachelor of performing arts (Pacific). Students are exposed to a range of performance work, generally with a Pacific focus, and are strongly encouraged to make contacts within the industry.

Chadwick, who has Samoan and European ancestry, attended Auckland Girls' Grammar School and graduated from Unitec in 1995 – the first Pacific Islander to do so. Her own experiences helped to shape the unique perspective of PIPA, which she wanted to run 'like an `aiga [family]'. Part of that sense of `aiga comes from post-diploma care. As Chadwick notes, 'It's not just about the students while they are with us, but where they go when they graduate.' Students are provided with a range of work opportunities.

Part of Auckland Theatre Company's brief is to collaborate with, celebrate and support 'the people and talent in South Auckland',[23] and PIPA has worked with ATC on a variety of projects, employing graduating students alongside professional actors and jointly staging several pantomimes with a strong Pasifika flavour. These include *Polly Hood in Mumuland* (2011) and *The Lolly Witch of Mumuland* (2015) by Lauren Jackson, and *Sinarella* (2012) by Chadwick and Sean Coyle. PIPA graduates such as Amanaki Lelei Prescott-Faletau and Troy Tu`ua have appeared in ATC productions, including *A Frigate Bird Sings* (2012).

In 2012 Chadwick wrote and directed her first play, *Galulolo (Tsunami)*, performed by graduating students at PIPA – a work that responds to the tsunami that devastated the south coast of Samoa on 29 September 2009.[24]

One of PIPA's most notable productions was *Where We Once Belonged*, directed by Chadwick and Anapela Polataivao (PIPA's head of acting) and initially staged at Mangere Arts Centre in November 2010.[25] Both women had acted in the 2008 ATC premiere of Dave Armstrong's adaptation of Sia Figiel's novel. For the PIPA production, with permission from Figiel and Armstrong, Chadwick sought to give the piece an authentic Samoan sensibility by having drummers and musicians on stage throughout and increasing the cast from five actors to 14: '... you can create the world of Samoa a lot more easily with more bodies. The market scene became more alive and you felt the impact of the "hiding". The feeling of humiliation was believable because you literally had the whole village watching.'

The primary difficulty faced by Chadwick was remaining true to Figiel's intentions while also honouring fa`asamoa.

> I had to change the first line [when a woman's vagina is mentioned] because one of the nights we performed it we had a group of people get up and walk out on the word 'vagina'. That was fine, because that was a reflection of where they were at, because the whole fa`asamoa culture is that you don't say certain things in front of your elders. We want to honour the fa`asamoa, but at the same time we want to have artistic licence to be able to tell the story and hello, it's not even our story. Those are Sia's words ... I had to choose my battles.

The PIPA production proved to be a critical and popular triumph lauded by Victor Rodger in his review, in which he compared it favourably to the ATC production as 'a completely different experience: richer and somehow more alive'.[26]

Tanya Muagututi`a, whose daughter Talia-Rae Mavaega graduated from PIPA in 2015 with a diploma in Pacific performing arts, comments: 'What Sean [Coyle] and Goretti [Chadwick] have done at PIPA is to bravely place Pacific performing arts on the highest platform, giving it the prestige, mana and recognition it deserves.'[27]

Mentoring programmes

A number of initiatives have existed to support and mentor new Pasifika playwriting. One of these, Writers' Block (2001–11), was initiated by Hone Kouka and Taki Rua with the aim of nurturing new Māori and Pacific Island writing, to develop full-length scripts for production, and to 'expand and build the body of work of Māori and Pacific Island writing'.[28] The best-known Pasifika writer to emerge from Writers' Block was Miria George, who co-founded Tawata Productions with Kouka in 2004. Tawata supports indigenous playwrights by workshopping plays – such as Moana Ete's *Ships* – through the annual Matariki Development Festival in Wellington.

A second initiative, Banana Boat, began with Playmarket in 2008 as a Pasifika writers' collective and became autonomous in 2010. Open to all, with preference given to Pasifika and Māori writers, it has offered a development programme called 'Enter the Banana'. This provides mentorship in the form of a dramaturg, workshop and public reading of new work by two writers each year. From 2010, David Mamea and Jenni Heka (on behalf of Banana Boat and Playmarket) offered several 'Newbie Writers' workshops as part of Auckland's Pasifika Festival.

Māori and Pasifika writers also have access to the Brown Ink programme run by Playmarket, which offers a one-day professional script clinic for a winning author. In 2010, its first year of operation, the selected play was *E Ono Tamai Pato* by Maureen Fepulea`i, on the subject of women survivors of domestic abuse. This developmental encouragement led to Fepulea`i's play winning 'Best New Play by a Pasifika Playwright' at the 2011 Adam New Zealand Play Awards.

Brown Ink runs other initiatives, such as Brown Ink Sessions, which include practical focused workshops such as those led by Victor Rodger and Stuart Hoar around the country in 2011. The Playmarket Brown Ink Playreading Tour 'introduces new writers to new audiences and is an opportunity for Playmarket to showcase emerging and talented writers and ... development programmes'.[29]

There have also been initiatives run by theatre companies, such as KKK's Kila Theatre Creatives and ATC Literary Unit's The Next Stage programme, which has supported rehearsed readings of works such as David Mamea's *Kingswood*.

Pasifika theatre in Wellington

While much of the energy of Pacific theatre currently lies in Auckland, there is also significant activity in Wellington. As well as work from The Conch, Whitireia Performance Centre, Toi Whakaari, BATS and the Matariki Development Festival, several other initiatives nurture new talent.

The Measina Festival, described as 'a celebration of Samoan culture, language and stories through dance, music and theatre', was first co-produced in 2014 by Jandals Inc and Pacific dance company Le Moana, whose members are graduates of the Whitireia Performance Centre.[30] In that first year, Jandals Inc revived their widely toured production of *Romeo and Tusi* and presented *IMPACT*, devised and choreographed by Taofi Mose-Tuiloma and Sasha Gibb. The piece reflected on the need for restoration following the 2009 Samoan tsunami.

The 2015 Measina Festival featured the premiere of the dance-drama *1918*, written and directed by Tupe Lualua, a lecturer at Whitireia and graduate from Victoria University's Pacific Studies programme. Like *IMPACT*, the work dramatises a catastrophic event, in this case the impact on Samoa of the 1918 influenza epidemic.[31] Also presented at the 2015 festival was a new work-in-progress, *Versions of Allah*, written and directed by Moana Ete.[32] Like Courtney Sina Meredith's *Rushing Dolls*, the play celebrates the diversity of experience for contemporary Samoan women by intercutting the stories of four cousins with that of their grandmother. It examines topics ranging from sexual harassment to contemporary conflicts in the Middle East.

Wellington's Kava Club has played a role in encouraging connections between performance and other art forms. Created by Mishelle Muagututi`a and others in 2014, the club is 'an inclusive art collective which brings together emerging to established Māori and Pasifika practitioners and advocates'.[33] Kava Club organises a monthly 'Chop Suey Hui', talanoa-style gatherings that foster community among its members. While it does not produce shows, it is another example of Pasifika practitioners creating support groups that benefit the development of contemporary art forms.

Forging links across the Pacific

Pasifika theatre in Aotearoa has developed networks and infrastructure alongside institutions such as the Department of Theatre and Dance at the University of Hawai`i, Kumu Kahua Theatre (Honolulu) and the Oceania Centre for Arts and Culture in Fiji, founded by Epeli Hau`ofa.

Practitioners such as Nathaniel Lees, Nina Nawalowalo, Victor Rodger and Fiona Collins have shared their expertise in the wider Pacific. Collins is a good example of the potential for interaction between theatre practitioners in Aotearoa and the Pacific Islands. Based at the National University of Samoa (NUS), she moves between Apia and Aotearoa facilitating relationships between Pasifika artists in both countries. Her artist's residency at NUS in 2009 led to her developing a performing arts foundation course in the department of expressive and practical arts. In 2010 she revised her first play, *My Penina* (2003), for Auckland's Herald Theatre, produced by Iosefa Enari and directed by Anapela Polataivao;[34] in 2011, working alongside Nathaniel Lees, she served as Samoan casting director in the filming of Tusi Tamasese's *The Orator* (*O Le*

Tulafale) (2011). This was the first feature film to be shot entirely in Samoa, in the Samoan language and with a Samoan cast and story, and received excellent reviews and screenings in international film festivals.[35]

In Apia, as part of Samoa–New Zealand Friendship Week (August 2012), Collins facilitated a performance event called 'Let Me Hear You Whisper', in which she performed with Joy Vaele and Olivia Taouma Levy. This was a 50-minute collection of monologues, poems, play excerpts, dance and music, and featured the work of writers such as Albert Wendt. The aim was to create 'a rich art out of the dynamic tension between New Zealand and Samoan cultures'.[36] Since 2013 she has run workshops and staged productions with local and New Zealand actors and set up a production house (Filet685) with Naea Asolelei To`alepai. Collins continues to write and direct her own scripts, including *Pele's Stars*, *Alofa* and her own adaptation of Sia Figiel's *Where We Once Belonged*.

Tours of New Zealand work to the Islands by Pacific Underground, The Laughing Samoans, KKK, MAU, Black Friars and The Conch, amongst others, have also showcased the Pasifika theatre of Aotearoa and built artistic links.

Another venture, Nina Nawalowalo's creation of a women's theatre company in the Solomon Islands with *Stages of Change*, has also had positive benefits for further collaboration. Just as Nawalowalo had brought Fijian artists to Aotearoa to perform in *Masi*, in 2016 she brought three women from *Stages of Change* to Auckland to perform alongside Tupe Lualua and Māori actor Awhina Rose-Henare Ashby in *Marama*, an image-based work that responded to the environmental impact of deforestation in the Pacific.

Cultural festivals also provide opportunities for artists from around the Pacific to interact. We have mentioned a number of these, such as Auckland's annual secondary schools' competition Polyfest, and the summer festivals held by Pacific Underground in Christchurch. Since 1992, Auckland's annual Pasifika Festival has become the largest Pacific Island gathering in Aotearoa. 'Villages' representing Pacific Island nations are built at the Western Springs venue to give visitors an experience of these cultures, including the presentation of food and cultural performances. In 1993 the Pasifika Festival expanded to include a venue for contemporary theatre as well.[37] For example, the 2009 programme featured MAU's *Tempest*, Fuemana's *Falemalama* and KKK's *Once Were Samoans*. As Auckland Museum Pacific collection curator Fulimalo Pereira notes, 'Festivals sustain cultural practices among Pacific Island communities and provide space for their development and transformation.'[38]

In the wider Pacific region the major performance gathering is the Festival of Pacific Arts (originally known as the South Pacific Festival of the Arts), which has been held every four years since 1972. The first was in Suva, where New Zealand drama was represented by Theatre Action's *Once Upon a Planet*. Alongside cultural performances from 21 Pacific countries, the second festival (Rotorua 1976) included Theatre Action's *Clowns*, Downstage's company-devised version of Janet Frame's *A State of Siege*, Bruce Mason's solo shows *Not Christmas but Guy Fawkes* and *The End of the Golden Weather*, and *Three Legends of Hatu Patu*, a play by Rotorua schoolchildren.[39] In more recent years, several Māori and Pasifika companies have presented traditional cultural performances alongside contemporary theatre works: The Conch, for example, presented *Vula* at the ninth festival in Palau.

The festival is not without its critics. Ian Gaskell explores the tensions in the festival between 'traditional' cultural performance and contemporary arts.[40] He questions the festival's notion of 'Pacificness', arguing that a pan-Pacific identity is 'an illusion', and that the festival presents 'an idyllic image of Pacific Island life that obscures the real social problems besetting its member countries'.[41] He cites his production at the 10th festival – of Fijian playwright Larry Thomas' *The Visitors*, which depicts violent racial tensions in Fiji – as an example of 'social reality' that contrasted markedly with the 'usual folkloric exhibition of song and dance that the festival customarily serves up as both touristic promotion and comforting self-image'.[42]

Gaskell's article illustrates some of the tensions in Pacific performance between 'cultural and political solidarity' and artistic practice.[43] Festivals and cultural performance play an important role in maintaining traditional Pacific cultures and languages. However, contemporary Pasifika theatre has used the tensions Gaskell mentions to create innovative artistic practice and to foster debate about the role of performance in society.

Conclusion
Floating Islanders

One of the biggest things for Pacific Island theatre was that from 1990 to 2000, the PI population [in New Zealand] grew by 40 per cent ... this Pacific theatre could only happen here.

OSCAR KIGHTLEY[1]

The evolution of Pasifika theatre in New Zealand, from its first seeding to the diversity and spirit of the work today, has been marked by a powerful sense of community, collaboration and strong family relationships that extend across generations. The feeling of 'family', mentioned often by those we interviewed, contributes to a complex network of kinship and creative connections between companies and individuals.

Pacific Island practitioners have achieved prominence as writers, directors, choreographers, actors, producers and film-makers. They demonstrate the ability to adapt, to be flexible, entrepreneurial, multi-skilled and inter-disciplinary. This fluidity arguably stems from a special position that Pasifika migrants hold in New Zealand, where they move within and between different sectors of society in a highly productive intercultural space. This is demonstrated vividly in the success of Pasifika comedy companies, where the liminal status of comedians enables them to be provocative, subversive and outrageous, and reflects the traditional function of fale aitu.

Collaborations between Pasifika theatre practitioners are significant in the wider cultural landscape of Aotearoa and the Pacific. Prior to the 1980s, Pasifika stories and characters were almost entirely absent. The cultural fluidity implicit in Makerita Urale's metaphor of 'floating Islanders' feeds this creative work. Pasifika artists are inspired by an eclectic range of sources, from fale aitu to commedia dell'arte, from *Think of a Garden* to *The Simpsons*, from Hone Kouka to Edward Albee, from Shakespeare to hip hop. Practitioners now move freely between live performing arts and other media.[2]

Pasifika artists have built and maintained a highly visible presence both locally and internationally. Many companies have reached out into the Pacific and beyond. Within New Zealand, venues such as the Mangere Arts Centre, educational institutions such as PIPA and writers' initiatives such as Brown Ink, as well as many theatre companies, have aided the development of a new generation of Pasifika practitioners. Reverend Mua Strickson-Pua notes that Pacific Underground, for example, have made theatre 'an accessible reality for our children, families and communities'.[3]

Evidence of the growing legacy of Pasifika theatre can be seen in the number of plays revived for performance. For example, 2012–13 saw new productions in Auckland of plays such as *A Frigate Bird Sings*, *Taro King*, *Niu Sila*, *Romeo and Tusi* and *Birds*. Dianna Fuemana, author of *Birds*, sees revivals as 'a sign of maturation: Pacific plays aren't disappearing when their playwrights move on'.[4]

Over three decades Pasifika theatre has generated a rich history. We have highlighted artists with roots in Samoa, Fiji, Tonga, Niue, the Cook Islands, Tokelau and New Zealand. From the outrageous humour of The Naked Samoans and the breath-taking imagery of The Conch to the skilful dramaturgy of John Kneubuhl and Victor Rodger, this is a diverse movement full of vitality and innovation. Pasifika theatre illustrates all the complexities of the fluid sense of cultural identity in migrant societies, and provides a dynamic exemplar of how migrant theatre movements can contribute to arts and culture on both local and international levels.

Appendix

A selected timeline of Pasifika productions 1981–2016

TITLE	AUTHOR	DIRECTOR / COMPANY	VENUE	DATES
1981				
Santa Claus of Rangiora	Kellee Rei-Harris & Mokalagi Tamapeau	TAOtahi	Botanic Gardens, Wellington	Summer
1982				
Atia	TAOtahi members	TAOtahi	Wellington & Auckland	May–Jun
1984				
Le Matau	Stephen Sinclair & Samson Samasoni	Helen Jarroe & Stephen Sinclair TAOtahi	New Depot, Wellington	3–18 Feb
1986				
South Pacific – The Rainbow	Simon Wilson & Rod Dunbar	Philippa Campbell	The Depot, Wellington	7 Mar–5 Apr
1987				
The Johnny Smith Myth	Eteuati Ete	Eteuati Ete	The Depot, Wellington	12–26 Jan
1988				
Feiva/Favour	John Kolia	Justine Simei-Barton, Pacific Theatre Inc	Little Maidment Theatre, Auckland	4–10 Aug
1989				
The Nine Night	Edgar White	Justine Simei-Barton, Pacific Theatre Inc	Little Maidment Theatre, Auckland	20–26 Jul
1990				
The Johnny Smith Myth	Eteuati Ete	Tommy Honey	The Depot, Wellington	Jan
Robeson – Song of Freedom	Andy Rashleigh	Justine Simei-Barton, Pacific Theatre Inc	Little Maidment Theatre, Auckland	Sep

TITLE	AUTHOR	DIRECTOR / COMPANY	VENUE	DATES
1991				
The Johnny Smith Myth	Eteuati Ete	Eteuati Ete	Taki Rua Depot, Wellington (Fringe Festival)	From 9 Jan
Horizons	Francis Serra [Simon Small]	Robert Gilbert, Whakarite Theatre Company	Performing Arts Centre, Christchurch	19 Oct–9 Nov
Lupe and Sina	Paul Simei-Barton	Justine Simei-Barton, Pacific Theatre Inc	Little Maidment Theatre, Auckland	6–21 Dec
1992				
Romeo and Juliet	William Shakespeare	Justine Simei-Barton & Alan Brunton, Pacific Theatre Inc	University of Auckland (Summer Shakespeare)	15 Feb–15 Mar
Think of a Garden	John Kneubuhl	Stuart Devenie (rehearsed reading)	Australasian Playwrights' Conference, Canberra	Apr
Horizons	Francis Serra [Simon Small]	Bert Van Dijk, Pacific Underground	Galaxy Theatre, Auckland	5–15 Aug
Horizons	Francis Serra	Bert Van Dijk	Taki Rua Depot, Wellington	19–29 Aug
Horizons	Francis Serra	Bert Van Dijk	Castle Theatre, University of Otago, Dunedin	2–5 Sep
Horizons	Francis Serra	Bert Van Dijk	Performing Arts Theatre, Christchurch	16–26 Sep
1993				
Think of a Garden	John Kneubuhl	Nathaniel Lees	Watershed Theatre, Auckland	11 Feb–6 Mar
Gifted and Fresh	Simon Small & Oscar Kightley	Pacific Underground	TIE Schools Tour	Apr–Nov
Illumina: The body in crisis	Lemi Ponifasio	Lemi Ponifasio, MAU	BATS Theatre, Wellington (Fringe Festival)	1–2 Apr
The Contest	Paul Simei-Barton	Justine Simei-Barton, Pacific Theatre Inc	Taki Rua Depot, Wellington	1–11 Sep
The Contest	Paul Simei-Barton	Justine Simei-Barton, Pacific Theatre Inc	Watershed Theatre, Auckland	16–26 Sep
Fresh off the Boat	Oscar Kightley & Simon Small	Nathaniel Lees, Pacific Underground	Rolleston Ave Theatre, Arts Centre, Christchurch	17 Nov–4 Dec
Voices On the Wind		Justine Simei-Barton, Pacific Theatre Inc	TIE North Island schools tour	1993–94
1994				
Fresh off the Boat	Oscar Kightley & Simon Small	Nathaniel Lees, Pacific Underground	Wellington Repertory Theatre	10–19 Mar
Who's the Flavour	Oscar Kightley	Pacific Underground	TIE schools tour	Term 1
Fresh off the Boat	Oscar Kightley & Simon Small	Nathaniel Lees, Pacific Underground	Herald Theatre, Auckland	7–22 Oct

TITLE	AUTHOR	DIRECTOR / COMPANY	VENUE	DATES
Tusitala and the House of Spirits	Paul Simei-Barton	Colin McColl & Justine Simei-Barton, Pacific Theatre Inc (workshop rehearsed reading)	Maidment Theatre, Auckland	3 Dec
Sons	Victor Rodger	Nathaniel Lees, Pacific Underground (workshop rehearsed reading)	Maidment Theatre, Auckland	4 Dec
Last Virgin in Paradise	Vilsoni Hereniko	Susan Wilson (Playmarket rehearsed reading)	Maidment Theatre, Auckland	Dec

1995

TITLE	AUTHOR	DIRECTOR / COMPANY	VENUE	DATES
Absolutely Fobulous	Victor Rodger & Others	Pacific Underground	Secondary schools tour	1995
Fagogo	(Samoan Story Telling)	A`oga Amata Training Institute	Taki Rua Depot, Wellington	8–10 Mar
Think of A Garden	John Kneubuhl	Nathaniel Lees	Taki Rua Depot, Wellington	8 Mar–8 Apr
Fresh off the Boat	Oscar Kightley & Simon Small	Nathaniel Lees	Downstage Theatre, Wellington	12–29 Apr
Ma Rainey's Black Bottom	August Wilson	Justine Simei-Barton, Pacific Theatre Inc	Herald Theatre, Auckland	31 Aug–23 Sep
Sons	Victor Rodger	David Fane, Pacific Underground	Court 2 Theatre, Christchurch	4–25 Nov
Lo`omatua: The ancient mother	Lemi Ponifasio	Lemi Ponifasio, MAU	Apia, Samoa	1995

1996

TITLE	AUTHOR	DIRECTOR / COMPANY	VENUE	DATES
Tatau: Rites of passage	Pacific Underground & Zeal Theatre	Stefo Nantsou, Zeal Theatre & Pacific Underground	Herald Theatre, Auckland	Feb
A Frigate Bird Sings	Oscar Kightley & David Fane	Nathaniel Lees	Downstage Theatre, Wellington (NZ International Arts Festival)	1–9 Mar
Coconuts With Juice	Oscar Kightley & Erolia Ifopo	Pacific Underground	Auckland primary schools	Mar
Tusitala and the House of Spirits	Paul Simei-Barton	Justine Simei-Barton, Pacific Theatre Inc	Taki Rua Depot, Wellington	29 Aug–21 Sep
Popo the Fairy	Makerita Urale	Erolia Ifopo	Taki Rua, Wellington	Oct
A Frigate Bird Sings	Oscar Kightley & David Fane	Nathaniel Lees	Watershed Theatre, Auckland	3–26 Oct
Su`e the Lost Son	Helen Tau`au Filisi	Helen Tau`au Filisi (school & community project)	Maidment Theatre, Auckland	5 Nov
Tatau: Rites of passage	Pacific Underground & Zeal Theatre	Stefo Nantsou, Zeal Theatre & Pacific Underground	Zeal Theatre, Bondi Pavilion, Sydney	Nov
One More for the Road	Lisa Tauoma & Paul Simei-Barton	Pacific Theatre Inc	TIE Auckland secondary schools	1996
Fuatia's Future	Charlie Oates Calico Young People's Theatre	Calico Young People's Theatre	TIE intermediate school tour	1996

TITLE	AUTHOR	DIRECTOR / COMPANY	VENUE	DATES
Romeo and Tusi	Erolia Ifopo & Oscar Kightley	Erolia Ifopo, Pacific Underground	TIE national schools tour	1996

1997

TITLE	AUTHOR	DIRECTOR / COMPANY	VENUE	DATES
Romeo and Tusi	Erolia Ifopo & Oscar Kightley	Pacific Underground (revised text)	Mona Vale Gardens, Christchurch	17 Jan–2 Feb
Bully For You	Erolia Ifopo	Erolia Ifopo, Pacific Underground	Schools tour	Mar–Jul
The Brownies: Fools of the Bacific (FOB)	Vela Manusaute & Canada Alofa	The Brownies	Taki Rua, Wellington; Court Theatre, Christchurch	To 3 May; To 29 Jun
Cunning Stunts	Victor Rodger	Conrad Newport	BATS Theatre, Wellington (Young and Hungry Season)	From 23 Jul
Illumina: The body in crisis	Lemi Ponifasio	Lemi Ponifasio, MAU	Taki Rua, Wellington	To 25 Oct
Dawn Raids	Oscar Kightley	Oscar Kightley, Pacific Underground	Herald Theatre, Auckland	11–29 Nov
Frangipani Perfume	Makerita Urale	Erolia Ifiopo	BATS Theatre, Wellington	16–23 Dec

1998

TITLE	AUTHOR	DIRECTOR / COMPANY	VENUE	DATES
Laumei: Return to paradise	Pacific Underground	Pacific Underground	Arts Centre, Christchurch	Feb
Eulogy	Oscar Kightley, David Fane, Peter Daube & Matt Chamberlain	Andrew Foster, Prague's Lost Tribe	Downstage Theatre, Wellington (Fringe Festival)	2–21 Mar
Lo`omatua: The ancient mother	Lemi Ponifasio	Lemi Ponifasio, MAU	Lake Taupo Arts Festival; Meteor Theatre, Hamilton	Feb; 30 Jun–2 Jul
Some Ghost to Watch Over Me	Tanya Muagututi`a	Pacific Underground	Arts Centre, Christchurch (Starving and Broke project)	To 21 Mar
Merchant of Aotearoa	Jamie Haugh	Shimpal Lelisi, Pacific Underground	Arts Centre, Christchurch (Starving and Broke project)	To 21 Mar
Fia Ola (dance)	Neil Ieremia (choreographer)	Black Grace Dance Company	Sky Theatre, Auckland (and national tour)	Apr
Faleaitu: House of spirits	Vela Manusaute & Canada Alofa	The Brownies	Downstage Theatre, Wellington; Auckland Town Hall; Ruby In The Dust, Dunedin; Great Hall, Christchurch	26 Apr; 27 Apr–3 May; 12–16 May; 19–23 May
Naked Samoans Talk About Their Knives	Oscar Kightley & David Fane	The Naked Samoans	BATS Theatre, Wellington (International Laugh! Festival); Southern Ballet Theatre, Christchurch; Herald Theatre, Auckland; BATS Theatre, Wellington	7–9 May; 13–16 May; 3–13 Jun; 29 Jun–11 Jul
Bare	Toa Fraser	Michael Robinson	Silo Theatre, Auckland	4–13 Jun
Frangipani Perfume	Makerita Urale	Hori Ahipene	Town Hall Concert Chamber, Auckland	24–28 Aug
Ava	Lemi Ponifasio	Lemi Ponifasio	Maidment Theatre, Auckland	9–12 Sep

TITLE	AUTHOR	DIRECTOR / COMPANY	VENUE	DATES
Sons	Victor Rodger	Christian Penny, Taki Rua Productions (revised text)	Downstage Theatre, Wellington	10–31 Oct
Swish	Nina Nawalowalo	Tom McCrory	Phoenix Theatre, Wellington	17–30 Nov
Dawn Raids	Oscar Kightley	David Fane, Pacific Underground	Court 2, Christchurch	18 Nov–12 Dec
Bare	Toa Fraser	Michael Robinson	BATS Theatre, Wellington	4–23 Dec
The Prospects	Oscar Kightley	Erolia Ifopo, Pacific Underground	TIE national tour	1998
Filo and the Magic Lamp	Tanya Muagututi`a & Others	Pacific Underground	TIE primary schools tour	1998

1999

TITLE	AUTHOR	DIRECTOR / COMPANY	VENUE	DATES
Island Mafia – The Family Story	Vela Manusaute		BATS Theatre, Wellington	To 28 Feb
Romeo and Tusi	Oscar Kightley & Erolia Ifopo	Erolia Ifopo, Pacific Underground	Frank Kitts Park, Wellington	13–20 Mar
Naked Samoans Go to Hollywood	Oscar Kightley & David Fane	The Naked Samoans	Auckland Town Hall; BATS Theatre, Wellington; Great Hall, Arts Centre, Christchurch	22–30 Apr; May; To 15 May
No. 2	Toa Fraser	Catherine Boniface	Silo Theatre, Auckland (New Works Festival)	16–26 Jun
Room 7	Tanya Muagututi`a	Erolia Ifopo, Pacific Underground	Primary schools tour	From 19 Jul
Malaga	Igelese Ete (composer), Jakki Leota-Ete (lyricist), Teokotai Paitai (choreographer)		Christchurch Town Hall (Christchurch Arts Festival)	30 Jul
Bare	Toa Fraser	Michael Robinson	Assembly Rooms, Edinburgh; Court 2, Christchurch	Aug; Sep
Sons	Victor Rodger	Christian Penny, Taki Rua Productions	Herald Theatre, Auckland	18 Sep–9 Oct
Bare	Toa Fraser	Michael Robinson	16th Ave Theatre, Tauranga	1–3 Nov
Coconuts	Eteuati Ete	Eteuati Ete	Phoenix Theatre, Wellington	3–24 Nov
Mapaki	Dianna Fuemana	Hori Ahipene	BATS Theatre, Wellington	9–13 Nov
No. 2	Toa Fraser	Catherine Boniface	Silo Theatre, Auckland	23–27 Nov

2000

TITLE	AUTHOR	DIRECTOR / COMPANY	VENUE	DATES
Bare	Toa Fraser	Michael Robinson	Downstage Theatre, Wellington	26 Jan– 5 Feb
Romeo and Tusi	Oscar Kightley & Erolia Ifopo	Erolia Ifopo, Pacific Underground	Outdoor Venues in Wellington Region: Harcourt Park, Upper Hutt; Outside Dowse Art Museum, Lower Hutt; Te Rauparaha Park, Porirua; Otaki Racecourse (Out and About Festival)	18–23 Mar
Naked Samoans: Wake me up before you go go	Oscar Kightley & David Fane	The Naked Samoans	The Boatshed, Wellington (International Laugh! Festival)	4–6 May

TITLE	AUTHOR	DIRECTOR / COMPANY	VENUE	DATES
He Kore Te Wiwia/ A Space Without Boundaries/Avanoa Leai Se Mea O Lai	Jerome Leota, Anapela Polataivao, Kayte Ferguson, Nina Nawalowalo	Nina Nawalowalo, Indecent Flesh Cooperative	BATS Theatre, Wellington	Jun
Mapaki	Dianna Fuemana	Hori Ahipene	Maidment Studio, Auckland; International Women's Playwrights Festival, Greece	Jun; Aug
Bone Flute Ivi Ivi – Ancient Winds Calling	Lemi Ponifasio	Lemi Ponifasio, MAU	Opera House, Wellington	19–21 Jul
No. 2	Toa Fraser	Catherine Boniface	Assembly Rooms, Edinburgh (Edinburgh Fringe Festival)	3–27 Aug
Bare	Toa Fraser	Michael Robinson	Opera House, Sydney, and Adelaide	18–28 Oct
New Works	Neil Ieremia (Choreographer)	Black Grace Dance Company	Herald Theatre, Auckland	22 Nov–2 Dec
Rangi and Mau's Fantastic Voyage	Tanya Muagututi`a	Pacific Underground	Schools tour	Term 2

2001

TITLE	AUTHOR	DIRECTOR / COMPANY	VENUE	DATES
Romeo and Tusi	Oscar Kightley & Erolia Ifopo	Pacific Underground	Christchurch Arts Centre (Pacific Arts Festival)	3 Feb
No. 2	Toa Fraser	Catherine Boniface	Downstage Theatre, Wellington Centrepoint Theatre, Palmerston Nth; New Plymouth (Taranaki Arts Festival)	29 Jan–9 Feb; 21 Feb–3 Mar; 17–18 Mar
The Native Chef	Erolia Ifopo	David Fane	Masi Café, Wellington (Fringe Festival)	16–17 Mar
Paradise	Toa Fraser	Tina Cook	Circa Theatre, Wellington	17 Mar–14 Apr
Bare	Toa Fraser	Michael Robinson	Maidment Theatre, Auckland	23–31 Mar
Our Back Yard	Neil Ieremia (Choreographer)	Black Grace Dance Company	Theatre Royal Christchurch and subsequent tour	29–30 Mar
Naked Samoans: The Trilogy	The Naked Samoans	The Naked Samoans	Herald Theatre, Auckland	19–30 Jun
Ifoga	Igelese Ete (Composer), Jakki Leota-Ete (Lyricist), Teokotai Paitai (Choreographer)	Tanya Muagututi`a & Sam Uta`i (producers)	Christchurch Town Hall (Christchurch Arts Festival)	27 Jul
Rangi and Mau's Fabulous Adventure	Pacific Underground	Pacific Underground	Telecom Pavilion, Christchurch	27–28 Jul
No. 2	Toa Fraser	Catherine Boniface	Christchurch Arts Festival; Fortune Theatre, Dunedin; Embassy Theatre Invercargill; Lawson Field Theatre, Gisborne; Rotorua Convention Centre; Hastings Blossom Festival; Nelson Arts Festival; Maidment Theatre, Auckland	27 Jul–5 Aug; 22–25 Aug; 28–29 Aug; 31 Aug–1 Sep; 6–7 Sep; 11–13 Sep; 27–29 Sep; 2–6 Oct
Rangi and Mau's Fantastic Voyage	Shimpal Lelisi	Pacific Underground	Schools tour	Aug
Jingle Bells	Dianna Fuemana	Dianna Fuemana	Maidment Studio Theatre, Auckland	10–27 Oct
Mapaki	Dianna Fuemana	Hori Ahipene	Pangea World Theater, Minneapolis, US	Nov 2001

TITLE	AUTHOR	DIRECTOR / COMPANY	VENUE	DATES
2002				
Naked Samoans: The trilogy	The Naked Samoans	The Naked Samoans	BATS Theatre, Wellington	11–26 Jan
Bone Flute Ivi Ivi – Ancient Winds Calling	Lemi Ponifasio	Lemi Ponifasio, MAU	Playhouse, Adelaide (Adelaide Festival of Arts)	7 Mar
Ranterstantrum	Victor Rodger	Colin McColl	Downstage Theatre, Wellington (NZ International Arts Festival)	8–17 Mar
The Native Chef	Erolia Ifopo		Waikato Museum of Art and History	26 Mar
Between the Islands	Karl Kite-Rangi	Karl Kite-Rangi	Wellington (Fringe Festival)	Mar
Naked Samoans: The trilogy	The Naked Samoans	The Naked Samoans	Herald Theatre, Auckland	1–17 May
Taro King	Vela Manusaute	Vela Manusaute & Anapela Polataivao, Island Players Theatre Company	Musgrove Studio, Maidment Theatre, Auckland	Jun
Island Girls	Oscar Kightley & Teuila Blakely	Island Players Theatre Company	Musgrove Studio, Maidment Theatre, Auckland	Jun
Rangi and Mau's Fantastic Voyage	Tanya Muagututi`a	Pacific Underground	Schools tour	Term 2
Feedback (musical)	Toa Fraser & Tim Finn	Catherine Boniface	Centrepoint Theatre, Palmerston North	8–29 Jun
Naked Samoans: The trilogy	The Naked Samoans	The Naked Samoans	Edinburgh (Fringe Festival)	Aug
Vula	Nina Nawalowalo & The Conch	Nina Nawalowalo, The Conch	BATS Theatre, Wellington	18–28 Sep
Wild Dogs Under My Skirt	Tusiata Avia	Tusiata Avia	Otago Settlers Museum, Dunedin	28 Sep–1 Oct
Through Windows	Susana Lei`Ataua	Brian Sergent	Circa Studio, Wellington	8–19 Oct
Wild Dogs Under My Skirt	Tusiata Avia	Tusiata Avia	Circa Studio, Wellington	14–19 Oct
The Sons of Charlie Paora	Lennie James	Samantha Scott, Massive Company	Herald Theatre, Auckland	Oct
Alisa	Tanya Muagututi`a	David Fane, Pacific Underground	Youth Centre, Christchurch and schools tour	8 Nov; Term 3
Rangi and Mau's Fantastic Voyage	Tanya Muagututi`a	Shimpal Lelisi & Tanya Muagututi`a, Pacific Underground	Youth Centre, Christchurch and schools tour	8 Nov; Term 2
2003				
Laughing With Samoans	Eteuati Ete & Tofiga Fepulea`i	The Laughing Samoans	Wellington Town Hall (Wellington Fringe Festival)	Feb
No. 2	Toa Fraser		King's Head Theatre, London	6 Feb–16 Mar
Tautala	Leilani Unasa	Leilani Unasa	Blue Note Bar, Wellington (Wellington Fringe Festival)	From 25 Feb
Surface (dance)	Neil Ieremia (Choreographer)	Black Grace Dance Company	TSB Theatre, New Plymouth; Sky City Theatre, Auckland	12–13 Mar; 26 Mar–5 Apr

TITLE	AUTHOR	DIRECTOR / COMPANY	VENUE	DATES
Island Divas	Lisa Taouma		Asia Society and Museum, New York, What Now? Contemporary art from the Pacific	Apr–May
Island Girls: The Remix	Teuila Blakely	Oscar Kightley, The Island Players	Maidment Studio Theatre, Auckland	Aug
Alisa	Tanya Muagututi`a	David Fane, Pacific Underground	Te Papa Marae, Wellington and schools tour	16 Aug; Term 3
The Packer	Dianna Fuemana	Dianna Fuemana	BATS Theatre, Wellington	26–30 Aug
The Songmaker's Chair	Albert Wendt	Nathaniel Lees, Auckland Theatre Company	Maidment Theatre, Auckland (Auckland Festival)	20–27 Sep
Paradise	Lemi Ponifasio	Lemi Ponifasio, MAU	Sky City Theatre, Auckland (Auckland Festival)	21–23 Sep
Naked Samoans Go Home	Oscar Kightley & David Fane	The Naked Samoans	Downstage Theatre, Wellington; Herald Theatre, Auckland (Auckland Festival)	23–27 Sep; To 4 Oct
Vula	Nina Nawalowalo & The Conch	Nina Nawalowalo, The Conch	Te Whaea Theatre, Wellington	23–30 Oct
Paradise	Lemi Ponifasio	Lemi Ponifasio, MAU	Venice Biennale International Theatre Festival	Oct

2004

TITLE	AUTHOR	DIRECTOR / COMPANY	VENUE	DATES
Alisa	Tanya Muagututi`a	Pacific Underground	Arts Centre, Christchurch Fa – Pacific Arts	Feb
The Songmaker's Chair	Albert Wendt	Nathaniel Lees	Soundings Theatre, Museum of NZ Te Papa Tongarewa, Wellington (NZ International Arts Festival)	27 Feb–3 Mar
My Penina	Fiona Collins	Fiona Collins & Tim Foley	Thistle Hall, Wellington (Fringe Festival)	From 8 Mar
Le Tauvaga (The Competition)	Louise Tu`u	Louise Tu`u	Metro Theatre (Mangere East Hall), Auckland	From 22 Mar
Niu Sila	Oscar Kightley & Dave Armstrong	Conrad Newport	Downstage Theatre, Wellington	2 Apr–1 May
Bare	Toa Fraser		Centrepoint Theatre, Palmerston North	3 Apr–1 May
Naked Samoans Go Home	Oscar Kightley & David Fane	The Naked Samoans	Gallagher Concert Chamber, Hamilton; Regent On Broadway, Palmerston North	8–10 Jul; 13 Jul
My Little Coconut Tree	Marisiale Tunoka	Richard Carlos Torr	Allen Hall Theatre, Dunedin	22–23 Jul
Naked Samoans Go Home	Oscar Kightley & David Fane	The Naked Samoans	Downstage Theatre, Wellington	26–31 Jul
Vula	Nina Nawalowalo	Nina Nawalowalo, The Conch	Palau, Micronesia (9th Festival of Pacific Arts)	Jul
Alisa	Tanya Muagututi`a	Pacific Underground	Great Hall, Arts Centre, Christchurch; Te Papa Marae, Wellington	Sep
Leaving the Underworld	Fiona Truelove	Nancy Brunning	BATS Theatre, Wellington	To 25 Sep
The Packer	Dianna Fuemana	Dianna Fuemana	Herald Theatre, Auckland	29 Sep–9 Oct
A Small Samoan Wedding	Eteuati Ete & Tofiga Fepulea`i	The Laughing Samoans	NZ Tour; Sydney; Suva; Rarotonga; Hawai`i; US	From Oct

TITLE	AUTHOR	DIRECTOR / COMPANY	VENUE	DATES
Taro King	Vela Manusaute	Vela Manusaute, Kila Kokonut Krew	BATS Theatre, Wellington	20–23 Oct
Niu Sila	Oscar Kightley & Dave Armstrong	Conrad Newport	Centrepoint Theatre, Palmerston North	21–23 Oct
My Penina	Fiona Collins	Tim Foley & Fiona Collins	Thistle Hall, Wellington	11–15 Dec

2005

TITLE	AUTHOR	DIRECTOR / COMPANY	VENUE	DATES
Alisa	Tanya Muagututi`a	Pacific Underground	Christchurch (Pacific Arts Festival)	Feb
Niu Sila	Oscar Kightley & Dave Armstrong	Conrad Newport	Maidment Theatre, Auckland; Wanaka (Festival of Colour)	3–19 Mar; 27 Apr–1 May
Vula	Nina Nawalowalo	Nina Nawalowalo, The Conch	Silo Theatre, Auckland	Mar
Playaz Night	Vela Manusaute	Vela Manusaute, Kila Kokonut Krew	Auckland Town Hall (NZ Comedy Festival)	5–6 May
Paradise	Lemi Ponifasio	Lemi Ponifasio MAU	Theater Der Welt, Amsterdam (Holland Festival)	23–25 Jun
Frangipani Perfume	Makerita Urale	Hori Ahipene	Telstra Clear Pacific Events Centre, Auckland	From 6 Jul
10 – A Decade of Works	Neil Ieremia (Choreographer)	Black Grace Dance Company (10th anniversary)	Viaduct Basin, Auckland	23 Jul–3 Aug
Leaving the Underworld	Fiona Truelove	Nancy Brunning	Maidment Studio Theatre, Auckland	6–13 Aug
The Sons of Charlie Paora	Lennie James	Samantha Scott, Massive Company	Downstage Theatre, Wellington; also Manukau, Hamilton, Gisborne	To 30 Aug
My Mother Dreaming	Dianna Fuemana	Dianna Fuemana	Herald Theatre, Auckland	9–14 Aug
Black Grace	Neil Ieremia (Choreographer)	Black Grace Dance Company	New Victory Theatre, New York	To 9 Oct
Old School	Eteuati Ete & Tofiga Fepulea`i	The Laughing Samoans	US, Hawai`i, Samoa, Australia, Fiji, NZ	From Oct
and what remains	Miria George	Hone Kouka, Tawata Productions	City Art Gallery, Wellington	16–19 Nov

2006

TITLE	AUTHOR	DIRECTOR / COMPANY	VENUE	DATES
The Songmaker's Chair	Albert Wendt	Dennis Carroll	Kumu Kahua Theatre, Honolulu	16 Mar–15 Apr
Once Were Samoans	Vela Manusaute	Anapela Polataivao & Vela Manusaute	Herald Theatre, Auckland	23–27 May
Vula	Nina Nawalowalo	Nina Nawalowalo, The Conch	Maidment Theatre; Auckland; The Playhouse, Sydney Opera House	25–27 May; 8–25 Jun
Hit the Curve	Paul Simei-Barton	Justine Simei-Barton, Pacific Theatre Inc	TIE secondary schools tour: Wellington, Hutt Valley, Porirua	12–28 Jun
Frangipani Perfume	Makerita Urale	Rachel House	Queensland (Dreaming Festival)	Jun
and what remains	Miria George	Hone Kouka	BATS Theatre, Wellington	25 Aug–2 Sep

TITLE	AUTHOR	DIRECTOR / COMPANY	VENUE	DATES
Requiem	Lemi Ponifasio & MAU	Lemi Ponifasio, MAU	Sky City Theatre, Auckland	16–17 Sep
Frangipani Perfume	Makerita Urale	Rachel House, Native Earth Performing Arts	Theatre Passe Muraille, Toronto; Firehall Arts Centre, Vancouver	27–30 Sep; 18–21 Oct
Off Work	Eteuati Ete & Tofiga Fepulea`i	The Laughing Samoans	Tour	From Oct
Falemalama	Dianna Fuemana	Dipankar Mukherjee	Pangea World Theater, Minneapolis, US	16 Nov
Requiem	Lemi Ponifasio & MAU	Lemi Ponifasio	Vienna (Festival for Mozart's 250th anniversary)	25–28 Nov
Requiem	Lemi Ponifasio & MAU	Lemi Ponifasio, MAU	Royal Flemish Theatre, Brussels	2–3 Dec
Naked Samoans Go Home (Again)	The Naked Samoans	The Naked Samoans	Auckland Town Hall	12–17 Dec

2007

TITLE	AUTHOR	DIRECTOR / COMPANY	VENUE	DATES
Off Work	Eteuati Ete & Tofiga Fepulea`i	The Laughing Samoans	Blaisdell Center, Honolulu	12 Jan
His Mother's Son	Leilani Unasa	Katrina Chandra Chickenhead Productions	BATS Theatre, Wellington	24 Jan–3 Feb
Mapaki	Dianna Fuemana	Hori Ahipene	Herald Theatre, Auckland	15–25 Feb
Wild Dogs Under My Skirt	Tusiata Avia	Tusiata Avia	Musgrove Studio, Maidment Theatre, Auckland	9–11 Mar
Tempest	Lemi Ponifasio	Lemi Ponifasio, MAU	MAU Theatre, Corban Estate, Auckland	11–16 Mar
Requiem	Lemi Ponifasio & MAU	Lemi Ponifasio	ASB Theatre, Auckland	22 Mar
Bare	Toa Fraser	Oliver Driver	Silo Theatre, Auckland	12 Apr–12 May
Being Brown	Michelle Johansson	Michelle Johansson, Black Friars	Herald Theatre, Auckland; Auckland (International Comedy Festival)	12–16 Apr; Apr
Goldilocks and the Three Little Puaka	Michelle Johansson	Michelle Johansson, Black Friars	Herald Theatre, Auckland; Auckland (International Comedy Festival)	19–20 Apr; Apr
Once Were Samoans	Vela Manusaute	Vela Manusaute & Anapela Polataivao, Kila Kokonut Krew	Herald Theatre, Auckland	22–26 May
Off Work	Eteuati Ete & Tofiga Fepulea`i	The Laughing Samoans	Founders Theatre, Hamilton	26 May
and what remains	Miria George	Hone Kouka	The Playroom, Cambridge, England (Pasifika Styles Performing Arts Festival)	31 May–1 Jun
Frangipani Perfume	Makerita Urale		Cambridge, England (Pasifika Styles Performing Arts Festival)	May
Niu Sila	Oscar Kightley & Dave Armstrong	Conrad Newport	Cambridge, England (Pasifika Styles Performing Arts Festival); Repertory Theatre, Christchurch; Theatre Royal, New Plymouth	May; 27–29 Jul; 3–5 Aug
His Mother's Son	Leilani Unasa	Katrina Chandra	Maidment Studio Theatre, Auckland	To 16 Jun
Once Were Samoans	Vela Manusaute	Vela Manusaute & Anapela Polataivao, Kila Kokonut Krew	BATS Theatre, Wellington	24–28 Jul

TITLE	AUTHOR	DIRECTOR / COMPANY	VENUE	DATES
Naked Samoans Go Home (Again)	The Naked Samoans	The Naked Samoans	TSB Showplace, New Plymouth (Taranaki Arts Festival)	29 Jul
My Name is Gary Cooper	Victor Rodger	Roy Ward, Auckland Theatre Company	Maidment Theatre, Auckland	20 Sep–13 Oct
Requiem	Lemi Ponifasio & MAU	Lemi Ponifasio, MAU	Southbank Centre, London	29–30 Sep
Crack Me Off	Eteuati Ete & Tofiga Fepulea`i	The Laughing Samoans	Aotea Centre, Auckland; Michael Fowler Centre, Wellington	26–27 Oct
and what remains	Miria George	Jason Te Kare, Radio New Zealand National	Radio New Zealand, National Programme	28 Oct
Lena	Jason Greenwood	Justine Simei-Barton, Pacific Theatre Inc	Herald Theatre, Auckland	3–10 Nov
Le Tauvaga	Louise Tu`u	Reading	Martin E. Segal Theatre Center, New York (World Indigenous Theatre Reading Series)	Nov

2008

TITLE	AUTHOR	DIRECTOR / COMPANY	VENUE	DATES
Vula	Nina Nawalowalo	Nina Nawalowalo, The Conch	Te Whaea Theatre, Wellington	14–17 Feb
Othello Polynesia	William Shakespeare	Michelle Johansson, Black Friars	Fale Pasifika, University of Auckland	16–18 Feb
Fragile Land	Tanika Gupta	Reading	Limelight, Aotea Centre, Auckland	4 Mar
bro'Town Live on Stage	The Naked Samoans	The Naked Samoans	St James Theatre, Wellington (NZ International Arts Festival)	4–5 Mar
No Names	Junior Williams	Reading	Limelight, Aotea Centre, Auckland	7 Mar
O Le Olaga (This is Life)	Victoria Schmidt	Reading	Limelight, Aotea Centre, Auckland	7 Mar
Where We Once Belonged	Sia Figiel/ Dave Armstrong	Colin McColl & Dave Fane	Downstage Theatre, Wellington; Concert Chamber, Auckland Town Hall	8–16 Mar; 27 Mar–19 Apr
Beige Against the Machine	James Nokise	Stand-up comedy	Classic Studio, Auckland	19–26 Apr
Vula	Nina Nawalowalo	Nina Nawalowalo	The Pit, Barbican Centre, London	23 Apr–3 May
Beige Against the Machine	James Nokise		Bluenote Bar, Wellington	29 Apr–3 May
Tempest II	Lemi Ponifasio	Lemi Ponifasio, MAU	Queen Elizabeth Hall, London	28 Jun
Falemalama	Dianna Fuemana	Dianna Fuemana	Pago Pago, American Samoa (10th Festival of Pacific Arts)	Jul
Polynation (performance poetry)	Selina Tusitala Marsh, Mua Strickson-Pua & others	Tusiata Avia	Auckland (Going West Books and Writers Festival); Queensland Poetry Festival	Jul; 23 Aug
Requiem	Lemi Ponifasio & MAU	Lemi Ponifasio	Lincoln Center, New York	Aug
Wild Dogs Under My Skirt	Tusiata Avia	Tusiata Avia	Powerhouse, Brisbane (Pasifika Festival)	27–30 Aug
Bare	Toa Fraser	Oliver Driver	Downstage Theatre, Wellington; Herald Theatre, Auckland	23 Sep–4 Oct; 8–18 Oct
The Chronicles	Legacy Dance Crew		Hawkins Theatre, Papakura, Auckland	21–22 Oct

TITLE	AUTHOR	DIRECTOR / COMPANY	VENUE	DATES
Once Were Samoans	Vela Manusaute	Anapela Polataivao, Kila Kokonut Krew	Metro Theatre (Mangere East Hall), Auckland (Manukau Festival Of Arts)	12–13 Nov
On a Different Shelf	Sandra Kailahi	Katrina Chandra, Kingston Productions & Stamp	Herald Theatre, Auckland	25–30 Nov
Frangipani Perfume	Makerita Urale	Staged Reading	La Mama, New York (New Indigenous Voices: Aotearoa 2008)	25 Nov
My Name is Gary Cooper	Victor Rodger	Staged Reading	La Mama, New York (New Indigenous Voices: Aotearoa 2008)	26 Nov
Prettyfull Woman	Eteuati Ete & Tofiga Fepulea`i	The Laughing Samoans	Tour	2008

2009

TITLE	AUTHOR	DIRECTOR / COMPANY	VENUE	DATES
Poly-Zygotic	Tupe Lualua, Taofi Mose-Tuiloma & Asalemo Tofete		BATS Theatre, Wellington (NZ Fringe Festival)	13–17 Feb
The Minister's Son	James Nokise	Sonal Patel, Not Even Broductions	BATS Theatre, Wellington	19–22 Feb
Prettyfull Woman	Eteuati Ete & Tofiga Fepulea`i	The Laughing Samoans	Tour	27 Feb
Falemalama	Dianna Fuemana	Dianna Fuemana	Auckland (Celebrate Pasifika)	Feb
Tempest: Without a body	Lemi Ponifasio	Lemi Ponifasio, MAU	ASB Theatre, Auckland	5 Mar
Falemalama	Dianna Fuemana	Dianna Fuemana	MAU Theatre, Corban Estate, Auckland	6–10 Mar
The Frogs	Aristophanes trans. David Barrett	Michelle Johansson, Black Friars	Hawkins Theatre, Papakura, Auckland	11–14 Mar
The Minister's Son	James Nokise	Sonal Patel	Galatos Theatre, Auckland	17–19 Mar
Once Were Samoans	Vela Manusaute	Anapela Polataivao, Kila Kokonut Krew	Globe Theatre, Palmerston North	25–26 Mar
Gathering Clouds	Black Grace	Neil Ieremia	Opera House, Wellington	26–28 Mar
The Minister's Son	James Nokise	Sonal Patel	Fortune Studio Theatre, Dunedin	31 Mar–4 Apr
Poly-Zygotic	Tupe Lualua, Taofi Mose-Tuiloma & Asalemo Tofete	Devised by the company	Downstage Theatre, Wellington (NZ Fringe Festival)	29 Apr–7 May
The Adventures of Jimi Samoa	James Nokise	Stand-up comedy	Comedy Underground, Auckland; Happy, Wellington	2–9 May; 12–16 May
Othello Polynesia	William Shakespeare	Michelle Johansson, Black Friars	Downstage Theatre, Wellington	2–6 Jun
Urban Hymns	Miria George	Fiona Truelove	BATS Theatre, Wellington, as part of Young and Hungry 09	10–25 Jul
Angels	Tanya Muagututi`a & Joy Vaele	Robert Gilbert, Pacific Underground & Court Theatre	Aranui High School, Christchurch; The Forge, Christchurch (Christchurch Arts Festival)	16–18 Jul; 22 Jul–15 Aug
Providence	Louise Tu`u	Louise Tu`u, We Should Practice (workshop presentation)	Metro Theatre (Mangere East Hall), Auckland	6 Aug
Yalewa	The Conch, Kasaya Manulevu	The Conch	BATS Theatre, Wellington (part of Conchus season)	18–29 Aug

TITLE	AUTHOR	DIRECTOR / COMPANY	VENUE	DATES
Who's Poppin? The Prequel	Sopa Enari		BATS Theatre, Wellington	2–5 Sep
Prettyfull Woman	Eteuati Ete & Tofiga Fepulea`i	The Laughing Samoans	Concert Hall, Queensland Performing Arts Centre, Brisbane	19 Sep
Naked Samoans Go Home	The Naked Samoans		ASB Theatre, Auckland (for Samoan tsunami)	7 Nov
Strictly Brown		Kila Kokonut Krew	Telstra Clear Pacific Events Centre, Auckland (For Samoan Tsunami)	8 Nov

2010

TITLE	AUTHOR	DIRECTOR / COMPANY	VENUE	DATES
Tempest: Without a body	Lemi Ponifasio	Lemi Ponifasio, MAU	Seymour Centre, Sydney (Sydney Festival Of The Arts); Théâtre De La Ville, Paris	10 Jan; 27–30 Jan
Joker's Guide to Armageddon	James Nokise	Stand-up comedy	Fringe Bar, Wellington	17–20 Feb
He Reo Aroha	Miria George & Jamie McCaskill	Hone Kouka, Tawata Productions	Soundings Theatre, Museum of NZ Te PapaTongarewa, Wellington (NZ International Arts Festival)	9–10 Mar
Sunameke (dance)		Julia Grey	Western Springs Lakeside Park, Auckland (Pasifika Festival)	13 Mar
Tautai	Iaheto Ah Hi	Oscar Kightley	Musgrave Studio, Maidment Theatre, Auckland	13–17 Apr
Fasitua Amosa is Ruufless!!	Fasitua Amosa	Stand-up comedy	The Basement Theatre, Auckland; Club Ivy, The Garden Club, Wellington	24 Apr–1 May; 12–15 May
Is This It?	James Nokise	Stand-up comedy	BATS Theatre, Wellington; Comedy Underground, Auckland	27 Apr–1 May; 4–8 May
Six Lessons and a Wedding	Michelle Johansson	Michelle Johansson, Black Friars	Drama Studio, University of Auckland	29 Apr–2 May
Rangi and Mau's Amazing Race	Tanya Muagututi`a, Joy Vaele, Raniera Dallas & Avefua Sua	Pacific Underground	Schools tour; Air New Zealand Foyer, Aotea Centre, Auckland	May–Jul; 17 Jul
Choka-Block	Eteuati Ete & Tofiga Fepulea`i	The Laughing Samoans	Queensland Performing Arts Centre, Brisbane	26 Jun
Birds With Skymirrors	Lemi Ponifasio	Lemi Ponifasio, MAU	Theater Der Welt 2010, Ruhr, Germany; Edinburgh International Festival	8 Jul; 17–18 Aug
His Mother's Son	Leilani Unasa	Katrina Chandra (reading)	Metro Theatre (Mangere East Hall), Auckland	15 Jul
My Penina	Fiona Collins	Anapela Polataivao	Herald Theatre, Auckland	2–7 Aug
Le Tauvaga – The Competition	Louise Tu`u	Iaheto Ah Hi (reading)	Metro Theatre (Mangere East Hall), Auckland	19 Aug
He Reo Aroha	Miria George & Jamie McCaskill	Hone Kouka, Tawata Productions	Glen Eden Playhouse, Auckland	25–28 Aug
Once Were Samoans	Vela Manusaute	Anapela Polataivao, Kila Kokonut Krew	Mangere Arts Centre, Auckland	10–12 Sep
Y Chromozone (dance)	various	Black Grace & others	Auckland Performing Arts Centre, Western Springs, Auckland	9 Oct
Strictly Brown 2	Kila Kokonut Krew	Kila Kokonut Krew	Manukau Festival of Arts	16 Oct

TITLE	AUTHOR	DIRECTOR / COMPANY	VENUE	DATES
Providence	Louise Tu`u	Louise Tu`u, We Should Practice	The Basement Theatre Studio, Auckland	20–23 Oct
We Can't Pay! We Won't Pay! (retold by Pani & Pani)	Dario Fo/ Pani & Pani	Goretti Chadwick, Anapela Polataivao, Auckland Theatre Company	Manukau Festival of Arts	Oct
Where We Once Belonged	Sia Figiel/ Dave Armstrong	Letti Chadwick & Anapela Polotaivao	Mangere Arts Centre, Auckland; Glen Eden Playhouse, Auckland	4–7 Nov
Tautai	Iaheto Ah Hi	Oscar Kightley	Mangere Arts Centre, Auckland	6–11 Dec
Once Were Samoans	Vela Manusaute	Kila Kokonut Krew	Brisbane (Pasifika Spectacular Festival)	2010

2011

TITLE	AUTHOR	DIRECTOR / COMPANY	VENUE	DATES
Mixed Nuts	Olivia Taouma-Levy	Lima Dance Productions	Mangere Arts Centre, Auckland (Auckland Fringe Festival)	24 Jan–26 Feb
Four Women	Leilani Esmae Sieni Salesa	Vela Manusaute, Kila Kokonut Krew	Centrepoint Theatre, Palmerston North	26 Feb –12 Mar
Pigs in the Yard	Kalisolaite `Uhila	Performance Art	Mangere Arts Centre, Auckland (Auckland Fringe Festival)	Feb
Take That! (dance)	Olivia Taouma-Levy	Olivia Taouma-Levy, Lima Dance Productions	Freeman's Bay Community Centre, Auckland	9–11 Mar
Samoa Mo Samoa	Jeanie Tualima	Edward Peni	Mangere Arts Centre, Auckland	22–26 Mar
Bare	Toa Fraser	Ian Hughes & Toa Fraser	Civic Theatre Auckland (for Christchurch earthquake victims)	25 Mar
Six Lessons and a Wedding	Michelle Johansson	Michelle Johansson, Black Friars	Mangere Arts Centre, Auckland	30 Mar–2 Apr
Polly Hood in Mumuland	Lauren Jackson	Goretti Chadwick, Auckland Theatre Company and PIPA	Mangere Arts Centre, Auckland	15–21 Apr
Uso	Michelle Johansson	Michelle Johansson, Black Friars	Downstage Theatre, Wellington	5–7 May
Kingdom of Lote	Suli Moa	Vela Manusaute & Anapela Polataivao, Kila Kokonut Krew	Mangere Arts Centre, Auckland	17–21 May
Public Service Announcements	James Nokise	Rachel Henry	BATS, Wellington (NZ International Comedy Festival)	20–21 May
Mapaki (scenes included in *Womanz Work! Plays From NZ Female Playwrights*)	Dianna Fuemana	K.C. Kelly, Ensembleimpact	Schools tour	31 May–8 Jul
Rangi and Mau's Amazing Race	Tanya Muagututi`a, Joy Vaele, Ave Sua & Raniera Dallas	Pacific Underground	Schools tour	June
Past, Present, Future (dance)	Keneti Muaiava		Metro Theatre (Mangere East Hall), Auckland	30 Jul–30 Aug
The Factory – A Pacific Musical	Vela Manusaute	Vela Manusaute & Anapela Polataivao, Kila Kokonut Krew	Mangere Arts Centre, Auckland	13 Aug–10 Sep
Public Service Announcements #2	James Nokise	Rachel Henry	BATS Theatre, Wellington	2–17 Sep

TITLE	AUTHOR	DIRECTOR / COMPANY	VENUE	DATES
Black Grace, Verse 2 (dance)	Neil Ieremia		Opera House, Wellington	12–13 Sep
Fasitua Amosa is Ruufless 2.0	Fasitua Amosa	Stand-up comedy	The Basement Theatre Studio, Auckland	4–8 Oct
Black Grace, Verse 2 (dance)	Neil Ieremia		Maidment Theatre, Auckland	5–11 Oct
Pigs in the Yard	Kalisolaite `Uhila	Performance art	The Performance Arcade, Aotea Square, Auckland	To 23 Oct
E Ono Tama`i Pato	Maureen Fepulea`i	Margaret-Mary Hollins Reading	Auckland, Wellington	Nov
Laugh You Long Time	Vela Manusaute	Kila Kokonut Krew	Mangere Arts Centre, Auckland	10 Dec
Being Brown	Michelle Johansson	Michelle Johansson, Black Friars	Mangere Arts Centre, Auckland	2011

2012

TITLE	AUTHOR	DIRECTOR / COMPANY	VENUE	DATES
Music and Me	Victoria Schmidt	Asalemo Tofete	Mangere Arts Centre, Auckland	13–18 Feb
Where We Once Belonged	Dave Armtrong/ Sia Figiel	Goretti Chadwick & Anapela Polataivao	Brisbane Powerhouse (World Theatre Festival)	15–18 Feb
Mixed Nuts 2: Underworld	Dance/ Promenade Theatre	Olivia Taouma	Mangere Arts Centre, Auckland	22–26 Feb
Providence	Louise Tu`u	Louise Tu`u, We Should Practice	Aotea Centre, Auckland (New Performance Festival)	24–25 Feb
Laugh You Long Time 2	Vela Manusaute & others	Stand-up comedy	Mangere Arts Centre, Auckland	25 Feb
Birds With Skymirrors	Lemi Ponifasio	Lemi Ponifasio, MAU	St James Theatre, Wellington (NZ International Arts Festival)	29 Feb–1 Mar
His Mother's Son	Leilani Unasa	Chris Molloy, Indigenous Theatre Group	Mangere Arts Centre, Auckland	29 Feb–3 Mar
Masi	The Conch	Nina Nawalowalo, The Conch	Soundings Theatre, Museum of NZ Te Papa Tongarewa, Wellington (NZ International Arts Festival)	2–6 Mar
Birds	Dianna Fuemana	Dianna Fuemana, Newwayintheatre	Mangere Arts Centre, Auckland	16–17 Mar
The Axe	Allen Curnow	James Wenley (rehearsed reading)	Drama Studio, University of Auckland	26 Mar
Sinarella	Goretti Chadwick & Sean Coyle	Goretti Chadwick & Anapela Polataivao, PIPA & Auckland Theatre Company	Mangere Arts Centre, Auckland	10–14 Apr
The Brave	Massive Company (devised)	Sam Scott & Carla Martell, Massive Company	Q Theatre, Auckland; Mangere Arts Centre, Auckland	17–22 Apr; 24–29 Apr
Fasitua Amosa is the Info-Crack Whore	Fasitua Amosa	Stand-up comedy	Cavern Club, Wellington; Vault, Q Theatre, Auckland	2–5 May; 9–12 May
Sky Blue	David Mamea	Radio play	Radio New Zealand, National Programme	13 May

TITLE	AUTHOR	DIRECTOR / COMPANY	VENUE	DATES
Tevita Manukia in Knock Knock	Tevita Manukia	NZ International Comedy Festival	The Classic Studio, Auckland	14–19 May
Plantation	Iaheto Ah Hi	Iaheto Ah Hi, Kinetic Wayfinding	Mangere Arts Centre, Auckland	15–19 May
Sunset Road	Miria George	Miria George, Tawata Productions	Circa Two, Wellington	20 Jun–7 Jul
Gaga: The Unmentionable	Louise Tu`u	Louise Tu`u	Galatos Theatre, Auckland	28 Jun
A Heart's Path	Suli Moa	Semi-staged reading	The Basement Theatre, Auckland, Rough, Raw and Ready Showcase	26 Jun
My Mother Dreaming	Dianna Fuemana	Semi-staged reading	The Basement Theatre, Auckland	29 Jun
At the Wake	Victor Rodger	Roy Ward	Centrepoint Theatre, Palmerston North	28 Jul–25 Aug
Taro King	Vela Manusaute	Vela Manusaute & Anapela Politaivao, Kila Kokonut Krew	Mangere Arts Centre, Auckland	15–24 Aug
Where We Once Belonged	Sia Figiel/ Dave Armstrong	Letti Chadwick & Anapela Polotaivao, PIPA	Glen Eden Playhouse, Auckland	23–26 Aug
Music and Me	Victoria Schmidt	Asalemo Tofete	BATS Theatre, Wellington	4–15 Sep
Hypothesis One	Fasitua Amoasa, Max Palamo, Beulah Koale, Shadon Meredith & Amelia Reid-Meredith (devisors)	Shadon Meredith & Amelia Reid-Meredith, Polynesian Laboratory	The Basement Theatre, Auckland	11–15 Sep
Heliaki: Tongan Contemporary Dance Theatre	Sesilia Pusiaki, Amanaki Prescott-Faletau	LIMA Productions	Mangere Arts Centre, Auckland	26–28 Sep
A Heart's Path	Suli Moa	Kate-Louise Elliott	Mangere Arts Centre, Auckland	To 28 Sep
Made in Samoa	Tofiga Fepulea`i	Stand-up comedy	Mangere Arts Centre, Auckland	30 Sep
Where We Once Belonged	Sia Figiel/ Dave Armstrong	Goretti Chadwick & Anapela Polataivao	Fortune Theatre, Dunedin	8–11 Oct
A Frigate Bird Sings	Dave Fane & Oscar Kightley	Alison Quigan, Auckland Theatre Company	Mangere Arts Centre, Auckland (Southside Arts Festival)	11–20 Oct
Culture Clash	Co-Theatre Physical	Beth Kayes	Auckland Performing Arts Centre, Auckland	26 Oct–3 Nov
Galulolo (Tsunami)	Goretti Chadwick	Goretti Chadwick, PIPA	Mangere Arts Centre, Auckland	31 Oct–4 Nov
Pacific Dance Choreolab (dance)			Mangere Arts Centre, Auckland	10 Nov
Gaga: The Unmentionable	Louise Tu`u	Louise Tu`u, We Should Practice	Old Folks Association Hall, Newton, Auckland	3–4 Dec
The Winged Thieves of Samoa	Leilani Unasa & Michelanne Forster	Fliss Higginson et al/ Calico Young People's Theatre	Whenuapai School, Auckland	2012
Funny Chokers	Eteuati Ete & Tofiga Fepulea`i	The Laughing Samoans	NZ & Australian tour	2012

TITLE	AUTHOR	DIRECTOR / COMPANY	VENUE	DATES
2013				
Absolutely Fobulous	Eteuati Ete & Tofiga Fepulea`i	The Laughing Samoans	NZ & Australian tour	2013
Romeo and Tusi	Erolia Ifopo & Oscar Kightley	Sasha Gibb, Jandals Inc	Whitireia Performance Centre, Wellington (Positively Pasifika Festival)	17–19 Jan
Masi	The Conch	Nina Nawalowalo, The Conch	Everest Theatre, Seymour Centre, Sydney	20–25 Jan
Black Faggot	Victor Rodger	Roy Ward, Multinesia Productions	The Basement Theatre, Auckland	16–20 Feb
Horses and other Farm Animals	Louise Tu`u	Louise Tu`u, We Should Practice	Whammy Bar, Auckland (Auckland Fringe Festival)	18–19 Feb
Fatu Na Toto – Planted Seeds (dance, oratory, music, song)	Tupe Lualua	Tupe Lualua, Le Moana Productions	BATS Theatre, Wellington	18–22 Feb
Mixed Nuts 3: Mythical (dance)		Olivia Taouma, LIMA Productions	Mangere Arts Centre, Auckland	27 Feb–2 Mar
The Factory – A Pacific musical	Vela Manusaute	Vela Manusaute & Anapela Polataivano, Kila Kokonut Krew	Q Theatre, Auckland	6–11 Mar
Le Tonu: The decision	Fasitua Amosa, Beulah Koale, Max Palamo	Shadon Meredith & Amelia Reid-Meredith, Polynesian Laboratory (PLab)	The Basement Theatre, Auckland	19–30 Mar
Romeo and Tusi	Erolia Ifopo & Oscar Kightley	Sasha Gibb, Jandals Inc	Aotea College, Porirua; Little Theatre, Lower Hutt	9–13 Apr; 16–19 Apr
Goodbye My Feleni	David Fa`auliuli Mamea	Shadon Meredith & Amelia Reid-Meredith, Hekama Creative & Chocolate Stigmata	The Basement Theatre, Auckland	16–25 Apr
James Nokise in So-So Gangsta	James Nokise	Stand-up comedy	Vault, Q Theatre, Auckland	27 Apr–4 May
Tautai	Iaheto Ah Hi	Oscar Kightley, Kinetic Wayfinding	Little Theatre, Library Building, Lower Hutt	29 Apr–2 May
Bare and *No. 2*	Toa Fraser	Robbie Magasiva/ David Fane	Mangere Arts Centre, Auckland	2–4 May
Mele Kanikau: A pageant	John Kneubuhl	Michelle Johansson	Fale Pasifika, University of Auckland	2–5 May
James Nokise in So-So Gangsta	James Nokise	Stand-up comedy	Fringe Bar, Wellington	7–11 May
Big Balls	Vela Manusaute	Stand-up comedy	Q Theatre Loft, Auckland (NZ International Comedy Festival)	7–11 May
Struggle Street (dance, music & drama performance)		Calvary Community	Mangere Arts Centre, Auckland	17–18 May
The Mau and the Visitor	Puloto Canada Alofa McCarthy	Puloto Canada Alofa McCarthy, Pacific Voice Productions	Mangere Arts Centre, Auckland	29 May–8 Jun

TITLE	AUTHOR	DIRECTOR / COMPANY	VENUE	DATES
Romeo and Tusi	Erolia Ifopo & Oscar Kightley	Sasha Gibb, Jandals Inc	Whitireia Theatre, Wellington	30 May–1 Jun
The Brave (devised)	Massive Company	Sam Scott & Carla Martell, Massive Company	Mangere Arts Centre, Auckland; Theatre Royal, New Plymouth	6–10 Aug; 20 Aug
Frangipani Perfume	Makerita Urale	Fiona Collins	National University of Samoa	8–10 Aug
The Mau and the Visitor	Pulotu Canada Alofa McCarthy	Pulotu Canada Alofa McCarthy, Pacific Voice Productions	Mangere Arts Centre, Auckland	12–16 Aug
Romeo and Tusi	Erolia Ifopo & Oscar Kightley	Sasha Gibb, Jandals Inc	Waikato University; Mangere Arts Centre, Auckland	22–24 Aug; 3–7 Sep
Niu Sila	Dave Armstrong & Oscar Kightley	Ben Crowder, Auckland Theatre Company	Clarence Street Theatre, Hamilton; St Margaret's College Chapel, Chchurch; Cashmere High School, Christchurch; Aranui High School, Christchurch; Old Library Arts Centre, Whangarei; Q Theatre Loft, Auckland; Suter Theatre, Nelson; Mangere Arts Centre, Auckland	13 Sept; 17–18 Sept; 19 Sept; 20 Sept; 26 Sept; 2–5 Oct ; 11–12 Oct; 15–25 Oct
Birds	Dianna Fuemana	Scotty Cotter, Sharu Loves Hats	The Basement Theatre Studio, Auckland	17–21 Sep
Digital Winds	Iaheto Ah Hi	Leilani Clarke & Iaheto Ah Hi, Kinetic Wayfinding & Martin Hautus Institute	Mangere Arts Centre, Auckland	24–28 Sep
Black Faggot	Victor Rodger	Roy Ward, Multinesia Productions	North Melbourne Town Hall, Australia	28 Sep–5 Oct
Fatu Na Toto – Planted Seeds (dance, oratory, music, song)	Tupe Lualua	Tupe Lualua	Q Theatre Loft, Auckland (Tempo Dance Festival)	12 Oct
Halfatasi	Refiner's Fire Collective		The Basement Theatre, Auckland ('The Feast')	15–19 Oct
Pacific Dance Presents Pacific Choreographers (dance)	Aruna Po-Ching, Filoi Vaila`au, Ula Naulutubutubu & Nikki Upoko		Q Theatre Loft, Auckland	16–17 Oct
James Nokise in So-So Gangsta	James Nokise	Stand-up comedy	Ombrellos, Dunedin	23–25 Oct
The Brave (devised)	Massive Company	Sam Scott & Carla Martell, Massive Company	Baycourt Theatre, Tauranga	24–25 Oct
Under the Fale	Pacific Underground	Pacific Underground, Festa, Free Theatre, Unitec School of Architecture	Christchurch, Open Air	26–27 Oct
Pacific Dance Choreolab 2013 (dance)	Amo Ieriko, Nikki Upoko, Santana Schmidt (choreographers)		Mangere Arts Centre, Auckland	2 Nov

TITLE	AUTHOR	DIRECTOR / COMPANY	VENUE	DATES
Don Ioane (*Don Juan* adapted with a Pacific twist)		Rachel House, PIPA	Mangere Arts Centre, Auckland	6–9 Nov
Speak Your Truth	Sela Faletolu	No Limits!	Court Theatre, Christchurch	10 Nov
Black Grace Presents Xmas Verses (dance)	Neil Ieremia (choreographer)	Black Grace	Herald Theatre, Auckland	27 Nov–1 Dec
Six Lessons and a Wedding	Michelle Johansson	Black Friars	National University of Samoa	3–5 Dec
Sai E	Lolo Fonua	Lolo Fonua, PIPA	Mangere Arts Centre, Auckland	4–6 Dec
My Father's Hands	Vela Manusaute & Stacey Leilua	Kila Kokonut Krew	Mangere Arts Centre, Auckland	9 Dec

2014

TITLE	AUTHOR	DIRECTOR / COMPANY	VENUE	DATES
Hi`iaka: Our pacific heroine emerges (dance)	Aruna Po-Ching & Tat Mahuru-Stanley (choreographers)	Aruna Po-Ching	Auckland Performing Arts Centre, Auckland	18 Jan
My Name is ... Pilitome	Vela Manusaute	Vela Manusaute, Kila Kokonut Krew	Martin Hautus Institute Performing Arts Centre, Auckland	27–31 Jan
Black Faggot	Victor Rodger	Roy Ward	Hannah Playhouse, Wellington	25 Feb–1 Mar
Stages of Change Project	The Conch	Nina Nawalowalo, The Conch	Solomon Islands, Papua New Guinea, Samoa, Brussels	Mar
Birds	Dianna Fuemana	Scotty Cotter, Sharu Loves Hats	BATS Theatre, Wellington (NZ Fringe Festival)	1–8 Mar
Stones in her Mouth	Lemi Ponifasio	Lemi Ponifasio, MAU	Opera House, Wellington (NZ International Arts Festival)	4–5 Mar
Black Faggot	Victor Rodger	Roy Ward, Multinesia Productions	Herald Theatre, Auckland	4–8 Mar
The Crimson House	Lemi Ponifasio	Lemi Ponifasio, MAU	St James Theatre, Wellington (NZ International Arts Festival)	5–6 Mar
Spiritus Aitu	Charlene Tedrow (choreographer), Grace Taylor (poet) & others	Ura Tabu Pacific Dance	Auckland Performing Arts Centre, Auckland	5–8 Mar
Elephants in the Garden of Gethsemane	Jay Williams	Phoenix NZ Performing Arts	Allen Hall, Dunedin (Fringe Festival)	15–16 Mar
Let's Talk about the Golliwogs	James Nokise	Stand-up comedy	Ombrellos, Dunedin (Fringe Festival)	20–22 Mar
James Nokise in the Bronaissance	James Nokise	Stand-up comedy	BATS Theatre, Wellington (NZ International Comedy Festival)	29 Apr–3 May
Romeo and Tusi	Oscar Kightley & Erolia Ifopo	Sasha Gibb, Jandals Inc	Whitireia Performance Centre, Wellington (Measina Festival)	28–31 May
Impact (dance)	Taofi Mose-Tuiloma & Sasha Gibb (choreographers)	Taofi Mose-Tuiloma & Sasha Gibb (devisors), Jandals Inc	Whitireia Performance Centre, Wellington (Measina Festival)	28 May–1 Jun
Fatu No Toto	Tupe Lualua	Tue Lualua, Le Moana	Whitireia Performance Centre, Wellington (Measina Festival)	30 May–1 Jun

TITLE	AUTHOR	DIRECTOR / COMPANY	VENUE	DATES
The Factory – A Pacific musical	Vela Manusaute	Vela Manusaute & Anapela Polataivao, Kila Kokonut Krew	Dunstan Playhouse, Adelaide; Riverside Theatre, Sydney; Canberra Theatre	12–14 Jun; 18–31 Jun; 24–25 Jun
Ships	Moana Ete	Moana Ete, Backyard Theatre	Gryphon Theatre, Wellington	5–19 Jul
Fresh Off Da Blane	Eteuati Ete & Tofiga Fepulea`i	The Laughing Samoans	Rotorua Civic Theatre	19 Jul
No Man's Land	Suli Moa	Ngapaki Moetara, Tales from the Kava Bowl	Shed 1, Corban Estate Arts Centre, Auckland	29 Jul–2 Aug
Fresh Off Da Blane	Eteuati Ete & Tofiga Fepulea`i	The Laughing Samoans	Nadi, Suva, Apia, Port Hedland, Kalgoorlie, Perth, Adelaide, Gold Coast, Brisbane, Wollongong, Sydney, Mt Isa, Rarotonga, Tutuila (American Samoa) and sundry NZ locations	1 Aug–13 Dec
Black Faggot	Victor Rodger	Roy Ward	Assembly Roxy – Upstairs, Edinburgh (Edinburgh Fringe Festival)	2–25 Aug
The Tautai of Digital Winds	Iaheto Ah Hi	Iaheto Ah Hi & Leilani Clarke, Kinetic Wayfinding	Mangere Arts Centre, Auckland	5–16 Aug
Kava Girls	Sani Muliaumaseali`i	Sani Muliaumaseali`i	Spotlites @ The Merchants' Hall, Edinburgh	10–25 Aug
Black Grace (dance, physical theatre, circus)		Neil Ieremia	Assembly Roxy, Edinburgh (Edinburgh Fringe Festival)	12–22 Aug
The Factory – A Pacific musical	Vela Manusaute	Vela Manusaute & Anapela Polataivao, Kila Kokonut Krew	Assembly Hall, Edinburgh (Edinburgh Fringe Festival)	12–25 Aug
Beauty and the Bro	James Nokise & Mel Parsons	Stand-up comedy	Mussel Inn, Golden Bay	14 Aug, followed by NZ tour 2 Sep–4 Oct
I Am	Lemi Ponifasio/MAU		Edinburgh Playhouse, Edinburgh	16–17 Aug
Sunset Road	Miria George	Miria George, Tawata Productions	Q Theatre Loft, Auckland	20–23 Aug
Goodbye My Feleni	David Mamea	Amelia Reid-Meredith & Shadon Meredith	Playhouse Theatre, Auckland	28–31 Aug
James Nokise's VIP – Voter Information Pack	James Nokise	Stand-up comedy	BATS Theatre, Wellington	29–30 Aug
The Merchant [of Venice]	William Shakespeare (adapted)	Michelle Johansson, Black Friars	Mangere Arts Centre, Auckland	3–6 Sep
Spiritus Aitu	Charlene Tedrow (choreographer), Grace Taylor (poet) & others	Ura Tabu Pacific Dance	NASDA Theatre, Christchurch	3–5 Oct
Sei `o Fafine	Sesilia Pusiaka	Sesilia Pusiaka	Aurora Centre, Christchurch; Kavanagh College Auditorium, Dunedin (Arts Festival)	10–12 Oct; 13–14 Oct
Sons	Victor Rodger	David Fane, Auckland Theatre Company	Mangere Arts Centre, Auckland	16–25 Oct

TITLE	AUTHOR	DIRECTOR / COMPANY	VENUE	DATES
Pacific Dance Presents Pacific Choreographers (dance)	Aruna Po-Ching, Filoi Vaila`au, Ula Naulutubutubu, Nikki Upoko		Q Theatre Loft, Auckland	16–17 Oct
James Nokise in So-So Gangsta	James Nokise	Stand-up comedy	The Manchester Ranch, Christchurch	16–18 Oct
Through My Father's Eyes	No Limits!		NASDA Theatre, Christchurch	23–25 Oct
Black Faggot	Victor Rodger	Roy Ward	Suter Theatre, Nelson (Arts Festival)	24–25 Oct
Black Grace Presents Xmas Verses (dance)	Neil Ieremia (choreographer)	Black Grace	Playhouse, Hamilton; Herald Theatre, Auckland; Whangarei	29 Oct–1 Nov; 5–9 Nov; 14 Nov
Fresh Off Da Blane	Eteuati Ete & Tofiga Fepulea`i	The Laughing Samoans	Theatre Royal, Nelson	1 Nov
Pure and Deep	Toa Fraser	Toa Fraser	Herald Theatre, Auckland	12–23 Nov
At the Wake	Victor Rodger	Roy Ward, Multinesia Productions	Herald Theatre, Auckland	25 Nov–6 Dec

2015

TITLE	AUTHOR	DIRECTOR / COMPANY	VENUE	DATES
My Name is Gary Cooper	Victor Rodger	David O'Donnell	Kumu Kahua Theatre, Honolulu	22 Jan–21 Feb
Girl on a Corner	Victor Rodger	Anapela Polataivao & Vela Manusaute, Multinesia Productions	The Basement Theatre, Auckland (Auckland Pride/Auckland Fringe)	9–14 Feb
I Wanna Be Na Nah Na Nah Nah	Tessa Mitchell, Stephen Bain & David Fane	Stephen Bain	A walking performance around Ponsonby, Auckland	12–22 Feb
Black Faggot	Victor Rodger	Roy Ward, Multinesia Productions	Centrepoint Theatre, Palmerston North	14–28 Feb
The Brave (devised)	Massive Company	Sam Scott & Carla Martell, Massive Company	Hannah Playhouse, Wellington	18–28 Feb
Mother/Jaw (dance)	Jahra 'Rager' Wasasala & Grace Woollett	Inspired by poetry of Arts Pasifika Emerging Artist award recipient Grace Taylor	The Basement Theatre, Auckland	25–28 Feb
I Am	Lemi Ponifasio	Lemi Ponifasio, MAU	ASB Theatre, Aotea Centre, Auckland	6–7 Mar
Rukahu	James Nokise	Not Even Productions	In Good Company, Wellington	10–14 Mar
HUA NUI: To be fruitful, to be productive (hula dance show)	Kumu Hula Aruna Po-Ching Kumu Hula Blaine Kamalani Kia		Shed 1, Corban Estate Arts Centre, Auckland	13 Mar
Impact (dance)	Taofi Mose-Tuiloma & Sasha Gibb (devisors)	Taofi Mose-Tuiloma & Sasha Gibb (choreographers)	Te Rauparaha Arena, Porirua	19 Mar
James Nokise in So-So Gangsta	James Nokise	Stand-up comedy	La Mama First Floor Theatre, New York	19–22 Mar

TITLE	AUTHOR	DIRECTOR / COMPANY	VENUE	DATES
The Lolly Witch of Mumuland	Lauren Jackson & Lolo Fonua	Alison Quigan & Troy Tu`ua, Auckland Theatre Company	Mangere Arts Centre, Auckland	11–18 Apr
My Name is ... Pilitome	Vela Manusaute	Vela Manusaute, Kila Kokonut Krew	4th Niue Arts And Cultural Festival	16 Apr
Get It Girl	Kolopa Simei-Barton & Denyce Su`a		Q Theatre Cellar, Auckland	25 Apr–2 May
Rushing Dolls	Courtney Sina Meredith	Rehearsed reading	Silo Theatre, Auckland	26 Apr
Big Words	James Nokise	Stand-up comedy	The Basement Theatre, Auckland; VK's Comedy & Blues Bar, Wellington	5–9 May; 12–16 May
1918 (dance drama)	Tupe Lualua	Tupe Lualua, Le Moana	Whitireia Performance Centre, Wellington (Measina Festival)	28–30 May
Six Lessons and a Wedding	Michelle Johansson	Michelle Johansson, Black Friars	Manakau Institute of Technology	Jun
Club Paradiso	Victor Rodger	Vela Manusaute, FCC	The Basement Theatre, Auckland	2–6 Jun
Marama	The Conch	Nina Nawalowalo, The Conch	John Dalton Theatre, Kerikeri	17–20 Jun
Rangi and Mau's Amazing Race	Tanya Muagututi`a, Joy Vaele, Ave Sua & Raniera Dallas	Joy Vaele Troy Tu`ua, & Pacific Underground	Te Oro Centre, Auckland	8–15 Jul
The Lolly Witch of Mumuland	Lauren Jackson & Lolo Fonua	Alison Quigan & Troy Tu`ua, Auckland Theatre Company	Selwyn Theatre, Kohimarama, Auckland	9–14 Jul
Kiwa	Black Friars	Black Friars	Oceanic Performance Biennial, Rarotonga; Auckland War Memorial Museum	11 Jul; 18 Jul
Fink About It	Eteuati Ete & Tofiga Fepulea`i	The Laughing Samoans	NZ, Australia, Fiji, Rarotonga, Tonga	24 Jul–5 Dec
1918 (dance drama)	Tupe Lualua	Tupe Lualua, Le Moana	Mangere Arts Centre, Auckland	27–30 Jul
Black Faggot	Victor Rodger	Roy Ward, Multinesia Productions	The Famous Spiegeltent, New Plymouth; TVNZ Festival Club, Arts Centre, Christchurch	18–18 Aug; 1–2 Sep
The White Guitar	Fa`amoana (John) Luafutu, Matthias Luafutu & Malo Luafutu (Scribe)	Nina Nawalowalo & Jim Moriarty, The Conch	Hannah Playhouse, Wellington	1–5 Sep
Frangipani Perfume	Makerita Urale	Ashley Demoville	Leeward Community College, University of Hawai`i	17–26 Sep
My Own Darling	Grace Taylor	Mia Blake, Auckland Theatre Company	Mangere Arts Centre, Auckland	16–24 Oct
Pacific Dance Choreolab Showing 2015 (dance)	Hadleigh Pouesi, Jahra 'Rager' Wasasala and Albert 'Bux' Fale (choreographers)		Corban Estate Arts Centre, Auckland	6 Nov
Versions of Allah	Moana Ete	Moana Ete	Wellington (Measina Festival)	2015

TITLE	AUTHOR	DIRECTOR / COMPANY	VENUE	DATES
2016				
1918 (dance drama)	Tupe Lualua	Tupe Lualua, Le Moana	San Diego (Fringe Festival)	2016
The Girl from Niue Island	Sinahemana Hekay & Vela Manusaute	Vela Manusaute, HM86 & Koli Mai A	Mangere Arts Centre, Auckland	19–30 Jan
Puzzy	Kiki/Victor Rodger	Anapela Polataivao, Lydia Zanetti & FCC	The Basement Theatre, Auckland	9–13 Feb
All Pearls Want to Return to the Sea	Julia Campbell		Wellington Museum	11–14 Feb
Samoa 101	Saufoi Tua Fa`avale	Sasha Gibb, Jandals Inc	Whitireia Performance Centre, Wellington	18–20 Feb
Marama	The Conch	Nina Nawalowalo, The Conch	Q Theatre Auckland (Auckland Arts Festival)	2–6 Mar
Ranterstantrum Redux (rehearsed reading)	Victor Rodger	Victor Rodger, FCC	University Bookshop, Dunedin; Auckland Performing Arts Centre, Auckland	7 Mar; 30 Apr
Dark Side of the Moon (poetry, music)	Jocelyn Fa`alavelave	Jocelyn Fa`alavelave & Sako	Dunedin (Fringe Festival)	8 Mar
Kelekele Mo`ui	Kalisolaite `Uhila	Performance Art	The Physics Room, Christchurch	8–12 Mar
Kingswood	David Mamea	Katie Wolfe, Auckland Theatre Company (rehearsed reading)	Auckland	23 Mar
Move	Iaheto Ah Hi & Leilani Clarke	Iaheto Ah Hi & Leilani Clarke, Kinetic Wayfinding	Te Oro Centre, Auckland; Mangere Arts Centre, Auckland	21–30 Apr; 23 May–4 Jun
Pigs on the Run	Devised by cast & directors	Troy Tu`ua & Alison Quigan	Mangere Arts Centre, Auckland	23–28 Apr
Niu Sila	Oscar Kightley & Dave Armstrong	Daniel Pengelly	Fortune Theatre, Dunedin	30 Apr–21 May
Sons	Victor Rodger	Victor Rodger, FCC (rehearsed reading)	Dunedin Public Art Gallery	1 May
Versions of Allah	Moana Ete	Rose Marie Kirkup, Ohokomo	BATS Theatre, Wellington (Kia Mau Festival)	7–11 Jun
The Vultures	Miria George	Miria George	BATS Theatre, Wellington (Kia Mau Festival)	8–18 Jun
Wahinetoa (dance)	Nikki Upoko, Katerina Fatupaito, Jahra Wasasala, Julia Mage`au Gray		Mangere Arts Centre, Auckland (Pacific Dance Festival)	15–16 Jun
Fatu na Toto (dance)	Le Moana & Tupe Lualua		Mangere Arts Centre, Auckland (Pacific Dance Festival)	17–18 Jun
The White Guitar	Fa`amoana John Luafutu, Matthias Luafutu & Malo Luafutu (Scribe)	Nina Nawalowalo & Jim Moriarty, The Conch	Hannah Playhouse, Wellington; Q Theatre Loft, Auckland	28 Jun–2 Jul; 6–15 Jul
Angels Re:born	Tanya Muagututi`a & Joy Vaele	Lavinia Uhila	The Basement Theatre, Auckland	16–30 Jul

TITLE	AUTHOR	DIRECTOR / COMPANY	VENUE	DATES
Thirsty	Ali Foa`i		BATS Theatre, Wellington; Pataka Art + Museum, Wellington	9–13 Aug; Dec
Club Paradiso/ Girl on the Corner	Victor Rodger	Victor Rodger, FCC (rehearsed reading)	Dunedin Public Art Gallery	10 Sep
Macbeth (adapted)	William Shakespeare	Michelle Johansson & Billy Revell, Black Friars	Mangere Arts Centre, Auckland	15–24 Sep
Wild Dogs Under My Skirt	Tusiata Avia	Anapela Polataivao, FCC	Mangere Arts Centre, Auckland	26 Sep–1 Oct
The White Guitar	Fa`amoana John Luafutu, Matthias Luafutu & Malo Luafutu (Scribe)	Nina Nawalowalo & Jim Moriarty, The Conch	Theatre Royal, Nelson (Nelson Arts Festival)	20–21 Oct
Frangipani Perfume	Makerita Urale	Anapela Polataivao, FCC (rehearsed reading)	Auckland Performing Arts Centre, Auckland	22 Oct
Brown: It's complicated	Antonia Stehlin	Antonia Stehlin	The Basement Theatre, Auckland	25–29 Oct
As Night Falls	Neil Ieremia (choreographer)	Black Grace Dance Company	Herald Theatre, Auckland	1–5 Nov
Pigs in the Yard II	Kalisolaite `Uhila	Performance Art/ Exhibition	Te Tuhi, Auckland	12 Nov–19 Mar 2017
Rukahu	James Nokise	Erina Daniels, Not Even Productions	BATS Theatre, Wellington	15–19 Nov
Purple Onion	Le Moana	Le Moana	Pataka Art + Museum, Wellington (Measina Festival)	1–3 Dec
Aumaga and *Shel We?* (dance)	Le Moana & Those Guys	Le Moana	Pataka Art + Museum, Wellington (Measina Festival)	1–3 Dec
Manu and *Wearing My Map* (dance)	Taofi Mose-Tuiloma & Julia Mage`au Gray (choreographers)	Jandals Inc, Le Moana	Pataka Art + Museum, Wellington (Measina Festival)	2–3 Dec
Talofa Papa	Kasiano Mita	Jandals Inc, Le Moana	Pataka Art + Museum, Wellington (Measina Festival)	3 Dec
Sau E Siva 2016 (dance)	Troy Tu`ua & others (choreography)	Sau E Siva Company	Mangere Arts Centre, Auckland	8–15 Dec
Island Time	Eteuati Ete & Tofiga Fepulei`a	The Laughing Samoans	NZ Tour	2016

For further details and updates on many productions, see Theatre Aotearoa: http://tadb.otago.ac.nz

Notes

Introduction

1. Teresia Teaiwa and Sean Mallon, 'Ambivalent kinships? Pacific people in New Zealand', in *New Zealand Identities: Departures and destinations*, eds James H. Liu et al. (Wellington: Victoria University Press, 2005), 207.
2. The word diaspora was originally used to describe how the Jewish nation became spread all over the world through mass migration over several centuries. It is now commonly applied to Pacific peoples because there are far more people of Pacific descent living in the US, Australia and New Zealand than in the islands themselves.
3. Makerita Urale, interview (1), 14 January 2011. All subsequent unattributed Urale quotes are from this interview.
4. Teaiwa and Mallon, 'Ambivalent kinships?', 225.
5. Hau`ofa's contribution to Pacific Studies includes founding (in 1997) and directing the Oceania Centre for Arts and Culture at the University of the South Pacific in Suva.
6. Epeli Hau`ofa, 'Our sea of islands', in *Inside Out: Literature, cultural politics, and identity in the New Pacific*, eds Vilsoni Hereniko and Rob Wilson (Lanham/Oxford: Rowman & Littlefield, 1999), 28; 30; 31.
7. Ibid., 32.
8. Eugenio Barba, *Beyond the Floating Islands* (New York: PAJ Publications, 1986), 193.
9. Ibid., 211.
10. In their study of dance in the South Pacific, Ralph Buck and Nicholas Rowe use the term 'moving ocean' to describe the 'crisscrossing pathways of migration that span millennia and continue to find new roots and connections between people and places'. 'Introduction' in *Moving Oceans: Celebrating dance in the South Pacific*, eds Buck and Rowe (New Delhi: Routledge, 2014), xxi.
11. Timote M. Vaioleti, 'Talanoa research methodology: A developing position on Pacific research', *Waikato Journal of Education*, 12 (2006), 23.
12. All participants were given the opportunity to correct their transcript or to comment further.
13. Ministry for Pacific Peoples: www.mpp.govt.nz/pacific-people-in-nz
14. We have not followed the convention of italicising words in Pasifika languages, since in many cases, like some Māori words, they have now come into common usage in New Zealand.
15. Karen Stevenson, *The Frangipani is Dead: Contemporary Pacific art in New Zealand* (Wellington: Huia, 2008), 26.
16. Victor Rodger, interview, 13 January 2011. All subsequent unattributed Rodger quotes are from this interview.
17. Jennifer Dann, 'Twelve Questions: Grace Taylor', *NZ Herald*, 20 October 2015: www.nzherald.co.nz/entertainment/news/article.cfm?c_id=1501119&objectid=11531659
18. Sheyne Tuffery, quoted in Stevenson, *The Frangipani is Dead*, 180.
19. Albert Refiti, 'Making spaces: Polynesian architecture in Aotearoa New Zealand', in *Pacific Art Niu Sila: The Pacific dimension of contemporary New Zealand arts*, eds Sean Mallon and Pandora Fulimalo Pereira (Wellington: Te Papa Press, 2002), 209.
20. Albert Wendt, 'Tatauing the post-colonial body', *SPAN: Journal of the South Pacific Association for Commonwealth Language and Literary Studies* 62 (2009), 88.

21. Lemi Ponifasio, quoted in Lisa Taouma, 'Gettin' jiggy with it', in *Pacific Art Niu Sila: The Pacific dimension of contemporary New Zealand arts*, eds Sean Mallon and Pandora Fulimalo Pereira (Wellington: Te Papa Press, 2002), 140.
22. Sean Mallon, *Samoan Art & Artists: O Measina a Samoa* (Nelson: Craig Potton, 2002), 24.
23. Albert Wendt, 'Towards a new Oceania', *Mana Review: A South Pacific journal of language and literature* 1:1 (1976), 52.
24. Fale aitu is also often spelled as a single word: faleaitu.
25. Also known as Caroline Sinavaiana-Gabbard.
26. Caroline Sinavaiana, 'Where the spirits laugh last: Comic theater in Samoa', in *Clowning as Critical Practice: Performance humor in the South Pacific*, ed. William E. Mitchell (Pittsburgh/London: University of Pittsburgh Press, 1992), 196.
27. Ibid., 212.
28. Ibid.
29. Vilsoni Hereniko, *Woven Gods: Female clowns and power in Rotuma* (Honolulu: University of Hawai`i Press, 1995), 166.
30. Victoria N. Kneubuhl, 'Traditional performance in Samoan culture: Two forms', *Asian Theatre Journal* 4:2 (1987), 167.
31. Sinavaiana, 'Where the spirits laugh last', 195.
32. John Kneubuhl and Vilsoni Hereniko, 'An interview with John A. Kneubuhl: Comic theatre of Samoa', *Mānoa*: *Writing from the Pacific Islands* 5:1 (1993), 103.
33. Anapela Polataivao, interview, 17 June 2012. All subsequent unattributed Polataivao quotes are from this interview.
34. Jamie C. Simpson, 'Performance and social inversion: The Samoan White Sunday', *Youth Theatre Journal* 19:1 (2005), 134–50 [147].
35. Ibid., 137.
36. Ibid., 134.
37. Finlay Macdonald, 'How to say sorry in Samoan', *New Zealand Listener*, 22 June 2002), 26.
38. 'Demographics of New Zealand's Pacific Population', Statistics New Zealand: www.stats.govt.nz/browse_for_stats/people_and_communities/pacific_peoples/pacific-progress-demography/geographical-distribution.aspx
39. Alice Te Punga Somerville, *Once Were Pacific: Māori connections to Oceania* (Minneapolis: University of Minnesota Press, 2012), xxii.
40. Makerita Urale, 'Godzone', *New Internationalist Magazine* 291 (1997): http://newint.org/features/1997/06/05/godzone/
41. Te Punga Somerville, *Once Were Pacific*, xxii.
42. *Act* was originally a quarterly produced by Downstage Theatre and the NZ Theatre Federation from 1967, later taken over by Playmarket until its demise in 1986.
43. Samson Samasoni, 'Māori and Pacific Island theatre in New Zealand: Past and future', *Act*, 11:2 (1986), 15–16.
44. Ibid., 15.
45. Anton Carter, 'Taking centre stage', in *Pacific Art Niu Sila: The Pacific dimension of contemporary New Zealand arts*, eds Sean Mallon and Pandora Fulimalo Pereira (Wellington: Te Papa Press, 2002), 154.
46. Ibid., 148.
47. Mallon, 'Theatre', in *Samoan Art & Artists*, 137–51.
48. Te Punga Somerville, *Once Were Pacific*, 158.
49. Simpson, 'Performance and social inversion', 147.
50. Ibid., 140

51. Christopher Balme and Astrid Carstensen, 'Home fires: Creating a Pacific theatre in the diaspora', *Theatre Research International* 26:1 (2001), 38.
52. Christopher B. Balme, *Pacific Performances: Theatricality and cross-cultural encounter in the South Seas* (Hampshire: Palgrave Macmillan, 2007), 191.
53. Diana Looser, 'A piece "more curious than all the rest": Re-encountering pre-colonial Pacific Island theatre, 1769–1855', *Theatre Journal* 63:4 (2011), 521.
54. Ibid., 539.
55. Diana Looser, 'Moving islands: Mapping the Samoan diaspora in contemporary transnational theatre from the South Pacific', *Contemporary Theatre Review* 22:4 (2012), 454.
56. Diana Looser, *Remaking Pacific Pasts: History, memory and identity in contemporary theater from Oceania* (Honolulu: University of Hawai`i Press, 2014), 238.
57. Kata Fülöp, 'Reverse chameleon in the Kiwi jungle: Identity construction of Pasifika theatre makers', (PhD diss., University of Canterbury, 2012).
58. Michelle Keown, *Pacific Islands Writing: The postcolonial literatures of Aotearoa/New Zealand and Oceania* (Oxford: Oxford University Press, 2007), 212–17.
59. Stevenson, *The Frangipani is Dead*, 140–46.
60. Ibid., 162.
61. Ibid., 164.
62. Ibid., 32–34.
63. Mark Houlahan, 'Shakespeare in the settlers' house', *Journal of New Zealand Literature*, 20 (2002), 119.
64. Ibid.
65. Mark Houlahan, '*Romeo and Tusi*: An eclectically musical Samoan/Māori *Romeo and Juliet* from Aotearoa/New Zealand', *Contemporary Theatre Review* 19:3 (2009), 279–88.
66. Philip Armstrong, 'Shakespeare and the space of adolescence', *English in Aotearoa* 47 (2002), 18–27.
67. Lisa Warrington, 'Comedy and irreverence: Rewriting Shakespeare in Aotearoa/New Zealand', in *Shakespeare's Legacy: The appropriation of the plays in post-colonial drama*, ed. Norbert Schaffeld (Trier: Wissenschaftlicher Verlag Trier, 2005), 130.
68. Julie McDougall, 'Māori and Pacific Shakespeares in Aotearoa/New Zealand' (MA diss., Victoria University of Wellington, 2006), 142.
69. Nicola Hyland, 'Wherefore art thou bro?' (PhD diss., University of Melbourne, 2012), 189.
70. Marc Maufort, *Transgressive Itineraries: Postcolonial hybridizations of dramatic realism* (Brussels: PIE Peter Lang, 2003), 131.
71. Marc Maufort, 'Voices of otherness: Multicultural dramaturgies in contemporary New Zealand', in *Identities in Process: Studies in comparative literature*, ed. Eduardo F. Coutinho (Rio De Janeiro: Aeroplano Editora, 2009), 67.
72. Marc Maufort, 'Positioning alterity: Multi-ethnic identities in contemporary New Zealand drama', *Cross-Cultures* 149:2 (2012), 257.
73. Marc Maufort and David O'Donnell (eds.), *Performing Aotearoa: New Zealand theatre and drama in an age of transition* (Brussels: Peter Lang, 2007).

1: The beginnings of Pasifika theatre

1. Eteuati Ete, interview, 15 June 2012. All subsequent unattributed Ete quotes are from this interview.
2. Makerita Urale, interview (3), 16 January 2014.

3. Sean Mallon notes that the group 'was formed just after the controversial Springbok rugby tour in 1981'. Sean Mallon, *Samoan Art & Artists: O Measina a Samoa* (Nelson: Craig Potton, 2002), 142.
4. From TAOtahi information sheet, supplied by Mokalagi Tamapeau, 28 July 2015.
5. For the production of *Le Matau*, the group's name was TAOtahi ma Uo ('TAOtahi and others').
6. Stephen Sinclair and Samson Samasoni, *Le Matau*, 1984, 53–54.
7. Ibid., 32.
8. Anton Carter, 'Taking centre stage', in *Pacific Art Niu Sila: The Pacific dimension of contemporary New Zealand arts*, eds Sean Mallon and Pandoro Fulimalo Pereira (Wellington: Te Papa Press, 2002), 154.
9. Mary Paul, review of *Le Matau*, *Act* 9:2 (1984), 20–21. The play was directed by Helen Jarroe and Stephen Sinclair.
10. Teresia Teaiwa and Sean Mallon, 'Ambivalent kinships? Pacific People in New Zealand,' in *New Zealand Identities: Departures and destinations*, eds James H. Liu et al. (Wellington: Victoria University Press, 2005), 219.
11. Carl Walrond, 'Cook Islanders: Alistair Te Ariki Campbell', Te Ara – the Encyclopedia of New Zealand: www.TeAra.govt.nz/en/photograph/852/alistair-te-ariki-campbell
12. See Howard McNaughton, *New Zealand Drama* (Boston: Twayne, 1981), 92.
13. Paul Millar, 'So dazzling a creature', in *Pacific Art Niu Sila*, 161.
14. Howard McNaughton, 'Drama', in *The Oxford History of New Zealand Literature in English*, ed. Terry Sturm (Auckland: Oxford University Press, 1998, 2nd edn), 361.
15. Eric Bradwell, 'The Man Called Jones', in *Seven One-Act Plays* (Wellington: Radio Publishing Co, 1933), 83.
16. John Thomson, *New Zealand Drama 1930–1980: An illustrated history* (Auckland: Oxford University Press, 1984), 55.
17. Bradwell, 'The Man Called Jones', 97.
18. Ibid., 84.
19. *Velvet Dreams* can be viewed at www.nzonscreen.com/title/velvet-dreams-1997
20. *The Axe* was published in 1949; a revised version was published in 1972 in an anthology of Curnow's plays.
21. Allen Curnow, 'The Axe', in *Four Plays* by Allen Curnow (Wellington: A.H. & A.W. Reed, 1972), 28.
22. James Wenley, 'Rediscovering the landmark New Zealand plays: The formative period of New Zealand drama', (MA diss., University of Auckland, 2013), 28.
23. Graeme Austin, review of *Hearts of Gold*, *Act* 8:5 (1983), 56.
24. McNaughton, 'Drama', 363.
25. Victor Rodger, interviewed by Lynn Freeman, *Standing Room Only*, Radio New Zealand, 7 August 2016: www.radionz.co.nz/national/programmes/standing-room-only/audio/201811158/pasifika-playwright-victor-rodger
26. Albert Wendt, 'Towards a new Oceania', *Mana Review: A South Pacific journal of language and literature* 1:1 (1976), 53.
27. Sarina Pearson, 'Film and photography', in *Pacific Art Niu Sila*, 176–77.
28. Hero Brown, 'Island current', *New Zealand Listener*, 19 October 1996, 40–41.
29. Fiona Collins, interview, 26 August 2016. All subsequent unattributed Collins quotes are from this interview.
30. Until its controversial closure, the Mercury (1968–92) was the largest professional theatre in New Zealand. See Nicholas Tarling, *Wit, Eloquence and Commerce: A history of Auckland's Mercury Theatre* (Auckland: Connacht Books, 2007).
31. Nathaniel Lees, '"Everything is family": David O'Donnell interviews Nathaniel Lees', in

Marc Maufort and David O'Donnell (eds), *Performing Aotearoa: New Zealand theatre and drama in an age of transition* (Brussels: PIE Peter Lang, 2007), 331.

32. Ibid., 331–32.
33. Mallon, *Samoan Art & Artists*, 150.
34. Theatre in Education originated in England in the 1960s. TIE brings together education and theatre, creating shows specifically for performance in schools.
35. Lees, '"Everything is family"', 333.
36. Mallon, *Samoan Art & Artists*, 142.
37. In 1989 the school became Te Kura Toi Whakaari o Aotearoa: New Zealand Drama School, commonly known as Toi Whakaari. Bill Guest, *Transitions: Four decades of Toi Whakaari: New Zealand Drama School* (Wellington: Victoria University Press, 2010), 122.
38. Other graduates, including Anapela Polataivao, David Fane and Victor Rodger, will be discussed in later chapters. Since 2008, Auckland's Pacific Institute of Performing Arts (PIPA) has also played a significant role in training Pasifika actors (see chapter ten).
39. Lani Tupu Snr, who migrated from Upolo to New Zealand in the early 1950s, is a matai (chief). In addition to his role in *Sons for the Return Home* and several later television dramas, Tupu Snr appeared in *Everyman* (1981) for Paul Maunder's bicultural company Theatre of the Eighth Day, and later became a board member of Toi Whakaari.
40. At that time Theatre Corporate, founded by Raymond Hawthorne in 1973, was Auckland's second professional theatre company.
41. Ete's father received the QSO in 2003. His mother received the Queen's Commemorative Medal in 1990 and a QSM in 2012, and was Wellingtonian of the Year Award winner in 2014 for her services to education.
42. Eteuati Ete, email to authors, 1 September 2015.
43. Te Ohu Whakaari ('The drama group') was one of the first Māori theatre companies, founded by Rangimoana Taylor c. 1982. Ete was also a member of Jim Moriarty's company Te Rakau Hua o te Wao Tapu ('The blossoming fruit tree of our sacred grove').
44. Queen Elizabeth II Arts Council was re-branded as Creative New Zealand in 1994.
45. Sima Urale, interview, 11 November 2014. All subsequent unattributed Sima Urale quotes are from this interview.
46. One of her brothers, Bill Urale, has achieved fame as hip hop recording artist King Kapisi.
47. 'Fifty percent of the applicants accepted for the 1988 intake were of Māori or Polynesian descent.' Guest, *Transitions*, 116. Cliff Curtis has subsequently become one of New Zealand's most successful actors with a Hollywood career, while Hori Ahipene became a writer, director and actor working in theatre and television.
48. Makerita Urale, interview (1), 14 January 2011.
49. The Depot's name comes from its first site in Courtenay Place, Wellington, beside the bus depot. It later moved to nearby Alpha Street. For short periods of time, the theatre was also known as The New Depot and Taki Rua Depot.
50. The original collective was Colin McColl, Jean Betts, Philippa Campbell, Fiona Johnstone, Alyson Baker, Richard Mudford, Phillip Mann and John Banas. See John Smythe, *Downstage Upfront* (Wellington: Victoria University Press, 2004) 245.
51. Sean Mallon, interview, 14 December 2011. All subsequent unattributed Mallon quotes are from this interview.
52. Paul Maunder, review of *South Pacific – The Rainbow*, *Illusions* 2, (1986), 30.
53. Helen White, review of *South Pacific – The Rainbow*, *Act* 11:2 (1986), 19.
54. Samson Samasoni, 'Rainbow play a Palagi vision', *New Zealand Times*, 23 March 1986, 35.

55. From 1992–94 the theatre was known as Taki Rua Depot. See Hone Kouka, 'Introduction', *Ta Matou Mangai* (Wellington: Victoria University Press, 1999), 17.
56. Makerita Urale, interview (1).
57. Directed by Erolia Ifopo with Sima Urale in the title role, *Popo the Fairy* was targeted at Aoga Amata (Samoan language preschools) and primary schools, and in 2001 toured to Samoa. It was later adapted as a children's book, *The Magic Seashell* (Wellington: Steele Roberts, 1999).
58. These companies will be discussed in detail in chapters two, three and four.
59. Makerita Urale, interview (3).
60. Jackie Pulani Johnson, 'Afterword: A portrait of John Kneubuhl', in *Think of a Garden and Other Plays* by John Kneubuhl (Honolulu: University of Hawai`i Press, 1997), 256. This essay provides a detailed biography of Kneubuhl.
61. Ibid., (stage direction), 79.
62. The Canberra workshop was jointly run by Playmarket and the Australian National Playwrights' Centre.
63. Mallon, *Samoan Art & Artists*, 150.
64. Ete played the boy David in the reading.
65. Lees, '"Everything is family"', 334–35.
66. Other Watershed cast members: Olivia Muliaumaseali`i (Lu`isa), John Callen (Frank), Afamasaga Agnes Rasmussen (Pito), Martyn Sanderson (Brother Patrick) and Henry Tuipea (Young David). The Watershed Theatre, founded by a co-operative including actors Michael Hurst and others, existed in various venues on the Auckland waterfront from July 1991–96.
67. Other Taki Rua cast members: K.C. Kelly (Frank), Le`autuli`ilagi Malaeta Sauvau (Pito), Desmond Kelly (Brother Patrick), Michael Poe Daniel/Semurana Bradbrook (Young David).
68. Lees, '"Everything is family"', 335.
69. Mallon, *Samoan Art & Artists*, 150.
70. Patrick Smith, review of *Think of a Garden*, *New Zealand Listener*, 20 March 1993, 46.
71. Lees, '"Everything is family"', 335–36.
72. Ibid., 337.
73. Ibid.
74. Laurie Atkinson, review of *Think of a Garden*, *Evening Post*, 10 March 1995.
75. Patricia Cooke, review of *Think of a Garden, NZ Herald*, n.d. (reproduced in *Australian and New Zealand Theatre Record*, March 1995).
76. Atkinson, review of *Think of a Garden*.
77. Susan Budd, review of *Think of a Garden*, *Capital Times*, 15 March 1995.
78. Established in 1992, the Wellington-based Chapman Tripp Theatre Awards were renamed the Wellington Theatre Awards in 2015.

2: Pacific Theatre Inc: A sense of Pasifika identity

1. 'Transforming Aotearoa's cultural landscape', *Spasifik*, Jan/Feb 2008, 18–19.
2. 'Director's Note', programme for *The Contest*, August 1993.
3. The fale aitu-inspired comedy duo The Brownies discussed in chapter 7 provides an example of work generated specifically from the groundwork laid by the Simei-Bartons and Pacific Theatre Inc.
4. Harvey Clark, 'Powerful messages in Pacific Theatre', *NZ Herald*, 3 August 1988, 18.
5. Justine Simei-Barton, interview, 16 December 2011. All subsequent unattributed Justine Simei-Barton quotes are from this interview.

6. Moriarty played Hamlet in Wellington in 1978 at the town hall concert chamber, with Don Selwyn as Claudius. Justine saw this production, directed by Paul Maunder, while a student at Porirua College.
7. Linda Herrick, 'Powerhouse of drama all ready to go', *NZ Herald*, 15 November, 2007.
8. Paul Simei-Barton, interview, 16 December 2011. All subsequent unattributed Paul Simei-Barton quotes are from this interview.
9. Sean Mallon, *Samoan Art & Artists: O Measina a Samoa* (Nelson: Craig Potton, 2002), 140.
10. 'Production Notes', programme for *The Contest*, August 1993.
11. According to the script, 'Feiva' means 'when you like something very much' (56). John Kolia is a playwright and novelist, largely unknown in New Zealand, whose novels include *Crocodile* and *The Late Dr Papua*.
12. John Kolia, *Feiva and Other Flexible Theatre* (Singapore: Koon Wah Printing, 1981), 58.
13. Ibid., 16–18.
14. Clark, 'Powerful messages in Pacific Theatre'.
15. Ibid.
16. Ibid. The *NZ Herald* notes that Zemke's fellow composer for *Feiva* was Monty Enges.
17. David Fane, interview, 15 December 2011. All subsequent unattributed Fane quotes are from this interview.
18. Shimpal Lelisi, interview, 19 June 2012. All subsequent unattributed Lelisi quotes are from this interview.
19. Clark, 'Powerful messages in Pacific Theatre'. Justine did not preclude Palagi or others from joining: 'I don't care where they come from, as long as they're interested, and keen, and committed.'
20. Ibid.
21. Konstantin Stanislavski (1863–1938) was a Russian actor, director, teacher and theorist whose books, including *My Life in Art* (1924) and *An Actor Prepares* (1937), have been enormously influential in actor training internationally. Peter Brook (born 1925) is a revered English director who has published several significant books on the craft including *The Empty Space* (1968) and *The Shifting Point* (1988).
22. Herrick, 'Powerhouse of drama all ready to go'.
23. Vela Manusaute, interview, 17 December 2011. All subsequent unattributed Manusaute quotes are from this interview.
24. Anapela Polataivao, interview, 17 June 2012. All subsequent unattributed Polataivao quotes are from this interview.
25. Clark, 'Powerful messages in Pacific Theatre'.
26. In her review of *Feiva*, Bernadette Rae commented that there were a number of mainly young female Polynesians enthusiastically responding in the audience.
27. Bernadette Rae, review of *Feiva/Favour*, *NZ Herald*, 6 August 1988, 13.
28. Robbie Shilliam, 'Keskidee Aroha: Translation on the colonial stage', *Journal of Historical Sociology* 24:1 (2011), 84.
29. The remaining cast members were Selina Crosbie, Kenti Apa, Esther Watkins and Roger Jolly. Crosbie, now known as Selina Tusitala Marsh, is a leading Pasifika poet.
30. David Fane stepped into the role when the Māori actor originally cast, Te Paki Cherrington, became ill and had to withdraw.
31. Bill Lennox, 'Back to the island', *New Zealand Listener*, 26 August 1989, 48.
32. Michael Billington, '*Robeson – Song of Freedom*', *The Guardian*, 31 March 1988, 21.
33. Sally Markham, 'Power of theatre reason for being', *Dominion Sunday Times*, 16 September 1990, 12.
34. Other cast members included John Kelleher (playing several roles) and Julie Watson as Edwina Mountbatten.

35. Markham, 'Power of theatre reason for being', 12.
36. Transcribed from a TV news item broadcast 5 December 1991, supplied by Justine Simei-Barton.
37. The book was Antony Alpers, *Legends of the South Seas* (London: J. Murray, 1970).
38. Red Mole, founded in 1974 by Brunton and Rodwell, was a politically active experimental theatre company. The dance company Limbs, co-founded in Auckland by O'Reilly and Chris Jannides, flourished from 1978–89.
39. According to Paul, Sally and Alan introduced them to a variety of theatre practitioners and writers, such as Eugenio Barba.
40. As Sally Markham observed, 'Here's hoping they bring it home to perform.' Markham, 'Power of theatre reason for being', 12.
41. Lisa Warrington, 'Theatre in 1990', *Journal of New Zealand Literature* 12 (1994), 30–31.
42. Peter Calder, 'Samoan life woven into pantomime', *NZ Herald*, 5 December 1991, 3. Since 2011, PIPA and ATC have produced a series of Polynesian pantomimes like *Polly Hood in Mumuland* and *Sinarella* (see chapter ten).
43. Mark Amery, review of *Lupe and Sina*, *STAMP*, January 1992, 22.
44. Calder, 'Samoan life woven into pantomime'.
45. The director's statement by Alan Brunton in the programme for *Romeo and Juliet* states: 'The poles that surround the ritual space make allusions to the tent-poles that prop up the shaman's tent of visions, to Verona's columns, to Shakespeare's Globe, and to the poles of the Samoan fale tele.'
46. Information drawn from a programme note for *Romeo and Juliet* (1992), and from Lisa Warrington, 'Comedy and irreverence: Rewriting Shakespeare in Aotearoa/New Zealand', in *Shakespeare's Legacy: The appropriation of the plays in post-colonial drama*, ed. Norbert Schaffeld (Trier: Wissenschaftlicher Verlag Trier, 2005), 129.
47. *Tagata Pasifika*, TVNZ broadcast February–March 1992. Clip provided by Justine Simei-Barton.
48. Ibid.
49. Aruna Po-Ching was later an actress, hula teacher, dancer and choreographer.
50. Herrick, 'Powerhouse of drama all ready to go'.
51. *Holmes Tonight*, TVNZ, 13 February 1992. Justine has responded to the criticism, saying: 'They were totally misinformed, and anyone claiming *Romeo and Juliet* is a love story between brother and sister, cousins or whatever, suggesting an incestuous relationship are idiots! You can quote me on that!' Justine Simei-Barton, email to authors, 10 December 2013.
52. Michael Neill, 'Post-colonial Shakespeare? Writing away from the centre', in *Post-Colonial Shakespeares*, eds Ania Loomba and Martin Orkin (London and New York: Routledge, 1998), 170–71.
53. *Voices on the Wind*, 'Teacher's notes', supplied by Paul Simei-Barton.
54. Albert Wendt, 'The contest', *Landfall 158* (1986), 144–53 [146]. The poem became Part 4 of Book One ('Beginnings') of *The Adventures of Vela* (Wellington: Huia Publishers, 2009, 23–34). In 2010 Wendt won the Commonwealth Writer's Prize for the Asia–Pacific region for this novel in verse.
55. Peter Calder, 'Creative Polynesian flame', *NZ Herald*, 4 November 1993, 1. The article celebrates the 'exciting rise' of Māori and Pacific Island theatre in Auckland in 1993, and while its focus is on John Kneubuhl's *Think of a Garden* and Hone Kouka's *Hide'n'Seek*, Pacific Theatre is noted for its staging of 'a bold and striking piece'.
56. Wendt, *The Adventures of Vela*, 24.
57. Wendt, 'The contest', 149.
58. Ibid., 150.

59. Ibid., 148.
60. Paul Simei-Barton, *The Contest*, unpublished ms. provided by playwright 1993, 50–51.
61. From *The Contest* programme's 'Production Notes'.
62. As Wendt described it, 'Someone suggested Vela Cooked / because he looked red and hot.' 'Vela's Beginnings', from *The Adventures of Vela*, 11.
63. Simei-Barton, *The Contest*, 3.
64. Ibid., 32–33. 'In *The Contest*, the flying fox represents what, for Wendt, remains an absolutely vital component of the native Pacific: the power of imagination.' April K. Henderson, 'Gifted flows: Making space for a brand new beat', in *The Contemporary Pacific* 22:2, 2010, 297. Henderson's article provides an excellent analysis of Wendt's 'great and epic story' (293), and also discusses the three-decade history of Samoan exposure to hip hop.
65. Junior: 'There's got to be more to fa`a Samoa than "shut up and do what you're told."' Simei-Barton, *The Contest*, 45.
66. The remaining four dancers were Aynsley Tapuvae, Misa Tupou, Mishelle Muagututi`a and Erolia Ifopo. Mishelle and Erolia were members of the recently formed Pacific Underground in Christchurch, discussed in chapters three and four.
67. Raewyn White, 'Dance works of 1993', *Illusions* 23 (1994), 35.
68. Ibid.
69. Sarah Catherall, 'Pacific Island renaissance staged', Press release, 31 August 1993.
70. Denis Welch, review of *The Contest*, *New Zealand Listener*, 16 October 1993, 43–44.
71. Susan Budd, '*Contest* proves a winner', *The Dominion*, 2 September 1993.
72. Laurie Atkinson, 'Explosion of theatrical energy in *The Contest*', *Evening Post*, 6 September 1993.
73. Budd, '*Contest* proves a winner'.
74. Calder, 'Creative Polynesian flame'.
75. August Wilson, *Three Plays*, Pittsburgh: University of Pittsbugh Press, 1991, 12.
76. Ibid., 29.
77. Ibid., 67.
78. Bernadette Rae, review of *Ma Rainey's Black Bottom*, *NZ Herald*, 1 September 1995.
79. Caroline Sinavaiana, 'Traditional comic theatre in Samoa: A holographic view', PhD thesis, University of Hawai`i, 1992. See introduction for more on her research.
80. Samoan-Hawaiian playwright Victoria Nalani Kneubuhl has also written a play about Stevenson's wife and her daughter: *Fanny and Belle* (2004).
81. David Fane and Whetu Fala both took roles in this early version, as did Hereniko.
82. Mark Amery, 'A Scot in Samoa', *New Zealand Listener*, 24 August 1996, 37.
83. They had earlier organised a series of comedy workshops, open not only to those who had performed with Pacific Theatre but to anyone who wanted to attend.
84. Stephanie Johnson, 'Jesting Samoan style', *New Zealand Listener*, 13 July 1996, 40.
85. Vilsoni Hereniko, among others, has drawn comparison between fale aitu and commedia dell'arte and other anti-establishment clowning. 'Clowning as political commentary: Polynesia, then and now', *The Contemporary Pacific* 6:1 (1994), 1–28.
86. Mallon, *Samoan Art & Artists*, 139. He spoke to Justine in 2000.
87. Justine Simei-Barton, email to authors, 9 January 2014.
88. Paul Simei-Barton, email to authors, 14 July 2015.
89. Paul Simei-Barton, *Tusitala and the House of Spirits*, unpublished ms, courtesy of the author, 7.
90. The full cast was: Martyn Sanderson (Robert Louis Stevenson), Sylvia Rands (Fanny Stevenson), Tim Raby (Joe Strong), Canada Alofa (Mata`afa/ Lafaele), Olivia Muliaumaseali`i (Lauli`i), Iosefa Enari (Siaki), Shimpal Lelisi (Talolo/Cokkie) and Tausili

Mose (Fa`auma). John Parker was designer, Helen Todd lighting designer and Mark Dashper musical director.

91. Robert Louis Stevenson, *Across the Plains with Other Memories and Essays* (London: Chatto & Windus, 1920), 248.
92. Earlier in the play they also draw comparison to the story of the fight between the Devil (Ti`apolo) and Mikaele the Archangel (Simei-Barton, *Tusitala and the House of Spirits*, 37).
93. Ibid., 48.
94. Ibid., 64.
95. Stevenson, *Across the Plains*, 250.
96. From an interview with Martyn Sanderson and Wanjiku Kiarie conducted by Martin Rumsby, reproduced in 'Testament of the Flying Fox', 25 August 2006: http://readingthemaps.blogspot.co.nz/search?q=tusitala
97. Susan Budd, 'Performances express essence of Samoa', *The Dominion*, 2 September 1996, 12.
98. Laurie Atkinson, '*Tusitala* shows off Samoan fun', *Evening Post*, 11 September 1996, 17.
99. Vaimoana Tapaleao, 'Transforming Aotearoa's cultural landscape', *Spasifik* Jan/Feb 2008, 38.
100. In 2005 Justine had returned to the theatre to direct a children's show, *The Little Mermaid*, a celebration of the 200th birthday of Hans Christian Andersen, at the Wellington Performing Arts Centre, reuniting with Sally Rodwell, who designed fish and bird masks for the project ('*Mermaid* play extended', *Dominion Post*, 12 April 2005, A12).
101. Dionne Christian, 'Grand inspiration out of a tiny island nation', *NZ Herald*, 1 November 2007.
102. Ibid.
103. Fiona Graham, 'Dramaturge as midwife: The writing process within a New Zealand community theatre project', *Journal of Writing in Creative Practice* 2:2 (2009), 209. Paul Maunder also discusses the project briefly in *Rebellious Mirrors: Community-based theatre in Aotearoa/New Zealand* (Christchurch: Canterbury University Press, 2013), 179–82. He refers to Justine as 'the logical person to direct the piece' (180).
104. Graham, 'Dramaturge as midwife', 214.
105. Tapaleao, 'Transforming Aotearoa's cultural landscape', 19.
106. Paul and Justine Simei-Barton, email to authors, 14 July 2015.

3: The Journey to Pacific Underground

1. From written material ('Fa`amalo congratulate Pacific Underground') provided by Rev Mua Strickson-Pua, 20 August 2015. All subsequent unattributed Strickson-Pua quotes are from this document. Rev Strickson-Pua (NZ-born of Samoan parentage) has been a champion of Pacific Island causes and a major supporter of Pacific Underground. He is a noted poet who co-founded Street Poets Black (1982) and pioneered Pasifika Art & Therapy Healing (PATH) 1995–2005.
2. David Fane, interview, 15 December 2011. All subsequent unattributed Fane quotes are from this interview.
3. New Zealand 2013 census: www.stats.govt.nz/Census/2013-census/profile-and-summary-reports/quickstats-culture-identity/pacific-peoples.aspx
4. Programme note, *Horizons* national tour, 1992.
5. Fuarosa Luafutu-Tamati, email to authors, 19 August 2015. All subsequent unattributed Luafutu-Tamati quotes are from this email.

6. Small, born in Christchurch in 1970, joined Puawai in February 1988 and trained there for 18 months. Robert Gilbert, born in Rotorua in 1964, began working professionally as an actor in Hamilton in 1981 as a trainee with Prospect Theatre Company, run by Lex Matheson and Sherril Cooper. During his time with the company, Gilbert also participated in TIE schools tours, which gave him vital experience that he would later put into practice with Whakarite Theatre Company.
7. Simon Small, email to authors, 3 August 2015.
8. Adapted for the stage by New Zealander Simon Phillips and directed by The Court's artistic director Elric Hooper, it ran from early December 1988 to January 1989.
9. A shorter version of the play had been performed in North Island marae venues in 1979, while this full-length version had played to acclaim in Christchurch in 1984 (programme note, *Sons of Sky and Earth*).
10. Elody Rathgen, review of *The Wide Open Cage*, *Press*, 5 July 1989, 8.
11. Robert Gilbert, interview, 19 December 2013. All subsequent unattributed Gilbert quotes are from this interview.
12. 'Brian Hannam', Playmarket: www.playmarket.org.nz/playwrights/brian-hannam
13. Erolia Ifopo, interview, 14 January 2011. All subsequent unattributed Ifopo quotes are from this interview.
14. 'The Native Chef', Unesco: http://webarchive.unesco.org/20160107120616/http://portal.unesco.org/culture/en/files/9157/10567060903the_native_chef.pdf/the%2Bnative%2Bchef.pdf. See also Kim Newth, 'Using "what's around"', *Press*, 12 June 1991, 20: 'Ifopo has a dancer's build and uses her hands expressively to elaborate her words ... From a young age she used to go to Samoan socials with her parents. She used to watch them waltz and loved the graceful way they moved. She also admired Samoan siva (dances) performed as special items at the socials. She enjoyed dancing for her grandfather, partially to overcome the language barrier that had developed because of her attending school [in Christchurch].'
15. Newth, 'Using "what's around"'.
16. Erolia Ifopo, email to authors, 15 December 2015.
17. Mishelle Muagututi`a, interview (1), 14 January 2011. All subsequent unattributed Mishelle Muagututi`a quotes are from this interview.
18. Tanya Muagututi`a, interview, 30 September 2010. All subsequent unattributed Tanya Muagututi`a quotes are from this interview.
19. Posenai Mavaega, interview, 30 September 2010. All subsequent unattributed Mavaega quotes are from this interview.
20. Adrienne Rewi, 'Theatre venture with NZ focus', *Press*, 23 January 1991, 20.
21. Court 2 (later known as The Forge) is a smaller studio space attached to the Court Theatre.
22. Michael O'Brien, review of *Big Bickies*, *Press*, 20 August 1990.
23. Rewi, 'Theatre venture with NZ focus'.
24. Although Gilbert is Pākehā, he was adopted and raised by a Ngāi Tahu father, and identifies strongly with aspects of Māori culture.
25. *Press*, 23 January 1991, 20.
26. Mishelle Muagututi'a, email to authors, 18 December 2013.
27. Anton Carter, interview, 16 June 2012. All subsequent unattributed Carter quotes are from this interview.
28. Oscar Kightley, interview, 18 June 2012. All subsequent unattributed Kightley quotes are from this interview.
29. Umaga co-founded the Contemporary Music Programme at Whitireia Polytechnic, and was awarded a QSM for services to the Pacific community in 2012.

30. Newth, 'Using "what's around"', 20.
31. Among those present was then-emerging Samoan/Rarotongan/Tahitian visual artist Michel Tuffery, who would co-design Kightley and Fane's *A Frigate Bird Sings* (1996), and who has subsequently become one of New Zealand's most respected Pasifika artists.
32. Small began writing *Horizons* during his term as writer-in-residence for Whakarite. 'I chose Francis Serra as a combination of my middle name and my mother's name.'
33. 'Playwright's note', *Horizons* programme, 1992.
34. This was noted by Lindsay Davis, in a review of *Horizons* (version 2): 'Ironically, Ifopo has never had the opportunity to act as a Samoan and instead often finds herself playing Māori characters, American Blacks or even Jamaicans!' (Lindsay Davis, *Presto* 3 (1992), 28).
35. Mishelle Muagututi`a, email to authors, 18 December 2013.
36. See Wellington's *Capital Times*, 25 August–2 September 1992: 'Horizons gives rein to Samoan myth'; and *Christchurch Star*, 17 October 1991, 15. According to Lindsay Clark's review in the *Press*, 21 October 1991, the play had been 'in work' since February 1990.
37. Christina Stachurski, review of *Horizons, Stage and Radio Record*, Winter (1990), 4.
38. Mike Houlahan, 'Traditions and tensions,' *Evening Post*, 19 August 1992.
39. Small studied Samoan language and culture at the Christchurch Polytechnic under Teta Pao-Kalolo.
40. From the 1992 re-drafted version of *Horizons* by Francis Serra. (Text transcribed from performance video supplied by Simon Small.)
41. Bronwyn Trudgeon, '*Horizons* gives rein to Samoan myth', *Capital Times*, 25 August 1992. Bert van Dijk arrived in Christchurch from the Netherlands in December 1991.
42. Mishelle Muagututi`a, email to authors, 18 December 2013.
43. Trudgeon, '*Horizons* gives rein to Samoan myth'.
44. *Horizons* touring leaflet, 1992.
45. Pacific Underground's logo was designed by Wellington artist Richard Arthur Kingsford in 1992, after discussion in a café with his friend Oscar Kightley. The design inspiration came from a tapa cloth on the wall of the café, combined with the target sight on the 'Public Enemy' logo. (Information provided by Mishelle Muagututi`a, October 2015.)
46. Simon Small and Oscar Kightley, introduction to *Fresh off the Boat* by Oscar Kightley and Simon Small (Wellington: Play Press, 2005), i. The introduction provides a detailed summary of both the writing process and the workshop.

4: Pacific Underground: The resounding beat

1. Fuarosa Luafutu-Tamati, email to authors, 19 August 2015. All subsequent unattributed Luafutu-Tamati quotes are from this email.
2. Anton Carter, interview, 16 June 2012. All subsequent unattributed Carter quotes are from this interview.
3. *Hide'n'Seek* was originally performed at Taki Rua in October 1992, and was rewritten for a larger-scale presentation at the March 1994 Wellington International Festival of the Arts.
4. Simon Small, interview, 5 November 2010. All subsequent unattributed Small quotes are from this interview.
5. Tanya Muagututi`a, interview, 30 September 2010. All subsequent unattributed Tanya Muagututi`a quotes are from this interview.
6. Oscar Kightley, interview, 18 June 2012. All subsequent unattributed Kightley quotes are from this interview.
7. Nathaniel Lees, interview, 16 June 2012.

8. David Fane, interview, 15 December 2011. All subsequent unattributed Fane quotes are from this interview.
9. Mishelle Muagututi`a, interview, 14 January 2011. All subsequent unattributed Mishelle Muagututi`a quotes are from this interview.
10. Karen Stevenson, *The Frangipani is Dead: Contemporary Pacific art in New Zealand, 1985–2000* (Wellington: Huia, 2008), 28.
11. Ibid.
12. Ibid.
13. Kightley and Small's writing influences included movies they were watching at the time. As Small notes: 'Our foundation for some of Samoa's rants was an Eddie Murphy movie [*Boomerang*, 1992], where he talks about playing pool as racist, because the white ball's killing all the coloured balls.'
14. Oscar Kightley and Simon Small, *Fresh off the Boat* (Wellington: Play Press, 2005), 24.
15. Ibid., 21.
16. Ibid., 4.
17. Ibid., 62.
18. Simon Small, email to authors, 3 August 2015.
19. David Mamea, interview, 28 November 2014. All subsequent unattributed Mamea quotes are from this interview.
20. Laurie Atkinson, *Evening Post*, 14 March 1994.
21. Susan Budd, *Dominion,* 17 April 1995. (A review of the revival at Downstage.)
22. Mark Cubey, *New Zealand Listener*, 8 October 1994, 47.
23. Mike Houlahan, *Evening Post*, 10 March 1994, 18.
24. Simon Small, email to authors, 3 August 2015.
25. Erolia Ifopo, interview, 14 January 2011.
26. Plot details were sourced from a flyer for *Gifted and Fresh*, supplied by Pacific Underground.
27. Mishelle Muagututi`a, email to authors, 9 December 2014. Rodger recalls: 'I did a first draft of 'Ab Fob' when I was at Toi Whakaari, but someone else must have done the draft that ended up being performed.' Victor Rodger, email to authors, 2 November 2015.
28. Joy Vaele, email to authors, 25 August 2015: 'I am Samoan, born and bred in Christchurch. Pacific Underground is my only form of training. I will be interning at Black Grace soon to learn more of the producing side of the theatre industry.' In 2014, Vaele was nominated best actress for the feature film *The Last Saint* at the NZ Film Awards.
29. Barbara Carpenter, email to authors, 13 October 2015. All subsequent unattributed Carpenter quotes are from this source. Having gained a BA in film & television at the New Zealand Broadcasting School, Carpenter is now a freelance writer/director/producer for TV. 'There is no doubt that I wouldn't be where I am if it wasn't for Pacific Underground. The importance of having a voice in anything I do was instilled into me from this company, along with the willingness to let me grow as an individual.'
30. *Bully For You* brochure, accessed from the Pacific Underground archive held at the Museum of New Zealand Te Papa Tongarewa.
31. Victor Rodger, 'Pacific writing in New Zealand: The niu wave': www.anzliterature.com/feature/pacific-writing-new-zealand-niu-wave/
32. Victor Rodger, interview, 13 January 2011.
33. Other cast members were: Iaheto Ah Hi (Sione), Toni Jones (Sandra), Wickham Pack (Nan) and Mishelle Muagututi`a (Sas), with David Fane as director.
34. Rodger notes: 'I'd met Dad a few times as a kid but this was the first time as a 19-year-old I had tried to establish a relationship with him.' Email to authors, 2 November 2015.
35. *New Zealand Listener*, 23 December 1995.

36. Tusiata Avia, Foreword to *Sons* by Victor Rodger (Wellington: Huia 2007), ix.
37. Jim Tully, 'Fine Pacific island portrait,' *Sunday Times*, 12 November 1995.
38. Christian Penny directed the revised text at Downstage in Wellington (October 1998), produced by Taki Rua, with a second season at Auckland's Herald theatre in September 1999.
39. 'Theatre is revelation: Stefo', by Shveata Chandel Singh, 23 July 2013: http://shveatachandel.blogspot.co.nz/2013/07/theatre-is-revelation-stefo.html
40. Ibid.
41. Tanya Muagututi`a, email to authors, 9 December 2014.
42. Michele Hewitson, review of *Tatau: Rites of passage*, *New Zealand Listener*, 13 April 1996, 40.
43. 'The first Samoan tufuga ta tatau to begin tattooing in New Zealand was Su`a Tavu`i Pasina Sefo Ah Ken. He arrived here in 1972. Later, he was followed and joined by his cousin Su`a Suluape Paolo II (1950–1999), who for a long time maintained the most visible presence and ongoing practice in New Zealand.' Sean Mallon and Uili Fecteau, 'Tatau-ed: Polynesian tatau in Aotearoa', in *Pacific Art Niu Sila: The Pacific dimension of contemporary New Zealand arts*, eds Sean Mallon and Pandora Fulimalo Pereira (Wellington: Te Papa Press, 2002), 23.
44. The premiere was in February 1996 at Auckland's Herald Theatre, followed by two weeks in November 1996 at Sydney's Bondi Pavilion for the Pacific Wave Festival.
45. *Tatau: Rites of passage* flyer from Sydney production, sourced from Pacific Underground archive held at the Museum of New Zealand Te Papa Tongarewa.
46. Hewitson, review of *Tatau.*
47. Christopher B. Balme, *Pacific Performances: Theatricality and cross-cultural encounter in the South Seas* (Hampshire: Palgrave Macmillan, 2007), 197.
48. Diana Looser, *Remaking Pacific Pasts: History, memory, and identity in contemporary theater from Oceania* (Honolulu: University of Hawai`i Press, 2014), 2.
49. Sarona Iosefa, 'Star-crossed lovers, Pacific issues,' *Press*, 15 January 1997, 13.
50. The choice of the name 'Heke' was a joking acknowledgement of Jake Heke in Alan Duff's *Once Were Warriors* (1990). The film version had screened in 1994. Also of note: Season 2 of *bro'Town* (TV3, 2005) featured an episode called *MorningSide Story* with similarities to *Romeo and Tusi.*
51. Oscar Kightley and Erolia Ifopo, *Romeo and Tusi*, unpublished ms. (Wellington: Playmarket, 2000), 44.
52. Ibid., 1.
53. Ibid., 5. Kightley and Fane would explore the tradition of the fa`afafine to more serious effect in *A Frigate Bird Sings*, discussed in chapter 5.
54. Shimpal Lelisi, interview, 19 June 2012. All subsequent unattributed Lelisi quotes are from this interview.
55. Posenai Mavaega, interview, 30 September 2010. All subsequent unattributed Mavaega quotes are from this interview.
56. 'Sarah Hunter hooked up *Romeo and Tusi* in Wellington for the International Festival of the Arts in 2000' (Erolia Ifopo, email to authors, 15 December 2015).
57. Purple for the Māori family, orange for the Samoan family, green for the Minister, red for the fa`afafine, blue for the helpers and black for the band.
58. Oscar Kightley, *Dawn Raids*, unpublished ms. (Wellington: Playmarket, 1997), 4.
59. Ibid., 8
60. Ibid., 10
61. Ibid., 71.
62. Ibid., 12.

63. Ibid.
64. Ibid., 7.
65. Kightley: 'Elvis features prominently in the play – he's a huge part of Pacific Island culture. There were photos on every living-room wall along with Jesus at Gethsemane, Jesus at the Last Supper' (Chris Bourke, 'Pacific's rude awakening', *Sunday Star-Times*, 2 November 1997, 3).
66. Ibid., 21.
67. Kightley, *Dawn Raids*, 40.
68. Ibid., 38.
69. Ibid., 58.
70. Ibid., 51.
71. Ibid., 32.
72. Ibid., 74.
73. Ibid., 72.
74. Marc Maufort, *Transgressive Itineraries: Postcolonial hybridizations of dramatic realism* (Brussels: PIE Peter Lang, 2006), 127.
75. *Dawn Raids* had a Christchurch season at Court 2 a year later (opening 18 November 1998), but has never subsequently been revived. It is due to be published by Playmarket in 2017.
76. *Theatre News*, Summer 98–99, 8.
77. Bernadette Rae, 'Chance lost to cast new light on dark episode', *NZ Herald* (Metro), 13 November 1997, 9.
78. New company members included Barbara Carpenter, Joy Vaele, Ave Robertson, Steve Tafea, Jamie Haugh, Shane Asi, Lupe Asi and Sonya Pegg.
79. Tessa Laird, 'Knights of the brown table', *New Zealand Listener*, 20 June 1998, 38–39.
80. The Soul Sisters were Tanya Muagututi`a, the late Jacky Sinclair-Phillips, Joy Vaele and Grace Vanilau.
81. Joy Vaele, email to authors, 1 December 2015.
82. Rosanna Raymond et al., 'Body beautiful: New Zealand fashion – Pacific style', in Mallon and Perieira, *Pacific Art Niu Sila*, 98.
83. Steph Walker, review of *Angels*, Theatreview, 27 July 2009: www.theatreview.org.nz/reviews/review.php?id=2387
84. Tanya Muagututi`a and Joy Vaele, *Angels*, unpublished ms. (Wellington: Playmarket, 2010), 30.
85. Walker, review of *Angels*.
86. Lindsay Clark, review of *Angels*, Theatreview, 18 July 2009: www.theatreview.org.nz/reviews/review.php?id=2368
87. A new production of the play, *Angels Re:Born*, was presented by the Auckland Theatre Company's Next Big Thing Youth Theatre Festival at Basement Theatre in July 2016, directed by Lavinia Uhila.
88. Laird, 'Knights of the brown table': 'Before and after the show, new musicians were given the chance to perform to a captive audience, a confidence building exercise for both parties.'
89. From the *Dawn Raids* programme notes, Herald Theatre, November 1997.
90. 'Pacific Underground releases Island Summer CD', *The Big Idea*, 21 October 2010: www.thebigidea.nz/stories/media-releases/185262-pacific-underground-releases-island-summer-cd
91. Tanya Muagututi`a, email to authors, 27 November 2015: '*Landmark* is a compilation CD that features two songs of mine, and songs from Beats'n'Pieces, Antsman [Anton

Carter], Scribe, Traveller and Charmed 1 [Nathan and Craig Chalmers], DJs Ali and Richie Broke, the late Hix Toto [who was a tutor at Puawai – George Kahi's nephew], The Naked Samoans, Cliff Mavaega, Ave Sua [and] the artwork of Jacob Luamanuvae, at the time a graphic design student at CPIT, now working in movies in the art department.'

92. Ibid.: '*Island Summer* captures the frontline musicians with Pos who are: Tanya Muagututi`a singer/songwriter, Andrew Sione (Tribalincs), Hemi Lesatele on second and third guitars, Seta Timo (LA Mitchell's Nativa Band) on bass guitar and Chris Searle, PU's resident drummer – [who have all] grown with the show since its beginning in 2005.'
93. Artists included Albert Wendt, Sarona Iosefa-Aiono, Tusiata Avia, Victor Rodger, Oscar Kightley, Simon Small, D Kamali and the Fika writers collective.
94. 'Ten – Pacific Arts Festival': www.eventfinda.co.nz/2010/feb/christchurch/ten-pacific-arts-festival. 'Various versions of *Rangi and Mau* were in demand and continued to tour schools for several years' (Tanya Muagututi`a, email to authors, 13 December 2015).
95. 'Pacific shows feature in Christchurch Arts Festival', 12 July 2005: www.nzmusician.co.nz
96. 'From under the fale Pacific Underground rises', *The Big Idea*, 24 October 2013: www.thebigidea.co.nz/connect/media-releases/2013/oct/135637-from-under-the-fale-pacific-underground-rises
97. Ibid.
98. Erolia Ifopo, email to authors, 15 December 2015.
99. From written material ('Fa`amalo congratulate Pacific Underground') provided by Rev Mua Strickson-Pua, 20 August 2015.
100. Tanya Muagututi`a, email to authors, 16 December 2015.

5: Pasifika Playwriting 1996–2012

1. *Between the Islands* was performed as part of the Taki Toru festival of Māori and Pasifika plays produced by Hone Kouka for the NZ Fringe Festival. It was based on Kite-Rangi's experience of returning to the Cook Islands to learn traditional navigation skills.
2. Albert Wendt, *The Songmaker's Chair* (Wellington: Huia, 2004), 1.
3. Mark Amery, 'Powerful production shows the Pacific way', *Sunday Star Times* March 1996, (n.d.).
4. Karangahape Road, at that time a red-light district in inner-city Auckland.
5. Oscar Kightley, interview, 18 June 2012. All subsequent unattributed Kightley quotes are from this interview.
6. David Fane, interview, 15 December 2011. All subsequent unattributed Fane quotes are from this interview
7. Makerita Urale, email to authors, 10 December 2015. Urale developed her career as a producer through her work as co-founder with Michel Tuffery and David Sa`ena on three Tu Fa`atasi Festivals (1994, 1996, 1998), which promoted the work of Pasifika artists (The Tu Fa`atasi Festival, Wellington: http://spasifikmag.com/issue51pacificfestivals/thetufaatasifestival/). In the NZ International Festival of the Arts, she line-produced the opera *Ricordi!* (1996) and the operatic work *Classical Polynesia* (1998) featuring Iosefa Enari.
8. Makerita Urale, interview (1), 14 January 2011.
9. Oscar Kightley, David Fane and Nathaniel Lees, 'A Frigate Bird Sings', in *Urbanesia: Four Pasifika plays* (Wellington: Playmarket, 2012), 23.
10. Niko Besnier, 'Crossing the boundaries', *Illusions* 25 (Winter 1996), 43.
11. Kightley, Fane and Lees, 'A Frigate Bird Sings', 94.
12. Ibid., 95–96.

13. Sean Mallon, interview, 14 December 2011. All subsequent unattributed Mallon quotes are from this interview.
14. 'Michel Tuffery is a New Zealand based artist of Samoan, Rarotongan and Mahoi Tahitian heritage': www.micheltuffery.co.nz/
15. Denis Welch, 'If the dress fits', *New Zealand Listener*, 4 May 1996, 41.
16. Stephanie Johnson, 'Shining reprise', *New Zealand Listener*, 2 November 1996.
17. Anita McNaught, 'Island queens', *Quote Unquote*, November 1996, 35.
18. Shimpal Lelisi, interview, 19 June 2012. All subsequent unattributed Lelisi quotes are from this interview.
19. Johnny Givins, 'A clean, simple, emotionally truthful production', Theatreview, 13 October 2012: www.theatreview.org.nz/reviews/review.php?id=5253
20. Ibid.
21. Makerita Urale, interview (3), 16 January 2014.
22. Ibid.
23. Makerita Urale, interview (2), 15 June 2012.
24. Denis Welch, 'Heaven scent', *New Zealand Listener*, 24 January 1998, 44.
25. Ibid.
26. Makerita Urale, 'Frangipani Perfume', in *Frangipani Perfume and Mapaki* (Wellington: The Play Press, 2004), 4.
27. Ibid., 6
28. Ibid.
29. Ibid., 26. The names Tivi (TV) and Naiki (Nike) parody elements of consumerism.
30. Ibid., 8.
31. Ibid., 35.
32. Makerita Urale, interview (2).
33. Fiona Collins, interview, 26 August 2016.
34. For example, Samoan poet Selina Tusitala Marsh elegantly summarises her experience of viewing *Frangipani Perfume* in her poem 'Where the girls are'. *Niu Voices: Contemporary Pacific fiction 1* (Wellington: Huia, 2006), 23–28.
35. www.creativenz.govt.nz/news/pacific-playwright-follows-her-sister-to-hawai-i
36. Along with Cook Islander Miria George's *and what remains*, *Niu Sila*, and work by Samoan performance artists Rosanna Raymond and Natasha Vaike.
37. 'New Indigenous Voices 2008': www.lamama.org/archives/2008/NewIndigenousVoice.html
38. Welch, 'Heaven scent', 44.
39. Makerita Urale, interview (1).
40. Dianna Fuemana, interview, 6 September 2012. All subsequent unattributed Fuemana quotes are from this interview.
41. Igelese Ete, 'Music notes', in Dianna Fuemana, *Two Plays: Falemalama and The Packer* (Wellington: Playmarket, 2008), 50.
42. Dianna Fuemana, *Two Plays: Falemalama and The Packer* (Wellington: Playmarket, 2008), 56.
43. Ibid., 70.
44. Ibid., 75.
45. *Birds* featured actors Ali Foa`i and Nora Aati.
46. Sharu Delilkan, 'Real, raw and revealing', Theatrescenes, 17 March 2012: www.theatrescenes.co.nz/review-birds-mangere-arts-centre/
47. Frances Walsh, 'Go coffee', *New Zealand Listener*, 30 October 1999, 34.
48. Toa Fraser, 'Bare', in *Two Plays* (Wellington: Playmarket, 2007), 44.
49. Fraser, 'Bare', 44.

50. Nik Smythe, 'The resultant standing ovation all but caused another earthquake', Theatreview, 27 March 2011: www.theatreview.org.nz/reviews/review.php?id=3867. The event raised over $83,000 for Christchurch.
51. Toa Fraser, 'No. 2', in *Two Plays*, (Wellington: Playmarket, 2007), 62.
52. Max Szalwinska, 'Keep it in the family', *The Scotsman*, 8 August 2000.
53. Nick Thorpe, 'Edinburgh Festival 2000 review – Theatre – *No. 2*', *The Independent*, 10 August 2000.
54. Timothy O'Brien, '*Paradise* invigorating theatre', *Dominion*, 19 March 2001.
55. Nina Nawalowalo, interview (1), 14 December 2011.
56. Kate Ward-Smythe, 'Great substance and wonderful comedy', Theatreview, 14 November 2014: www.theatreview.org.nz/reviews/review.php?id=7613
57. James Wenley, '*Pure and Deep* – review', *Metro*, 18 November 2014.
58. Wendt, *The Songmaker's Chair*, 2. 'Moana-nui-a-kiwa' is a Māori name for the Pacific Ocean.
59. Wendt: 'I'd written a couple of short one-act plays in the 60s when I was teaching at Samoa College. I had an idea for a longer work about three generations of a Samoan family living in Auckland, but it took a while to come to fruition.' Iain Sharp, 'Pacific pen', *Sunday Star Times*, 23 November 2003, 28.
60. Nathaniel Lees, interview, 16 June 2012. All subsequent unattributed Lees quotes are from this interview.
61. 'A promise comes to life', *NZ Herald*, 10 September 2003.
62. Wendt, *The Songmaker's Chair*, 1.
63. Ibid., 15.
64. Ibid., 103.
65. Ibid., 99.
66. Ibid., 17.
67. Tui Atua Tupua Tamasese Efi and Tamasailau Sua`ali`i-Sauni (eds), *Su`esu`e Manogi – In search of fragrance: Tui Atua Tupua Tamasese Ta`isi and the Samoan indigenous reference* (Samoa: Centre for Samoan Studies, National University of Samoa, 2009).
68. Melani Anae, 'Review of *The Songmaker's Chair*', *The Contemporary Pacific* 17:1 (2005), 272.
69. Wendt, *The Songmaker's Chair*, 116.
70. Nathaniel Lees, email to authors, 29 August 2016.
71. Frances Edmond, 'Dressed Samoans talk, and talk, about their lives', *New Zealand Listener*, 27 September 2003.
72. Anae, 'Review of *The Songmaker's Chair*'.
73. Joseph T. Rozmiarek, '"Chair" Samoan drama of kin, traditions', *Honolulu Advertiser*, 18 March 2006.
74. Robert Sullivan, 'Review of *The Songmaker's Chair*', *The Contemporary Pacific* 19:2 (2007), 653.
75. Robyn McLean, 'A question of family', *Dominion Post*, 27 February 2004, 7.
76. Gibson Group, TV3, 1993–97.
77. Dave Armstrong interview, 16 January 2011. All subsequent unattributed Armstrong quotes are from this interview.
78. John Smythe, 'Another classic Kiwi play', *National Business Review*, 8 April 2004.
79. Oscar Kightley and Dave Armstrong, 'Niu Sila', in Dave Armstrong and Oscar Kightley, *Two Plays* (Wellington: Playmarket, 2009), 68.
80. Ibid., 69.
81. Ibid., 72.

82. Judith Raiskin, 'Telling tales out of school: Sia Figiel and indigenous knowledge in Pacific Islands literature', in *Gender and Globalization in Asia and the Pacific: Method, practice, theory*, eds Kathy E. Ferguson and Monique Mironesco (Honolulu: University of Hawaii Press, 2008), 19.
83. Dave Armstrong, *Where We Once Belonged*, unpublished ms. (Wellington, Playmarket, 2008), 29.
84. Ibid., 54.
85. Lynn Freeman, 'Highly polished production of important, heartfelt work, *Capital Times*, 13 March 2008.
86. Sian Robertson, 'The discomfort of change: Moving and funny', Theatreview, 30 March 2008: www.theatreview.org.nz/reviews/review.php?id=1326
87. David Mamea, interview, 28 November 2014. All subsequent unattributed Mamea quotes are from this interview.
88. In the 2014 production of *Goodbye My Feleni*, directed by Amelia Reid-Meredith in Auckland, the roles were taken by Dominic Ona Ariki (Tama), Pua Magasiva (Ioane), Shadon Meredith (Simi) and Shimpal Lelisi (Ete). Sound design was by Posenai Mavaega and Tanya Muagututi`a.
89. David Mamea, *Goodbye My Feleni*, unpublished ms., 2013, 2014 (supplied by author), 6.
90. Oscar Kightley and David Fane had written *Eulogy*, performed at Downstage in March 1998, which tells a story of people interned on Somes Island in Wellington Harbour during World War II and includes two Samoan characters.
91. Ibid., 16.
92. Ibid., 17.
93. One of Mamea's brothers died in 2000, and the shock of that loss crops up frequently in his writing.
94. *Le Matau* (1984) by Sinclair and Samasoni opens with a rendition of 'Goodbye My Feleni' to farewell Ioane as he migrates from Samoa to Aotearoa.
95. Inaugurated in 2007 by Playmarket, the Adam New Zealand Play Award 'recognises and celebrates the best in new writing for the theatre': www.playmarket.org.nz/news/adam-nz-play-award-winners-2015. To qualify for entry, plays must not have had a professional production. The Best Pasifika Playwright Award was established in 2011, when it was won by Maureen Fepulea`i for *E ono tama`i pato*. Jonathan Riley won with *Makigi* in 2012.
96. Victor Rodger, interview, 13 January 2011. All subsequent unattributed Rodger quotes are from this interview.
97. There was a strong Polynesian solidarity in Rodger's year at Toi Whakaari, which included Māori actors Tanea Heke, Waimihi Hotere and Mitch Tawhi Thomas, and Tongan Misa Tupou. Tupou later moved to Hawai`i, where he became director of the Oahu Fringe Festival.
98. In fact it was Michael Smythe, commenting on Sian Robertson's review, who said: 'Could this play ... only have been written by a New Zealander? It is an astute allegory that has left me reflecting for days on colonisation and globalisation ...', Theatreview, 24 September 2007: www.theatreview.org.nz/reviews/review.php?id=966
99. Victor Rodger, 'My name is Gary Cooper', in *Urbanesia: Four Pasifika plays*, (Wellington: Playmarket, 2012), 184. It is a historical fact that children were named after the famous visitor as a mark of honour.
100. Ibid., 171.
101. For one discussion of the Mead controversy see Alice Dreger, 'Sex, lies and separating science from ideology', *The Atlantic*, 15 February 2013: www.theatlantic.com/health/archive/2013/02/sex-lies-and-separating-science-from-ideology/273169/

102. Rodger, 'My name is Gary Cooper', 206.
103. Natasha Hay, 'Naked ambition', *New Zealand Listener*, 13 October 2007, 49.
104. Rodger, 'My name is Gary Cooper', 252.
105. Diana Looser, 'Moving islands: Mapping the Samoan diaspora in contemporary transnational theatre from the South Pacific', *Contemporary Theatre Review* 22:4 (2012), 465.
106. This refers to the 1988 TV mini-series *Emma: Queen of the south seas* starring Nicaraguan Barbara Carrera as the Samoan Queen Emma.
107. Rodger, 'My name is Gary Cooper', 236.
108. Cast: Robbie Magasiva (Gary), Roy Snow (Nick), Nora Aati (Teuila), Jennifer Ward-Lealand (Connie), Goretti Chadwick (T), Anapela Polataivao (Salamoana), Leisha Ward-Knox (Jennifer), Damien Harrison (Joel).
109. Hay, 'Naked ambition'.
110. Sian Robertson, 'Sex, lies and photographs', Theatreview, 24 September 2007: www.theatreview.org.nz/reviews/review.php?id=966
111. Paul Simei-Barton, '*My Name is Gary Cooper* at Maidment Theatre', *NZ Herald*, 10 July 2007.
112. Looser, 'Moving islands', 465.
113. Paloma Fresno-Calleja, 'Revised spectacles: Literary transformations of Hollywood's Pacific narratives'' *Journal of Postcolonial Writing* 49:3 (2013), 275.
114. Moana Nepia, 'Sensual complexity', Theatreview, 24 January 2015: www.theatreview.org.nz/reviews/review.php?id=7693
115. Ward directed both the premiere of *After the Wake* at Centrepoint Theatre in 2012 and the 2014 Auckland production (by Multinesia Productions).
116. Sharu Delilkan and Tim Booth, 'In the wake of genius', Theatre Scenes, 28 November 2014: www.theatrescenes.co.nz/tag/victor-rodger/
117. Lyn Gardner, 'Black Faggot – rough-and-ready agitprop', *The Guardian*, 19 August 2014.
118. Cameron Woodhead, 'Theatre Review: *Black Faggot*', *Sydney Morning Herald*, 30 September 2013.
119. Natasha Hay, 'Rodger that', *New Zealand Listener*, 16 February 2013, 45–46.
120. Dionne Christian, 'Writer and star venture to dark side', *NZ Herald*, 31 May 2015: www.nzherald.co.nz/entertainment/news/article.cfm?c_id=1501119&objectid=11457576
121. Ibid.
122. McNaught, 'Island queens', 35.

6: MAU and The Conch: Bodies, images and light

1. Nina Nawalowalo, interview (1), 14 December 2011. All subsequent unattributed Nawalowalo quotes are from this interview.
2. See Murray Edmond, 'Lighting out for paradise: New Zealand theatre and the "other" tradition', *Australasian Drama Studies* 18 (1991), 183–206.
3. Core members of the Pacific Sisters include Selina Forsyth, Rosanna Raymond and Feeonaa Wall (Samoan), Niwhai Tupaea, Suzanne Tamaki and Lisa Reihana (Māori), Ani O'Neill (Cook Islander) and Jaunnie Ilolahia (Tongan). See Jacqueline Charles Rault, 'More than simply traditional: The Pacific Sisters', *Pacific Arts* 10:2 (2010), 5–15.
4. Shigeyuki Kihara is a multimedia and performance artist who uses photography to explore themes of Pacific culture, identity, indigenous spirituality, colonialism, stereotypes, gender roles and consumerism. Kihara was born in Samoa and is of Japanese and Samoan descent: www.metmuseum.org/exhibitions/listings/2008/shigeyuki-kihara

5. Black Grace's work has been described as 'highly physical, rich in the storytelling traditions of the South Pacific': www.blackgrace.co.nz/about
6. Butoh pioneer Hijikata Tatsumi christened this new form 'Ankoko Butoh' (dance of darkness). Sondra Fraleigh et al., *Hijikata Tatsumi and Ohno Kazuo* (New York/London: Routledge, 2006), 7.
7. Lemi Ponifasio, interview with Kim Hill, *Saturday Morning*, Radio New Zealand, 1 February 2014: www.radionz.co.nz/national/programmes/saturday/audio/2584267/lemi-ponifasio-theatre-of-power
8. Makerita Urale, interview (2), 15 June 2012.
9. P.W., review of *Illumina: Aria*, *Hawkes Bay Herald Tribune*, 21 June 1997.
10. Ann Hunt, review of *Illumina: The body in crisis*, *Dominion*, 5 April 1993.
11. Ibid.
12. Christopher B. Balme, *Pacific Performances: Theatricality and cross-cultural encounter in the South Seas* (Hampshire: Palgrave Macmillan, 2007), 213.
13. Lisa Taouma, 'Gettin' jiggy with it', in *Pacific Art Niu Sila: The Pacific dimension of contemporary New Zealand arts*, eds Sean Mallon and Pandora Fulimalo Pereira (Wellington: Te Papa Press, 2002), 140.
14. Balme, *Pacific Performances*, 213.
15. Analysis of *Lo`omatua: The ancient mother* is based on David O'Donnell's viewing of the production at the Meteor Theatre, Hamilton, 30 June 1998, as part of the first FUEL Festival. See also Geoffrey Milne's 'Cross-Tasman reflections' in *Eureka Street* 8:7 (1998), 43.
16. Anton Carter, interview, 16 June 2012.
17. Sellars is one of America's leading contemporary theatre directors.
18. See http://mau.co.nz/
19. Analysis of *Requiem* is based on David O'Donnell's viewing of the production, KVS Royal Flemish Theatre, Brussels, 2006.
20. Sam Trubridge, review of *The Crimson House*, Theatreview, 7 March 2014: www.theatreview.org.nz/reviews/review.php?id=6805
21. Quoted in Taouma, 'Gettin' jiggy with it', 140.
22. Lemi Ponifasio, Artist's Talk, New Zealand International Festival of the Arts, 6 March 2014, personal notes.
23. In his analysis of MAU's *Paradise* (2003) Balme notes, 'Almost total darkness represented the beginning of the world when in Polynesian cosmology there was eternal night caused by the seamless embrace of Rangi the sky god and Papa the earth goddess.' Balme, *Pacific Performances*, 214–15.
24. 'Delivering the tension of unnoticeable change', Selecon, 27 January 2009: www.seleconlight.com/index.php?option=com_content&view=article&catid=2&id=2685
25. Ponifasio, Artist's Talk.
26. Trubridge, review of *The Crimson House*.
27. Albert Wendt, foreword to *Bone Flute Ivi Ivi* programme, 2000.
28. Ponifasio, Artist's Talk.
29. Transcribed from Kim Hill interview, 1 February 2014.
30. Programme note, *Stones in her Mouth*.
31. Poi is a dance form in which women swing white balls on string in complex patterns requiring skill and coordination.
32. Nathaniel Lees, interview, 16 June 2012.

33. Programme note, *Birds with Skymirrors*.
34. Analysis of *Birds with Skymirrors* is based on the authors' viewing of the production staged at the NZ International Festival of the Arts, 1 March 2012.
35. The image is similar to the bird/men featured in paintings by New Zealand artist Bill Hammond, which often have an ecological theme.
36. On the same day that MAU performed *Birds with Skymirrors* in Wellington, (1 March 2012) it was announced that the government of Kiribati was negotiating with Fiji to buy thousands of acres to re-settle its population due to the threat of rising seawaters.
37. Taouma, 'Gettin' jiggy with it', 140.
38. Sondra Fraleigh, *Butoh: Metamorphic dance and global alchemy* (Chicago: University of Illinois Press, 2010), 31.
39. Louise Tu`u, interview, 17 December 2011. All subsequent unattributed Tu`u quotes are from this interview.
40. Vela Manusaute, interview, 17 December 2011.
41. Tom McCrory, interview, 27 January 2012. All subsequent unattributed McCrory quotes are from this interview.
42. The Conch: www.theconch.co.nz/
43. The Conch, mission statement: www.facebook.com/TheConchNZ
44. Robert Bennett trained in mime at the Rose Bruford College of Speech and Drama and l'École Jacques Lecoq in Paris, and founded Mime International in Wellington in 1975. He retired in 2003.
45. Based in Switzerland, Mummenschanz creates a 'non-verbal theatrical language' using masks, bodies and movement: www.mummenschanz.com. Decroux (1898–1991) was a French actor, specialising in corporeal mime. Polunin, creator of stage spectacles such as *Slava's Snowshow* (1993), is a Russian performance artist and clown.
46. Richard McDougall is a former World Open champion for Close Up Magic and a gold star member of the Inner Magic Circle.
47. Kieve is a leading illusion designer and magic consultant for stage and screen, whose credits include innovative magic effects on the films *Harry Potter and the Prisoner of Azkaban* (2004), *Hugo* (2011) and on many West End and Broadway shows such as *Matilda the Musical* (2011) and *Ghost the Musical* (2011): www.stageillusion.com. *The Guardian*'s Michael Billington named him 'The invisible genius of British theatre'.
48. Nina Nawalowalo: www.theconch.co.nz/projects/past/vula
49. Timothy O'Brien, review of *A Space without Boundaries*, *Dominion Post*, 21 December 2000.
50. Collins and Lei`ataua are playwrights as well as actors. Lei`ataua's *Through Windows* (2002) was stage-managed by Tausili Mose at Circa theatre.
51. Collins had previously worked as an assistant to Neil Ieremia when he was establishing Black Grace. Inspired by other Pasifika playwrights, Collins wrote and performed her first play *My Penina* in the 2004 Wellington Fringe Festival, for which she won Best Play, with Tusiata Avia as both actor (Mele) and script advisor. See Chapter 10 for further discussion of Fiona Collins.
52. Parts of this discussion of *Vula* have been previously published in David O'Donnell, 'Issues in PI women's theatre: *Vula* and *Frangipani Perfume*', in *Illusions: New Zealand moving image and performing arts criticism* 36 (Winter 2004), 32–35.
53. Stephen Blackburn received one of two Chapman Tripp awards for this production, the other going to composer Gareth Farr.
54. Jenny Stevenson, review of *Vula*, *Dominion Post*, 20 September 2002.
55. John Smythe, review of *Vula*, *National Business Review*, 27 September 2002.

56. 'For centuries ... Fijians have been performing meke, a traditional dance that passes on knowledge and genealogies ... Fijians are all similar in that they all need, want and will come together to dance the meke.' Sachiko Miller, 'Treasuring the meke in a modern Fiji', in *Moving Oceans: Celebrating dance in the South Pacific*, eds Ralph Buck and Nicholas Rowe (New Delhi: Routledge 2014), 119.
57. Kasaya Manulevu, interview, 11 November 2014. All subsequent unattributed Manulevu quotes are from this interview.
58. Moai are the giant carved heads on Rapa Nui (Easter Island).
59. Salesi Le`ota interview, 3 March 2012. All subsequent unattributed Le`ota quotes are from this interview.
60. Paul Kieve, interview, 14 December 2011.
61. Parts of this discussion of the performance of *Masi* have been previously published in Lisa Warrington and David O'Donnell, 'Unfolding the cloth: Patterns of landscape and identity in the Conch's *Masi*', in *Enacting Nature: Ecocritical perspectives on indigenous performance*, eds Birgit Dawes and Marc Maufort (Brussels: Peter Lang, 2014), 199–217.
62. The Conch: www.theconch.co.nz/
63. Nina Nawalowalo, email to authors, 7 December 2015.
64. Rodger, 'My name is Gary Cooper', *Voices Against Violence*, as told to Kate Burry and Connie Grouse (Auckland: British Council New Zealand, 2015), 33–34.
65. 'Inspiring workshop for youth takes them behind closed doors at Te Papa': www.voxy.co.nz/national/5/251593

7: Comedy for the kitchen or the lounge?

1. Eteuati Ete, interview, 15 June 2012. All subsequent unattributed Ete quotes are from this interview.
2. Vela Manusaute, interview, 17 December 2011. All subsequent unattributed Manusaute quotes are from this interview.
3. Canada Alofa appeared in this production as Mata`afa and Lafaele.
4. Sarina Pearson, 'Subversion and ambivalence: Pacific Islanders on New Zealand Prime Time', *The Contemporary Pacific* 11:2 (1999), 367.
5. Ibid., 368.
6. Unless otherwise indicated, sketch material quoted from The Brownies appears on their DVD *Comedy At Its Best* (2000), and has been transcribed from the live show as it appears on the DVD.
7. Transcribed from Kila Kokonut Krew, *Laugh You Long Time*, DVD (2011). In discussing traditional fale aitu, John Kneubuhl sees a very different attitude to that exemplified here by The Brownies: 'There is a tendency to say that Samoans laugh at the white man and by laughing at the white man put him down. That's not true. That's the modern sympathiser trying to make Samoans act like political agitators against colonial government. Samoans will laugh at other Samoans rather than at the white man.' (Kneubuhl and Hereniko, 'An interview with John A. Kneubuhl: Comic theatre of Samoa', *Mānoa: Writing from the Pacific Islands* 5:1 (1993), 103.
8. Julie Malo, 'Brown boys in the ring',' *The Southland Times*, 19 April 1998.
9. Christine Robertson, 'Life is hard – and hilarious', *Evening Post*, 30 April 1997.
10. Oscar Kightley interview, 18 June 2012. All subsequent unattributed Kightley quotes are from this interview.
11. In subsequent productions Robbie Magasiva and Iaheto Ah Hi also played roles.
12. Pearson, 'Subversion and ambivalence', 383.

13. Susan Budd, review of *Naked Samoans: The trilogy*, *NZ Herald*, 21 June 2001: www.nzherald.co.nz/lifestyle/news/article.cfm?c_id=6&objectid=195961
14. Sima Urale, interview, 11 November 2014.
15. David Fane, interview, 15 December 2011.
16. Frances Edmond, 'Beyond a joke', review of *Naked Samoans: The trilogy*, *New Zealand Listener*, 18 May 2001, 55.
17. All quotations from *Naked Samoans: The trilogy* have been transcribed from the 2002 *Tagata Pasifika – The Naked Samoans* documentary, NZ On Screen: www.nzonscreen.com/title/tagata-pasifika-the-naked-samoans-2001
18. Anon., review of *Naked Samoans: The trilogy*, *The Scotsman*, 12 August 2002: www.scotsman.com/news/naked-samoans-the-trilogy-1-616764. Linda Herrick noted this review in 'Och aye, talofa', *NZ Herald*, 19 August 2002.
19. Karen Stevenson, *The Frangipani is Dead: Contemporary Pacific art in New Zealand 1985–2000* (Wellington: Huia, 2008), 26.
20. www.nzonscreen.com/title/tagata-pasifika-the-naked-samoans-2001
21. Helena Grehan, 'Black & tran: A comedy that laughs in the face of racism?', *Australasian Drama Studies* 42 (2003), 115.
22. Ibid, 117.
23. Christopher B. Balme provides a description and analysis of *Naked Samoans Go Home* in chapter eight of *Pacific Performances*, 210–12.
24. www.nzonscreen.com/title/tagata-pasifika-the-naked-samoans-2001
25. Elizabeth Mitchell had been a journalist with Kightley at the *Auckland Star* in the late 1980s, and became the producer of *bro'Town.*
26. This was a catch phrase on the show.
27. *bro'Town* was also adapted as a stage show and performed at the St James Theatre, Wellington, in March 2008 as a festival offering, featuring the TV cast. See Robbie Ellis's review, '*bro'Town* live on stage', 6 March 2008: www.scoop.co.nz/stories/HL0803/S00091/arts-festival-review-brotown-live-on-stage.htm
28. NZ Film Commission: 'Top twenty New Zealand Films released at New Zealand box office (to 21 September 2016)': www.nzfilm.co.nz/sites/nzfc/files/Top%2020%20September%202016_0.pdf
29. The Laughing Samoans: www.laughingsamoans.com/about/. The first show – with Tofiga Fepulea`i as MC and Ete as the main act – also featured Samoan/Welsh comedian James Nokise, who has since established a solo stand-up career, often containing pointed political commentary, as in *James Nokise's V.I.P. – Voter Information Pack* (2014) or *Let's Talk about the Golliwogs* (2014).
30. *Off Work* (2006), transcribed from the DVD of the live performance.
31. Unnamed reviewer, 'Reviews', *Waikato Times*, 17 May 2010, 5.
32. *Off Work* (2006), transcribed from the DVD of the live performance.
33. A hāngi is the Māori practice of cooking food buried beneath layers of earth. A hongi is part of a traditional greeting ritual, in which the participants formally press their noses and foreheads together.
34. Robertson, 'Life is hard – and hilarious'.
35. Manusaute has subsequently commented: 'We went to Niue (with *My Name is ... Pilitome*) in 2015 and we performed, and it was welcomed. Our comedy worked there, it worked on YouTube, it worked everywhere else.' Vela Manusaute, email to authors, 27 November 2015. The show was performed on 16 April 2015 at the 4th Niue Arts and Cultural Festival.
36. Dave Armstrong, interview, 16 January 2011.

8: Kila Kokonut Krew: 'From the Pacific we rise'

1. 'Pacific peoples in Auckland: Results from the 2013 census': www aucklandcouncil.govt.nz/EN/planspoliciesprojects/reports/Documents/pacificpeoplesinaucklandrresultsfrom2013census201510.pdf
2. 'New Generation Awards', The Arts Foundation: www.thearts.co.nz/new_generation_awards.php
3. Anapela Polataivao, interview, 17 June 2012. All subsequent unattributed Polataivao quotes are from this interview.
4. Vela Manusaute, interview, 17 December 2011. All subsequent unattributed Manusaute quotes are from this interview.
5. Actor/director Michael Hurst has played a central role in the development of professional theatre in Auckland, and is well known for his roles in the American television series *Hercules: The legendary journeys* (1995–99) and *Xena: Warrior princess* (1995–2001), both filmed in New Zealand.
6. Vela Manusaute, email to authors, 27 November 2015.
7. The studio is an intimate black box theatre, now called the Musgrove Studio.
8. Pua Magasiva played the title role in the films *Sione's Wedding* and *Sione's 2: Unfinished business*.
9. Francis Till, review of *Island Girls*, *NZ Herald*, 24 June 2002.
10. Vela Manusaute, 'Taro King', in *Urbanesia: Four Pasifika plays* (Wellington: Playmarket, 2012), 110.
11. Ibid.
12. Ibid., 158.
13. Ibid., 164.
14. Johnny Givins, review of *Taro King*, Theatreview, 16 August 2012: www.theatreview.org.nz/reviews/review.php?id=5048
15. Information taken from former Kila Kokonut Krew website.
16. Kila Kokonut Krew 'Mission statement': www.facebook.com/Kila-Kokonut-Krew-92837192322/
17. *Playaz Night*: www.indoanswer.com/clip/Playaz-Nite-Music-video/xMht7kYyEOM
18. The awards were founded by actor Kip Chapman in 2009 and originally known as the Hackman Theatre Awards, a reference to Wellington's Chapman Tripp Awards.
19. Sian Robertson, 'Inspires the most hilarity', Theatreview, 23 May 2007: www.theatreview.org.nz/reviews/review.php?id=776
20. John Smythe, review of *Once Were Samoans*, Theatreview, 24 July 2007: www.theatreview.org.nz/reviews/review.php?id=870
21. Information drawn from Lynn Freeman's interview with Staccy Leilua and Anapela Polataivao, *Arts on Sunday*, Radio New Zealand, February 2011: www.radionz.co.nz/national/programmes/artsonsunday/20110213
22. Freeman, *Arts on Sunday*.
23. John Ross, review of *Four Women*, Theatreview, 28 February 2011: www.theatreview.org.nz/reviews/review.php?id=3694
24. Theatreview, May 2011: www.theatreview.org.nz/reviews/production.php?id=2143. In chapter nine we discuss earlier Tongan short plays, written and staged by Michelle Johansson.
25. Sharu Delilkan, review of *Kingdom of Lote*, Theatrescenes, 18 May 2011: www.theatrescenes.co.nz/review-kingdom-of-lote/

26. Suli Moa, *Kingdom of Lote*, (Wellington: Playmarket, 2011), 18.
27. Creative New Zealand Arts Pasifika awards, 2013.
28. Vela Manusaute, email to authors, 27 November 2015.
29. Paul Simei-Barton, review of *The Factory*, *NZ Herald*, 15 August 2011.
30. This discussion of *The Factory* is based on the authors' viewing of the production at Q Theatre on 9 March 2013.
31. Stacey Leilua, personal communication, 9 March 2013.
32. Janet McAllister, review of *The Factory*, *NZ Herald*, 7 March 2013.
33. *The Factory* web series: http://thefactorystory.co.nz/. Janet McIver was production manager for *An Angel At My Table* (1990), *Once Were Warriors* (1994) and *Whale Rider* (2002). Robin Scholes is a founding partner of production company Communicado, and the producer of films such as *Once Were Warriors* (1994), *Mr Pip* (2013) and the Samoan film *The Tattooist* (2007). Michael Bennett is an award-winning writer and director whose credits include the feature film *Matariki* (2010) and the TV series *Kaitangata Twitch* (2010). Joe Lonie is a music video director and was a member of the funk rock band Supergroove.
34. Patrick McDonald, 'Two sparkling talents shine and subvert', *The Advertiser* (Adelaide), 14 June 2014, 54.
35. 'FCC's aims are to encourage the FLOW of truthful acting; to CREATE space for Polynesian stories and to CONNECT young Polynesian practitioners with seasoned industry veterans': www.facebook.com/FCC-683693461740982/
36. Analysis of *Club Paradiso* is based on the authors' viewing of the production on 5 June 2015.

9: Pasifika women writers 2002–15: 'Born restless'

1. Courtney Sina Meredith, Introduction to *Rushing Dolls in Urbanesia: Four Pasifika plays* (Wellington: Playmarket, 2012), 265.
2. Associate Professor Hon. Luamanuvao Winnie Laban, commenting at a Pasifika writers' talanoa held by the IIML at Victoria University, 6 August 2016.
3. Dale Husband, 'Tusiata Avia – painful explorations', *E-Tangata*, 18 October 2015: http://e-tangata.co.nz/news/tusiata-avia-painful-explorations
4. Tonya Turner, 'Skirts will be rattled', *Courier Mail* (Brisbane), 23 August 2008, 15. Theroux's book was entitled *The Happy Isles of Oceania: Paddling the Pacific*.
5. 'Who loves who more?' *Wild Dogs Under My Skirt*, Wellington: Victoria University Press, 2004, 42. See also 'Tamaiti':

   Fale hits the kids with the broom.
   What are you smiling for?
   Break your mouf
   Break your bones
   Cook you in da oven. (38)
6. Tusiata Avia, *Wild Dogs Under My Skirt*, (Wellington: Victoria University Press, 2004), 46.
7. Turner, 'Skirts will be rattled', 15.
8. Avia, *Wild Dogs Under My Skirt*, 16.
9. Ibid, 18.
10. Rebecca Fox, *Otago Daily Times*, 28 September 2002.
11. Nicholas Wright, 'The task of the Tusitala: Tusiata Avia's *Wild Dogs Under My Skirt*', in *Journal of Commonwealth Literature*, Vol 46:2 (2011), 225.
12. Sue Gough, 'Wild act unleashed', *Courier Mail* (Brisbane), 30 August 2008, 56.

13. www.spasifikmag.com/1septwilddogsundermyskirt/
14. Alice Te Punga Somerville, *Once Were Pacific: Māori connections to Oceania*, Minneapolis: University of Minnesota Press, 2012, 117.
15. Siobhan Harvey, 'Goddess of poetry', *New Zealand Listener*, 14 February 2009.
16. Bill Manhire: http://vup.victoria.ac.nz/brands/Tusiata-Avia.html
17. Meredith, Introduction to *Rushing Dolls in Urbanesia*, 265.
18. https://courtneymeredith.com
19. Working Titles is an initiative of the Silo Theatre in Auckland, whose brief is to support 'adventurous new work and cultivate exciting New Zealand theatre for future Silo programming': http://silotheatre.tumblr.com/post/102414433873/working-titles-2015. *Rushing Dolls* was named joint Best Play by a Woman Playwright at the 2011 Adam NZ Play Awards.
20. Courtney Sina Meredith, 'Rushing Dolls', in *Urbanesia: Four Pasifika plays* (Wellington: Playmarket, 2014), 266.
21. Ibid., 297.
22. Ibid., 278.
23. Ibid., 277–78.
24. Ibid., 307.
25. Victor Rodger, 'Pacific writing in New Zealand: The niu wave': www.anzliterature.com/feature/pacific-writing-new-zealand-niu-wave/
26. Creative Talanoa, 'An amazing poet, youth development worker and teaching artist: Grace Teuila Taylor': https://creativetalanoa.com/tag/grace-teuila-taylor
27. She was also the Auckland Writer's Festival Poetry Idol winner in 2008, and a recipient of the 2012 World of Difference award 'for her dedication and involvement in the community': www.tautai.org/artist/grace-taylor/
28. Paula Green: https://nzpoetryshelf.com/2013/12/02/grace-taylors-debut-poetry-collection-is-tender-strong-and-essential/comment-page-1/
29. 'Twelve questions: Grace Taylor', *NZ Herald*, 20 October 2015: www.nzherald.co.nz/entertainment/news/article.cfm?c_id=1501119&objectid=11531659
30. Grace Teuila Evelyn Taylor, 'What is Afakasi?', *Afakasi Speaks* (Honolulu: Ala Press, 2013), 21.
31. James Wenley, Theatre Scenes, 14 July 2014: www.theatrescenes.co.nz/review-the-selecta-auckland-theatre-company/
32. Stephen Austin, 'Brave, thoughtful, exciting, smart and evocative', Theatreview: www.theatreview.org.nz/reviews/review.php?id=7221
33. Wenley, Theatre Scenes.
34. 'Twelve questions: Grace Taylor', *NZ Herald*, 20 October 2015.
35. Paul Simei-Barton, *NZ Herald*, 19 October 2015: www.nzherald.co.nz/entertainment/news/article.cfm?c_id=1501119&objectid=11531167
36. Nik Smythe, 'Arresting eloquence', Theatreview, 18 October 2015: www.theatreview.org.nz/reviews/review.php?id=8602
37. 'Twelve questions: Grace Taylor', *NZ Herald*, 20 October 2015.
38. Louise Tu'u interview, 17 December 2011. All subsequent unattributed Tu`u quotes are from this interview.
39. We Should Practice: http://weshouldpractice.com/about/
40. Tu`u's father comes from Asau in Savai`i, while her mother is from Salamumu in Upolu.
41. Formerly known as the Auckland Secondary Schools Māori and Pacific Islands Cultural Festival.
42. Louise Tu`u, *Le Tauvaga*, unpublished ms. (Wellington: Playmarket, n.d.), 16.
43. Ibid., 25.

44. Tu`u: 'I was experimenting with languages, so in that particular draft I think most of the dialogue is in French. I don't speak French, just asked a mate to translate all this text.'
45. The Auckland Playwrights Collective provides workshops and rehearsed readings in front of an audience to help new and emerging writers: www.tapac.org.nz/events-read_raw_submissions-54
46. Māori actor Te Paki Cherrington passed away in September 2013.
47. Louise Tu`u, *Providence*, unpublished ms. (Wellington: Playmarket, 2008), 25.
48. Janet McAllister and Paul Simei-Barton, 'Theatre reviews: Best of 2010,' *NZ Herald*, 18 December 2010. There were no specific reviews for the 2010 season of *Providence*, as reviewer tickets were not issued. (Louise Tu`u, email to authors, 18 October 2015).
49. Vanessa Byrnes, 'Waiting for more', Theatreview, 25 February 2012: www.theatreview.org.nz/reviews/review.php?id=4528
50. James Wenley, 'Performance wrap-up', Theatre Scenes: www.theatrescenes.co.nz/new-performance-wrap-up-show-pony-providence-and-wake-less/
51. Louise Tu`u, email to authors, 18 October 2015.
52. Louise Tu`u, *Gaga: The unmentionable*, in *Talanoa: Four Pacific plays*, (Auckland: Little Island Press, 2017), 'About the Play', 179. Tu`u adds, 'Incidentally, Gagana is also a bird in Russian folklore with an iron beak and copper claws.'
53. Ibid., 183.
54. Ibid., 197.
55. Michelle Johansson, interview, 20 July 2016. All subsequent unattributed Johansson quotes are from this interview.
56. The name was chosen after Revell and Sila were selected to travel to London's Globe Theatre with the Shakespeare Globe Centre New Zealand Young Shakespeare Company.
57. Johansson, Michelle (2011), *Six Lessons and a Wedding*, unpublished ms, supplied by author, 7.
58. Ibid.
59. Ibid., 14.
60. Albert Wendt, email to authors, 3 September 2016, quoting his letter to Michelle Johansson.
61. Michelle Johansson, 'Cultural crisis in postcolonial Pacific theatre: John Kneubuhl's *Mele Kanikau: A pageant*', *AlterNative* 10:2 (2014), 120.
62. Ibid., 113.
63. Aaron Taouma, 'Cultural essence thoroughly examined', Theatreview, 4 May 2013: www.theatreview.org.nz/reviews/review.php?id=5865
64. Denyce Su`a's *Talosaga* – a tribute to her father – was performed in 2015 as part of her master's in drama at Auckland University. Su`a, a performer with Sam Scott's Massive Company, joined Black Friars to play Portia in *The Merchant of Venice* (2014). Revell's *IN/SECURITY* – which 'riffed off John Godber's *Bouncers*' – was performed at the Musgrove Studio in 2015. Tongan Timote Mapuhola's *Broken Pieces* was a finalist in Playmarket's 'Playwrights B425' competition, 2016.
65. Leilani Unasa, *His Mother's Son*, unpublished ms. (Wellington: Playmarket, 2012), 7.
66. Leilani Unasa, interview, 18 June 2012. All subsequent unattributed Unasa quotes are from this interview.
67. The play was also staged at the Musgrave Studio, Maidment Theatre, Auckland, in June 2007, with Dianna Fuemana and Jonathan Riley (as Stephen) replacing Truelove and Meredith.
68. *His Mother's Son* publicity material: www.theatreview.org.nz/reviews/production.php?id=265

69. In 2012 Unasa re-worked *His Mother's Son* as a two-hander, which arguably strengthens the inter-generational cycles it deals with, as both generations are played by the same two actors. Presented at Mangere Arts Centre directed by Chris Molloy, this production by the Indigenous Theatre Group featured Michael Koloi (Tasi/ Stephen) and Jenni Heka (Rachael/Sita)
70. Unasa, *His Mother's Son*, 12.
71. In 2007 Pacific Theatre staged Jason Greenwood's *Lena*, which also deals with an afakasi story.
72. Katrina Chandra, interview, 17 December 2011.
73. *Stage Adventures: Eight classroom plays* (Wellington: Playmarket, 2014).
74. www.women.govt.nz/inspiring-women/leilani-unasa
75. Miria George, quoted by Adam Goodall, 'A woman, leaving: An oral history of *and what remains*', 18 July 2016: http://pantograph-punch.com/post/a-woman-leaving-an-oral-history-and-what-remains
76. Te Punga Somerville, *Once Were Pacific*, 182–83.
77. Goodall, 'A woman, leaving'.
78. Miria George, *and what remains* (Wellington: Tawata Press, 2007), 20: Solomon: 'Sixteen percent of this country was a problem that we were forced to solve.'
79. In Wellington, at Circa, Māori actors Rob Ringiao Lloyd and Tina Cook played Ina and the mother; George removed the latter role for the Auckland production, which featured two actors with Cook Island ancestry – Taungaroa Emile (Ina) and Nathan Mudge (Luka).
80. Sharu Delilkan, review of *Sunset Road*, Theatrescenes: www.theatrescenes.co.nz/review-sunset-road-tawata-productions/
81. Husband, 'Tusiata Avia – painful explorations'.

10: Building the future

1. Katrina Chandra, interview, 17 December 2011. All subsequent unattributed Chandra quotes are from this interview.
2. Ibid.: 'Ngā Tohu o Uenuku translates as the site of creativity, the place of the rainbow, and Uenuku is an old name for Mangere.'
3. www.rdtpacific.co.nz/projects-item/mangere-arts-centre. Mangere Arts Centre was first proposed in 1993, and building was officially begun in August 2009. The project was funded by the Manukau City Council. The iconic nature of the building, designed by Auckland company Creative Spaces, led to it becoming a finalist in the Prague Quadrennial 2011 architecture exhibition.
4. Chandra left the Mangere Arts Centre at the start of 2012 to take up a job in Melbourne. She was followed by Kate Louise Elliott (2012–13) and Alison Quigan (as performing arts manager) from May 2013. Both women brought considerable theatre expertise to the centre.
5. 'Mangere Arts Centre's first birthday': www.localist.co.nz/auckland/articles/mangere-arts-centres-first-birthday
6. The production featured Aleni Tufuga, Anapela Polataivao, Fasitoa Amosa, Glen Jackson, Nora Aati, Stacey Leilua, Suli Moa and Vela Manusaute, with lighting and sound by Katrina Chandra.
7. Chandra had wanted *Tautai* to be the inaugural production, since at the time Iaheto Ah Hi was living in Mangere, and this would have reinforced the sense of community that the centre wished to promote. Kinetic Wayfinding was founded in March 2013 by Leilani Clarke and Iaheto Ah Hi. The company's mission is: 'the development and

delivery of high quality New Zealand theatre with a focus on urban Pasifika-inspired stories': www.facebook.com/Kinetic.Wayfinding

8. Johnny Givins, 'Too many strings tangle the story', Theatreview: www.theatreview.org.nz/reviews/review.php?id=6331
9. Founded in 2012 by Natalie Malietoa-Moa.
10. Founded in Auckland in 2010, Pacific Dance New Zealand (PDNZ) offers a range of services that includes 'supporting emerging dance practitioners through our choreographic labs': www.pacificdance.co.nz/profile.php
11. The Dusky Maidens were Nastassia Wolfgramm, Yvonne Taufa and Joanna Mika-Toloa.
12. Raewyn Whyte, 'Mixed Nuts – a local showcase', Theatreview, 25 February 2011: www.theatreview.org.nz/reviews/review.php?id=3677. New *Mixed Nuts* programmes were presented at the Auckland Fringe in 2012 and 2013.
13. www.circuit.org.nz/event/kalisolaite-uhila-pigs-in-the-yard-ii
14. Jandals Inc began in December 2012 as 'an organization that is committed to the development and longevity of ethnic arts in Wellington, creating a place/pathway for future Pacific practitioners': www.facebook.com/JandalsInc
15. Sharu Delilkan, 'Straight from the heart,' Theatrescenes: www.theatrescenes.co.nz/review-a-hearts-path-tales-from-the-kava-bowl/
16. Aaron Taouma, 'Cultural essence thoroughly examined', Theatreview, 4 May 2013: www.theatreview.org.nz/reviews/review.php?id=5865
17. *Puzzy* (2016), directed by Anapela Polataivao and dramaturged by Victor Rodger for FCC, was the first play by Hawaiian-based Samoan/Filipina actor Kiki (Kiana Rivera), who appeared in the Honolulu productions of *My Name is Gary Cooper* and *Frangipani Perfume* in 2015.
18. Unitec graduates include Nastassia Wolfgramm, Fasitua Amosa and Stacey Leilua, among many others.
19. www.tapac.org.nz/
20. Whitireia Performance Centre is a part of Whitireia New Zealand, formerly known as Whitireia Community Polytechnic.
21. Victor Rodger, 'By turns moving, hysterical and thought provoking', Theatreview: www.theatreview.org.nz/reviews/review.php?id=3514
22. Goretti Chadwick, interview, 16 March 2013. All subsequent unattributed Chadwick quotes are from this interview.
23. www.atc.co.nz/participate/southside-programme
24. 'Goretti Chadwick – A story from the heart', *Spasifik* 52 (Sept/Oct 2012), 43. Chadwick: 'The idea actually came from a discussion I had with a dear friend of mine, Victor Rodger.'
25. In 2012 it toured to Brisbane's Powerhouse, 15–18 February, as part of the World Theatre Festival, and played at Auckland's Glen Eden Playhouse (23–26 August) and Dunedin's Fortune Theatre for the Arts Festival (8–11 October).
26. Rodger, 'By turns moving'.
27. Tanya Muagututi`a, email to authors, 16 December 2015. Talia-Rae's teachers at PIPA also included David Fane and Vela Manusaute.
28. Writers' Block Mission Statement, supplied by Hone Kouka, 7 February 2011.
29. 'Playmarket Brown Ink Sessions', Theatreview: www.theatreview.org.nz/news/news.php?id=878.
30. 'Tupe Lualua to showcase new work at Measina Festival', *KC News*, June 2015: www.kcnews.co.nz/story.php?storyID=9661
31. In 2016 Le Moana took *1918* to the San Diego Fringe festival where it received excellent reviews and won the Critic's Pick award.

32. Moana Ete is a 2010 graduate of Toi Whakaari and is following in the footsteps of her father, Eteuati Ete.
33. 'About Kava Club': www.facebook.com/kavaclub
34. Collins was joined in the cast by Aleni Tufuga and Iaheto Ah Hi.
35. 'Samoan feature film first', Ministry of Culture and Heritage: www.mch.govt.nz/news-events/news/samoan-feature-film-first. Lees was associate producer and casting director.
36. '"Whispers" about Friendship Week', *Samoa Observer Online*: http://live.isitesoftware.co.nz/samoa2012/news///index_dynamic/containerNameToReplace=Middle/focusModuleID=3709/overideSkinName=newsArticle-full.tpl. 'Let Me Hear You Whisper' is the title of a popular Samoan song.
37. 'History of Pasifika': www.aucklandnz.com/pasifika/pasifika-festival-history
38. Fulimalo Pereira, 'Arts specific: Pacific peoples and New Zealand's arts', in *Tangata o le Moana: New Zealand and the people of the Pacific*, eds Sean Mallon, Kolokesa Māhina-Tuai and Damon Salesa (Wellington: Te Papa Press, 2012), 305–33 (320).
39. The 1976 festival's souvenir programme can be accessed at http://digitool.auckland.ac.nz/R/?func=dbin-jump-full&object_id=30142&local_base=GEN01
40. Originally from Canada, Gaskell was for several years professor of theatre arts at the University of the South Pacific in Suva, Fiji. He directed the premiere productions of several plays by indigenous Fijian playwright Larry Thomas.
41. Ian Gaskell, 'Truth, identity and a sense of "Pacificness"', *Australasian Drama Studies* 55 (2009), 133.
42. Ibid., 143.
43. Ibid., 146.

Conclusion

1. Oscar Kightley, interview, 18 June 2012.
2. As Teaiwa and Mallon observe of Samoan-born Oscar Kightley, 'He is very much a product of New Zealand as is evident from the ease with which he moves across the boundaries of sports journalism, comedy, theatre and television.' Teresia Teaiwa and Sean Mallon, 'Ambivalent Kinships? Pacific people in New Zealand', in *New Zealand Identities: Departures and destinations*, eds James H. Liu et al. (Wellington: Victoria University Press, 2005), 220.
3. From written material ('Fa`amalo congratulate Pacific Underground') provided by Rev Mua Strickson-Pua, 20 August 2015.
4. 'Pacific theatre picks up the pace', *NZ Herald*, 14 September 2013, 9

Bibliography

Interviews with authors

Dave Armstrong, 16 January 2011
Anton Carter, 16 June 2012
Goretti Chadwick, 16 March 2013
Katrina Chandra, 17 December 2011
Fiona Collins, 26 August 2016
Eteuati Ete, 15 June 2012
David Fane, 15 December 2011
Dianna Fuemana, 6 September 2012
Robert Gilbert, 19 December 2013
Erolia Ifopo, 14 January 2011
Michelle Johansson, 20 July 2016
Paul Kieve, 14 December 2011
Oscar Kightley, 18 June 2012
Nathaniel Lees, 16 June 2012
Shimpal Lelisi, 19 June 2012
Salesi Le`ota, 3 March 2012
Tom McCrory, 27 January 2012
Sean Mallon, 14 December 2011
David Mamea, 28 November 2014
Kasaya Manulevu, 11 November 2014
Vela Manusaute, 17 December 2011
Posenai Mavaega, 30 September 2010
Mishelle Muagututi`a, 14 January 2011
Tanya Muagututi`a, 30 September 2010
Nina Nawalowalo, (1) 14 December 2011; (2) 15 June 2012
Anapela Polataivao, 17 June 2012
Victor Rodger, 13 January 2011
Paul Simei-Barton, 16 December 2011
Justine Simei-Barton, 16 December 2011
Simon Small, 5 November 2010
Louise Tu`u, 17 December 2011
Leilani Unasa, 18 June 2012
Makerita Urale, (1) 14 January 2011; (2) 15 June 2012; (3) 16 January 2014
Sima Urale, 11 November 2014

Books, chapters & articles

Alpers, Antony (ed.), *Legends of the South Seas*, London: J. Murray, 1970.

Armstrong, Philip, 'Shakespeare and the space of adolescence', *English in Aotearoa* 47 (October 2002): 18–28.

Avia, Tusiata, *Wild Dogs Under My Skirt*, Wellington: Victoria University Press, 2004.

Balme, Christopher B., *Pacific Performances: Theatricality and cross-cultural encounter in the South Seas*, Hampshire: Palgrave Macmillan, 2007.
Balme, Christopher and Astrid Carstensen, 'Home fires: Creating a Pacific theatre in the diaspora', *Theatre Research International* 26(1) (March 2001): 33–46.
Barba, Eugenio, *Beyond the Floating Islands*, New York: PAJ Publications, 1986.
Besnier, Niko, 'Crossing the boundaries', *Illusions* 25 (Winter 1996): 43–45.
Bradwell, Eric, 'The man called Jones', in *Seven One-Act Plays*, Wellington: NZ Radio Record/ British Drama League, 1933, 83–97.
Buck, Ralph and Nicholas Rowe (eds), *Moving Oceans: Celebrating dance in the South Pacific*, New Delhi: Routledge, 2014.
Burry, Kate and Connie Grouse (eds), *Voices Against Violence*, Auckland: British Council New Zealand, 2015.
Carter, Anton, 'Taking centre stage: Pacific theatre in New Zealand', in *Pacific Art Niu Sila: The Pacific dimension of contemporary New Zealand arts*, Sean Mallon and Pandora Fulimalo Pereira (eds), Wellington: Te Papa Press, 2002, 146–59.
Curnow, Allen, *Four Plays*, Wellington: A.H. & A.W. Reed, 1972.
Figiel, Sia, *Where We Once Belonged*, Auckland: Pasifika Press, 1996.
Fraleigh, Sondra, *Butoh: Metamorphic dance and global alchemy*, Chicago: University of Illinois Press, 2010.
Fraleigh, Sondra and Tamah Nakamura, *Hijikata Tatsumi and Ohno Kazuo*, New York, London: Routledge, 2006.
Fraser, Toa, *Two Plays: Bare and Number 2*, Wellington: Playmarket, 2007.
Fresno-Calleja, Paloma, 'Playing (with) stereotypes in postcolonial Pacific theatre', *Journal of Commonwealth Literature* 45 (2010): 171–88.
------ 'Revised spectacles: Literary transformations of Hollywood's Pacific narratives', *Journal of Postcolonial Writing*, 49(3) (2013): 265–77.
Fuemana, Dianna, *Two Plays: Falemalama and The Packer*, Wellington: Playmarket, 2008.
Fulop, Kata, 'Reverse chameleon in the Kiwi jungle: Identity construction of Pasifika theatre makers', PhD diss., University of Canterbury, 2012.
Gaskell, Ian, 'Truth, identity and a sense of "Pacificness"', *Australasian Drama Studies* 55 (2009): 132–49.
George, Miria, *and what remains*, Wellington: Tawata Press, 2007.
Graham, Fiona, 'Dramaturge as midwife: The writing process within a New Zealand community theatre project', *Journal of Writing in Creative Practice*, vol. 2, no. 2 (2009): 209–16.
Grehan, Helena, 'Black & tran: A comedy that laughs in the face of racism?', *Australasian Drama Studies*, 42 (2003): 112–22.
Guest, Bill, *Transitions: Four decades of Toi Whakaari: New Zealand Drama School*, Wellington: Victoria University Press, 2010.
Hamilton, Andrew, 'Nineteenth-century French missionaries and fa`a Samoa', *Journal of Pacific History* 32(2) (1998): 163–77.
Hammer, Anita, *Between Play and Prayer: The variety of theatricals in spiritual performance*, Amsterdam/New York: Rodopi, 2010.
Hau`ofa, Epeli, 'Our sea of islands', in *Inside Out: Literature, cultural politics, and identity in the new Pacific*, Vilsoni Hereniko and Rob Wilson (eds), Lanham/Oxford: Rowman & Littlefield, 1999, 27–38.
Hazou, Rand, 'Real men at play: Massive Company's *The Brave*', *Australasian Drama Studies* 68 (April 2016): 97–117.
Henderson, April K., 'Gifted flows: Making space for a brand new beat', *The Contemporary Pacific*, vol. 22, no. 2 (2010): 293–315.
Hereniko, Vilsoni, 'Clowning as political commentary: Polynesia, then and now', *The Contemporary Pacific*, vol. 6, no. 1 (Spring 1994): 1–28.

------, *Woven Gods: Female clowns and power in Rotuma*, Honolulu: University of Hawai`i Press, 1995.
Houlahan, Mark, 'Shakespeare in the settlers' house', *Journal of New Zealand Literature* 20 (2002): 112–24.
------, '*Romeo and Tusi*: An eclectically musical Samoan/Māori *Romeo and Juliet* from Aotearoa/New Zealand', *Contemporary Theatre Review* 19(3) (2009): 279–88.
Hyland, Nicola, 'Wherefore art thou bro?', PhD diss., University of Melbourne, 2012.
Icons from Te Papa: Pacific, Wellington: Te Papa Press, 2006.
Ifopo, Erolia, 'The native chef', Paper/presentation at UNESCO Pacific Region of Experts on Arts Education, Nadi, Fiji Islands, November 2002: http://webarchive.unesco.org/20160107120616/http://portal.unesco.org/culture/en/files/9157/10567060903the_native_chef.pdf/the%2Bnative%2Bchef.pdf
Jackson-Bourke, Leki, et al., *Talanoa: Four Pacific plays*, Auckland: Little Island Press, 2017.
Johansson, Michelle, 'Cultural crisis in postcolonial Pacific theatre: John Kneubuhl's *Mele Kanikau: A Pageant*', *AlterNative* 10:2 (2014): 110–22.
------, '"Coz Tybalt shanked Romeo's dox": Poly-nizing Shakespeare on the Southside', *English in Aotearoa*, no. 88 (April 2016): 15–20.
Johnson, Jackie Pualani, 'Afterword: A portrait of John Kneubuhl', in *Think of a Garden and Other Plays*, John Kneubuhl, Honolulu: University of Hawai`i Press, 1997, 251–66.
Keown, Michelle, *Pacific Islands Writing: The postcolonial literatures of Aotearoa/New Zealand and Oceania*, Oxford: Oxford University Press, 2007.
Kightley, Oscar and Simon Small, *Fresh off the Boat*, Wellington: The Play Press, 2005.
Kightley, Oscar and Dave Armstrong, 'Niu Sila', in Dave Armstrong, *Two Plays*, Wellington: Playmarket 2009.
Kightley, Oscar, David Fane and Nathaniel Lees, 'A Frigate Bird Sings', in *Urbanesia: Four Pasifika plays*, Wellington: Playmarket, 2012, 11–96.
King, Michael, *Being Pakeka Now: Reflections and recollections of a white native*, Auckland: Penguin, 1999.
Kneubuhl, John, *Think of a Garden and Other Plays*, Honolulu: University of Hawai`i Press, 1997.
Kneubuhl, John A. and Vilsoni Hereniko, 'An interview with John A. Kneubuhl: Comic theatre of Samoa', *Mānoa: A Pacific Journal of International Writing* 5(1) (1993): 99–105.
Kneubuhl, Victoria N., 'Traditional performance in Samoan culture: Two forms', *Asian Theatre Journal* 4(2) (1987): 166–76.
Kolia, John, *Favour and Other Flexible Theatre*, Singapore: Koon Wah, 1981.
Kouka, Hone, 'Introduction', in *Ta Matou Mangai: Three plays of the 1990s*, Hone Kouka (ed.), Wellington: Victoria University Press, 1999, 9–28.
Lees, Nathaniel, '"Everything is family": David O'Donnell interviews Nathaniel Lees', in *Performing Aotearoa: New Zealand theatre and drama in an age of transition*, Marc Maufort and David O'Donnell (eds), Brussels: PIE Peter Lang, 2007, 331–47.
Looser, Diana, 'A piece "more curious than all the rest": Re-encountering pre-colonial Pacific Island theatre, 1769–1855', *Theatre Journal* vol. 63, no. 4, December 2011, 521–40.
------, 'Moving islands: Mapping the Samoan diaspora in contemporary transnational theatre from the South Pacific', *Contemporary Theatre Review* 22(4) (2012): 451–66.
------, *Remaking Pacific Pasts: History, memory and identity in contemporary theater from Oceania*, Honolulu: University of Hawai`i Press, 2014.
McDougall, Julie, 'Māori and Pacific Shakespeares in Aotearoa/New Zealand', MA diss., Victoria University of Wellington, 2006.
McNaughton, Howard, *New Zealand Drama*, Boston: Twayne, 1981.

------, ‘Drama’, in *The Oxford History of New Zealand Literature in English* (2nd edn), Terry Sturm (ed.), Auckland: Oxford University Press, 1998, 321–93.
Mallon, Sean, *Samoan Art & Artists: O Measina a Samoa*, Nelson: Craig Potton, 2002.
Mallon, Sean and Pandora Fulimalo Pereira (eds), *Pacific Art Niu Sila: The Pacific dimension of contemporary New Zealand arts*, Wellington: Te Papa Press, 2002
Mallon, Sean, Kolokesa Mahina-Tuai and Damon Salesa, *Tangata o le Moana: New Zealand and the people of the Pacific*, Wellington: Te Papa Press, 2012.
Mallon, Sean and Uili Fecteau, ‘Tatau-ed: Polynesian tatau in Aotearoa’, in *Pacific Art Niu Sila: The Pacific dimension of contemporary New Zealand arts*, Sean Mallon and Pandora Fulimalo Pereira (eds), Wellington: Te Papa Press, 2002, 21–37.
Manusaute, Vela, ‘Taro King’, in *Urbanesia: Four Pasifika plays*, Wellington: Playmarket, 2012, 97–164.
------, ‘My Name is Pilitome’, in *Talanoa: Four Pacific plays*, Auckland: Little Island Press, 2017, 1–52.
Marsh, Selina Tusitala, ‘Where the Girls Are’, in *Niu Voices: Contemporary Pacific fiction 1*, Wellington: Huia, 2006, 23–28.
Maufort, Marc, *Transgressive Itineraries: Postcolonial hybridizations of dramatic realism*, Brussels: PIE Peter Lang, 2006.
------, ‘Voices of otherness: Multicultural dramaturgies in contemporary New Zealand’, in *Identities in Process: Studies in comparative literature*, Eduardo F. Coutinho (ed.), Rio De Janeiro: Aeroplano Editora, 2009, 63–73.
------, ‘Positioning alterity: Multi-ethnic identities in contemporary New Zealand drama’, *Cross/Cultures* 149(2) (2012): 257–77.
Maufort, Marc and David O’Donnell (eds), *Performing Aotearoa: New Zealand theatre and drama in a age of transition*, Brussels: PIE Peter Lang, 2007.
Maunder, Paul, ‘Searching for a third world culture in Aotearoa’, *Illusions* 2 (Winter 1986): 29–31.
------, *Rebellious Mirrors: Community-based theatre in Aotearoa/New Zealand*, Christchurch: Canterbury University Press, 2013.
Meredith, Courtney Sina, ‘Rushing Dolls’, in *Urbanesia: Four Pasifika Plays*, Wellington: Playmarket, 2012, 259–312.
Millar, Paul, ‘So Dazzling a Creature’, in *Pacific Art Niu Sila: The Pacific dimension of contemporary New Zealand arts*, Sean Mallon and Pandora Fulimalo Pereira (eds), Wellington: Te Papa Press, 2002, 161–73.
Miller, Sachiko, ‘Treasuring the meke in a modern Fiji’, in *Moving Oceans: Celebrating dance in the South Pacific*, Ralph Buck and Nicholas Rowe (eds), New Delhi: Routledge 2014, 119–31.
Neill, Michael, ‘Post-colonial Shakespeare? Writing away from the centre’, in *Post-Colonial Shakespeares*, Ania Loomba and Martin Orkin (eds), London: Routledge, 1998, 164–85.
O’Donnell, David, ‘Shaping the future: Pacific playwrights in New Zealand’, in Laurie Atkinson with David O’Donnell (eds), *Playmarket 40: 40 Years of playwriting in New Zealand*, Wellington: Playmarket, 2013, 92–97.
------, ‘Re-claiming the “fob”: The immigrant family in Samoan drama’, in Marc Maufort and David O’Donnell (eds), *Performing Aotearoa: New Zealand theatre and drama in an age of transition*, Brussels: PIE Peter Lang, 2007, 307–30.
------, ‘Issues in PI women’s theatre: *Vula* and *Frangipani Perfume*’, *Illusions: New Zealand moving image and performing arts criticism* 36 (Winter 2004): 32–35.
O’Donnell, David and Bronwyn Tweddle, ‘Toa Fraser: Shifting boundaries in Pacific Island comedy’, *Australasian Drama Studies* 42 (April 2003): 123–37.

------, 'Naked Samoans: Pacific Island voices in the theatre of Aotearoa/New Zealand', *Performance Research* 8(1) (2003): 51–60.

Pearson, Sarina, 'Subversion and ambivalence: Pacific Islanders on New Zealand prime time', *The Contemporary Pacific* 11(2) (1999): 361–88.

------, 'Film and photography: Picturing New Zealand as a Pacific place', in *Pacific Art Niu Sila: The Pacific dimension of contemporary New Zealand arts*, Sean Mallon and Pandora Fulimalo Pereira (eds), Wellington: Te Papa Press, 2002, 175–89.

Pereira, Fulimalo, 'Arts specific: Pacific peoples and New Zealand's arts', in *Tangata o le Moana: New Zealand and the people of the Pacific*, Sean Mallon, Kolokesa Māhina-Tuai and Damon Salesa (eds), Wellington: Te Papa Press, 2012, 305–33.

Raiskin, Judith, 'Telling tales out of school: Sia Figiel and indigenous knowledge in Pacific Islands literature', in *Gender and Globalization in Asia and the Pacific: Method, practice, theory*, Kathy E. Ferguson and Monique Mironesco (eds), Honolulu: University of Hawai`i Press, 2008, 15–36.

Raymond, Rosanna, Jakki Leota-Ete and Shigeyuki Kihara, 'Body beautiful: New Zealand fashion – Pacific style', in *Pacific Art Niu Sila: The Pacific dimension of contemporary New Zealand arts*, Sean Mallon and Pandora Fulimalo Pereira (eds), Wellington: Te Papa Press, 2002, 90–101.

Refiti, Albert, 'Making spaces: Polynesian architecture in Aotearoa New Zealand', in *Pacific Art Niu Sila: The Pacific dimension of contemporary New Zealand arts*, Sean Mallon and Pandora Fulimalo Pereira (eds), Wellington: Te Papa Press, 2002, 209–25.

Rodger, Victor, *Sons*, Wellington: Huia, 2007.

------, 'My Name is Gary Cooper', in *Urbanesia: Four Pasifika plays*, Wellington: Playmarket, 2012, 165–257.

------, *Black Faggot and Other Plays*, Wellington: Victoria University Press, 2017.

Samasoni, Samson, 'Māori and Pacific Island theatre in New Zealand – past and future', *Act: Theatre in New Zealand*, vol. 11, no. 2, (April 1986): 15–16.

Sanderson, Martyn, 'Testament of the Flying Fox'. Interview with Martyn Sanderson and Wanjiku Kiarie conducted by Martin Rumsby: http://readingthemaps.blogspot.co.nz/search?q=tusitala

Shilliam, Robbie, 'Keskidee Aroha: Translation on the colonial stage', *Journal of Historical Sociology*, vol. 24, no. 1, March 2011, 80–99.

Simpson, Jamie C., 'Performance and social inversion: The Samoan White Sunday', *Youth Theatre Journal* 19(1) (2005): 134–50.

Sinaviana, Caroline, 'Comic theater in Samoa as indigenous media', *Pacific Studies*, vol. 15, no. 4, December 1992, 199–209.

------, 'Traditional comic theatre in Samoa: A holographic view', PhD diss., University of Hawai`i at Manoa, 1992.

------, 'Where the spirits laugh last: Comic theater in Samoa', in *Clowning as Critical Practice: Performance humor in the South Pacific*, William E. Mitchell (ed.), Pittsburgh/London: University of Pittsburgh Press, 1992, 192–218.

Singh, Shveata Chandel, 'Theatre is revelation: Stefo': http://shveatachandel.blogspot.co.nz/2013/07/theatre-is-revelation-stefo.html

Smythe, John, *Downstage Upfront: The first 40 years of New Zealand's longest-running professional theatre*, Wellington: Victoria University Press, 2004.

Stevenson, Karen, *The Frangipani Is Dead: Contemporary Pacific art in New Zealand, 1985–2000*, Wellington: Huia, 2008.

Stevenson, Robert Louis, *Across The Plains with Other Memories and Essays*, London: Chatto & Windus, 1920.

Strange, Glyn, *The Little Theatre: Golden years of the New Zealand stage*, Christchurch: Clerestory Press, 2000.

Taouma, Lisa, 'Gettin' jiggy with it', in *Pacific Art Niu Sila: The Pacific dimension of contemporary New Zealand arts*, Sean Mallon and Pandora Fulimalo Pereira (eds), Wellington: Te Papa Press, 2002, 132–45.

Tapaleao, Vaimoana, 'Transforming Aotearoa's cultural landscape', *Spasifik* (Jan/Feb 2008): 38.

Taylor, Grace Teuila Evelyn, 'What is Afakasi?', *Afakasi Speaks*, Honolulu: Ala Press, 2013.

Tarling, Nicholas, *Wit, Eloquence and Commerce: A history of Auckland's Mercury Theatre*, Auckland: Connacht Books, 2007.

Teaiwa, Teresia and Sean Mallon, 'Ambivalent kinships? Pacific people in New Zealand', in *New Zealand Identities: Departures and destinations*, James H. Liu, Tim McCreanor, Tracey McIntosh and Teresia Teaiwa (eds), Wellington: Victoria University Press, 2005, 207–29.

Te Punga Somerville, Alice, *Once Were Pacific: Māori connections to Oceania*, Minneapolis: University of Minnesota Press, 2012.

Thomson, John, *New Zealand Drama 1930–1980: An illustrated history*, Auckland: Oxford University Press, 1984.

Tu`u, Louise, 'Gaga the Unmentionable' in *Talanoa: Four Pacific plays*, Auckland: Little Island Press, 2017, 177–202.

Urale, Makerita and Dianna Fuemana, 'Frangipani Perfume' *and* 'Mapaki', Wellington: The Play Press, 2004.

Urale, Makerita, *The Magic Seashell*, Wellington: Steele Roberts, 1999.

Urbanesia: Four Pasifika plays, Wellington: Playmarket, 2012.

Va`ai, Letuimanu`asina Dr Emma Kruse, 'Religion', in *Samoa's Journey 1962–2012: Aspects of history*, Leasiolagi Malama Meleisea, Penelope Schoeffel Meleisea and Ellie Melesia (eds), Wellington: Victoria University Press, 2012, 77–96.

Va`ai, Silafau Dr Sina, Saumaeafe Dr Vanya Taule`alo, Fiona Collins, Solomona Susau, Maluiao Leua Latai and Apulu Lance Polu, 'Arts, literature and the media', in *Samoa's Journey 1962–2012: Aspects of history*, Leasiolagi Malama Meleisea, Penelope Schoeffel Meleisea and Ellie Melesia (eds), Wellington: Victoria University Press, 2012, 173–205.

Vaioleti, Timote M., 'Talanoa research methodology: A developing position on Pacific research', *Waikato Journal of Education* 12 (2006): 21–34.

Warrington, Lisa, 'Theatre in 1990', *Journal of New Zealand Literature*, 12 (1994): 5–44.

------, 'Comedy and irreverence: Rewriting Shakespeare in Aotearoa/New Zealand', in *Shakespeare's Legacy: The appropriation of the plays in post-colonial drama*, Norbert Schaffeld (ed.), Trier: Wissenschaftlicher Verlag Trier, 2005, 125–40.

------, '"Look here, upon this picture, and on this": Representations of *Hamlet* in Aotearoa/New Zealand, 1993–2007', *Contemporary Theatre Review*, 19(3) (2009), 305–16.

Warrington, Lisa and David O'Donnell, 'Unfolding the cloth: Patterns of landscape and identity in The Conch's *Masi*', in *Enacting Nature: Ecocritical perspectives on indigenous performance*, Birgit Dawes and Marc Maufort (eds), Brussels: PIE Peter Lang, 2014, 199–217.

Wendt, Albert, 'The contest', *Landfall 158* (June 1986): 144–53.

------, *The Songmaker's Chair*, Wellington: Huia, 2004.

------, *The Adventures of Vela*, Wellington: Huia, 2009.

------, 'Tatauing the post-colonial body', *SPAN: Journal of the South Pacific Association for Commonwealth Language and Literary Studies*, 62 (December 2009): 83–103.

------, 'Towards a new Oceania', *Mana Review: A South Pacific journal of language and literature*, vol. 1, no. 1 (1976): 49–60.

Wenley, James, 'Rediscovering the landmark New Zealand plays: The formative period of New Zealand drama', MA diss., University of Auckland, 2013.
White, Edgar, *The Nine Night & Ritual By Water*, London: Methuen, 1984.
White, Raewyn, 'Dance works of 1993', *Illusions*, 23 (July 1994): 28–35.
Wilson, August, *Three Plays*, Pittsburgh: University of Pittsburgh Press, 1991.
Wright, Nicholas, 'The task of the Tusitala: Tusiata Avia's *Wild Dogs Under My Skirt*', *The Journal of Commonwealth Literature*, 46(2) (June 2011), 219–36.

Unpublished playscripts (1)

Accessed from Playmarket: www.playmarket.org.nz

Armstrong, Dave, *Where We Once Belonged*, 2008.
Fraser, Toa, *Paradise*, 2001.
Hannam, Brian, *The Waitara Purchase*, 1973.
Kightley, Oscar, *Dawn Raids*, 1997.
Kightley, Oscar and Erolia Ifopo, *Romeo and Tusi*, 2000.
Kouka, Hone and Hori Ahipene, *Hide 'n' Seek*, 1992.
Manusaute, Vela, *Once Were Samoans*, 2008.
Moa, Suli, *Kingdom of Lote*, 2011.
------, *A Heart's Path*, 2012.
------, *No Man's Land*, 2013.
Muagututi`a, Tanya and Joy Vaele, *Angels*, 2010.
Rodger, Victor, *Ranterstantrum*, 2002.
Sinclair, Stephen and Samson Samasoni, *Le Matau*, 1984.
Tu`u, Louise, *Le Tauvaga*, n.d.
------, *Providence*, 2008.
------, *Horses and Other Farm Animals*, 2013.
Unasa, Leilani, *His Mother's Son*, 2012.

Unpublished playscripts (2)

Ah Hi, Iaheto, *Tautai*, 2010 (Kinetic Wayfinding, provided by Iaheto Ah Hi).
------, *Digital Winds: Part 3 of the Stingray Trilogy*, 2014 (Kinetic Wayfinding, provided by Iaheto Ah Hi).
Atia, 1982, original music & lyrics by Danny Goddard, Felicity Day, Samson Samasoni (provided by TAOtahi).
Brunton, Alan, Justine Simei-Barton and William Shakespeare, *Romeo and Juliet*, 1992 (Pacific Theatre Inc, provided by Paul and Justine Simei-Barton).
Roberts, Hemi, *Manawhenua*, n.d. (provided by Robert Gilbert).
Johansson, Michelle, *Six Lessons and a Wedding*, n.d. (provided by Michelle Johansson).
Mamea, David, *Goodbye My Feleni*, 2013 and 2014 versions (provided by David Mamea).
Rei Harris, Kellee and Mokalagi Tamapeau, *Santa Claus of Rangiora* (1981) (provided by TAOtahi).
Simei-Barton, Paul, *The Contest*, 1993 (Pacific Theatre Inc, provided by Paul and Justine Simei-Barton).
Simei-Barton, Paul, *Tusitala and the House of Spirits*, 1996 (Pacific Theatre Inc, provided by Paul and Justine Simei-Barton).
Small, Simon (as Francis Serra), *Horizons*, 1991 (viewed on videotape provided by the author.)

DVD/internet

Bennett, Michael, *The Factory* web series, devised and written by Michael Bennett (Kila Kokonut Krew and Jump Film and Television, 2013): http://thefactorystory.co.nz
Bennett, Simon (director) *Sione's 2: Unfinished business* (South Pacific Pictures, 2012).
The Brownies, *Comedy At Its Best* (Video-aau Productions, n.d).
bro'Town Series 1–5 (Sony Pictures Home Entertainment, 2004–09).
Fraser, Toa (director), *No. 2* (Numero Films Ltd, 2006).
Graham, Chris (director), *Sione's Wedding* (South Pacific Pictures, 2006).
Kila Kokonut Krew, *Laugh You Long Time* (Kila Kokonut Krew Entertainment, 2011).
Maunder, Paul (director), *Sons for the Return Home* (Pacific Films, 1979).
The Laughing Samoans, *Laughing With Samoans* (Double E Productions, 2003).
------, *Off Work* (Double E Productions, 2007).
------, *Funny Chokers* (Double E Productions, 2012).
Tamasese, Tusi (director), *The Orator* (Blueskin Films Ltd, 2011).
Tagata Pasifika – The Naked Samoans, NZ on Screen: www.nzonscreen.com/title/tagata-pasifika-the-naked-samoans-2001

New Zealand Theatre databases

Theatre Aotearoa, the New Zealand theatre database: http://tadb.otago.ac.nz
Theatreview: www.theatreview.org.nz

Index

Page numbers in **bold** refer to illustrations.